for Kate Zhou,

who studies the

happier time that came

<u>after</u> this period of

campaigns, monitors, and

violence.

Lyn White

Policies of Chaos

WRITTEN UNDER THE AUSPICES OF THE
CENTER OF INTERNATIONAL STUDIES,
PRINCETON UNIVERSITY

LYNN T. WHITE III

Policies of Chaos

The Organizational Causes of Violence in China's Cultural Revolution

Princeton University Press
Princeton, New Jersey

Library of Congress Cataloging-in-Publication Data

White, Lynn T.
  Policies of chaos : the organizational causes of violence in
China's cultural revolution / Lynn T. White III.
      p.   cm.
  Bibliography: p.
  Includes index.
  ISBN 0-691-05546-7
  1. China—History—Culture Revolution, 1966-1969.   2. China—
Politics and government—1949-1976.   I. Title.
DS778.7.W47 1988   88-15235
951.05′6—dc19   CIP

For my father
and my mother

Contents

Acknowledgments

Where do debts for a book begin? With the author's parents, always. This applies even to works about countries less famous for their stress on filiality than China. My father knew before his death about the joint dedication of this book, and he was pleased.

Any study in the social sciences or humanities inevitably owes much to the people about whom it is written. Here, they are the residents of Shanghai from 1949 to 1968. I hope they and other Chinese may find some interest in reflections by a foreigner. The diffuseness of important obligations is astounding. This author is beholden to many teachers of diverse things at earlier times: a Latin instructor at an Oakland, California, junior high school; a professor at Williams College who taught about India; many professors in graduate school at Berkeley; colleagues here at Princeton; and others too numerous to name.

My specific debts are myriad too. Feng Shengping, Li Cheng, Long Fu, and other Chinese (some of whom requested anonymity) have helped by reading and marking a draft. Richard Madsen, Lucian W. Pye, Raymond F. Wylie, my wife Barbara-Sue, and her mother, Doris Mount, went over the text and suggested specific changes. Oral comments or correspondence on my ideas, though not on the text itself, came from a distinguished further group of China hands: John K. Fairbank, Philip Kuhn, Benjamin Schwartz, Ezra Vogel, Allen Whiting, and David Zweig.

Margaret Case managed the book through the Press. Let me vouch to other authors in the China field that Princeton University Press is a most professional and encouraging publisher with which to work. Carolyn Wenger went over the text in detail and with great sensitivity, trying to improve my style; I give her a huge vote of thanks for making this book clearer than it would otherwise be. Gretchen Oberfranc commanded the computers to do the typesetting from my files. Harriet Hitch took charge of the flyleaf and catalog description. Jane Low (whose family originated in Shanghai) and Alessandra Bocco handled the logistics of publication. With the book in production, I still do not know all the people at Princeton University Press to whom I owe thanks; but they are a splendid team.

I thank Harcourt Brace Jovanovich for permission to reprint in chapter 5 first lines from a selection in *E. E. Cummings: Complete Poems, 1913–62* (New York, 1963).

My institutional debts for support of research in this project are also several. The Joint Committee on Contemporary China of the Social Sciences

Research Council and the American Council of Learned Societies supported this work generously, as did Princeton University and its Woodrow Wilson School, with whose Center of International Studies I have been associated throughout the project. Universities Service Centre, Hong Kong, provided essential facilities for my interviewing and library work. More diffuse institutional debts, not directly connected with this project, are also important: The University of California Center for Chinese Studies, Berkeley, was the place where I cut my teeth in the China field. The Harry Frank Guggenheim Foundation, which has particular interest in study of the causes and prevention of violence, has funded my next project about the lessening of social tensions in China after 1978. The Shanghai Academy of Social Sciences and the University of Hong Kong have also helped that research on the altogether happier topic of China's reforms, which will become a sequel to the book now in your hands.

None of the people or organizations mentioned above should be held responsible for my own tendency to error, but I owe them all a great deal.

Barbara-Sue, Jeremy, and Kevin have put up with this over many years; and for that and much more, they have my love.

Princeton, Shanghai, and Hong Kong, 1988

Abbreviations

BR	*Beijing Review*
CCP	Chinese Communist Party
CNA	*China News Analysis*, Hong Kong
CPSU	Communist Party of the Soviet Union
CR	Cultural Revolution
CYL	Communist Youth League
DGB	*Dagong bao* (L'Impartial), Shanghai, Tianjin, and Hong Kong
ECMM	*Extracts from China Mainland Magazines*, Hong Kong
GMD	Guomindang
GMRB	*Guangming ribao* (Bright daily), Beijing
GRRB	*Gongren ribao* (Workers' daily), Beijing
HQ	*Hongqi* (Red Flag), Beijing
JFRB	*Jiefang ribao* (Liberation daily), Shanghai
LDB	*Laodong bao* (Labor news), Shanghai
NCNA	*New China News Agency*, Shanghai unless noted
PLA	People's Liberation Army
PRC	People's Republic of China
QNB	*Qingnian bao* (Youth news), Shanghai
RMRB	*Renmin ribao* (People's daily), Beijing
SEM	Socialist Education Movement
SCMM	*Survey of China Mainland Magazines*, Hong Kong
SCMP	*Survey of the China Mainland Press*, Hong Kong
SHGS	*Shanghai gongshang* (Shanghai industry and commerce)
SHGSZL	*Shanghai gongshang ziliao* (Materials on Shanghai industry and commerce)
SHNL	"Shanghai Newsletter," in *South China Morning Post*, Hong Kong
SHWB	*Shanghai wanbao* (Shanghai evening news)
SN	*Shanghai News*
URI	Union Research Institute, Hong Kong
WHB	*Wenhui bao* (Documentary news), Shanghai
XDRB	*Xingdao ribao* (Singapore daily), Hong Kong
XMBWK	*Xinmin bao wankan* (New People's evening gazette), Shanghai
XMWB	*Xinmin wanbao* (New people's evening news), Shanghai
XWRB	*Xinwen ribao* (News daily), Shanghai
YB	*Yi bao* (Further news), Shanghai
ZGQN	*Zhongguo qingnian* (China youth), Beijing
ZGQNB	*Zhongguo qingnian bao* (China youth news), Beijing
ZW	*Zhanwang* (Prospects), Beijing

Romanizations

This book romanizes Chinese in pinyin. The system is difficult for English readers, because it uses frequent *q*'s, *x*'s, *z*'s, and *zh*'s as initial consonants. It is nonetheless favored in the People's Republic of China, is now standard, and is scarcely more counterintuitive than the Wade-Giles system (the main alternative, developed by British missionaries and diplomats).

Chinese, like any other language, has a distinctive sound system. Exact equivalents with English are impossible to reproduce in a printed list, but the table below can convey approximate Chinese sounds. Here are the pinyin symbols whose values differ most from what English readers expect. The number of items is kept small so that they may be remembered: only five consonants that begin syllables, plus four endings. Readers who follow this table—and say other pinyin as if it were English—will not quite be speaking Chinese, but they will also not be far wrong.

Pinyin	=	English
c-	=	ts-
q-	=	ch-
x-	=	sh-
z-	=	dz-
zh-	=	j-
-i	=	*
-ian	=	-ien
-ong	=	-ung
-ui	=	-way

---

* The -*i* is variant and stands for English -ee after most initial consonants (that is, labials *b*-, *m*-, *p*-; dental stops and liquids *d*-, *l*-, *n*-, *t*-; and palitals *j*-, *q*-, and *x*-), -r after *ch*-, *r*-, *sh*-, *zh*- (retroflexes), and deep -uh after *c*-, *s*-, *z*- (dental sibilants). This -*i* (the main flaw in pinyin) may be confusing at first. The rest of the system is straightforward enough, and even the -*i* comes with practice.

Policies of Chaos

CHAPTER 1

What the Cultural Revolution Was, and Why It Happened

Why is fire hot, or water deep?
—CHINESE PROVERB

Why did the Cultural Revolution occur? What made urban Chinese attack each other in the streets? How could a polity whose precepts of organization came from either Lenin or Confucius fall apart so completely? Why in 1966 did so many Chinese—as most of them now think—go politically berserk? This remains a question on China's agenda, even though there are reasons for many Chinese to forget about it. Such a searing experience shapes attitudes toward the future.

Because this mass movement wounded many patriotic Chinese deeply, they ask how it happened, who or what gave rise to it, whom or what to blame. Uncertainty about the Cultural Revolution's cause haunts current politics, even though many Chinese look back on their actions in that time with a sense of embarrassment. The major novelist Ba Jin, whose wife died during the turmoil, expresses a commonly held view: "I am sure it would be impossible that anyone who did not experience the Cultural Revolution directly, or has never been forced to dig deep into his soul and reveal all the ugliness that he found, could understand what actually happened."[1] Yet Ba Jin does not pretend to tell us why the Cultural Revolution occurred. It was, for many, a personal experience so traumatic that a rational or cause-seeking analysis of its origins, such as this book attempts, may seem too shallow an approach. Many people nonetheless want to know why the violence occurred, because they want to prevent anything like it from happening again.

ALTERNATIVE DEFINITIONS OF THE CULTURAL REVOLUTION

The CR, or Cultural Revolution, is often understood in narrow and official terms, as the peak of Party Chairman Mao Zedong's reign in China. Its

---

[1] Ba Jin, *Random Thoughts*, trans. Geremie Barmé (Hong Kong: Joint Publishing Co., 1984), pp. xv–xvi.

beginning is ordinarily defined by events in high-level politics (even though most Chinese best remember its effects at street level). Some say it started with a speech that Mao's defense minister Lin Biao gave in September 1965; others refer to an editorial that Yao Wenyuan published in October of that year.[2] Some say the CR started with an inspirational statement by Mao himself on May 16, 1966.

The end of the CR is even harder to pinpoint, but it is also usually measured by the headlines of high politics. A Party Congress was held in 1969, after most of the random violence had subsided; and this meeting ended the Cultural Revolution, according to some. Lin Biao's power and life ended in September 1971; if the CR is conceived as a gradual military takeover, this reversed it. Mao finally died in 1976, so that year is most often (and officially) taken as the end of the Cultural Revolution. Such a view implies Mao should be credited or blamed for the whole episode.

Chinese memories of the Cultural Revolution make it a time of apparently senseless violence, a holocaust-like event that needs to be understood so it will never be allowed to recur. If this definition becomes primary, the most relevant years are 1966–68, when the ordinary lives of many Chinese urban people were most disrupted. This book defines the CR mainly in terms of its violence and chaos. But the origins of the movement may at first seem harder to think about when its definition becomes less superficial and less dependent on news stories about high-level politics and ideas from Beijing. One of the purposes of this book is to show that the Cultural Revolution's standard definition, in both scholarly and official literatures, has obscured a search for the roots of its violence. The Cultural Revolution is defined in this book on a scope appropriate for that search—even at the risk of using its name in a new way.

"Gang of Four" Maoist leadership is still the usual answer to questions about the cause of the Cultural Revolution: a few high-placed members of the Party elite inspired hundreds of millions of people to work for a more egalitarian China—and to throw out their rivals in Beijing who had different goals. Mao condoned the criticism even of Communist officials in order to realize his own visions. This kind of explanation is useful for an analysis of Mao and a few of his friends or rivals. They had remarkable passions, which had important effects.

But China is a big place. Its politics cover more than four or five people.

---

[2] Yao, the Chairman's main polemicist, was a Shanghai newspaperman later dubbed one of the "Gang of Four." The other three were Mao's wife Jiang Qing, Shanghai union organizer Wang Hongwen, and Shanghai politician-journalist Zhang Chunqiao.

The usual elite-oriented explanation of the Cultural Revolution throws light on some of the causes of the movement, but it begs too many important questions: Why were revolutionary ideas growing so luxuriantly in large urban groups by the mid-1960s? Why did individuals become so interested in them? If the radical seed germinated in the minds of a few national leaders, how could they scatter it with such signal success, so widely and quickly? What was in China's ground to make it flourish? Were the underlying reasons for the Cultural Revolution's violence explicit in statements of that time? Why were the victims of such diverse kinds, including previous officials as well as previous outcasts? To what extent were the motives of the city people who made this "revolution" all the same, irrespective of the groups from which they came? Why were the conspirators and the victims in this movement at various stages so often similar (or indeed, the very same people)? Is it most persuasive to place blame for this holocaust only on Mao, or on Chinese traditions that change very slowly, or on some inherent flaw of socialism, or on the means by which the state activated any such broad factors in the specific motives of millions?

Such questions cannot be answered if the CR is seen as comparable only to a natural disaster, such as an earthquake, whose causes may never be adequately known. Many presume that something in the psychology of mass behavior, some native human aggressiveness—but random, inexplicable, indelible, like a lightning bolt or wildfire, a deep fault in the earth or original sin—is the center of the problem. The causes of such disasters can seldom be sufficiently shown. "Herd instinct" was important at this time; people were afraid of being left outside the circle of the legitimate community. In a slogan of that period, people said they would "rush wherever Chairman Mao points." The application of physical and animalistic metaphors to the Cultural Revolution seems difficult to avoid, because they accurately describe the terror that many Chinese still recall. But such metaphors cannot be completely satisfactory. This book tries to go beyond them. Even if they are true to the underlying causes of the event, they do not show conditions whose absence would have precluded the Cultural Revolution. Even natural disasters have causes, and it is worthwhile to try and understand them. In any case, it will not do to begin with concepts implying that the explanatory task here is mostly impossible.

Even if there are frightening monsters in the caves of the human soul (or the Chinese soul), their existence would not explain why they emerged in 1966—and why they stay safely underground most of the time.[3] Compari-

---

[3] This is not the place for a disquisition about the un-Chinese quality of any explanations

sons of paranoia and conspiracy terrors under Mao with those under Hitler or Stalin show that social doctrines do not account for the intensity of activities such leaders foster.[4] But why do such fearsome options in politics become attractive to wide masses of people at some times and places and not at others? Why do people make these choices, rather than select alternatives equally available in their cultures and ideologies? If high leadership was the only cause, why were so many followers enthusiastic enough to obey orders for violence against their neighbors?

EXPLANANDUM AND HYPOTHESES

The answers we find depend largely on the questions we ask. The main characteristic of the Cultural Revolution—the main thing to be explained about it—is in retrospect its violence. Yet many past writings have centered on other aspects of it. The best Chinese book on the Cultural Revolution, and most Western books about it, are play-by-play narrative accounts.[5] Interpretive studies have emerged in both Chinese and other languages, and it is clear that many possible questions about the Cultural Revolution are legitimate matters for study.

If this event is seen mainly as a psychological ordeal for millions who survived it, then a current practical issue is one of therapy.[6] Major national

---

referring to inherent human sin. But for more about "great tradition" views of original goodness, see Wm. Theodore de Bary, ed., *Sources of Chinese Tradition* (New York: Columbia University Press, 1960), esp. 1: 99–100 (a general and explicit rejection of Xun Zi's views in favor of Mencius's), and Donald J. Munro, "Man, State, and School," in *China's Developmental Experience*, ed. Michel Oksenberg (New York: Praeger, 1973), esp. pp. 121–33. More important, on the "little tradition" of folk-Buddhistic views of human nature, see Wolfram Eberhard, *Guilt and Sin in Traditional China* (Berkeley and Los Angeles: University of California Press, 1967), pp. 18–23.

[4] This book's emphasis on "monitors" is indebted to ongoing research by Andrew G. Walder, who nonetheless does not treat monitoring as a policy. His use of literature on comparative communism and of theory that sees violence as "deviance" confirming a system (as in Kai T. Erikson, *Wayward Puritans: A Study in the Sociology of Deviance* [New York: Wiley, 1966]) may be less appropriate to the subject of this book than reliance on theorists like Clifford Geertz or James Scott, who view cultures or systems as inconsistent. For a defense of the former position, see David Elkins and Richard Simeon, "A Cause in Search of Its Effect, or What Does Political Culture Explain?" *Comparative Politics* 11 (January 1979): 127–46; and see note 110 below and the concluding chapter.

[5] See Yan Jiaqi and Gao Gao, *Zhongguo "wenge" shinian shi* (A history of the decade of China's "Cultural Revolution") (Hong Kong: Dagongbao Press, 1986).

[6] Anne F. Thurston's *Enemies of the People: The Ordeal of the Intellectuals in China's Great Cultural Revolution* (New York: Knopf, 1987) is a testimonial to human suffering in the CR. As Thurston could be first to point out, this topic can have no exhaustive treatment. An-

officials have said that about one hundred million people (one-tenth of the country's population) suffered in the Cultural Revolution.[7] Some were victimized directly; others, by association with close relatives. Some say that twenty million people died in the Cultural Revolution.[8] A much lower estimate of these fatalities (by a Western scholar who successfully debunks inflated casualty figures in Chinese campaigns) numbers the deaths at about one million. But as this same, more conservative estimator points out: "The Cultural Revolution, even aside from its deaths, was a tragedy of immense proportions, devastating in its impact on the Chinese people."[9] No one knows the exact number of deaths or victims in this event. The meaning of statistics in holocausts is difficult to comprehend. Not enough can be done to alleviate the sense of guilt among survivors, their fears that the movement might recur, and the wounds that many Chinese still feel.[10] An outsider may be in a position to offer clinical advice for the victims, but that is not the aim of this book. An attempt to understand the hurt in terms of its social causes is the main goal here.

If the Cultural Revolution is conceived as a set of policies handed down from Beijing—and this is the most common conception of it—then a careful look at very few top leaders should suffice to describe it. But in this book, the CR is defined as an act of violence by and against millions of people. So it is necessary to look for explanations broadly, among a great many actors. Studies of labeled social groups, of dyadic relations between monitors and clients, and of the results of institutionalized campaign violence will forward an understanding of why old authorities collapsed and new local leaders became so ambitious so unexpectedly.

This book aims at finding the reasons for massive political frustration among many urban Chinese by the mid-1960s. It is partly concerned with leaders—official local bosses, as well as informal leaders of self-conscious groups that were not necessarily official. But the main question concerns

---

other contribution is Arthur Kleinman's *Social Origins of Stress and Disease: Depression, Neurasthenia, and Pain in Modern China* (New Haven: Yale University Press, 1985).

[7] See Andrew J. Nathan, *Chinese Democracy* (New York: Knopf, 1985), p. 5.

[8] Any casualty estimate for the CR partly depends, of course, on the definition of its time period. For figures, see Alan P. L. Liu, *How China is Ruled* (Englewood Cliffs, N.J.: Prentice-Hall, 1986), p. 48. See also Lu Ken, "Hu Yaobang fangwen ji" (Interview with Hu Yaobang), *Baixing yuekan* (*Baixing Monthly*, Hong Kong), December 1985, p. 32.

[9] Stephen Rosskamm Shalom, *Deaths in China Due to Communism: Propaganda versus Reality* (Tempe: Center for Asian Studies, Arizona State University, 1984).

[10] Anne F. Thurston, "Victims of China's Cultural Revolution: The Invisible Wounds," parts 1, 2, *Pacific Affairs*, 57, no. 4, 58, no. 1 (1984–85, 1985): 599–620 (esp. p. 605), 5–27. Thurston uses interviews to explain the depth of the scars. Concerning survivors' guilt and fears of recurrence, see pp. 7–17.

both leaders and their followers: Why did people ostracize each other? Why did they cut each other off, within their daily work units? Why did they go on the streets to attack many whom they did not even know? The isolation and humiliation were even harder for many victims of the CR to bear than was the torture.[11] Perhaps widespread frustrations would not have erupted so violently without encouragement from Mao and his well-known "gang." But it is unclear how four or five people could have produced such extensive, thorough, highly motivated fury among millions, however much their policies justified violence.

This book argues that the specific causes of the Cultural Revolution as a mass movement lay in administrative policies used in the whole pre-1966 history of the PRC. Especially important were three institutionalized policies whose effectiveness cumulated only gradually. These implementing, administrative policies were means by which the Party tried to achieve ambitious goals with scarce resources.

1. Official good and bad *labels* for groups, such as "cadres" or "proletarians," "rightists" or "capitalists," made people acquire concrete interests in seeing these labels used in their favor and not to their harm. These labels created "status groups," which became conscious of their shared interests in official allocations of jobs, housing, services, places in schools, and rights to live in cities. The labels created new kinds of collective group consciousness.

2. Official support for designated *bosses* and monitors raised individuals' dependence on particular leaders in units where they worked or studied. This dependency also lessened individuals' ability to find alternative livelihoods outside those units. Such policies forced people into clientage more surely than the feudal legacy of Confucian patriarchy ever did. State support for strong hierarchy in local units created a situation that made it "rational" for individual actors to behave as if maintaining links with their official bosses was the touchstone for all they did in public. These policies bred both adulation and resentment of patrons. By the mid-1960s, many urbanites were ready to follow orders for "struggle" against either the designated leaders or their local rivals, depending on how they had fared as individuals with the pre-CR local monitor.

3. Official *campaigns* frightened citizens into avid compliance with state policies. These movements reduced short-run administrative costs for an understaffed Party needing support for revolutionary social programs. But the campaigns also legitimated violence. "Killing chickens to scare monkeys"

[11] Thurston, "Victims," p. 605.

(*sha ji jing hou*) had become normal workaday policy by August 1966, when a relaxation of previous police controls on urban politics allowed many new groups and individuals to conflict with each other—and to use similar violence for their own ends.

None of these policies was foreordained by Communist or Chinese traditions, both of which come in many possible forms. Unstable policy has usually been explained as the result of tensions among elites, though not on the local level. This may seem tenable, or at least interesting, when a central participant was that most engaging loose cannon, Mao Zedong. But a reason for the ever-changing policies from Beijing lies in the results, for gaining mass compliance, of vacillation itself. Constant unpredictability, when backed by state force, tends to scare people. It is an administrative policy that raises the chances of (and lessens the costs of) public compliance with any other policies.

An emphasis on tensions among the national elite obscures this link. *All* top leaders benefit from the effects of their unpredictability at lower levels. The habit of campaigns strengthens the government, no matter which faction wins in Beijing. The dependence of subordinates on monitors is also an interest of all members of the Party's highest ranks, whatever their policy differences on more substantive issues. The broad constituency that positive labels created for the Party also was a benefit for all of the most important leaders. For the whole period from 1949 to 1966, and for all top leaders, standard operating procedures involved labeling people, enmeshing them in hard-to-change patronage networks, and legitimating campaign violence. These were general habits that cut the expense of garnering mass compliance with revolutionary rule. Such patterns had long-term costs (the most important was the Cultural Revolution), but these were not easy to foresee. For a decade and a half, many immediate victories of good-label groups, tight hierarchy, and brief campaigns obscured the bigger, unintended consequences of these effective techniques of short-term manipulation.

The widespread habit of force arose not just from struggle among a few politicians, or just from patriarchal flaws in Chinese culture, or just from the allure of proletarian social ideals or contrastive, vivid political symbols. It stemmed mainly from the gap between the Party's shortage of capable revolutionaries and its need for mass compliance. The socialization of Chinese to follow the Party Chairman was important, especially in 1966 when the movement began. But groups' and individuals' accumulated reaction to administrative policies in the entire period after 1949 was the main cause of the Cultural Revolution's forcefulness.

THE IMPORTANCE OF LABELED STATUS GROUPS

This chapter contains generalizations that later evidence will confirm; but first, the theses set forth above deserve to be made more explicit. The inherent confusion of the Cultural Revolution militates against any final analysis of it. The constituencies most relevant to this mass movement were not just elite factions in Beijing. Nor were they economically generated classes. They were status groups. The first topic concerns how they arose.

The "class" label of an urbanite was not hard to determine. All city people were categorized under one of several fixed titles, depending on the type of income source of the household head in 1949, namely,

> worker (*gongren*)
> peasant (*nongmin*) of various kinds
> capitalist (*zichan jieji*)
> landlord (*dizhu*)
> petty bourgeois (*xiao zichan jieji*)
> vagabond (*youmin*).

Urbanites were assigned to such "classes" in the early 1950s, as soon as the Party began personal dossiers or updated the old GMD files. The designations might be reviewed anytime, at the initiative of either the individual or the bureaucracy. A person could argue for a better label, and some designations were created to relieve servants of the state from worrying about personal liability in "class" struggle campaigns. These special titles were

> revolutionary cadre (*geming ganbu*),
> revolutionary soldier (*geming junren*), or
> dependant of revolutionary martyr (*geming lieshi jiashu*).[12]

"Intellectual" (*zhishi fenzi*) was not a class designation, though "student" (*xuesheng*) became common as a quasi–class category, a bit like the three honor-laden labels for state functionaries. Household registration books (*huji bu*) contained only the most important labels, but the dossiers (*dang'an*) in police stations and work-unit security offices included more extensive records. Many kinds of application forms asked for self-reporting of

---

[12] See Richard Curt Kraus, *Class Conflict in Chinese Socialism* (New York: Columbia University Press, 1981), pp. 24, 185.

class and other labels. These were usually accurate, since officials could easily check them against police files.

Communist Party cadres tended to discriminate, especially after the Antirightist Campaign of mid-1957, against people in cities who had "bad" labels (usually "bourgeois" but also often "intellectual" or "rightist"). The dossiers allowed bureaucrats to give people public advantages or stigmas. School admissions, good jobs, avoidance of rural work assignments, rights of association, housing, food, and much else became subject to official rationing on the basis of class labels (such as "capitalist" or "worker") and other political labels (such as "rightist" or "model"). Because Chinese workplaces, schools, and residential areas were increasingly centralized, with a few leaders controlling ever more of the resources that people needed for leading contented lives, individuals had no choice except to confirm tight local authority structures by obeying the designated leaders, especially during "class" struggles. Labeling thus interacted with monitoring and campaigning to shape the incentive structures of both officials and ordinary urbanites.

This pattern was a syndrome, a self-confirming "loop," a habit to save costs in preserving the new order. But the administrative policies that created it did not come into full force suddenly in 1949. Many members of the Chinese Communist Party were originally from rather-well-to-do social groups, which the syndrome finally oppressed most, though most of the cadres avoided harm to themselves on this basis before 1966. Party members' intentions were often divided. The CCP took far more than a decade to garner resources even for partial realization of the totalist concepts idealized in the notion of "proletarian dictatorship." The head of steam, built up to free the Party's scarce personnel for revolutionary functions, eventually became a crucial cause of violent ostracism in the Cultural Revolution.

Individuals' consciousness about class labels became more political than social. These designations were formally recorded, during the early 1950s, in the household registration books.[13] Such labels did not describe China's actual classes, because they did not distinguish people according to current links with the forces and relations of economic production, which the revolutionary government had already begun to change.[14] But the labels gradu-

---

[13] For more, see Lynn White, "Deviance, Modernization, Rations, and Household Registration in Chinese Cities," in *Deviance and Social Control in Chinese Society*, ed. R. W. Wilson, S. Greenblatt, and A. Wilson (New York: Praeger, 1977), pp. 151–72.

[14] This is not the book for a discourse on the evolution of the concept of class, but it is worth noting that most of the Marxist innovators since Marx and Engels (Bernstein, Kautsky, Lukács, Gramsci, Althusser, Poulantzas, and others) have spent much of their intellectual effort

ally created mass political groups, which acquired common interests and the potential for common consciousness.

Such groups were usually unorganized. Some Party cadres nonetheless increasingly encouraged proletarian-labeled people to form clubs, and these efforts reached a high level of activity by the mid-1960s. After August of 1966, many kinds of citizens could join political groups on practically any basis, and data presented below show that labels affected these decisions. Associate interviews give evidence of the importance of political labels for individuals' lives before the Cultural Revolution. So do recent Chinese novels, short stories, and autobiographical accounts.[15]

Class labels recorded in the household books could be important, but even more important were those in the secret files (*dang'an*) that each person's work unit kept. When applying for a job in a state organization, it was usual to fill out a form indicating one's class and other particulars—which the authorities might or might not check.[16] Labels such as "rightist" (*youpai fenzi*) or "bad element" (*huai fenzi*) that resulted from investigations would be noted. An individual often did not have any way of knowing on what evidence such "black materials" had been compiled. Political labels largely determined individuals' life chances in China throughout the third quarter of this century.

Youths with good group designations—"cadre" even more than "worker," and especially the "five red type" (*hong wu lei*)—began the violence in 1966. Political resentment of negative labels was slower to be articulated, partly because these categories were crosscut by nationalistic identifications. The Communist government had previously laid claim to

---

trying to capture the practical virtues of making economically generated classes almost synonymous with Weberian "status groups." See Martin Carnoy, *The State and Political Theory* (Princeton: Princeton University Press, 1984). The labeled classes that the PRC used were closer to status groups, despite some of their names; the simplest way to define them is to look at the registration books and security dossiers.

[15] "The Wounded" literature (*shanghen wenxue*), named for Lu Xinhua's 1977 story of that name, chronicles the harm done to people who had bad labels. See Lu Xinhua et al., *The Wounded: New Stories of the Cultural Revolution*, trans. Geremie Barmé and Bennet Lee (Hong Kong: Joint Publishing Co., 1979); see also Perry Link, ed., *Stubborn Weeds: Popular and Controversial Chinese Literature after the Cultural Revolution* (Bloomington: Indiana University Press, 1983), and autobiographical accounts that make the same point: Liang Heng and Judith Shapiro, *Son of the Revolution* (New York: Random House, 1983); Yue Daiyun, with Carolyn Wakeman, *To the Storm: The Odyssey of a Revolutionary Chinese Woman* (Berkeley and Los Angeles: University of California Press, 1985). The finest novel in this genre is Dai Houying's *Ren a, ren*, translated as *Stones of the Wall* (New York: St. Martin's Press, 1985).

[16] In the Cultural Revolution, Red Guards often went to rural areas where bureaucrats whom they wished to attack had grown up, to check the accuracy of urban records. This practice was called "outside investigation" (*wai diao*).

patriotism from the entire population. There was scant legitimate opportunity for the offspring of families labeled capitalist, or worse, to oppose affirmative action in the life chances for proletarians directly. When they finally did so, during the Cultural Revolution, their action came in the form of extreme violence against bureaucrats as a new class. Claiming rights to a place in the sun, many children of the bad-labeled groups were only in 1966 able to attack people whom they disliked, especially when some proletarians joined them. When police controls were relaxed in August 1966 (by Mao for his own reasons), youths of various backgrounds seized the opportunity to attack Party bureaucrats who had administered affirmative action in favor of labeled proletarians and cadres.

The ironies in this situation were poignant. Many bourgeois-labeled people joined some workers to create an ostensibly "Great Proletarian" Cultural Revolution. To live down their pasts, as well as to have revenge on the bureaucrats who repressed them, they often joined the most radical groups. These bands sometimes also attacked older intellectuals who had class labels similar to their own. The status quo found its most ardent defenders—whose methods often came to resemble police conservatism—among the supposedly revolutionary proletariat.

Could there have been such a sharp divergence between the rhetoric of the movement and the personal impulses behind it? Data presented below show there could be and was. Bourgeois intellectuals have been radical before, and worker-leaders have been conservative. Extreme radicalism has generally been a phenomenon of well-to-do groups at times of revolution (even in pre-industrial societies).[17] Much evidence, below, will show it remained so in China.[18]

These ironies should not, however, obscure the role of proletarian-labeled people, who often sensed the frustration—and the continuing informal social prestige—of bourgeois-labeled people. Thus cadre-related groups developed an interest in purging corruption (except favoritism to themselves) from the ranks of their own protectors. They hoped to assure the Party's revolutionary legitimacy for the future. These people, advantaged by the label system, might otherwise lose benefits that had become well established by the 1960s. They initiated and joined attacks against officials whose wrongdoing was so obvious, it became a threat to the whole system that

[17] See Alfred Cobban, *The Social Interpretation of the French Revolution* (Cambridge: Cambridge University Press, 1964).

[18] More is in Lynn White, "Bourgeois Radicalism in the 'New Class' of Shanghai," in *Class and Social Stratification in Post-Revolution China*, ed. James L. Watson (Cambridge: Cambridge University Press, 1984), pp. 142–74.

helped them.[19] And they usually led the battle against intellectuals and rightists, their potential rivals for local leadership.

In most cities, two loose coalitions of Red Guard factions therefore
emerged—and made war on each other. One of them defended the previous
regime and its policies, insofar as this was feasible for particular bureaucrats
who had good reputations. This first coalition included many of the earliest-
formed Red Guard groups (whose members claimed to be "red" because
they had proletarian or cadre backgrounds, though critics called them "factions to protect emperors" [*baohuang pai*]). The other coalition was generally more radical, because its members wanted more changes of previous
bureaucrats. It included groups that claimed the label "rebel faction" (*zaofan pai*) because of attacks on bureaucratic cadres. Some members had
bourgeois class labels and had been excluded from the first-formed Red
Guard groups because they did not come from worker or cadre families. A
recent PRC appraisal uses the same distinction when it refers to "the two
types of factional organization in the Cultural Revolution." One of these
"rebelled against leading cadres, and the other protected leading cadres."[20]

At first, capitalist-labeled people could not participate in the Cultural
Revolution because of their class stigma. Intellectuals among them were far
more active than businessmen or other nonproletarians, and students became the core of many "rebel factions." People labeled bourgeois had mostly
developed habits of political quietude after the fearsome campaigns against
them in the 1950s; but as the Cultural Revolution developed, the local political opportunities available to these people became more important than
their labels.

The sequence of ostracism and violence has been a common theme of
many similar movements in the past. Since the first modern revolution, the
Puritan one in England, there has been a record of attacking traditions,

---

[19] Another Chinese literary genre, called "reportage" (*baogao wenxue*), provides vivid ex-
posés of such corruption. See especially the famous report that gives the main title to Liu Binyan's *People or Monsters? And Other Stories and Reportage from China after Mao*, ed. Perry
Link (Bloomington: Indiana University Press, 1983). See also the famous play "What If I Really
Were," by Sha Yexin et al., in *Stubborn Weeds*, pp. 198–250, in which major characters are
corrupt cadres. Even the Central Committee's *Resolution on CCP History (1949–81)* (Beijing:
Foreign Languages Press, 1981), p. 47, admitted that "it remains difficult to eliminate the evil
ideological and political influence of centuries of feudal autocracy. . . . This meant that conditions were present for the overconcentration of Party power in individuals and for the development of arbitrary individual rule."

[20] "Thirteen Questions on Repudiating the Great Proletarian Cultural Revolution," *Jiefang-
jun bao* (Liberation army news) (Beijing), July 14, 1984, esp. question 9. The terms *baohuang
pai* and *zaofan pai* can be found in many articles and in the author's interviews of Cultural
Revolution participants, conducted from 1967 to 1984 in Hong Kong and Princeton.

smashing idols, renaming places, and killing "counterrevolutionaries" that makes for fearsome history wherever it has occurred. France had its guillotines. The early revolutionary United States had tar-and-featherings. In China, as in other countries, such violence winds down as leaders in many groups come to believe that the costs of acrimony between them outweigh the benefits of reconciliation for their own status groups. As local leaders who have various kinds of actual functions in society come to terms, China's upheaval may develop more like the English and the French revolutions than the Russian one, with which it is almost always compared.

China's CR engaged "masses"—large groups in cities—but not mainly the hopeless or the powerless. It mobilized local leaders and their families to preserve or restore privileges. It spurred capitalist-labeled (especially intellectual) families to correct injustices against themselves. It also motivated cadres' families to defend their gains of previous years. Personal and material, not just collective and ideal, motives were essential on all sides of the Cultural Revolution.

THE IMPORTANCE OF BOSSES AND PATRONAGE

The CR was also a struggle for personal freedom, not just for group interests. A promising line of research stresses the importance of "clientelism" in China and other socialist states.[21] Tight, patriarchal authority relations are normal in many Chinese work units, and rebellion against them is a natural reaction for members who feel oppressed. The domain of a patron in China is the work "unit" (*danwei*). These come in many different sizes, mostly larger than families, with smaller units nested inside of larger ones— for instance, a ward within a hospital, within a medical college, within a health "system."[22] The boss in a large unit is normally collective, rather than a single person.

In the years preceding the Cultural Revolution, usually one member of

[21] See Jean C. Oi, "Communism and Clientelism: Rural Politics in China," *World Politics* 37, no. 2 (1985): 238–66. Andrew G. Walder is at work on a book that may explore the importance of clientelism in cities, notably among industrial workers, during the Cultural Revolution. The most relevant published work is his *Communist Neo-Traditionalism: Work and Authority in Chinese Industry* (Berkeley and Los Angeles: University of California Press, 1986). See also John Wilson Lewis, *Political Networks and the Chinese Policy Process* (Stanford, Calif.: Northeast Asia–United States Forum, 1986).

[22] A "system" is a *xitong*. Gail E. Henderson and Myron S. Cohen's *The Chinese Hospital: A Socialist Work Unit* (New Haven: Yale University Press, 1984) provides the fullest survey in English of such authority relations during a calm period.

the leadership was dominant and was seen by higher authorities as the person in charge of the unit. He was in most cases a male Party secretary, frankly called the "boss" (*daitou ren*). Subjugation to such a monitor, when he was hostile, was called "wearing small shoes" (*chuan xiaoxie*). For underlings, poor relations with the official patron meant difficult work assignments, slow promotions, and general unpleasantness.

Soviet-imported institutions strengthened and officialized Chinese traditions of patronage. These habits are more specifically Leninist than Communist. People in China have long been arranged according to strong "dyadic" bonds between leaders and followers. Families have naturally nurtured such relations, and many other social groups—not just in China, but especially there—have tried to replicate the warmth and order of family links. These old patterns were intensified by the norms of Communist discipline that underlay new laws and institutions for a "New China" built in the 1950s on models from the USSR.

Mass groups are usually too large, however, for the people in them to know each other well. They become less effective as face-to-face relations are divided into many levels of hierarchy. Members may still have a warm sense of the political effectiveness that sheer numbers give them in this kind of organization; but if they think that immediate patrons treat them unfairly, and if higher patrons in a bureaucratized network do not have time to judge all such cases, the viability of the clientelist system decreases. As an administrative device, the system is most effective when underlings in it cannot switch out of the unit to which they are assigned. They then have more incentive to obey the designated monitor.

Analysis of mass groups needs to be complemented by patron-client analysis, which can explain political changes in local communities and work units. The argument for the importance of clientelism is sometimes presented as if it were incompatible with label/"group" and campaign/"totalitarian" explanations of action. Analysts favoring the patronage model point out that relevant groups in China are only sometimes articulated and sometimes self-conscious. Also, totalitarian campaigns only sometimes give positive incentives to actors (for example, to activists).[23] But patron-client bonds are only some of the political links that affect urban Chinese. There is nothing wrong with casting diverse analytic nets, and it is practical to note that labeling and campaigning share a similarity with designating patrons:

[23] See Walder, *Communist Neo-Traditionalism*, pp. 5–7. But a footnote (p. 7) puts Communist states' "distinctive variety of 'pluralism' . . . beyond the scope of this book." See more below, in the concluding chapter.

all three were policies. As later chapters will show, these forms of inquiry complement each other, despite the logical tensions between them. A full explanation of the CR will take the frequency of strong small-unit rule in China seriously, just as it will also take seriously the importance of mass social forces. What unifies these two types of analysis is not that they are based on the same logic for explaining action, but that they are both based on specifiable government policies, accumulating from 1949 to 1966.[24]

THE IMPORTANCE OF CAMPAIGNS

Group consciousness created by labels, along with inflexible dyadic relations created by patronage policies, might not have influenced Chinese so deeply by 1966 if administrative violence had not become legitimate normal policy. In the West during the late 1960s there was some bias against discussing the Cultural Revolution's violence. This movement's antibureaucratic ideas were exciting. Western intellectuals had seldom experienced revolutions directly, and the CR's ideals seemed more salient in the late 1960s than its violence. Only in retrospect has attention focused on the ways the Cultural Revolution ate its children. Its idealism surely increased the ruthlessness of its actors.

A complete list of all China's campaigns before the Cultural Revolution is not necessary here, partly because Ezra Vogel has abstracted their general form:

> The speed-ups [in a campaign] form a pattern found not only in collectivization, but also in land reform and later in the Great Leap Forward and the Cultural Revolution. The pattern is one of careful planning and groundwork at all levels, then a sudden increase in the targets set by superiors in the hierarchy. After a sudden burst of all-out mobilization, the new targets are "achieved." Targets are raised several times until the final goal is reached. This is followed by readjustment to correct for "paper successes" and problems arising because of the hasty campaign. The leaders do not spell out in their writings the logic behind the waves of assault.[25]

[24] The accumulating effectiveness of the three administrative policies stressed in this book was an uneven, not a steady, phenomenon. For example, there was some lessening of pressure in the period before 1963, and the 1962–66 period was ambivalent, with political claims important in some spheres but weak in others. See later chapters below on this.

[25] Ezra F. Vogel, *Canton under Communism: Programs and Politics in a Provincial Capital, 1949–1968* (Cambridge: Harvard University Press, 1969), pp. 167–68.

This method of administration is designed more to achieve results than to plan them. It aims at effectiveness more than predictability. It seems to be most useful when the "organizational weapon" that is launching assaults has too few resources to achieve goals without keeping subordinates or non-members off balance. Not only do campaigns lower the need for administrative resources because they raise compliance through inspiring fears of repression. Just as important, they gather new administrative resources by raising hopes of career advancement among activists.

The Chinese government from 1949 to 1966 was effective at social reform in part because it combined progressive policies with implementation by scaring people, changing goals in movements often and unpredictably, and saddling established institutions with work teams of outsiders who impressed the power of the state on local leaders. Such procedures are not like those of "legal-rational" modern bureaucracies, but they bring change quickly. For an administration in a hurry, they seem (and are) temporarily cost-effective.

Campaign policies have achieved progressive goals in concentrated doses. But the chapters below will show that the Chinese state often lacked the personnel who might have allowed it to consolidate its gains from these movements. The campaign method, which requires even more implicit or explicit violence than other kinds of government policy, was more costly in the long run than was evident immediately. Sometimes campaigns were temporarily relaxed or restricted to limited sectors of society (as was the case for a while after 1961). By the mid-1960s, however, in an atmosphere of tension that labeling and patronage policies had brought and after campaigns had legitimated force in politics, a relaxation of police controls brought an explosion from people who could then use violence for their own purposes.

These three kinds of administrative policy are more important together than separately. Labeling policies and patronage policies both breed consciousness of interests—in groups and individuals, respectively. Labels make groups, and similarly favored or disfavored people can guess their allies on that basis, while they can also still act individually. Mandating official patrons gives each person a boss, and individuals can act together on that understanding to support or topple the patron. Campaigns provide a context in which these perceptions can spur violence that seems rightful. A conclusion of this book is that differences in the logic of causal explanation between these three factors are less important than their ability to account for events together, because they interact with each other.

INTERNATIONAL COMPARISONS AND
THE STAGES OF REVOLUTIONS

Many people think of revolutions as sudden. They are violent, and a blow is supposed to strike in an instant. But actually, revolutions take years. The English Revolution executed King Charles; but its origins can be traced at least a century before its high tide, and it was partly reversed in the Stuart Restoration.[26] Before 1789, France was home to many political ideas; afterward, chaos reigned for the better part of a decade until international war gave reasons for unity. The Mexican Revolution may be the most-long-drawn-out of all; it sputtered on for more than a century after 1810. In Russia, a separation of 1917 from 1905, or especially from Stalin's violence in the 1930s, would hide many important continuities. It should come as no surprise that China's case is similar; the Cultural Revolution is one event in a linked series.

Clear threads of nationalist and revolutionary sentiment tie together the gigantic and bloody Taiping Rebellion of 1850–64, the Republican Revolution of 1911, the anti-imperialist strikes in Chinese cities of the 1920s, the resistance against Japan from 1937 to 1945, the Civil War until 1949, and campaigns in the PRC after 1949. Among these surges of China's century-long turbulence, the Cultural Revolution could eventually prove to be the last major instance, because its violence divided rather than legitimated a social elite. In this, it differed from most earlier whirlpools in the current. Mass upheavals appear to come in bunches over long periods of time. They may be unexpected but are not instant. There is enough evidence from countries like England, France, and the United States to suggest that extended periods of relative calm may follow revolutions or their equivalents, after these storms pass. Revolutions take a while to mature, because they are made of resources, not just ideals. Eventually, they also seem to wind down.

China is not the first country whose revolution has seen alternating waves of emphasis on stability and change. The radical Robespierre killed the more moderate Danton; but a few years later, France had an emperor. Struggles between visionaries and realists dominated the first decade of Soviet politics—until Stalin's reforms created a kind of solid order. Choices made in periods of postrevolutionary tension, and lessons that people draw retrospectively, can shape a nation's politics for a long time. In Russia, the eval-

---

[26] Lawrence Stone's *The Causes of the English Revolution, 1529–1642* (New York: Harper and Row, 1972) deals with the prelude.

uation of Stalin is still a prime question of public life, though he died several decades ago. Many bureaucrats (in the KGB and other elites that Stalin established) still value his role in creating the modern Soviet state. But others look to rejection of Stalinism as the touchstone of progress. Maoism in many ways differed from Stalinism, but Mao and Stalin both endorsed sharp political intervention in citizens' lives. The Cultural Revolution bred a quietism and cynicism, a knowledge that political will can fail to bring intended results.[27] Reactions to Mao's Cultural Revolution will structure Chinese politics for many years. They show a pattern recognizable in other revolutions that wound down more quickly than the Russian one has done.

PREVIOUS RESEARCH ON THE STAGES OF CHINA'S REVOLUTION

The Liberation of 1949 and the Great Leap Forward of 1958 are the events in the PRC that scholars have explained best, although several years passed before there was any academic consensus on what these occasions meant. More than a decade after the founding of the PRC, most American attention even in academic circles focused on how the United States had "lost" China. The scholarly questions of the 1950s derived more from ideologies than from less constrained efforts of interpretation. Anecdotes, play-by-play accounts of specific events, and narrative histories were dominant genres in the field. Were Mao and his colleagues merely agrarian reformers, or full-fledged Leninists? Had the USSR's role in China's revolution been crucial? Was Mao merely the newest and poorest of the totalitarians—just another version of Stalin or Hitler? These were the main perceived issues. Categories of thought among American China hands were inseparable from the categories of U.S. politics in the 1950s.

In 1962, when Chalmers A. Johnson's book *Peasant Nationalism and Communist Power* appeared, the questions of this debate shifted.[28] Because that analysis treated communism as a subtype of nationalism, and because the new approach related the growth of Communist groups in North China

[27] A vivid treatment of such cynicism is Liu Xinwu's story "Awake, My Brother!" in *The Wounded*, pp. 179–203.

[28] *Peasant Nationalism and Communist Power: The Emergence of Revolutionary China, 1937–1945* (Stanford, Calif.: Stanford University Press, 1962). *The China Quarterly*, published in London, appeared in 1959; this journal's first articles included thoughtful statements of 1950s positions, and it soon became a medium for new research of many kinds.

to the context of war against Japan, academic interest moved from more abstract questions of ideology to functional questions, especially to the means by which the CCP gained a mass constituency. Johnson's thesis was contested by scholars who said the Party's social policies were crucial to Communist gains in politics, but the issues he raised are still the framework of serious debate on the PRC's beginning.[29] It took more than a dozen years after 1949 to set the parameters of this controversy, to focus on the resources that created the event of 1949, and to shape the question of what caused it.

Just one other event in CCP history has received a similarly thorough airing by academics. The Great Leap Forward of 1958 affected the lives of more Chinese more deeply than any campaign since then. Western scholars, looking at the gigantic upheaval of the Leap, initially had scant idea what to make of it. Anecdotes, summaries of CCP policy ideals, and critiques (sympathetic or unsympathetic, liberal or egalitarian) did not add up to any coherent sense of what had happened. In the mid-1960s, however, with the publication of works by Franz Schurmann, James Townsend, William Skinner, and Audrey Donnithorne, an implicit consensus arose from disparate researches: the Leap concerned organization.[30] It was an attempt to mobilize social energies by a Party that was interested in maximizing its impetus through "human organization," not just in allocating resources efficiently through "technical organization." One way to specify this trade-off between mobilization and efficiency was to look at China in terms of its many social cells, which could nest inside each other. Another was to look at the contrasts between different kinds of decentralization. The event was thus defined; it was a gigantic administrative experiment. It could be comprehended by theories of organization in economic infrastructure (for example, grain trade) and by attention to the sizes of management units. The controversy

---

[29] The best-known study along these lines is Mark Selden's *The Yenan Way in Revolutionary China* (Cambridge: Harvard University Press, 1971). Lucian Bianco's *The Origins of the Chinese Revolution, 1915–1949* (Stanford, Calif.: Stanford University Press, 1971) tends toward the same conclusions—but by emphasizing the concrete, harsh similitude between incursions of poverty and incursions of the Japanese army into peasants' lives, Bianco attempts some synthesis of the "peasant nationalism" and "social revolution" views. Like the French existentialist he is, Bianco writes beautifully about all this, without finalizing it absolutely.

[30] Franz Schurmann, *Ideology and Organization in Communist China* (Berkeley and Los Angeles: University of California Press, 1966); James R. Townsend, *Political Participation in Communist China* (Berkeley and Los Angeles: University of California Press, 1967); Audrey Donnithorne, *China's Economic System* (New York: Praeger, 1967); and G. William Skinner, "Marketing and Social Structure in Rural China," a three-part series in *Journal of Asian Studies* 24, nos. 1–3 (1964–65).

over the relative importance of different-sized units continues, especially in discussions of Chinese fiscal arrangements.[31] Like the debate about 1949, it has nurtured insights into problems that go far beyond the event on which it first focused.

The Cultural Revolution has spawned even more books than the Liberation or Leap. Many have praised or lambasted its policy ideals, provided accounts of politics among a very few top leaders, or explored the drama in particular institutions. Some of the liveliest books have come from Westerners who taught at Chinese universities in 1966–69.[32] Red Guards have also reported their experiences.[33] Interpretations of the Cultural Revolution, even by Chinese who suffered it, have often stayed fairly close to the categories that were already implicit in (or contrary to) statements of that time—although recent reports have stressed the random violence then, as some older accounts did not.[34]

These treatments are well informed, but only a few stand back from the passions of the CR to ask what caused it. A senior China hand, assessing his colleagues' overall work on the Cultural Revolution twenty years after that movement began, rightly gave them high marks in analyzing its immediate causes, but low marks for their attempts to find its fundamental causes.[35]

[31] See Thomas Lyons, *Economic Integration and Planning in Maoist China* (New York: Columbia University Press, 1987), and aspects of Thomas G. Rawski's forthcoming *Chinese Management Capabilities: Industrial Technology*. For earlier work, see Audrey Donnithorne, "China's Cellular Economy: Some Economic Trends Since the Cultural Revolution," *China Quarterly* (hereafter CQ), 52 (October–December 1972): 605–12, and Donnithorne, "Comment: Centralization and Decentralization in China's Fiscal Management," CQ 66 (June 1976): 328–39; Nicholas R. Lardy's "Comment" immediately follows in the same issue. A major new contribution to this long-debated subject is Barry Naughton's, "The Economy of the Cultural Revolution," in *New Perspectives on the Cultural Revolution*, ed. William Joseph, Christine Wong, and David Zweig (Cambridge: Harvard University Press, 1988).

[32] Victor Nee, *The Cultural Revolution at Peking University* (New York: Monthly Review Press, 1969); William Hinton, *Hundred Day War: The Cultural Revolution at Tsinghua University* (New York: Monthly Review Press, 1972); Colin Mackerras and Neale Hunter, *China Observed: 1964–1967* (London: Pall Mall, 1968); and Hunter, *Shanghai Journal: An Eyewitness Account of the Cultural Revolution* (New York: Praeger, 1969)—to name just a few of the books.

[33] Gordon A. Bennett and Ronald N. Montaperto, *Red Guard: The Political Biography of Dai Hsiao-ai* (Garden City, N.Y.: Doubleday, 1972); Ken Ling, *The Revenge of Heaven: Journal of a Young Chinese* (New York: Putnam, 1972); Gao Yuan, *Born Red* (Stanford, Calif.: Stanford University Press, 1987); and Liang and Shapiro, *Son of the Revolution*.

[34] See especially the autobiography by Nien Cheng, *Life and Death in Shanghai* (London: Collins, 1986).

[35] Lucian W. Pye, "Reassessing the Cultural Revolution," *China Quarterly* 108 (December 1986): 597–612.

Past answers to this question fall into several categories, which have been explored in other books that provide background for the more syncretic and policy-centered explanation adopted here.[36]

The next five subsections below deal with past approaches to the task of explaining the CR. The present project tries to organize them into a framework sufficient to explain the violence. It would be easy for a hasty reader of this book to get the impression that it arbitrarily rejects alternative views, tossing them away so as to get to the main hypothesis. But in fact, the effort here is aimed at showing what each of them can and cannot explain, so as to move toward a more comprehensive explanatory structure that includes them.

Common explanations of the CR emphasize social ideals, conflicts in Beijing, Mao's personality, the attractiveness of revolutionary symbols, or high-level impatience about national development. None of these approaches is wrong, even though the inadequacies of each will be discussed immediately below. The problem with most of them is that, even if they show whence ideas for action came in the CR, they do not demonstrate why so many people took up those ideas with such verve. They need to be supplemented—not supplanted—by an explanation of why high leaders and ideal notions were followed in such a singularly unusual, violent way by so many people. For that, it is not enough to talk about culture, ideology, top politicos, or symbols (all of which come in many types, of which only some were important by 1966). Why did particular options in these fields seem cogent to so many then? Labels, monitors, and campaigns—administrative policies arising from the CCP's lack of adequate resources to attain its ambitious goals quickly—put urban Chinese in a mood to act radically by 1966. The purpose here is not to reject previous explanations of the CR, but to show their scope. It is necessary to establish the mentalities of China's urban audience by the

---

[36] Despite some questioning here, I am in debt to previous works on the CR by many authors. Richard Baum, Marc Blecher, Anita Chan, Lowell Dittmer, John Gardner, Hong Yung Lee, John Wilson Lewis, Roderick MacFarquhar, Stanley Rosen, Susan Shirk, Tang Tsou, Andrew Walder, and Gordon White are certainly among them. This work on the CR may differ mostly in the attempts (1) to use local newspapers from the 1950s and early 1960s along with interviews and later 1960s sources; (2) to consider economic and cultural actors together—workers, not just students, and residents, not just cadres; (3) to admit both rational/individual and symbolic/group bases of action; and especially (4) to identify public reaction to previous *policies* as the spurs of mass violence in 1966, and concurrently to identify cultures as underlying factors that explain too much and Beijing leaders as precipitating factors that alone explain too little. This approach could not exist, however, without reference to earlier contributions by many others.

mid-1960s in order to see why diverse people affected and responded so forcefully to the ideals and leadership factors that many previous analyses have emphasized.

THE CR AS AN EXPRESSION
OF EGALITARIAN-COLLECTIVIST IDEALS

A commonsense approach in explaining human behavior is to ask the participants why they act as they do. The first answers to this question, for this stage of the Chinese revolution as for previous ones, were mostly ideological. The movement was seen as a class struggle against "capitalist roaders" who promoted material incentives in socialist China. The movement was not, in this view, mainly an adulation of Mao, or an elite power struggle, or a celebration of symbols devoid of social aims, or a clash of mass social groups. Instead, it was what people said it was: an effort to impose a more ideal revolutionary order on factories, communes, the army, and schools. Many of Mao's ideals were obviously praiseworthy.[37]

K. S. Karol spoke of the Communist purposes of the CR, not its causes.[38] Richard Pfeffer said the CR was an "authentic" revolution because Mao's intention was to create a new governing superstructure.[39] William Hinton wrote that such policies would change people, until finally no social classes would exist.[40] The Committee of Concerned Asian Scholars decided that "[t]he Great Proletarian Cultural Revolution was . . . the struggle to determine which line China would follow," especially in terms of goals such as equality, community, Chinese independence, and passing the torch of revolution across generation gaps.[41]

Yet Mao was less consistently anticapitalist than his most famous rivals. Liu Shaoqi and Peng Zhen were the main Communist leaders opposing non-

---

[37] Karl Polanyi's, *The Great Transformation* (New York: Rinehart, 1944) can be read for an argument that egalitarian and collectivist ideals are an essential ingredient of development, needed to regulate the effects of commoditization on modern efficient markets of human labor, environs, and earnings.

[38] K. S. Karol, *The Second Chinese Revolution*, trans. M. Jones (New York: Hill and Wang, 1974).

[39] Richard Pfeffer, "The Pursuit of Purity: Mao's Cultural Revolution," *Problems of Communism* 18, no. 6 (November–December 1969): 12–25.

[40] William Hinton, *Turning Point in China: An Essay on the Cultural Revolution* (New York: Monthly Review Press, 1972).

[41] *China! Inside the People's Republic* (New York: Bantam Books, 1972), pp. 72, 102–3. A careful book on idealism is Jean Daubier's *A History of the Chinese Cultural Revolution*, trans. Richard Seaver (New York: Random House, 1974).

Party intellectuals' "blooming" during 1957. Mao favored criticism from non-CCP people, at least for a while, in order to improve the quality of the cadres' performance. Peng Zhen went so far as to compare the 1957 rightists with Chiang Kai-shek and Wang Jingwei (China's chief collaborator with Japan).[42] Separating the ideological disputes of these leaders from their factional conflicts may be difficult in relation to any short time period, but over the long haul none of them was entirely inflexible. The CCP's top leaders conferred often with each other. They largely agreed on methods for implementing administration in New China—especially on the three policies for labels, patrons, and campaigns that are stressed in this book. They might apply these ideas differently at various times; but they were neither so diverse among themselves nor so consistent over time as they are often depicted in efforts to explain the Cultural Revolution on grounds of their social ideals.

What the participants said was populist and egalitarian. They said it even as they fought each other; so their pronouncements hardly explain their fighting. They all stressed conspiracies of national and class betrayal, as well as loyalty to an emperor-like leader; but this hardly explains the variety of directions their violence took, since it was aimed at each other. Social idealism in the CR may be a corollary of the violence, but the former is not convincing as a causal explanation of the latter. Ideals and violence may have had common origins in many individuals' and groups' reactions to earlier manipulation.

Then too, Maoism is not such a unified philosophy that clear deductions can be made from it. In a trenchant review of many major—and diverse—scholarly interpretations of "Mao Zedong thought," Nick Knight shows that

[t]he Mao texts do not speak for themselves; they are activated anew by each fresh reading, activated in ways which produce different emphases, different and at times sharply conflicting interpretations. . . . These instances of critique and counter-critique have done little more than reveal that the scholars involved are in disagreement; appeals to mutually exclusive assumptions and different empirical realities do not constitute the basis for fruitful debate.[43]

---

[42] Roderick MacFarquhar, *The Origins of the Cultural Revolution* (New York: Columbia University Press, 1974), 1: 290, quoting *RMRB*, August 7, 1957.

[43] Nick Knight, "The Marxism of Mao Zedong: Empiricism and Discourse in the Field of Mao Studies," *Australian Journal of Chinese Affairs* 16 (July 1986): 18–19.

Unlike some other totalitarians, Mao was not a riveting public speaker. His personal appearances were rare and somewhat random, and his speeches rambled. They did little to aid people who wanted to apply his thought accurately. Mao's sweeping ideas allowed vast room for different uses and interpretations, and he often refused to take sides in public disputes of which he was aware. His quotations were always available in the "little red book," but they are various enough for practically any purpose.[44] What his texts say, to the extent it can be specified, is less important than the many interpretive readings Chinese gave them and the functions people made them serve.

The less outside analysts knew about China, the clearer their descriptions became—and the more full of praise (if they were politically on the Left) or condemnation (if on the Right). Leo Huberman and Paul Sweezy, for example, rejected the idea that the CR arose from either mass or elite power struggles; they echoed contemporary Chinese statements that its purpose was to lead China into communism.[45] Stephan Possony, from the Right, wrote that Mao's reckless idealism gave America a chance to recruit anti-Maoists in China's military for opposing the USSR.[46] Since the Chinese media were describing the turmoil in philosophical terms, it was hardly surprising that outsiders drew their own very diverse conclusions on this Cultural Revolution, as if it were a seminar in political philosophy.

THE CR AS A RESULT OF POWER STRUGGLE

More cautious approaches to the problem often combined ideal analysis with a particular emphasis on elite power struggles. An object of this book is to complement rather than contradict some fine previous reports about China's national leaders. A bibliography on this subject would take a volume in itself.[47] The best reference, *The Origins of the Cultural Revolution* by Roderick MacFarquhar, includes two volumes thus far and will contain three when complete. It mainly concerns "the thinking, actions, and interaction of the Chinese leaders. . . . Mao Tse-tung, who made the Cultural

[44] An atypical but striking example is in Cheng, *Life and Death in Shanghai*, e.g., p. 291.

[45] Leo Huberman and Paul Sweezy, "The Cultural Revolution in China," *Monthly Review* 18, no. 8 (1967): 1–17.

[46] Stephan T. Possony, "The Chinese Communist Cauldron," *Orbis* 13, no. 3 (1969): 783–821.

[47] James C. F. Wang's, *The Cultural Revolution in China: An Annotated Bibliography* (New York: Garland, 1976), esp. chaps. 1, 2, mostly concerns this.

Revolution, Liu Shao-ch'i, who was cast as its Lucifer, and Chou En-lai, who survived it and its subsequent reverberations."[48]

Mao's personal role in encouraging the Cultural Revolution—especially in relaxing police controls during August 1966 and stirring up Red Guards to "seize power"—was a necessary cause of what happened and explains some of its aspects. If the Cultural Revolution can be boiled down to the question, "Why did Mao do this," it is possible to discuss many of the movement's most famous events. If the CR is defined entirely in terms of actions that required the approval of Mao, it is possible to write, as Harold Hinton has, that

> [t]he origins of the Cultural Revolution, therefore, can hardly be attributed, as some analysts propose, to basic sociological causes, such as discontent among students and industrial workers over inadequate job opportunities and rule by the Party apparatus.... The inspiration and leadership of the Cultural Revolution were Mao's, and without his initiative there would have been no Cultural Revolution.[49]

The only difficulty is that, while the CR indeed could not have taken place without Mao's instigation, the Chairman provides no sufficient explanation of why the event grew so large and so violent. Politics that widely invades personal and family life, as Robert C. Tucker has pointed out, presumes a totalitarian leader—a Hitler or Stalin or Mao.[50] Historical cases certainly suggest that charismatic leadership is a necessary condition for such an enthusiastic movement. Scholars may oversimplify their task, however, when they imply that the CR arose only because of Mao's call and not because of motives in the wide population which heard him. Klaus Mehnert, for example, writes that the Red Guards did not rise of their own will but were mobilized by Mao exclusively for his own purposes. This view makes the CR

---

[48] MacFarquhar, *The Origins*, 1: 3. The second volume was published in 1983; the third is forthcoming. Earlier, somewhat similar contributions were made by Byung-joon Ahn, *Chinese Politics and the Cultural Revolution: The Dynamics of Policy Processes* (Seattle: University of Washington Press, 1966); Richard Baum, *Prelude to Revolution: Mao, the Party, and the Peasant Question, 1962–66* (New York: Columbia University Press, 1975); and Richard Baum and Frederick C. Teiwes, *Ssu-Ch'ing: The Socialist Education Movement of 1962–1966* (Berkeley: University of California Center for Chinese Studies, 1968).

[49] Harold C. Hinton, *An Introduction to Chinese Politics* (New York: Praeger, 1973), p. 57.

[50] Robert C. Tucker, "Does Big Brother Really Exist?" *Wilson Quarterly* 8, no. 1 (1984): 106–17.

"a revolution from above," in which mass groups and social factors played an inessential role.[51]

There are at least three big questions that need to be raised about such explanations: First, why should anyone expect the motives of millions to serve or parallel the designs of a few top leaders? Second, what is the basis for assuming that the differences between these high politicos drove events more powerfully than their consensus, which had a more certain and long-lasting effect on state policies? Third, why is it necessary to rely on tentative data about the suspected preferences of atypical people, instead of the far more extensive and verifiable data available about the actual situations of many average people, as firmer grounds for explaining what happened to the many?

Analysts who are sensitive to the history and culture of Chinese politics stress the likely importance of factional alignments. But it is difficult to move from this insight to specific conclusions, for several reasons. First, potential leadership struggles in China are not always actualized. As Parris Chang has shown, even Mao Zedong often had to cooperate with leaders who had different social preferences, in a complex process of "conflict and consensus-building."[52] Severe elite conflict may always be potential below the surface; but in some periods, both before the CR and afterward, it has not occurred.

Second, Lowell Dittmer gives evidence to suggest that Mao was reconciled to Liu Shaoqi as late as October 1966—long after the CR had begun—and only later changed his famous mind.[53] Mao's intentions were unclear and vacillating, usually open to new options. The irresolvability of conflict among leaders in Beijing (and also among leaders in Shanghai, as described below) almost surely postdated mass conflict in the streets.

Third, it is questionable whether the particular disagreements among the Beijing elite—especially the differences over agricultural policy after the post-Leap rural failures—could motivate a CR that was mostly urban. Much of the scholarly literature traces the main roots of the CR to Liu's, Deng's, and other leaders' disdain for Mao's collectivization policies during the Leap

[51] Klaus Mehnert, *Peking and the New Left: At Home and Abroad* (Berkeley: University of California Center for Chinese Studies, 1969). See also Cheng Chu-yuan, "The Power Struggle in Red China," *Asian Survey* 6, no. 9 (1966): 469–83, and Gene T. Hsiao, "The Background and Development of 'The Proletarian Cultural Revolution,'" *Asian Survey* 7, no. 6 (1967): 389–404.

[52] Parris H. Chang, *Power and Policy in China*, enlarged ed. (University Park: Pennsylvania State University Press, 1978), e.g., p. 2.

[53] Lowell Dittmer, "The Cultural Revolution and the Fall of Liu Shao-ch'i," *Current Scene* 11, no. 1 (1973): 1–13. A PRC informant doubts Mao's avowals of willingness to work with Liu, but the mootness of this point mainly underlines the need for an analysis that goes far beyond high leaders.

of 1958–59.[54] This detailed work offers a good understanding of the animus of a few Politburo members toward Mao. It is a highly indirect means of trying to explain why so many city folk began to attack each other so bitterly several years later, in 1966.

Conflicts among famous people in Beijing were nonetheless a necessary precipitating factor of the Cultural Revolution, even if not a sufficient condition to explain its mass violence. This "power-struggle" cause of the event still receives attention, mainly because Mao often kept the pivotal role among the Beijing actors.[55] But a more specific reason for the Chairman's importance lies in the social effects of Central Committee directives during 1966. Mao himself penned the "May 16 Circular"—an inspirational polemic that legitimated criticism of certain Central Committee documents.[56] The "Sixteen Points" of August 7, 1966, passed by the committee at Mao's instigation, forbade police from preventing the formation of political organizations that would before then have been routinely repressed. But administrative techniques using labels, patronage, and campaigns had not divided the top leaders in principle (even when particular styles of implementing these and other policies divided them). Liu Shaoqi was as fond of such techniques as Mao Zedong. Central elite conflicts have been overemphasized by the literature as a reason for the CR.

[54] Liu—and Deng—were on Mao's side during the Leap. For relevant views, see Tai Sung An, *Mao Tsetung's Cultural Revolution* (Indianapolis, Ind.: Bobbs-Merrill, 1972); Franz Michael, "The Struggle for Power," *Problems of Communism* 16, no. 3 (1967): 12–21; James T. Myers, "The Fall of Chairman Mao," *Current Scene* 6, no. 10 (1968): 1–18; and, to a large extent, Roderick MacFarquhar, *The Origins*, all of which link the CR closely to leadership disagreements about rural policies. MacFarquhar's careful study, however, casts doubt on links to other policy disagreements that most articles infer from questionable post-1965 evidence. Notably, he does not depict Liu Shaoqi as a special advocate of Soviet-style models in China; and his work on many such points is a good corrective to other analyses based on fewer data. See also Lowell Dittmer, *Liu Shao-ch'i and the Chinese Cultural Revolution: The Politics of Mass Criticism* (Berkeley and Los Angeles: University of California Press, 1974).

[55] A recent contribution along these lines is Andrew Hall Wedeman's *The East Wind Subsides: Chinese Foreign Policy and the Origins of the Cultural Revolution* (Washington, D.C.: Washington Institute Press, 1987). Wedeman argues that power, not policy, was the only serious issue in Beijing—and specifically that Zhou Enlai became radical in the CR because the premier realized that only Mao, not Liu, could protect him. If this was all true, as it may have been, then it still made little difference to the vast majority of participants in the CR. For related reasons, the present book does not fall into any of the "descriptive typologies" in Kuo Tai-chün and Ramon H. Myers, *Understanding Communist China: Communist China Studies in the United States and the Republic of China, 1949–1978* (Stanford, Calif.: Hoover Institution Press, 1986). The book in your hands assumes no monolithic CCP, nor an essentially developmentalist regime, nor a mainly socialist one, nor a CCP whose internal top struggles (personalized or other) determine all important politics. These types, used by scholars in the United States and elsewhere, are all top-down analyses; they all neglect the other direction.

[56] The "May 16 Circular" and "Sixteen Point Decision" are printed in Daubier, *A History*, pp. 289–305.

Maoists were not so locally organized, ideologically consistent, or exclusively identifiable as the power-struggle explanation of the CR suggests. Liuists did not exist in coherent groups during the two years of violence after 1966. Yet power struggle between factions, presumably extending from Beijing down to local work units, has been the most enduring of all explanations of the CR. It has been discussed so extensively, for such a long time, that many people implicitly define the CR as if power struggle were its main or only possible meaning. Many who have previously thought a good deal about the CR will have trouble with this book, until they realize that their past attention to Beijing power struggles is inconsistent with their own knowledge of the extent of local disorganization, disloyalty, and chaos after 1966.

The May and August 1966 decisions were crucial to starting the CR, but they tell little about the mass political energy it released. Earlier central decisions, which divided the top leadership, reveal even less. They do not explain the violence. Mao led something like a coup in 1966, but not all coups produce Cultural Revolutions. Academic traditions in sinology have inclined even contemporary China hands to rely on official documents, especially from the capital, as basic sources of information. Useful as these policy statements are, they do not get to the experiences of most Chinese. Local newspapers and interviews suggest other factors that yield different reasons for the extent of the conflict. The official high road in China studies fails to traverse most of the country.

THE CR AS A RESULT OF MAO'S PERSONALITY

One of the most interesting specific models of the origins of the Cultural Revolution treats Chairman Mao's psychology. This approach suffers the same problems of any other that assumes a high leadership can thoroughly control such a huge population. But because Mao obviously inspired much, and because Chinese who participated in the CR blame or praise him readily, this approach nonetheless deserves serious attention.

Robert Lifton believes Mao had an "activist response" to his anticipated death. Mao launched a "quest for rebirth" of Chinese society. He tried to control his environment "through behavior determined by intra-psychic needs no longer in touch with the actualities of the world."[57] This arresting theory does not claim to explain everything about the Cultural Revolution

---

[57] Robert J. Lifton, *Revolutionary Immortality: Mao Tse-tung and the Cultural Revolution* (New York: Vintage Books, 1968), p. 32.

(which is just as well), but it explores the purist symbols of the CR's politics and can contribute to an understanding of the movement's language.

The cult of Mao became state policy. Should it, however, be used to explain conflict or unity? Mao abetted it consciously, but many people and groups adopted it for their own ends too. Both sides in a battle might justify their attacks on each other in terms of loyalty to the godlike Chairman. The Mao cult in local situations usually bore a quite indeterminate relation to Mao's desires. The leader cult was an index, more than a cause, of mass anxiety and political passion in the CR. It was extremely important. But like the violence with which it correlated, it is something to be explained more than something useful for explaining further effects, a symptom more than a cause. What is remarkable is not that a leader asked for blind support, but that so many wholeheartedly gave it. The reasons for this, as for the extensive violence, can be sought in the experiences of China's urban masses during many previous years and in their consequent mentalities by the mid-1960s.

Many biographers of Mao, notably Ross Terrill, document the extent to which the Chairman became willful and senile in the CR and "lost all collegial sense," ending with a "fractured vision."[58] Even the Central Committee's *Resolution on CCP History* notes that "Comrade Mao Zedong's prestige reached a peak and he began to get arrogant. . . . He gradually divorced himself from practice and from the masses, acting more and more arbitrarily and subjectively, and increasingly put himself above the Central Committee of the Party."[59] Actually, many "masses" thought Mao was close to them in the CR. To its credit, however, the *Resolution* goes on to explain that "blaming this on only one person or on only a handful of people will not provide a deep lesson for the whole Party or enable it to find practical ways to change the situation." Instead, it blames the "evil ideological and political influence of centuries of feudal autocracy," which created conditions "for the over-concentration of Party power in individuals and for the development of arbitrary individual rule and the personality cult in the Party."[60] Men of affairs in China, like many who have written from outside, thus stress not only the faults of Mao but also the pattern of his leadership style as an important contributing factor to the Cultural Revolution.[61]

By far the most powerful explanation of this type is a Marxist one, a 1980

---

[58] Ross Terrill, *Mao: A Biography* (New York: Harper and Row, 1980), e.g., p. 324 or 366.

[59] *Resolution on CCP History*, p. 46.

[60] Ibid., p. 47.

[61] For example, Stanley Karnow, *Mao and China: From Revolution to Revolution* (New York: Viking, 1972), and Edward E. Rice, *Mao's Way* (Berkeley and Los Angeles: University of California Press, 1972).

essay entitled "Mao Zedong and the Cultural Revolution," by Chinese dissident Wang Xizhe.[62] Wang argues that Mao after 1956 was a Stalinist, a
firm supporter of bureaucratic rule in the imperial mold—with himself as
emperor. Mao's occasional antibureaucratic statements were purely tactical
politics, Wang says. Mao designed these egalitarian-sounding outbursts to
gain popular support, but never to threaten the apparat he created. In the
tradition of Marx's "Eighteenth Brumaire of Louis Bonaparte," Wang points
out that a majority of Chinese (the peasants) were willing to support a charismatic dictator who was "fascist" despite his Communist trappings. Wang
emphasizes old Chinese political culture and Mao's ability to capitalize on
the peasants' penchant to adulate a leader.

Traditional authority relations, in China as elsewhere, are partly based
on pomp, dignity, and "community."[63] In this sense, they are like politics
even in states that rotate their kings by elections.[64] Wang points to the rural-
egalitarian bases of Mao's dictatorship. The CR began and had its apogee,
however, in the most modern Chinese cities, such as Shanghai, where politics
is also crucially based on efficiency, the specialization of functions, new culture, and "society." From such cities, it spread to the country;[65] and Wang's
account by itself does not show why the flow was in that direction. He describes the kind of charisma Mao wielded, without showing why specific
modern and urban groups responded to it first and most powerfully, and
without suggesting what those groups were.

Wang realizes the possibility of an explanation of the CR based on mass
groups; but as a Marxist, he is limited by an inability to conceive any "social
contradiction" except between economically generated classes.[66] In one of

[62] Joseph Morrison's translation of Wang Xizhe's stirring essay is in *On Socialist Democracy and the Chinese Legal System*, ed. Anita Chan, Stanley Rosen, and Jonathan Unger (Armonk, N.Y.: Sharpe, 1985), pp. 177–260. Wang has been jailed for making statements of this
sort in media not under Party control, even though his ideas are an exceptionally consistent,
frank, unexpurgated representation of the way some leaders in China's reform government also
view the CR.

[63] See Harry Eckstein, "The Idea of Political Development: From Dignity to Efficiency,"
World Politics 34, no. 4 (1982): 451–86, and Clifford Geertz, *Negara: The Theatre State in
Nineteenth-Century Bali* (Princeton: Princeton University Press, 1980).

[64] See Clifford Geertz, "Centers, Kings, and Charisma: Symbolics of Power," in *Local
Knowledge* (New York: Basic Books, 1983), pp. 121–46.

[65] The best recent accounts, about a village in Guangdong, are Richard Madsen's, *Morality
and Power in a Chinese Village* (Berkeley and Los Angeles: University of California Press,
1984), and Anita Chan, Richard Madsen, and Jonathan Unger's, *Chen Village: The Recent
History of a Peasant Community in Mao's China* (Berkeley and Los Angeles: University of
California Press, 1984).

[66] Chan, Madsen, and Unger, *On Socialist Democracy*, pp. 256–59.

the few equivocal parts of an otherwise cocksure "Eighteenth Brumaire," Wang admits: "If we try to understand the Cultural Revolution from a different perspective by taking Mao Zedong's Cultural Revolution as being in opposition to the people's Cultural Revolution and then say that the Cultural Revolution was a product of sharpening contradictions within Chinese society, this makes some sense."[67] Such an approach is essential to this book. It is inconsistent with an emphasis on the causal importance of Mao's personality separate from the context of opportunities and resources he faced, especially among millions of very local leaders in cities.

THE CR AS AN EXERCISE IN SYMBOLS

Personalities other than Mao made this movement. Many analysts therefore approach it in terms of symbolic gestures, whose active form was seen as more important than their psychological or social content. One Red Guard interrupted the poster writing of another to ask, "How did you get to be so dedicated and enthusiastic?" The reply was general, all about signs of growth and strength: "I want to exercise myself. I want to collect experience. Supporting the Great Cultural Revolution is a great chance for us young people to develop ourselves."[68]

Michael Walzer, studying the "zealous, systematic, sustained politics" of radicalism in early revolutionary Europe, cogently shows how it flourished among "masterless men" whose interests went far beyond material benefits. Radicalism in its Puritan form, for example, was not a phenomenon of impoverished groups. It grew among merchants and gentlemen. This early radicalism combined—as Mao did—an interest in personal development with a crusading, war-loving spirit. As the Huguenot enthusiast de Mournay put it, "La paix est un grand mal, / La guerre est un grand bien . . . Paix est propre au meschant, / La guerre au vray chrétien."[69]

Mao was famous for saying "It is right to rebel" and "I like chaos"—and this sense of a need for tumult grew easily among youths in small groups throughout China that rejected rigid traditions. The CR explicitly delegitimated traditional moral codes, and many of the "children of Mao" were

---

[67] Ibid., p. 259.

[68] Liang and Shapiro, *Son of the Revolution*, p. 118.

[69] Michael Walzer, *The Revolution of the Saints: A Study in the Origins of Radical Politics* (Cambridge: Harvard University Press, 1965), pp. 8, 91, 309.

educated to despise order.[70] An emphasis on the uses of mayhem, an ambivalent attitude toward authority, can flourish not only in a socialist form, but in any set of symbols directed to change. Lucian Pye theorizes that pressures of social development have undermined the traditional Chinese social order, especially in warm but authoritarian families, so that individuals in cities are now cast adrift to find themselves.[71] A related theory, by Richard Solomon, associates traditional Confucian authority and compliance with the "oral" stage of personality formation.[72] Rural Chinese communities have long needed to be solidaristic in organizing work, lest they fail for lack of enough to eat.[73] Solomon's theory links Mao's introspective and scatological style with "anal" themes that condone struggle, aggression, and chaos to purge China's old society. A recent Hong Kong author, Sun Longji, thinks "the deep structure of Chinese culture" leads to a "disorganization of self," allowing a Cultural Revolution to occur—even though he also says this is the result of "something 'deeper' than political or even social causation."[74] Various reasons might be offered for the rise of such symbols; in any case, they seem to take on a life of their own.

Analysis of political symbols can be accomplished with fewer brave assumptions than full explanations of their origins need to attempt. The terms used by participants in the CR tended to be more stable in their formal patterns than in their referents. As a Red Guard explained: "The *People's Daily*

[70] See Anita Chan, *Children of Mao: Personality Development and Political Activism in the Red Guard Generation* (Seattle: University of Washington Press, 1985); see also David M. Raddock, *Political Behavior in Adolescents in China: The Cultural Revolution in Kwangchow* (Tucson: University of Arizona Press, 1977).

[71] Lucian W. Pye, *The Spirit of Chinese Politics: A Psychocultural Study of the Authority Crisis in Political Development* (Cambridge: MIT Press, 1968). See also his *China: An Introduction*, 3d ed. (Boston: Little, Brown, 1984), in which this kind of theme (pp. 214ff.) is combined with less psychological interpretations (pp. 287ff.).

[72] Richard H. Solomon, *Mao's Revolution and the Chinese Political Culture* (Berkeley and Los Angeles: University of California Press, 1971), e.g., the concluding chapter, pp. 510–26. See also Solomon's lighter book in collaboration with Talbott Huey, *A Revolution Is Not a Dinner Party: A Feast of Images of the Maoist Transformation of China* (Garden City, N.Y.: Doubleday, 1975).

[73] See Lynn White, "Agricultural and Industrial Values in China," in *Value Change in Chinese Society*, ed. Richard Wilson, Sidney Greenblatt, and Amy Wilson (New York: Praeger, 1979), pp. 53–69, for a nonpsychological argument linking details of work in the rice and wheat crop cycles with needs for coordinated, authoritarian collectivism, which could provide enough food for the population. Culture may come more from agriculture than from independent personalities.

[74] Sun Longji, *Zhongguo wenhua de "shenceng jiegou"* (The "deep structure" of Chinese culture) (Hong Kong: Jixian she, 1983); short selections and other items by Sun are in *Seeds of Fire: Chinese Voices of Conscience*, ed. Geremie Barmé and John Minford (Hong Kong: Far Eastern Economic Review, 1986), p. 31.

. . . told us to 'repudiate all monsters and ghosts,' but it never really helped us to define 'monster' or 'ghost.' This left room for different interpretations and caused factionalism."[75] Ambiguous communications had diverse uses in CR politics. Chairman Mao often issued "latest directives" that were received in conflicting groups. These might do violent battle with each other, because they interpreted his words differently, while all claimed fealty to the Chairman in Beijing.[76]

Even in the top leadership, interpretations of terms often varied wildly. High members of the Central Committee held conflicting concepts of an idea as important as "class":

> Mao said, "We need not concern ourselves with class or stratum, but with power holders. . . . The focal point is the Party." Someone then inquired of Mao, "In what designation should we count these children of landlords and rich peasants who participate in labor?" Mao replied, "As they are commune members, of course it should be peasant!" Li Xuefeng, however, objected that this designation was too vague: "Poor peasants and middle peasants are also called commune members, therefore this designation cannot resolve the question of class. . . ." But Zhou Enlai sided with Mao, interjecting, "Ordinary peasant! Just call them peasants."[77]

It is clear that top leaders at this time had scant consensus on what "class" meant. Mao often favored vague definitions of the term, because that habit would concentrate criticism against bureaucrats.

Lowell Dittmer, after a comprehensive analysis of the symbolism of CR polemics, concludes that its language "can provide general guidelines for a social movement in the context of widespread uncertainty. . . . Cultural Revolution polemic succeeded in symbolizing and legitimating the expression of the masses' repressed grievances and demands, [though] it also unleashed strong tendencies toward polarization and anarchy."[78]

This approach, which links a communications system to a system of meaning, deals with the expression of grievances mainly in linguistic terms.

---

[75] In Ronald N. Montaperto, "From Revolutionary Successors to Revolutionaries," in *Elites in the People's Republic of China,* ed. Robert A. Scalapino (Seattle: University of Washington Press, 1972), pp. 592–93.

[76] On the functions of normative ambiguity, see Lynn White, "Shanghai's Polity in Cultural Revolution," in *The City in Communist China,* ed. John Wilson Lewis (Stanford, Calif.: Stanford University Press, 1971), pp. 366ff.

[77] This confusion on the Central Committee, December 20, 1964, re class, is quoted in Kraus, *Class Conflict,* pp. 86–87.

[78] Lowell Dittmer, "Thought Reform and Cultural Revolution: An Analysis of the Symbolism of Chinese Polemics," *American Political Science Review* 71, no. 1 (1977): 83.

The CR clearly brought certain forms of symbolization to the fore. Contrasts between blackness and light (especially the bright red-yellow sun), secret procedures and open ones, dirt and purity, passive flight and violent activism—all these together formed a Manichaean syntactic structure inherent to the style of the CR. A symbolist approach to the movement can be tightly structured. Even if it can only indirectly get to the individual motives and social causes of action in the CR, it has the advantage of dealing in categories made by the participants themselves—the ones that a researcher can most fully replicate in his or her own mind.

For purposes of this book, the most important aspect of such symbols is their invasiveness. The Party (like Red Guard units copying it in the CR) was to be an "organizational weapon," a system that legitimately invades its environment rather than adapting.[79] But during the Cultural Revolution, campaigns created a situation in which any group could harass its enemies violently in the name of "the people" or the prophetic Chairman. Mao's use of activist symbols in organization lent legitimacy to CR factionalism.

Such symbols still do not identify *which* groups and individuals establish violent factions to correct specific grievances. They provide information on the form of legitimate opportunities, but not on which of these options are actually taken. Specifying these things requires knowledge of more substantive issues of the time, as well as a look at preceding years for clues on how groups formed and people fared.

THE CR AS A RESULT
OF CONFLICTING DEVELOPMENT NEEDS

A more comprehensive but difficult approach relates the CR to modernization. This method is somewhat like the organizational treatment that has best explained the Great Leap Forward. "Red" styles of work are seen as useful for encouraging political loyalty in a gigantic developing state with very imperfect communications. "Expert" or "instrumental" values are also

[79] Lenin has not often been blamed for the CR by Western scholars, maybe because he too was an intellectual. A case might be made, however, on the basis of Philip Selznick's *The Organizational Weapon: A Study of Bolshevik Strategy and Tactics* (New York: McGraw-Hill, 1952), and using Karl Mannheim's concept of "ideology" or Franz Schurmann's "practical ideology," that policies like labeling, monitoring, and campaigning are Leninist. They design a "system" to invade rather than adapt functionally to its environment. See Schurmann, *Ideology and Organization*. Rightist regimes, however, could use and have used such policies too; so they are not just Leninist but deserve to be identified more generally. They might, for example, appear in Islamic or South African or Israeli forms (and have partly done so).

needed, to give China the power that comes from a reliable bureaucracy. Because these two sets of requisites conflict, political instability is constant; China follows a zigzag course, emphasizing one, then the other.[80] Cyclic policy, sometimes red and sometimes expert, shows a quasi-modern attempt to specialize these two inherently different aspects of China's development over time.

As a side effect, though, this cycle also demoralized thirty million or so basic-level cadres by the mid-1960s. When attacked, these bureaucrats tended to retreat rather than protect themselves.[81] In this view, the CR continued earlier movements, especially the Socialist Education Campaign of the early 1960s. Richard Baum, Doak Barnett, Michel Oksenberg, and others have interpreted even the early events of the CR in modernization terms.[82] One reason for the CR's particular virulence was the quick recruitment of specialists as Party members from 1947 until 1957.[83] In the mid-1960s, the CCP still contained many people of nonproletarian class backgrounds, and Mao's desire to modernize China by finding social energy in class struggle conflicted with the interests of many intellectuals and experts who were needed to develop the country. Mao's "revolutionary pragmatism" condoned violence for the purpose of "unfreezing" China's bureaucracy.[84]

Explanations of the CR in terms of China's modernization can be devel-

---

[80] Richard D. Baum predicted such swings before the CR in " 'Red and Expert': The Politico-Ideological Foundations of China's Great Leap Forward," *Asian Survey* 4, no. 9 (1964): 148–57.

[81] See Richard Baum and Frederic Teiwes, "Liu Shao-ch'i and the Cadres' Question," *Asian Survey* 8, no. 4 (1968): 323–45. See also Baum's "Elite Behavior under Conditions of Stress: The Lesson of the 'Tang-ch'uan Pai' in the Cultural Revolution," in *Elites in the People's Republic of China*, ed. Robert A. Scalapino (Seattle: University of Washington Press, 1972), pp. 540–74. Baum's work, especially his scattered essays that complement *Prelude to Revolution* crucially, add up to a major statement on the links between bureaucracy and development needs. Karl Polanyi, in his *The Great Transformation*, describes development as two processes together: the increase of efficient market allocation of land, labor, and money as commodities, and the increase of regulation against certain bad effects of that efficiency.

[82] This interpretation is from Michel Oksenberg, "China: Forcing the Revolution to a New Stage," *Asian Survey* 7, no. 1 (1967): 1–15. See also Doak A. Barnett's lectures at Princeton, published as *China after Mao* (Princeton: Princeton University Press, 1967), and Richard D. Baum, "Ideology Redivivus," *Problems of Communism* 16, no. 3 (1967): 1–11. Edward Friedman strongly relied on development explanations too, emphasizing the "cultural givens of modernization" in "Cultural Limits of the Cultural Revolution," *Asian Survey* 9, no. 3 (1969): 188–201.

[83] Donald W. Klein, "A Question of Leadership: Problems of Mobility Control and Policymaking in China," *Current Scene* 5, no. 7 (1967): 1–8.

[84] Harry Harding, Jr., "China: Toward Revolutionary Pragmatism," *Asian Survey* 11, no. 1 (1971): 51–67.

oped into sophisticated, multifactor historical interpretations. Domestic needs, and even ideas about Mao's personality, can be considered along with Beijing's international concerns during the mid-1960s.[85] Yet this approach is almost too comprehensive, too systematic, to show why the cycle reached such an extreme peak in 1966. The social ideals of the CR are better covered than its violence, in this treatment of the problem. It explains a movement, but hardly a trauma.

THE CR AS A RESULT OF
RECURRENT ADMINISTRATIVE POLICIES

An effort to specify the CR's political constituencies can give the violence a more verifiable and broad-based cause. Data about individuals and local group leaders do not assume an identity of interests between top politicians and ordinary citizens. They need not rely on premises about conflicts between Mao and Liu (who usually cooperated), or about the omnipotence of symbolic styles, the psychological needs of personalities, the tight requisites of modernization, or rigid links between social ideals and individual behavior.

Academic research on previous stages of the Chinese revolution (especially those which ended in 1949 and 1958) stabilized only after a stress on intentions was replaced by an emphasis on groups, organizational resources, and the links of politics to people's daily lives. A similar approach may help for the CR. Chalmers Johnson was one of the first scholars to take mass interests in the CR seriously and to emphasize that Mao could only conduct "emergency salvage operations" in contexts he did not control.[86] As Johnson emphasized, the bureaucracy had ossified by the mid-1960s, and Party leaders were unable to make the CCP responsive to the needs of mass groups. Mao used students and others to purge bureaucrats, but finally he had to bring in the army.

Other analysts, including Michel Oksenberg and John W. Lewis, linked policy positions to occupational groups.[87] But the political stances of many

[85] For example, see Brian Hook, "The Post-Plenum Development of China's Proletarian Cultural Revolution," *World Today* 22, no. 11 (1966): 467–75, and "China's Cultural Revolution: The Preconditions in Historical Perspective," *World Today* 23, no. 11 (1967): 454–64.

[86] Chalmers A. Johnson, "China: The Cultural Revolution in Structural Perspective," *Asian Survey* 8, no. 1 (1968): 1–15.

[87] See Michel Oksenberg's "Occupational Groups in Chinese Society and the Cultural Revolution," in Chang Chun-shu, James Crump, and Rhodes Murphey, eds., *The Cultural Revo-*

mass groups defied exact definition. Ideological concepts, obviously important to the participants, tended to throw as much shadow as light on their
motives. John Gittings made an early attempt to cut this knot by casting
doubt on the descriptive accuracy of group categories used officially in the
movement.[88] He distinguished a leftist group of "have-not underemployed
students and workers" from a rightist "awkward coalition of Army leaders,
Party bureaucrats, and government administrators."

Evidence from Red Guard newspapers suggested that groups defined by
social class labels were important in the movement. Evidence for the radicalism of capitalist-labeled student Red Guards threw doubts, however, on
the possibility of a straightforward logic to order this chaos. China watchers
mainly noticed that, after the formation of many diverse Red Guard groups
in 1966, two large coalitions emerged in each major city by 1967.

Shanghai had its radical "Red Revolutionaries" and its more conservative
"Scarlet Guards." Wuhan had its "Workers' General Headquarters" and its
"Million Heroes." In Guangzhou, radical "Red Flags" conflicted with more
establishmentarian "East Winds." Beijing had an "Earth Faction" and a
"Heaven Faction" (the latter, named after an aviation institute, opposed old
Party leaders less virulently than the former, whose first members came from
a geology institute). Even Wuzhou had an iconoclastic "Revolutionary Rebel
Grand Army" and an "Alliance Command" that attacked the Party authorities less. The Grand Army was always relatively radical and willing to attack local Party committee leaders, whereas the Alliance Command was
more inclined to attack deputy leaders or scapegoats—at least until the top
leaders' positions became untenable.

Hong Yung Lee and Stanley Rosen have gathered extensive data about
this cleavage in Guangzhou. Lee draws the following conclusions: The radical group was diverse, comprising many youths and even pedicab drivers,

---

lution: 1967 in Review (Ann Arbor: University of Michigan Center for Chinese Studies, 1968),
pp. 1–44, which distinguishes seven such occupations and assesses their respective influences
on policy. Oksenberg later convened a conference at Ann Arbor concerning Chinese interest
groups; many of the papers appear in Victor C. Falkenheim, ed., *Citizens and Groups in the
Policy Process of the People's Republic of China* (Ann Arbor: University of Michigan Press,
1987). E. Stuart Kirby, "The Framework of the Crisis in Communist China," *Current Scene* 6,
no. 2 (1968): 1–10, uses a similar framework. So do several chapters (including those by
J. Lewis and L. White) in John W. Lewis, ed., *The City*. See also David S. G. Goodman, ed.,
Groups and Politics in the People's Republic of China (Armonk, N.Y.: Sharpe, 1985).

[88] Gittings refers to "a growing mood of anti-intellectualism, supposedly aimed at bourgeois intellectuals but clearly directed at the new type of revolutionary intellectual thrown up
by the Cultural Revolution"; see his "The Prospects of the Cultural Revolution," in *China after
the Cultural Revolution* (New York: Vintage, 1970), pp. 69, 72, extracted from an article in
Bulletin of the Atomic Scientists 25, no. 2 (1969).

as well as various others who were discontented with their lot. These radical Red Flags in Guangzhou communicated with their allies in other provinces more often than did their rivals. The many radical publications more often opposed army policy and fought the "Great Alliances and Three-in-One Combinations" that eventually gave the military more influence in civilian affairs. The radicals more often criticized head Party secretaries, especially those having openly political functions, whereas the East Winds sought targets among deputy heads and specialists. Radical journals more often launched broadsides against whole Party committees, not just individual scapegoats. They sometimes upheld "factionalism" as having revolutionary potential, and they stressed criticism of "power-holders . . . in the Party." But the East Winds, more often from cadre families, attacked "monsters and freaks," especially non-Party intellectuals who had capitalist class labels.[89]

Rosen, using interviews of two thousand Guangzhou students who became Red Guards, found that about three-quarters of the radical Red Flags came from families with "middle and bad" labels. Four-fifths of the more establishmentarian East Wind Red Guards were from families of workers, soldiers, and officials.[90] Marc Blecher and Gordon White, studying local CR politics in a technical unit, found that over two-thirds of its employees with proletarian class backgrounds joined the conservative group, whereas a similar portion of the employees of "bad" or "mediocre" class backgrounds joined the radicals.[91]

"Workers" were generally found in both coalitions (though the conservative alliance contained more of them), because of big differences between less-favored contract workers and more-favored union workers.[92] But sometimes, conflicts were ostensibly between groups of people having different kinds of labels. In Guangzhou, an establishmentarian Red Guard newspaper described a rival, more radical, less proletarian faction as follows: "[W]hen they were oppressed, to effect their own liberation they displayed a definite quality of resistance, objectively a definite revolutionary quality. But they

[89] Hong Yung Lee, *The Politics of the Chinese Cultural Revolution: A Case Study* (Berkeley and Los Angeles: University of California Press, 1978), pp. 302–22.

[90] Stanley Rosen, *Red Guard Factionalism and the Cultural Revolution in Guangzhou (Canton)* (Boulder, Colo.: Westview, 1982), p. 147. Seventy-four percent of the Red Flags were capitalists, clerks, and professionals, but 81 percent of the East Winds were from approved-label families.

[91] Marc J. Blecher and Gordon White, *Micropolitics in Contemporary China: A Technical Unit during and after the Cultural Revolution* (White Plains, N.Y.: Sharpe, 1979), p. 81. The existence of a small third faction, mostly proletarian, slightly complicated matters in this unit.

[92] See Lynn White, "Workers' Politics in Shanghai," *Journal of Asian Studies* 26, no. 1 (1976): 99–116.

rebelled out of selfishness (even to the point of acting to benefit the interests of their own reactionary class)."[93]

Radical groups commandeered trains more often than conservatives, partly for politics, partly for the fun of "revolutionary tourism," and partly to move away from their dossiers at a crucial time of class struggle. When radical Red Guards from Shanghai and elsewhere came to Beijing, they met protests from conservatives. As a handbill written by local Beijing people put it,

> Like a swarm of wasps, you sons and daughters of landlords, rich peasants, counterrevolutionaries, bad elements, and rightists have descended on the capital with great pomp and speed! Let us tell you, we allow only the children of the five red categories to come. . . . Some of you have the family background of capitalists; your uncles have spent a number of years in the people's prisons, and some of your uncles were historically counterrevolutionaries. . . . You, a bunch of bad eggs, the Red Guards and the Five-Red category children of Beijing do not welcome you. We want you to get out of here, and at once.[94]

The CR clearly unleashed frustrations in groups labeled by class categories. Radical groups attracted not just "capitalists" who failed to shed their labels but also contract workers and intellectuals with grudges against bureaucrats. And the turmoil gave many individual cadres a chance to confirm their own positions as bosses in local units—and to put down socially prestigious but bad-labeled notables who had the personal skills to replace them. Rivalry among leaders within units was evident in the CR, and it displayed a frequent pattern: Pre-CR heads of units, when they were not vulnerable to charges of previous corruption, naturally led conservative groups. But deputy heads tended to join radical factions. Bosses did not disappear in this period, but previously monitored sub-bosses often claimed more authority.

The language of this movement has a formal intensity showing the extent of mass frustration in China by the mid-1960s. But the articulated ideals of the CR fail to describe its main constituencies—either groups or individuals—accurately. The words of the campaign also fail to show how resources differed among its political groups. Ideology throws practically no light on

---

[93] Quoted from the tabloid *Xiaobing* (December 9, 1967) in Rosen, *Red Guard Factionalism*, p. 235. Another translation of the same revealing source appears in Lee, *The Politics of the Chinese*, p. 321.

[94] Kraus, *Class Conflict*, pp. 121–22.

who moved to violence at the local level, and why. That calls for a look at administrative policies and resources in the 1950s and 1960s.

RESEARCH PLAN

Two big problems with many published explanations of the Cultural Revolution, which do not take groups or patron-client relations seriously, may be described in general terms. First, these explanations are seldom "behavioral." They emphasize intentions, policies, dreams of high leaders, ideologies, and isms associated with the likes of Mao Zedong or Liu Shaoqi. They tell little about the actions of millions of participants, about the social origins or work contexts of the actors, about the real experiences of their lives. These reports look at the ideals of the Cultural Revolution, which were important, but not at the material bases essential to its occurrence.

Second, many works in this field have dealt too exclusively with public reasons, not personal ones.[95] The latter are difficult to isolate. The top political leaders, whose histories are somewhat documented but whose motives were seldom clear, lived in part of the old imperial palace, close to each other but far from the environment of China's masses. The personal motives for the Cultural Revolution should be sought in terms of much larger casts of characters. If Chinese people are like others (and an opposite assumption would end most hopes of understanding), they act for themselves as well as for their groups. Their individual motives deserve more attention, just as their material conditions do. The situations in which urban Chinese actually found themselves, before the mid-1960s, can be understood only after an exploration of the effects of policies on their physical circumstances and individual motives.

Analysts must find ways to look at the Cultural Revolution in terms of personal or concrete interests, without foreswearing an examination of the collective or normative factors that were also obvious in this movement. In rough terms, workers and managers spend a great amount of time arranging external, physical situations—the workers mostly for themselves, and the managers often for larger groups. Intellectuals and urban residents, on the other hand, spend a relatively great amount of time thinking about meanings and styles—the intellectuals for their larger communities, and the residents in local contexts. In actual fact, of course, all these people do all these things.

---

[95] An exception—though it is not designed mainly to explain the Cultural Revolution—is Susan L. Shirk's *Competitive Comrades: Career Incentives and Student Strategies in China* (Berkeley and Los Angeles: University of California Press, 1981).

These groups overlap, even though they can be distinguished, roughly but adequately, for purposes of analysis: people acting on material problems can be called "workers" or "managers," and those involved with symbolic ones can be named "students" or "residents."

The book centers on these groups. Chapter by chapter, it discusses workers and managers together, and students and residents together.[96] This approach (like any other) has its shortcomings; but a look at its comprehensiveness is in order. "Analytic" approaches to causation, centered on the human mind and values, contrast with "synthetic" ones, which tend to stress the concrete environs of actors.[97] This distinction between meanings and facts is pervasive in social science.[98] China hands have often based their notions on this difference between norms and concrete situations.[99] Students and residents have much to do with the former, and managers and workers with the latter.

[96] Manager-cadres and workers may in particular situations have hierarchical relations to each other, but they are considered together here because they deal with material problems in society, not because managers direct workers.

[97] The "analytic" tradition is represented by Aristotle or Descartes; the "synthetic," by Dewey or Hegel. See Stephen C. Pepper, *World Hypotheses: A Study in Evidence* (Berkeley and Los Angeles: University of California Press, 1970). David Hume, *A Treatise of Human Nature* (1739), finds the two sources of knowledge in impressions and ideas; Immanuel Kant, *The Critique of Pure Reason* (1781), describes the bases of knowledge in sensations and understandings. The dichotomy between sensed *Evidenz* and subjective *Sinn* (meaning) has long haunted Western epistemology. See Talcott Parsons, *The Social System* (Glencoe, N.Y.: Free Press, 1961), pp. 5–6, and especially his *The Structure of Social Action* (New York: McGraw-Hill, 1937), pp. 44–47. (With his usual flair for phrasing, Parsons calls perceived facts "the situational referent.") Karl Mannheim, *Ideology and Utopia: An Introduction to the Sociology of Knowledge* (London: Routledge, 1936), Philip Selznick, *The Organizational Weapon*, and Franz Schurmann, *Ideology and Organization*, suggest that norms can perform either of two functions: "utopian" norms cause a group to invade its environment (as a Leninist party or "organizational weapon" does), or a "total ideology" helps it adapt to its environment (as most functional systems do). Schurmann follows this and suggests uses of "practical" and "pure" ideologies in China. Functional analysis of ideology is the surest kind, so long as it is not imposed too heavily on actual thought; see Raymond F. Wylie, *The Emergence of Maoism* (Stanford, Calif.: Stanford University Press, 1980), p. 273.

[98] Albert O. Hirschmann, *Exit, Voice, and Loyalty: Responses to Decline in Firms, Organizations, and States* (Cambridge: Harvard University Press, 1970), shows why economists should pay more attention to political "voice" (protests about unsatisfactory organizational performance) to supplement their conventional emphasis on "exit" (reduction of resources from the outside; e.g., when a consumer leaves a firm's market). Hirschmann is able, in this way, to show the relation of politics to economics. He links ideal norms to the concrete individuals and groups that exit or complain when the norms are not met.

[99] A recent example is the difference between "internal remedialism-radicalism" and "external remedialism-rationalization" in Harry Harding, Jr.'s *Organizing China: The Problem of Bureaucracy, 1949–1976* (Stanford, Calif.: Stanford University Press, 1981). Internal remedialism and radicalism refer to meaning-evidence issues, and external remedialism and rationalization refer to whole-collectivity issues. Many other recent books could be cited.

A distinction between public and private (like the norm-fact difference mentioned above) is very old in social thought.[100] It has shaped modern social science as deeply as the fact-meaning difference.[101] Sociologists contrast two types of bond that hold actions together: community and society. The first is based on a premise that social data can be understood as generated together, while the second assumes they arise separately, even if society involves their coordination.[102] A writer can decide to look at data as separate, or instead to assume their mutual dependence.[103] Managers and student intellectuals have more to do with groups, whereas individual workers or residents tend to look more to their own affairs. There is no sure way to say that either of these epistemologies is generally better than the other, so this book uses both.

Questions can easily be raised about this method,[104] but the proof of any pudding will be in the eating. The main reason for mentioning such broad categories here (situation/meaning and collective/locality) is that they specify no interpretation of the events these chapters attempt to explain, even though they allow a comprehensiveness in organizing the available information.

This book will try to give a picture of what it was like to be an urban Chinese (a worker, manager, student, or resident) from 1949 to 1966. The

[100] See E. E. Schattschneider, *The Semisovereign People* (Hinsdale, Ill.: Dryden, 1975), esp. pp. 6–10. Classic works on this are Plato's *Republic* (in which Socrates argues that the just man is concerned not for himself alone) and Aristotle's *Politics*. See also Albert O. Hirschmann, *Shifting Involvements: Private Interest and Public Action* (Princeton: Princeton University Press, 1982).

[101] A four-quadrant design can be drawn to generate Parsons's famous functions—"adaptation," "goal attainment," "integration," and "latent pattern maintenance and tension management"—and its axes are the same as those which make Pepper's types of epistemologies. This chart is like the one (whose dimensions are unlabeled) in Talcott Parsons and Neil J. Smelser, *Economy and Society* (Glencoe, N.Y.: Free Press, 1956), p. 19. This way of looking at Parsons's categories reduces their number from four to two: a collective-individual dimension and a fact-meaning one.

[102] Albert Hirschmann shows the continuing usefulness of this old difference for present thinking. There is no need to cite more than the title *Shifting Involvements*.

[103] Aristotle or Dewey use "dispersive" premises; Descartes or Hegel prefer "integrative" ones. See Pepper, *World Hypotheses*. Aristotle, Descartes, Hegel, and Dewey could be ranged in quadrants of a field generated by the analytic-synthetic and dispersive-integrative dimensions. Those quadrants can respectively be called (in Pepper's terms) formalist, mechanist, organicist, and contextualist. Pepper categorizes—and then evaluates—major groups of epistemologists in this way.

[104] This procedure is not Hoyle, according to many. A trait or function is not a thing or group. The advantage of the approach here, so long as not too much is made of it, is that it gives some confidence that the functions of the groups considered exhaust a logical field. Even Talcott Parsons and Neil Smelser suggest institutions and groups of people specializing in four broad types of functions such as are offered here. They label the quadrants of a diagram at least with broad terms such as "economy" and "polity." See *Economy and Society*, fig. 3, p. 53.

aim is like that of anthropology.[105] Some think there is no way to use sociologists' methods for anthropologists' goals, but diversity of the categories of research here (which are functionalist) and the conclusions (which concern memories and lessons) will in practice confirm the test the book makes, in an effort to cover many angles in seeking the causes of the Cultural Revolution.[106]

PERIODIZATION

A crucial third dimension, along with that between facts and meanings and that between levels of analysis, is naturally time. Each of the four categories above evolved specific interests many years before the CR. Historical narrative is obviously one way to look at such development. Most of this book's chapters are therefore arranged chronologically, and they come in groups of two: for each period, the first concerns workers and managers, and the second concerns students and residents. These pairs cover five periods. Specific dates dividing the times are approximate, because the events flow from each other and overlap. A list with suggestive descriptions here may serve to begin the discussion:

Institutions define new groups: May 1949–March 1956
Transition to socialism: March 1956–July 1957
Rightists, Leap, and depression: July 1957–January 1962
Recovery to revolution: January 1962–May 1966
Cultural Revolution: May 1966–January 1969

There is no hope of attempting to describe this movement for all parts of the country. Again, representing the field concretely will be more fruitful than trying to exhaust it logically—and this implies an emphasis on data

[105] See Clifford Geertz's essays "Thick Description" and "Deep Play" in his *The Interpretation of Cultures* (New York: Basic Books, 1973), pp. 3–30, 412–53. See also Geertz's later articles in *Local Knowledge*. He stresses groups' perceptions in *The Social History of an Indonesian Town* (Cambridge: Harvard University Press, 1965).

[106] A similar combination of symbolic, functionalist, and rational-actor methods is used in Richard Madsen's *Morality and Power*. Madsen distinguishes two cockfight-like symbols in his village, and they are alternative leadership styles. They have different functions, and peasants choose rationally between them. See also Geertz's discussion of the Brahmana ordination ceremony (a symbol very unlike the cockfight) in "Deep Play," *The Interpretation of Cultures*, p. 452. The quiet, untumultuous Brahmana ceremony is as "like Bali" as the cockfight, and it might be used to organize a different essay on culture there. For more on presentational categories that differ from the parameters of the main thesis here, see the introduction to chapter 10.

from one city. Beijing, the national capital, would hardly be appropriate for the new concerns of this study. If the extensiveness and quality of data were to decide the focus, the choice would be Guangzhou; but the best current books on the movement largely concern students in that city, and it is better to try for coverage elsewhere.[107] No place is typical in China, but data of many kinds are superb from the nation's largest city, Shanghai.[108] The East China metropolis was the political base of radical leaders later known as the Gang of Four. This study is not absolutely confined to Shanghai, but continuing attention to that place makes the story livelier.[109]

CONCLUSION

This book is about the beginnings of the Cultural Revolution in its main sense—its harshness. The emphasis here on groups, individuals, and campaign politics is an implicit departure from the "totalitarian model" and from other consensus models of society. That may at first seem strange, since the topic is a violent movement under a charismatic leader much famed for his thoughts. Yet the choice of analysis depends on what one is trying to explain, and the object here is not to show how official policies arose. It is, instead, to see why violence arose.

Only people near the "bottom" of the political system had power to bring so much turbulence.[110] The emphasis here on long-term administrative policies—and on the unintended, reactive policies that small groups and individuals evolved over long periods to deal with these impositions from Beijing—suggest a lesson that is practical as well as analytic. Labeling people, enmeshing them in hard-to-change patronage networks, and legitimating violence against them are techniques that may mobilize resources and save costs temporarily, but not always in the long run.

[107] Rosen, *Red Guard Factionalism*, and Lee, *The Politics of the Chinese Cultural Revolution*.

[108] For more on the sources for this project, and on the importance for it of local newspapers (especially non-Party papers), see the introduction to the Bibliography, below. Many items listed there, including some by the present author, provide more on Shanghai's role in modern China's politics and economy—a topic not directly relevant to the explanatory project of this book, but fascinating in its own right.

[109] This author has previously written a book about Shanghai, which of course influences the choice of focus. See *Careers in Shanghai: The Social Guidance of Individual Energies in a Developing Chinese City* (Berkeley and Los Angeles: University of California Press, 1978).

[110] The most important recent contribution to the study of political power in small communities seems to be James C. Scott's *Weapons of the Weak: Everyday Forms of Peasant Resistance* (New Haven: Yale University Press, 1985).

If so, many explanations of the Cultural Revolution are *too broad*. They tend to neglect the specific powers of state policies and the powers of mass actors by 1966. Permanent flaws of patriarchy in Chinese culture or dubious idealism in Communist ideology may indeed relate to some underlying causes of the CR; but specific coercive measures to promote group labels, personal control, and frightening campaigns channeled these cultural or ideological tendencies powerfully, so as to instigate the violent result rather than a more peaceful one. There may well be some Chinese cultural or Communist ideological tendencies toward such policies. But these penchants do not produce the chaos of a Cultural Revolution all the time. Culture, by a sturdy definition, offers a much thicker array of inconsistent options than straight deductions from it usually imply. Any "culture," framing enough of the environment of those who use it to deserve that name, is probably too various to determine specific behavior. Consistency is not its hallmark; long-term usefulness is.[111]

A framework to explain the Cultural Revolution must take account of the fact that its targets were of such diverse kinds. Some people were attacked because of their bad labels; some had mainly done their regular bureaucratic jobs and thus created resentments; still others had led activist, unusual, frightening campaigns. Only a mixture of different group, individual, and normative logics of action (which can, however, be unified in terms of state policy) can explain this variety of targets. Different new and old subcultures affected what both the victims and the attackers did. They were not all deviants or assistants, helping indirectly or directly to define the boundaries of a society based on consensus. Some were wayward Communists, but others were really not Communists at all.[112] Communism (or any other ism) arises

---

[111] This contrasts with the definition of more consistent, less option-filled, and less useful kinds of "culture" found, for example, in Elkins and Simeon, "A Cause in Search of its Effect, or What Does Political Culture Explain?"—even though this book's overall thesis finds "structural" causes of the CR to be more immediate than Chinese cultural ones. The difference arises not from disagreement with what Elkins and Simeon say about the requirements of explanation, but instead from conflicts between the subcultures of the state and those of many people. No unified set of "premises" necessarily joins these. Note the apology in that article (p. 136) that the reasons for preferring "structural explanations" are just "practical."

[112] For an extreme but valid example, see Cheng, *Life and Death in Shanghai*. The approach here differs from that in Erikson, *Wayward Puritans*, because it assumes no implicit or explicit agreement on social values and no necessary role for the state in setting such values (though Kai Erikson's historical narrative suggests the Massachusetts Bay polity did more to create an atmosphere of paranoia than his theory stresses). The approach here assumes instead that individuals, groups, and countercultures can create really new and different norms, which have a potential for changing societies rather than just reconfirming them. The means for this are explored in books by a very different author, Erik H. Erikson: *Childhood and Society* (New York:

as one political choice in a broader cultural context of alternatives. Such an ideology is not a culture, even though it also offers flexible inconsistencies sufficient to cast doubt on many kinds of deductions that might be attempted from it.

Other explanations of the CR seem *too narrow*, however, relying excessively on the ideals or psychoses of a single Mao. All the top Party leaders from 1949 to 1966—not just Mao—saw political labeling, appointing bosses for each unit, and scary campaigns as administratively needed; these policies do not reliably distinguish them. Some precipitating factors of the CR lie in Beijing, to be sure; but it is necessary to go beyond these, to find why the response on the streets was so forcible.

An explanation of the CR in terms of mass leadership groups, their members' torn motives in small clientelist networks, and their resources can complement the usual emphases on voluntarist ideology, Communist education (as distinct from allocation policies), and official aims in explaining what happened. The motives of the relevant urbanites can now be defined in light of everything above.

1. Their constituencies were not economic classes but political status groups, created by government programs using class-label and patronage categories to save costs in policy implementation during earlier years.

2. The leadership and most of the membership of such groups can be described better by words like "intellectual" or "cadre" than by words like "capitalist" or "worker."

3. Not everyone in Chinese cities joined the movement. Policy reports tell little about nonparticipation.

4. As the movement developed after 1965, immediate local factors also became important. Various factories, schools, and neighborhoods produced different kinds of groups. Differences in signals from Beijing, at the times when mass groups found leaders or mobilized for conflict, also created variations among them.

5. Actual or threatened violence became an increasingly legitimate norm from 1949 to 1966, because the administrative habit of campaigning allowed the Party to save costs by deploying a small staff to pursue huge goals. Violence spread quickly in urban China when Beijing's policy in August

---

Norton, 1963), chap. 7, and *Young Man Luther* (New York: Norton, 1958). An emphasis on the fact of inconsistent culture, despite what states claim, was long ago offered in Ralf Dahrendorf's "Out of Utopia: Toward a Reorientation of Sociological Analysis," *American Journal of Sociology* 64 (September 1958): 115–27.

1966 disallowed police counteraction. At that time, people who disliked their labels or their bosses rose up to change them.

An approach to the Cultural Revolution in terms of mass groups, tensions between individuals, and administrative violence can achieve only a historical explanation. Analytic understanding is all we can expect from such an exercise. Yet this may give hints on better policies for other places and future times. There seems no alternative, for anyone who wishes to treat the Cultural Revolution with an aim to observe actions, not just ideals, from the viewpoints of people, not just politicians.

CHAPTER 2

Workers and Managers:
New Democracy vs. Socialism, 1949–1956

He who seeks the salvation of the soul, of his own and of others, should not seek it along the avenue of politics, for the quite different tasks of politics can only be solved by violence.
—MAX WEBER

The stage must be set to depict the context in which CCP administrative policies accumulated to create a Cultural Revolution. The drama opens in a place where labeled groups of people were already important, where labor-management relations were highly clientelist, and where civil violence was widespread. To change these patterns, the revolutionary government mandated new constituencies, fostered new local leaderships, and threatened the previous threateners. This process brought basic change. But when continued later, it restored the old patterns, even though the actors were new. A more sensitive, admittedly difficult, policy would have been first to use these techniques to free people from their old burdens, but then to ease state controls for the sake of further development.

The story begins with a brief overview of these patterns among managers and workers in Shanghai before 1949. Management of resources had long been the main job in cities like Shanghai where the Cultural Revolution was most severe. Material benefits for individuals and small groups have always been the wellsprings of Shanghai's growth. The first large social groups to become conscious of common interests in this materialistic city were commercial traders. They were divided by language (Ningbo and other Wu dialect groups, Cantonese, Europeans). But all were together on the market. Shanghai's business was business, and the city's economic importance preceded its political prominence. It has seldom served as an administrative capital for any region beyond its suburbs. Until the middle of the last century, Hangzhou, Suzhou, and Nanjing, all older centers in East China near Shanghai, had far richer political traditions.[1]

---

[1] For more data, see Lynn White, "Non-Governmentalism in the Historical Development of Modern Shanghai," in *Urban Development in Modern China*, ed. Laurence J. C. Ma and Edward W. Hanten (Boulder, Colo.: Westview, 1981), pp. 19–57.

OLD SHANGHAI ECONOMIC GROUPS,
PATRONAGE, AND TERROR

Shanghai's modern development began in the 1840s, with the arrival of foreign trading firms after the Opium War.[2] The Small Sword and Taiping rebellions in the next decade spurred the city's growth. Foreigners protected it because of their interests in private commerce. When rebels threatened the property and lives of inland Chinese, a flood of refugees came to this place where businesses financed a small protective militia.

The money that Chinese and foreign entrepreneurs brought to Shanghai created an industrial proletariat, and workers were recruited for specific industries from specific inland locales. Labor contracts, secret societies, and "same-place associations" of immigrants from particular areas all rose together. Same-place association leaders usually also served as labor bosses. Indirect payment of wages through labor foremen was widespread.[3] These contractors' links to their hirelings were dyadic. The labor patrons assumed a general responsibility for protecting and supplying their subordinates, in exchange for fealty and hard work. The relationship was clientelist, hierarchical, and (ideally if not in practice) family-like. Hiring was arranged through patron-client networks.

Guilds (*gongsuo*) also grew, in many industries, out of co-provincials' associations that established workshop rules and product standards. Such associations often had rituals honoring local deities. When they were concurrently economic groups, they venerated "ancestral masters" (*zushi*), thought to be the original inventors of the relevant trade techniques. For example, Lu Ban was the spirit master of carpenters and masons. His followers celebrated the saint's day each year with banquets and theatrical performances. These festivities also included religious rites, at which the labor bosses officiated.

In 1921, each of Shanghai's eight carpentry guilds represented various stages of work—and various provinces. Nonprovincials were generally excluded from the labor-supplying clubs. For example, Shanghai's dyers in 1921 were all Hunanese.[4] The Small Sword Society, which had long organ-

---

[2] A basic book is Rhoads Murphey's *Shanghai: Key to Modern China* (Cambridge: Harvard University Press, 1953).

[3] The same-place associations were called *tongxiang hui*. See Jean Chesneaux, *The Chinese Labor Movement, 1919–1927*, trans. Hope M. Wright (Stanford, Calif.: Stanford University Press, 1968), esp. pp. 89–94.

[4] Ibid., esp. pp. 113–18. See also Stanford University China Project, *East China*, Subcontractor's Monograph HRAF-29, Stanford 3 (New Haven: Human Relations Area Files, 1956), pp. 148–49, 359–62.

ized the city's seamen, boatmen, and dockhands, kept that union monopoly on the port for many decades. Underworld secret societies, notably the "Green Gang" (*Qingbang*), involved leaders of these work associations and were active in politics. Not only did they help maintain the division of people into categories by geographic origin, they also supported the patronage pattern and attempted to terrorize anyone who resisted this system effectively.

Societies of this sort helped Sun Yat-sen during the 1911 revolution against the Manchu dynasty. Especially after the May 30 Incident of 1925, in which British-officered police shot into a group of demonstrators protesting the murder of a Chinese worker by a Japanese, the Communist Party also had great success in organizing trade unions, now along more modern lines.[5] Chinese nationalism made for cooperation between the workers' guilds, the Guomindang, and the Communists at this time, even though old and new styles of organization varied greatly among them. Progressive parts of Shanghai's trade union movement flourished in the mid-1920s, under Communist leaders.

The main secret societies, however, helped Chiang Kai-shek in his 1927 coup against Communists in Shanghai.[6] A few even helped the Japanese during the wartime occupation. None of this, however, fundamentally changed the way in which individuals were recruited for urban labor. The clientelist pattern remained strong for a long time; Shanghai workers depended on their patrons for physical security and wages.

By the end of the war against Japan, even a Communist writer admitted, "Most labor disputes are mediated by the Government. . . . In the process of these disputes, many enlightened capitalists did their best to make the necessary improvements for workers, even in this poor economic situation."[7] The urban Communist Party, far from trying to rouse the proletariat against managers before 1949, was eager to forge a worker-capitalist alliance against Chiang Kai-shek. For a long period, from the 1920s well into the 1950s, labels like "patriot" or "pro-GMD" defined good or bad categories in the Communist Party more than labels like "worker" or "capitalist" did.

Entrepreneurs' tensions with the GMD had an old history. Socialist ideals long inspired Sun Yat-sen's party, which had cordial relations with Lenin's party in the 1917–27 period. Chiang's 1927 coup relied more on support

---

[5] See many PRC publications on these 1920s exploits—for example, Huang Yifeng and Zhou Shangwen, *Shanghai gongren sanci wuzhuang qiyi* (Three armed uprisings of the Shanghai workers) (Shanghai: Renmin chuban she, 1979).

[6] The most famous report of the 1927 coup is a novel, André Malraux's *Man's Fate* (*La condition humaine*), trans. Haakon Chevalier (New York: Random House, 1934).

[7] *Qunzhong* (Masses) (Shanghai), 13, nos. 11–12 (1946): 29.

from workers in secret societies than from capitalists. Even after 1927, the Nanjing militarists and secret-society worker-leaders both milked Shanghai's rich capitalist tax base, kidnapped the offspring of businessmen who would not pay protection money, and eroded the political power of capitalists.[8] Japanese occupation troops, with their quisling version of the Guomindang under collaborator Wang Jingwei, continued the tradition of quasi-official threats and taxation against the capitalists who remained in Shanghai.[9] Official conflict with capitalists was usual in pre-1949 Shanghai, even when the government was the GMD. A climate of violence affected all aspects of Shanghai's politics and culture in the 1920s and 1930s, and because of war again in the 1940s.[10]

Wu Zhongyi, who owned three-tenths of the shares in Shanghai's largest cloth company, the Xinshen Textile Corporation, spent time during the 1940s in jails run both by the Japanese and Chiang Kai-shek. The Nationalist government, at a time of skyrocketing inflation during the Civil War after 1945, demanded all of that company's cloth—at state-fixed prices. Wu fled to Hong Kong in 1948. It is small wonder that he and Rong Yiren (the major owner of the same corporation, and Shanghai's richest capitalist) returned in 1949 to posts of honor under the Communist regime.[11] (Rong later served as a capitalist deputy mayor of Shanghai for nearly a decade under the CCP.)

Left-leaning journals in 1948 emphasized the importance of giving individual bourgeois enough material incentives to conduct their businesses. A writer for a leftist magazine quoted the complaints during the Civil War of

[8] This is the thesis of Parks M. Coble, Jr., *The Shanghai Capitalists and the Nationalist Government, 1927–1937* (Cambridge: Harvard University Press, 1980).

[9] Marie-Claire Bergère, " 'The Other China': Shanghai from 1919 to 1949," in *Shanghai: Revolution and Development in an Asian Metropolis*, ed. Christopher Howe (Cambridge: Cambridge University Press, 1981), p. 23.

[10] The literature in Chinese on this era (variously from the PRC, Taiwan, and Hong Kong, both fiction and history) is much too vast to cite here. There is more in Japanese, French, and other languages. No British brigadier could retire without giving the world his memoirs of Shanghai (for further references, see White, "Non-Governmentalism"). Also available in English are Chinese accounts such as Pan Ling's *Old Shanghai: Gangsters in Paradise* (Hong Kong: Heinemann, 1984) and her *In Search of Old Shanghai* (Hong Kong: Joint Publishing Co., 1982), as well as translations of famous novels such as Mao Tun's *Midnight* (Beijing: Foreign Languages Press, 1957). The best history will be in forthcoming work on the links between Shanghai culture and police coercion in the 1920s and 1930s, from Frederic Wakeman, Jr.

[11] Barry Richman, *Industrial Society in Communist China* (New York: Random House, 1969), pp. 904–6. Members of the Rong family who were more suspicious of the Communists created major textile and dying works in Hong Kong, but Rong Yiren experienced all the PRC movements through the era of the Four Modernizations, when he was featured in efforts to expand China's external trade.

a factory owner: "In the last few months, I did over a billion *yuan* of business; but even if I had plenty of orders now, I wouldn't be able to pay the interest, [because] imported raw materials have to be bought in foreign currency. Who has enough of that now?"[12] This journal also quoted capitalists who spoke directly against the GMD: "Tax rates are so high, everybody cooks his books."

Many bourgeois managers therefore acquiesced in the change to a Communist regime in 1949. Of course, they had no choice. But their experiences with the GMD government had often been dismal. The devils they did not know well—who in 1949 were the Communists—might prove less bad than the devils they understood. The peasants of the Red Army, who came into the city on May 26, 1949, were new in the direct experience of the vast majority of both workers and managers. That Communist army had been recruited far away, largely on the North China plain. Although some of the Communist officers knew Shanghai, no urban constituency at that time had been crucial to their victory.

The People's Liberation Army soldiers took care to arrive in trucks decked with red flowers and with large portraits of Mao Zedong and Zhu De, though pictures of Stalin were sensitively omitted. For a time, many workers and managers were fairly well united in hopes the new leaders might be uncorrupt. Entrepreneurs and intellectuals of course knew that peasants and soldiers in the newly arrived army might not perceive them as the salt of the earth. But most of them were unsure what to expect, and the coercive CCP challenge to their own positions had not yet begun.

MANAGERS' HESITANT SUPPORT FOR THE NEW REGIME

The peasant army lacked enough expert personnel to monitor, much less control, vital aspects of China's largest city. All economic "units" were ordered to carry on as before. In the municipal bureaucracy, 95 percent of the GMD employees—49,000 of them—stayed at their posts.[13] Zhao Zukang, the GMD's acting mayor of Shanghai for a few days when the Red Army marched in and also head of the GMD's Public Works Bureau, remained in the city—and much later became a deputy mayor under the new regime. The government established a Military Control Commission, at whose office all

---

[12] *Zhanwang* (Outlook) (Shanghai), 2, no. 4 (1948).
[13] Chen Yi, "Two Months' Work in Shanghai," *China Digest* September 21, 1949, pp. 8–9.

ex-GMD functionaries had to register. But they were almost universally kept at their jobs, which the incoming army had scant manpower to staff. In later years, this CCP shortage of personnel led to a rationing of trusted monitors and to Party sponsorship of patronage. But at first, it mainly meant that the new state could not control most local leaders.

Communist inspectors moved into a few important offices and were regarded as "suspicious," because they asked continually for explanations of any procedures they did not understand.[14] This pattern, in which a few monitors looked over the shoulders of many businessmen to check rather than perform managerial work, became usual in the city. It was common for small units, at least through the Transition to Socialism of 1956 (and even in the workers' propaganda teams of the Cultural Revolution).

At a few important offices and firms, some high-echelon managers revealed in 1949 that they had long been secret Communists. The head of the Activities Brigade of the Shanghai office of the GMD's Central Bureau, who had previously been active in suppressing independent democrats for the GMD, proved to be a CCP member. The manager of the Min'an Insurance Company turned out to be a Communist, as did many others who dumbfounded their colleagues by such revelations.[15] Entrepreneurs such as Rong Yiren, if they did not move too much money to Hong Kong and outwardly cooperated with the new regime, were dubbed "national capitalists"—a label of dubious honor, which generally matched their own uncertain feelings.[16]

Shanghai's economy depended very largely on foreign trade before 1949; so the boycott of China trade by the United States and its allies in 1950 caused a local depression. Six thousand firms in the city had to close during the first five months of 1950. Another 3,100 "suspended operations" (but did not formally close) in the first nine months.[17] Most managers of firms that were not operating filed official papers to close their businesses, but the government generally denied these requests; and some resumed operations by the middle of the year. By May 1950, the authorities encouraged entrepreneurs' applications to found new firms. Within five months, almost 2,500

[14] *Monthly Report* (Shanghai), June 30, 1949.

[15] Sima Lu, *Douzheng shiba nian* (Eighteen years of struggle) (Hong Kong: Zilian chuban she, 1967), pp. 181–83.

[16] Interviews in Hong Kong provide important evidence for this. See also, for example, Sima Lu's book, cited in note 15 above.

[17] *Current Background* (Hong Kong), October 16, 1950, p. 53, includes monthly figures for closures, suspensions, resumptions, and newly opened firms. The text is based on addition of these numbers, which are sometimes divided between industrial and commercial firms on a monthly basis. Closures increased sharply until May; and suspensions, until June.

such licenses had been granted for commercial businesses alone. The exigencies of the embargo and the Korean War created strong demand for new supplies. The war in particular promoted a small renaissance of capitalism in early Communist Shanghai.

Business conditions were not, however, as in the old days. Capitalist managers of many large plants (though not in the overwhelming majority of small ones) were supposed by May 1950 to join "labor-capital consultative committees" (*laozi xieshang hui*), in which the officials urged workers and entrepreneurs to agree on wage and salary cuts for the duration of the economic crisis.[18] This program and others like it brought capitalist managers together with worker-leaders and soldier-monitors. It began to create records in which each group of people was clearly inventoried, labeled, distinguished from the others. A new leadership to manage Shanghai's economy was only in embryo by 1950, and serious "class struggle" was still impracticable because of economic needs. The state nonetheless began to label capitalists and workers more comprehensively, and to mediate between them in large firms.

Bourgeois patriotic youth from Shanghai helped staff many work teams in the national land reform campaign of 1950.[19] Some also helped in urban monitoring jobs and as soldiers in Korea. "Military cadres' schools" (*junshi ganbu xuexiao*) by late 1950 enrolled large numbers of such youths. In subsequent years, those who proved their activism were admitted to the Party.[20] Capitalist youths might in this way establish their usefulness and live down their dubious family backgrounds. Their label was slightly embarrassing, but they could adopt a better-sounding one at that time by being patriotic.

PARTIAL RESISTANCE TO THE NEW REGIME AMONG WORKERS

Because businessmen's success at this time clearly depended on accommodation to the new regime, many entrepreneurs cooperated well with officials despite obvious dangers for them in the new state ideology. But workers were not under these constraints. The traditional labor-boss organization of Shanghai's proletariat, which the GMD had often used but never fully controlled, was still strong in important parts of the city and in industries such

[18] *LDB*, May 13, 1950.

[19] See Chen Yuan-tsung, *The Dragon's Village* (New York: Pantheon, 1980).

[20] See *NCNA*, December 13, 1950, and Chen, *The Dragon's Village*. Relevant later articles are in *NCNA* (May 1, 1954) and *JFRB* (May 18, 1954).

as construction and transport. As a Communist labor organizer mourned in 1950, "The organization of unions, in lines of business where other associations [*banghui*] have great power, is very complex. Therefore, unified leadership is very difficult."[21] In the Shanghai Electric Cable Factory, for example, true-blue proletarians were responsible for Luddite sabotage when Communist organizations tried to control them. During March 1950, a group of over eighty workers in this factory met "to instigate labor discord" and "to destroy machinery with explosives."[22]

The Party in Shanghai tried to co-opt as many union groups as it could. The most important leader of local CCP union work, speaking to labor organizers studying together in a class, urged them to

> respect the old workers and the spontaneous [*zisheng*] leaders of various sections. Old workers are experienced and trusted by other workers. As for the spontaneous leaders [that is, pre-1949 labor heads], no matter how they established their prestige, they have good relationships and contacts with the workers. Therefore when we cooperate with them, we are also cooperating with all the other workers.[23]

The continuing power of the old patron-client system was thus recognized bluntly. This Communist spokesman also emphasized how much variation existed among old proletarian groups, and he stressed that organizers should "take care of workers in various associations [*bangpai*]." He said, "There have been different associations because of objective conditions. They did not form into groups by themselves. Therefore, we should not discriminate against them. We should help them and educate them, so that they may be adept at becoming masters of the country."

Patrons of secret societies, who were mostly of impeccable proletarian background and had large worker followings—but had engaged before 1949 in racketeering—presented the Communists with a major quandary. The Party had insufficient staff to suppress these gangs quickly. So it forgave

---

[21] *LDB*, January 14, 1950.

[22] *NCNA*, November 4, 1950. The article asserts that these workers were associated with the GMD, though it gives no evidence to substantiate that claim. These events, maybe because they were so sensitive, were not reported until several months after they occurred. For earlier examples of Luddism, in 1918, see Jean Chesneaux, *The Chinese Labor Movement, 1919–1927*, trans. Hope M. Wright (Stanford, Calif.: Stanford University Press, 1968), pp. 127–29.

[23] Shanghai zonggonghui wenjiao bu (Shanghai General Federation of Labor, Culture and Education Department), *Quanguo gonghui gongzuo huiyi teji* (Speeches from the National Union Work Conference) (Shanghai: Laodong chuban she, 1950) (hereafter *Union Work*), report of Liu Changsheng, pp. 28–30.

cooperative old labor leaders in exchange for their support. The most breathtaking example in Shanghai was Huang Jinrong (alias Huang Mapi, "Pockmark Huang"). Leftist papers called him "the number-one celebrity and secret society leader." But as late as May 19, 1951, he made "confessions to show his determined support for the People's Government."[24] Huang had begun as an apprentice in a shop that mounted paintings. He decided this work "had no future." So he joined the French Concession police, where he rose to the post of chief detective and emerged as head of the Green Gang. In effect, Huang gave the French merchants protection, and they gave him an area in the middle of China's largest city where he had effective sovereignty to sell opium and run other underworld businesses. He snuffed out all crime that he did not control. Drug dealers in Huang's area felt it safe to put their names and return addresses on packages of opium.[25] Huang sometimes cooperated with Chiang Kai-shek, but as later Communist reports admitted,

> Many people acknowledged him as a "teacher," and he thus acquired numerous disciples, who in turn retained their own disciples. With so many followers directly and indirectly claiming his patronage, there were bound to be a number of bad ones who perpetrated wicked deeds and bullied people. Huang had been too old to look after things, though he could not escape the responsibility of being overindulgent.[26]

This was a weak Communist reprimand for Shanghai's biggest racketeer. But he was a proletarian, and he was powerful. He was allowed to retire quietly, because most of his network of clients could thus be brought under Communist patrons at the least cost.

By a mixture of co-option and force, the Party made slow inroads on the power of traditional unions. Financial regulations nonetheless suggest that co-opted leaders, even new ones without pre-1949 patronage, tended to follow the old habits:

> Most unions are rich. They have huge amounts of money, but they do not use it to benefit their members. In financial work, there is anarchy and no discipline. Responsible staff can draw money easily. . . . Embezzlement and extravagance are frequent. The leaders of local unions seldom show their financial reports to higher-level unions or to their members. . . . Most

[24] *DGB* (Shanghai), May 20, 1951.
[25] Coble, *The Shanghai Capitalists*, pp. 37–38.
[26] *DGB* (Shanghai), May 29, 1951.

high-ranking union cadres get their living expenses on the supply system [*gongji zhi*]. They need not worry about their living; so they do not care about the finances of the unions.[27]

Even large unions in the Shanghai General Federation did not have to deposit any of their funds in the People's Bank until more than a year after Liberation.[28]

The regime could effectively use force against other kinds of proletarian organizations, such as Taoist cults (*hui dao men*), which had never provided major protection or provision for their members.[29] But the Party's main approach to workers' secret societies (*banghui*) was to co-opt as many high leaders as would cooperate, to punish others when they could be suppressed without political costs, and to hope that ordinary members would increasingly follow the new regime. Even in the Taoist organizations, only a few leaders were harmed. A newspaper urged that "the masses of members must save themselves from the pit of fire by withdrawing from reactionary cults and severing all relations with them. . . . No further action will be taken against these people."[30] "Ordinary officers" in these cults were assured of safety, so long as they would register with the police and promise to change their ways. Millenarian societies were too popular and large for the Party to monitor very thoroughly or soon. In Tianjin, the coastal city most like Shanghai in North China, one of every five adults was a member of a cult society in 1949.[31]

In sum, the Communist Party during the early 1950s had loyalty problems among workers, not just among capitalist managers. Some bourgeois did not oppose a radical approach to Shanghai's economic problems. Many workers remained in clubs that were still highly independent of the government. At the same time, "class" lines were being drawn. Capitalists were increasingly distinguished from proletarians, even though they staffed vital offices in the city—including many then implementing policies to centralize Shanghai and instill loyalty to New China. Patronage policies were not lessened under the new regime. At first, networks of clients were co-opted, pre-

[27] Shanghai zonggonghui caimao chu (Shanghai General Federation of Trade Unions, Finance Division), *Gonghui caimao gongzuo* (Union finance work) (Shanghai: Laodong chuban she, 1951), pp. 1–11.

[28] *LDB*, November 23, 1950.

[29] The most important of the Taoist cults was the Yi Guan Dao, against which decisive action was taken only in 1953, when military courts tried some leaders (*JFRB*, June 8, 1953).

[30] *JFRB*, June 13, 1953.

[31] On this and other topics relevant to this chapter, see Kenneth G. Lieberthal, *Revolution and Tradition in Tientsin, 1949–1952* (Stanford, Calif.: Stanford University Press, 1980).

sumably in hopes that later their members could be transformed into good revolutionaries. The Party's lack of monitors, in relation to the size and complexity of China's largest city, required that many of its early policies be nonradical.[32]

ORGANIZING MORE LOYAL UNIONS

The Party's main problem in Shanghai immediately after Liberation was a lack of sufficient personnel who were both loyal and educated. The first official advantages for workers arose not just on ideological grounds, but also because the Communists needed to offer more incentives to skilled staff. Less than a month after the Red Army marched into the city, the Education Department of the Shanghai General Federation of Trade Unions sponsored "cadre training courses for employees," aimed at experienced workers and technicians especially from plants in critical businesses that GMD capitalists had abandoned.[33] Forty percent of these new worker-cadres were from chemical factories, and another 30 percent were from textile plants. In some important organizations, the Communists needed to train new monitors quickly, because the Party had few or none there before 1949.

Other industries, such as public utilities and electric machinery, were represented hardly at all in this program, either because control of them was deemed less urgent or possible, or because they could be monitored indirectly through government offices. Liaison stations (*lianluo zhan*) and work groups (*gongzuo zu*) were nonetheless created in the old administrative districts of the electric machinery union. "Preparation committees" (*choubei weiyuanhui*) tried to register educable workers in smaller factories.[34] Since most Shanghai workers were in firms employing fewer than a dozen hands, the Party's task, in attempting to tap the energies of this scattered proletariat, was gigantic.

By August 1949, six hundred "preparation committees" had formed in Shanghai, and each was supposed to "summon activists" and "elect back-

---

[32] A related argument, but for rural areas, is in Vivienne Shue's *Peasant China in Transition: The Dynamics of Development toward Socialism, 1949–1956* (Berkeley and Los Angeles: University of California Press, 1980).

[33] *Zhigong ganbu xunlian ban; LDB*, July 23, 1949.

[34] *LDB*, July 13, 1949. For example, this issue of *LDB* refers to a "Shanghai Eastern District Small Iron Foundries' Employees' Union Preparation Committee" (Hudong qu xiaoxing tiegongchang zhigong lianhe choubei weiyuanhui), which coordinated at least 104 factories employing about two thousand workers. The committee clustered these into thirty-nine small groups (*xiao zu*), but it is clear that many smaller foundries had not yet registered.

bone elements" to monitor the urban economy.[35] These programs gave participating workers a sense of pride, a sense of official and labeled identification as a group—and a sense that new cadres would later be promoted to better managerial jobs because of state patronage.

Such sponsorship of workers followed the classic Leninist precepts that Soviet experts recommended for China.[36] But they were much easier to implement in some trades than others. "Educational workers," mostly teachers, began to form unions only at the end of 1949. The proletarian status and fortunes of this literate group were to become major issues in Shanghai for the next three decades. Street cleaners, garbage collectors, night-soil carriers, and match dippers also formed unions rather slowly.[37] These diverse groups had low official priority as early as 1950; and in later years, they contributed to a mixed, officially created underclass of petty intellectuals and contract workers.

Transport and construction laborers were also relatively slow to form new unions, but for an entirely different reason: these workers had formed the bastion of the most powerful secret societies. The regime therefore had to concentrate its scarce staff in the most vital offices. The Shanghai Railroad District, long a government monopoly of obvious military and economic importance, was given a new union structure by early 1950.[38] The thirty-five thousand workers were spread among five railway lines: "Ning-Hu" to Ningbo, "Hu-Hang" to Hangzhou, "Ning-Wu" to Wuhu, "Zhe-Gan" connecting Ningbo and Nanchang, and "Nan-Xin" connecting Nanchang and Jiujiang. The division of these workers into separate lines was deemed consistent with a policy of creating industrial unions (*chanye gonghui*). This program of unionization was mainly designed to use proletarian solidarity for more efficient management, not for further revolution.

An obvious prerequisite to socialist nationalization was the monitoring of Shanghai's economy.[39] For this purpose, it was vital that the Party recruit workers such as boatmen, who could watch trade flows. Not until mid-1950 was the Shanghai Civilian Boats Association set up, with six separate unions

[35] *Union Work*, report of Liu Changsheng to a study class of Shanghai worker-cadres on August 3, 1949, pp. 25–26.

[36] Gilbert Rozman, *A Mirror for Socialism: Soviet Criticisms of China* (Princeton: Princeton University Press, 1985), chap. 3.

[37] *LDB*, December 10, 1949.

[38] *LDB*, January 18, 1950.

[39] See Lynn White, "Low Power: Small Enterprises in Shanghai," *China Quarterly* 73 (March 1978): 45–76. Similar rural issues are treated in Dorothy J. Solinger, *Chinese Business under Socialism* (Berkeley and Los Angeles: University of California Press, 1984), esp. pp. 138–53.

for workers on coal barges, lighters, small open boats, sampans, fertilizer carriers, and ferries.[40] Boat people—a subethnic group in Shanghai as elsewhere in China—were important but difficult for the new government to organize, for many reasons: They were powerful because their functions were vital to urban supply, their quasi-ethnic separateness divided them from other proletarians, their residences in boats on the water were elusive to pin down, and they had been highly organized in ritual societies before 1949.

Shanghai's government tried to persuade boatmen to move their homes ashore.[41] State companies invested in tugboats, which could economically pull canal and river craft hitched together in long trains. Incentives of this sort proved necessary, before the highly mobile, elusive boat people came under the state's thumb. Many trades, which depended on materials the boats hauled, could not be collectivized before transport was brought under control. Boat people were an essential source of economic information the Party needed, before it could socialize Shanghai.

Trusted workers were invited to join "people's security teams" and "discipline teams," whose organizations were military in style.[42] These teams mostly supplied factory watchmen. But their educated members were prime recruits for new jobs in socialist monitoring, especially after training in the city's "military cadres' schools." Forty percent of the students at these institutions in 1951 came from worker backgrounds, even though Shanghai's Public Security Bureau, which ran them, was only 20-percent proletarian.[43]

By the middle of 1951, after the temporary closure of most textile factories because of blockaded cotton supplies, an All-Shanghai Workers' Discipline Congress was held, at which proletarians heard they were the salt of the earth.[44] Union rules specified that new propagandists were to be "found" among the proletariat, and they were clear candidates for Party membership.[45] The CCP slowly began its attempt to create a new leadership in Shang-

---

[40] *LDB*, May 16, 1950. This Shanghai Minchuan Weiyuanhui was established simultaneously with the China Seamen's Union (Zhongguo Haiyuan Gonghui) (ibid.).

[41] Shanghai did not follow Canton's practice of establishing an "urban district on the water" (*shuishang qu*), although Shanghai built many on-land accommodations for boat people.

[42] *Renmin baoan dui* and *jiucha dui*. *LDB*, July 23, 1949, reported that 250 activist workers had formed the "East Shanghai Heavy Industry Discipline Team," which was based on previous people's security teams.

[43] *Junshi ganbu xiao*; *LDB*, June 12, 1951.

[44] Ibid.

[45] Shanghai zonggonghui wenjiao bu (Shanghai General Federation of Trade Unions, Culture and Education Department), *Gongchang zhong de xuanquan gudong gongzuo: gonghui*

hai's economy, not by overturning patronage patterns of the poor but by co-opting and renaming them.

By the autumn of the next year, the General Federation of Trade Unions had organized over 90 percent of Shanghai's regular, noncontract workers.[46] The government did not reach all workers in this way, but it forged links with many. It had to influence the city's labor organizations before it could socialize the economy. What the workers knew about their firms—and what they might tell the understaffed Party, if they could be wooed—was the main prerequisite to socialism in Shanghai.

THE COSTS OF SUPPORT FROM LABELED WORKERS

Special treatment of the labeled proletariat became a major government expense. This led to restrictions of the number of workers covered by union benefits, because of cost. For example, the government paid 75 percent of the wage and rice allowances for workers at textile factories shut down during the early 1950s blockade of cotton imports.[47] Red tape slowed the procedure for obtaining worker insurance. Consents from both unions and managements were imposed, to slow the extension of benefits to new workers. The Labor Bureau in one short period turned down 55 percent of unions' applications for labor insurance, on the ground that the paperwork was not yet complete.[48] National rules, in effect, encouraged state companies to hire nonunion workers. For example, the rules specified that all nonmedical benefits should be provided to nonunion employees at only half the usual rate.[49] By May 1, 1952, only 376,000 Shanghai workers had received health protection under the laws.[50] This was a small fraction even of the unionized proletariat.

Basic-level union activities were financed by dues, but higher union offices got revenues from levies on enterprise payrolls. Government subsidies paid only for the financial auditing of unions' accounts.[51] There was obvious

---

gongzuo cankao ziliao (Propaganda and education work in factories: Reference documents for union work) (Shanghai: Laodong chuban she, 1950), pp. 10–13.

[46] *LDB*, September 30, 1952. There were 1,290,000 of these workers all told, in 22 major industries and 50,380 basic-level units whose average membership was 23 (ibid.).

[47] *LDB*, June 6, 1951.

[48] *LDB*, March 20, 1951.

[49] *Current Background*, February 23, 1951, p. 1.

[50] *SN*, May 1, 1952.

[51] Shanghai zonggonghui caimao chu, *Gonghui caiwu gongzuo*, pp. 68–69.

high-level concern that local proletarian leaders might use union funds to line their own pockets.

By the middle of 1950, the city government was restricting its activities to "jobs, instead of relief" (*yi gong dai zhen*) for unemployed workers. Leading city officials, however, preferred to supply railroad tickets for emigration inland. In June 1950, only two hundred unemployed people were hired through official agencies in all of Shanghai, though during later months the number increased somewhat as the unemployed were recruited to "recondition parks, repair roads, work in quarries, dredge ditches, and deepen waterways."[52]

The traditional apprenticeship system was maintained, but a union publication warned that "[t]he wages of apprentices should not be too high. Their main aim is to be trained, not to make money; so their wages should be just enough for living. . . . If the wages of apprentices are too high, the responsible staff of enterprises will be loath to employ them."[53] At this time, unions codified high qualifications for apprenticeships, including semiannual examinations not linked to specific trades and three-year terms before the apprentices could be certified as regular workers.

The financial crunch, resulting from the 1950–51 blockade, sharpened the stratification between unionized and ephemeral workers—even though the union members did not yet receive many benefits from their more official, labeled status. Permanent workers (*guding gongren*) were fully supported and had job security. Contract workers (*hetong gongren*) had fixed, sometimes long-term, contracts that were generally honored but did not provide real job security. Temporary workers (*linshi gongren*) had short-term, nonenforceable contracts—or none at all. Finally, enterprises could save overhead as well as labor costs by using out-contract workers (*waibao gongren*), who usually did piecework in their homes or in neighborhood workshops. This structure for Shanghai's labor market preceded the household registration and ration systems, and it preceded class-label tests for access to education. But it was an early, important example of official ranking for a large labeled category of the city's population.

At the top of this structure, among workers at least, were those chosen to be Party members in unions. They were charged with responsibility "for assuring that, among the laboring masses, the decisions of the Party become

[52] *LDB*, March 2, 1951.

[53] Shanghai zonggonghui diaocha yanjiu shi (Shanghai General Labor Federation, Investigation and Research Office), *Gonghui qinggong gongzuo* (Youth work in the unions) (Shanghai: Laodong chuban she, 1951), pp. 1–2.

the decisions of the masses . . . so that work is carried out smoothly."[54] These rules minced no words: "The chief mission of unions is to work for the realization of production plans." But union leaders were not to accomplish this through encouraging class struggle. On the contrary, they were supposed "to harmonize relations between capitalists and workers, so that the national bourgeoisie will develop production."

THE KOREAN WAR AND
PATRIOTIC CONTROL OF CAPITALISTS

Nothing integrates a society like external war.[55] After Chinese troops crossed the Yalu River into Korea during late October 1950, the effects on politics in Shanghai were enormous. At first, the Party hoped to train mostly proletarian-background new leaders in the war. The military cadres' schools of Shanghai organized a Committee to Recruit Students, working mainly in workers' districts. Factory laborers could take the entrance exam even if they had only completed primary education, but a bourgeois student first had to finish at least the second year of middle school.[56] Workers comprised only 12 percent of the applicants, but 40 percent of admissions.[57] Links between industries, schooling, and militias can be traced back to the nineteenth century and before.[58] The effects of the Korean War in Shanghai strongly revived this tradition (and were carried into later decades too, when factory militias became important politically).

A kind of "war communism" developed, in which the Party encouraged entrepreneurs, especially in war-related industries such as drugs and machinery, to produce as much as possible. Capitalism's short renaissance in 1951 was not limited to war industries. For example, a businessman who had not been wealthy before Liberation established a publishing business that year on the basis of a large loan from the People's Bank. He was fully in charge of his firm, and he was allowed to hire mostly temporary rather than unionized workers, at low wages. When he was dissatisfied with his employees, he fired them. More than one hundred had met that fate by the mid-1950s. In

[54] *Union Work*, quotes on pp. 26, 27, 31.
[55] See Lewis Coser, *The Functions of Social Conflict* (Glencoe, N.Y.: Free Press, 1956).
[56] *Chaosheng weiyuanhui; LDB*, December 5, 7, 1950.
[57] *LDB*, December 12, 19, 1950.
[58] Frederic Wakeman, Jr., *Strangers at the Gate: Social Disorder in South China, 1839–1861* (Berkeley and Los Angeles: University of California Press, 1966), pp. 64–69, notes the link between Confucian *shexue* schools and *tuanlian* militias in Canton during the 1840s, for example.

the next five years, this businessman managed to multiply the capital value of his enterprise a hundredfold, apparently without breaking any laws.[59]

These trends acted against stronger state control of the economy. By late 1951, a labor shortage plagued Shanghai's state-run factories, because wages in private plants were higher. State cadres deprecated "job jumping." The *Liberation Daily* expressed official hopes for merchants' acquiescence to state control: "Under the economic system of New Democracy, various kinds of enterprises must avoid blind competition and mutual discrimination. They must render mutual help to each other, so as to seek common progress."[60]

At the beginning of 1952, Shanghai banks reduced interest rates for commercial loans.[61] This was a period in which many Shanghai capitalists, if they had some government support, could run enterprises personally. Many did so, even as directors of state-owned industries.[62] The war also gave many an old firm a new lease on life. Shanghai in 1951–52 was short of electrical equipment, and Chen Huasheng, head of the Wahson Electric Fan Company, was allowed to expand his operation—and to keep it formally a private enterprise for the next half decade.[63]

The Korean War also created a sense of national emergency, giving the Party wide popular support to apply new and strict standards of behavior among both capitalists and CCP members. Corruption was redefined at this time.[64] Unemployed workers helped clean the city physically. Political dissent was easier to suppress in time of war, and institutions or persons with foreign cultural backgrounds could be reformed and made more Chinese. Above all, the Party publicized the punishments it gave to a few of its own

[59] *XWRB*, June 23, 26, 1957. The article specifies that the entrepreneur, Huang Miaofu, did not repent his success. It cites no illegality on his part, even though it suggests individuals should not increase capital so quickly. Huang had some advantages, because he was a "dependent of a military martyr" (*junlie shu*).

[60] *JFRB*, October 11, 1951.

[61] *NCNA* (Beijing), June 21, 1952, and *DGB* (Hong Kong), January 12, 1952.

[62] A Shanghai example, much discussed during the Cultural Revolution, was the Yong'an (Wing On) Department Store. For details that overstate capitalists' freedoms in the 1950s, see the article by Fan Xiubing [pseud.], *RMRB*, August 20, 1967.

[63] Interview with an ex-worker in the Huasheng Electric Factory, URI, Hong Kong. "Wahson" fans, named for the entrepreneur who founded the company, are of high quality and are exported. When the plant became "joint state-private" in 1956, the Party secretary taking charge assumed the pseudonym Chen Hua (the first two characters of the founder's full name, which could also be translated as "Arrange China")—a minor gloss on the Chinese revolution's incompleteness.

[64] See Lynn White, "Changing Concepts of Corruption in Communist China," in *Changes and Continuities in Chinese Communism: The Economy, Society, and Technology*, ed. Yuming Shaw (Boulder, Colo.: Westview, 1988).

high cadres for political corruption. The secretary general of the Shanghai Municipal Party Committee, Li Yu, was removed for "arrogance and abuse of his position." Two members of the committee's Economic and Finance Department, a leading official of the General Federation of Trade Unions, another in the power company, and the ex-chief of the Training Department of the Public Security Bureau were among the CCP personnel purged at this time.[65] The CCP first and very publicly monitored itself (or at least resolved intra-Party conflicts with a purge that looked like a cleaning) before moving on to attempt more control of other organizations.

In such a context, the Party could also garner support for a major public attack against corruption among capitalist entrepreneurs. A "Three Anti" Campaign against official corruption thus undergirded the simultaneous "Five Anti" Campaign against economic wrongdoing.[66] This provided the government with extensive information that would be needed to create a planned economy later.

The Five Anti Campaign was the first major movement against Shanghai capitalists, and it was coercive on the local level. A decision in early 1952 to have workers run it, rather than let the capitalists' Federation of Industry and Commerce fight economic corruption, was the most crucial early intervention by Communist state power against bourgeois businessmen.[67] In the first major use of institutional violence against capitalists, the Five Anti Campaign became a series of struggle meetings for "tiger hunting."

Tax evasion was the usual charge proven against capitalists. By the end of 1951, the Municipal Tax Bureau had found over 50,000 evading companies, owing a total of 260 trillion yuan. By the end of December in the next year, another 106,000 tax shirking companies were found; but they were apparently smaller, because only 70 trillion yuan more of revenue was recouped.[68] The guilty firms ranged from small "traveling merchants" to large steel mills.[69]

Itinerant merchants, who were supposed to remit sales taxes they collected

[65] See *JFRB*, March 2, 1952.

[66] The "Five Antis" were bribery, tax evasion, stealing state property, cheating on contracts, and theft of economic secrets—all of which had, to some extent, been taken for granted traditionally. See John Gardner, "The Wu-fan Campaign in Shanghai: A Study in the Consolidation of Urban Control," in *Chinese Communist Politics in Action*, ed. A. Doak Barnett (Seattle: University of Washington Press, 1969), pp. 447–76.

[67] The federation's committees were put under new auspices at a meeting reported in *JFRB*, February 7, 1952, in which Shanghai Party secretaries Sheng Peihua and Pan Hannian criticized the federation for too little activity in the campaign.

[68] *RMRB*, December 30, 1953.

[69] *NCNA*, February 18, 1952.

on behalf of the government, were especially difficult for the Tax Bureau to monitor. It established a system of "business record books," but to little avail. A law decreed: "When goods are loaded or unloaded in wharfs or other transport stations, traders will present their record books to be checked by the responsible staff. In this way, they will be exempt from having to prepay tax as a guarantee."[70] Compliance was raised by the sometimes effective power of police on transport routes.

Supply markets provided the Party's main leverage over most small shops (before the shortages and rationing of the mid-1950s). Tea shops were urged to form "joint purchasing small groups" under the state Tea Company.[71] Workers' consumer cooperatives, designed "to reduce exploitation by middlemen," applied further pressure on private capitalists.[72] By September 1951, there were about three hundred such co-ops in Shanghai, having an aggregate membership of half a million people and advertising goods at "cheaper than market prices." These institutions could change the basis of livelihood for small capitalists selling goods whose supply the government could monitor.

Control could also threaten production, however. Some early labeling in Shanghai was designed to counteract this effect by emphasizing the importance of production. In the Five Anti Campaign, as soon as companies were found to be "law abiding or basically law abiding," laudatory certificates to that effect were awarded, presumably to ease their disquiet.[73] By the same token, the principle of labeling was firmly established in this campaign. The label "capitalist" was clearly bad, and "workers" in their firms were encouraged to lead Five Anti criticisms. Directives from the municipal Party were ambiguous: On one hand, these ordered that struggle meetings should not be held during work hours, "because this brings much loss of business."[74] On the other, they affirmed unmistakably that the role of managers was to "support the aims of the Party and the development of the state" and to "become law-abiding agents of capital"—not necessarily to make a profit for themselves or pay their employees too generously.[75] When a group is labeled (as capitalists were in the Five Anti Campaign) and when the label

[70] *SHGSZL* 2, no. 38 (1951): 1373; the books were *yingye jilü bo.*
[71] *Liangou xiaozu; SHGSZL* 3, no. 39 (1952): 2545. The company was the Guoying Chaye Gongsi, Huadong Qu Gongsi. There were two waves of effort to put these shops in groups. The first, in 1951, established ten groups; the second began in May 1952 and set up four groups. Each group contained about fourteen shops.
[72] *JFRB*, November 14, 1951.
[73] *LDB*, April 15, 1952.
[74] *XWRB*, January 3, 1953.
[75] Speech by Pan Hannian, *JFRB*, May 19, 1952.

categorizes victims for a "ritual of struggle,"[76] an administrative result is that they are claimed as instruments of the leaders conducting the ritual.

In a few firms by 1952, workers had already become factory managers. When a capitalist owner of a steelworks was arrested for embezzlement, his place as manager was taken by a proletarian Party member.[77] A chemical factory, also short of executives after the Five Anti Campaign, promoted fifteen workers to fill the directorship, deputy directorships, and department headships.[78] The Railroad District promoted 160 "first class workers" in April 1952, and labor union heads were also replaced by Five Anti activists.[79] Labels, especially those denoting enthusiasm for the regime, obviously affected careers by this time.

The Shanghai Workers' Political School began two-month training courses in March 1952 to provide loyal cadres for management posts.[80] About 40 percent of the first three classes (each with about one thousand nascent managers) joined the Party upon graduation. They were sponsored for membership by the school's own CCP organization.[81] Others had been Party members in their factories before they enrolled. They went for training to become official monitors in their units.

Proletarian resentment against capitalists was a real phenomenon in Chinese cities during the early 1950s. And the Party began to do more then to stir feelings against bourgeois whom local CCP bosses distrusted. Lu Wenfu's novella *The Gourmand* reveals both the resentment that the CCP exploited and the extremes to which labeling could go. Because fiction is a good way to describe motives, a brief summary of this story can throw light on worker-capitalist relations. The narrator is Gao Xiaoting, who as a boy from a poor family was a servant in the house of Zhu Zhizhi, a capitalist. Zhu had no regular work and was a connoisseur of food. Just before 1949, the proletarian Gao joined the Party, later obtaining rights to cadre status. He was assigned to oversee the management of a restaurant. Zhu, a frequent customer there, still led a comfortable life after the revolution; but he broke no laws. "He did not smoke opium, he did not gamble, he had no interest in prostitutes. Besides enjoying delicious food, he did nothing. He could not be

---

[76] See Richard Madsen, *Morality and Power in a Chinese Village* (Berkeley and Los Angeles: University of California Press, 1984), e.g. pp. 22ff., for much more on "ceremonies of innocence" and "rituals of struggle."

[77] *LDB*, March 23, 1952. The new manager had worked in the steel company's molding shop for fourteen years and was not a demobilized soldier (ibid.).

[78] *LDB*, April 15, 1952.

[79] *LDB*, April 23, 1952.

[80] *NCNA*, May 12, 1952.

[81] *LDB*, May 10, July 29, September 23, 1952; *SN*, June 28, September 9, 1952.

put into the category of counterrevolutionary." This maddened Gao, who remained radical from the early 1950s until the Cultural Revolution, when he got revenge against Zhu.[82] The novella is striking for several reasons—not least for its explicit connection of early 1950s labeling with political motives in the late 1960s.

This book sardonically criticizes its proletarian narrator for pettiness. Despite the proletarian cadre's long history of vituperation against a "parasite capitalist," the story shows that he could do nothing substantial for the revolution. *The Gourmand* is a model history of the development of friction between officially labeled groups. The story satirizes the viewpoint of a worker-manager, whose character defects become obvious without the author ever having to express his own views directly. Political labeling conflicted with the incomplete change of social elites after 1949. An ex-proletarian "new class" soon became frustrated, as did the old elite that was its natural rival.

The other side of this coin is that bourgeois-labeled families increasingly feared ostracism. As time went by, people with bad labels were more willing to do anything that might raise their political legitimacy. Even capitalists could prove their patriotism, making public self-sacrifices for the sake of national progress. Proletarians—especially upwardly mobile worker cadres—could advance themselves in the same way.

These patterns continued for at least three decades after 1949, but they were already evident by the early 1950s. New clubs were established for unionized workers' leisure time activities. Many of the beneficiaries were not actually workers, but bureaucrats. In November 1952, for example, the South Shanghai Workers' Club was opened to serve 160,000 proletarians and cadres in four urban districts.[83] Such facilities were not for all; they were for loyalists in the new management class, whose numbers were increasing even though most of Shanghai's business was still conducted by older elites.

Not until December 1952 did any general registration of business establishments in Shanghai begin.[84] District branches of the Federation of Industry and Commerce had formed only a month earlier.[85] For three and a half years, from mid-1949 until late 1952, the Party achieved its aims among most Shanghai capitalists by external pressures against them (largely from

---

[82] Lu Wenfu, *Meishi jia* (The gourmand), *Shouhuo* (Harvest) 1 (January) 1983.

[83] *SN*, November 6, 1952.

[84] *SHGSZL* 3, no. 97 (1952): 5798.

[85] *SHGSZL* 3, no. 93 (1952): 5609.

workers), rather than by encouraging any but the most loyal of them to participate actively in the federation.

Some managers nonetheless received congratulations for having helped in the Five Anti movement.[86] This campaign had hurt production because of its effects on capitalists. The Party acquired a stake in regularizing the status of bourgeois, to restore their incentive to work—and thus in distinguishing Party members it could trust from those about whose loyalty it had doubts. At the conclusion of the Five Anti Campaign, the government gave its approval for an East China Trade Fair aimed at increasing business.[87] Because tax delinquency had been the most common specific charge against capitalists, "mutual help groups" and "workers' tax aid groups" drew up "plans of payment" for bourgeois businessmen unable to remit their taxes immediately.[88]

Economic revival was more important than socialist control in 1952, and it made the urban economy harder for the Party to monitor. The number of light industrial factories in Shanghai was 38 percent higher in 1952 than it had been in 1950.[89] Because of the Five Anti Campaign, private firms' output was less in 1952 than it had been the previous year; but it picked up again in 1953.[90] Three years after the establishment of Communist government in Shanghai, the future of relations between types of local leaders was at least as unclear as it had been in 1949.

CONSOLIDATING THE NEW ELITE'S GAINS AGAINST CAPITALISTS

The state became accustomed to the revenue that pressure against businessmen could bring, and it increasingly fostered a rival elite of local activists who hoped to discomfit or displace them. Even after the end of the Five Anti Campaign in July 1952, more worker-cadres were designated to gather information about capitalist managers. The Tax Bureau in September of the following year conducted a "random check" of returns from about three thousand firms and found that 85 percent "employed methods to evade tax. . . . As many as seventy-seven techniques were found to have been

---

[86] *NCNA*, April 21, 1952.
[87] *NCNA*, July 23, 1952.
[88] *SHGSZL* 3, no. 31, (1952): 2118.
[89] *NCNA*, February 2, 1953.
[90] *RMRB*, March 3, 1954.

used."[91] Even though the Five Antis had ended, businessmen who were caught in sharp practices during September 1953, and in similar campaigns of 1955 and later, were vilified as "traitorous merchants."[92]

A decision was made to separate the schools for proletarian and capitalist leaders. The system of "Party schools" (*dang xiao*) was open to CCP members exclusively, and the "socialist academies" (*shehui zhuyi xueyuan*) were for capitalists and members of "democratic parties."[93] This segregation meant that Shanghai's up-and-coming proletarian leadership avoided contamination from established businessmen and intellectuals. But it also legitimated the principle that these leaderships should not work together. The content of study in the schools was similar, strongly emphasizing Marxist ideology. The reason for the segregation was social and political, rather than curricular.[94]

In December 1953, the Party announced vague future plans for a "Transition to Socialism."[95] The Five Anti Campaign had already established the legitimacy of using violence to change urban economic institutions, and it was no secret that the ruling Party was Communist. So this policy of socialism came as no great surprise to capitalists. But it represented a change of emphasis from the "New Democratic" propaganda of 1949, which assured the bourgeoisie of a long-term role in New China. And capitalists could see that the Party's plans for nationalization were ambitious. Socialization could be realized only by campaigns threatening dire consequences for individual capitalists who did not cooperate. The Party in 1953–54 still lacked sufficient staff to manage all of Shanghai's enterprises effectively. Also, the partial rejuvenation of capitalism to aid the army in the Korean War had not yet entirely ended.

More and more firms nonetheless came under state planning, mostly as enterprises that were "joint state-private" (*gongsi heying*). The government acquired shares of private firms, which were transferred to the state in payment of high fines arising from the Five Anti Campaign. Occasionally the

[91] *GMRB*, September 8, 1953.

[92] *Jianshang*; *XWRB*, September 11, 1985.

[93] Interview, Hong Kong; see also *NCNA*, November 22, 1951.

[94] There were also cadres' schools (*ganbu xuexiao*), which an interviewee said were mostly "for training low-level technicians and political cadres." The academic standards at these schools were "not especially high," although they did give some loyal and intelligent ex-peasants and ex-soldiers a start on careers in Shanghai.

[95] Robert Loh, as told to Humphrey Evans, *Escape from Red China* (New York: Coward-McCann, 1962), pp. 130–33.

state bought shares outright. Or it acquired them by confiscation from GMD refugees and others who left for places like Hong Kong. By 1951, about 10 percent of the Chinese government's budget came from confiscations; but with the Five Antis of 1952, the figure rose to 23 percent.[96] By early 1954, "Tax Bureau checks of enterprises, late in the previous year, revealed 81 percent of firms evading taxes."[97] So individual capitalists were again called into meetings, along with their families and especially their wives, to encourage compliance with new imposts.[98] No one doubted that the label of a household head would pertain to all its members, and in these meetings it began to mean more than just a description of the sources from which the family received income. Meetings began to turn such labels into political and moral judgments about people.

Stiff criminal sentences were imposed for economic crimes. One capitalist, in the auto repair business, had hired technicians away from other firms (apparently state or joint ones) and had thus encouraged "a blind movement of labor," unauthorized by the bureaucracy. He received a three-year sentence in prison. Another entrepreneur was jailed for opening his own factory without a license—and promising his laborers union memberships.[99] The problem with these entrepreneurs, from some CCP cadres' standpoint, was that they weakened the potential monopoly of hiring that the new would-be patrons envisaged.

This sort of pressure also created tax revenues beyond the government's expectations. During 1953, the whole city managed to pay one-third more taxes than in 1952; and this performance was repeated in 1954. During two well-publicized months of 1955, state revenues exceeded the expected quota. Wealthy Shanghainese also bought more "State Economic Construction Bonds" than expected in that period.[100] Such pressure on capitalists had many effects. For one thing, an increased number of entrepreneurs closed their firms or asked to do so.[101]

---

[96] Because of remittances between government levels, and because some big firms cross jurisdictional boundaries, these figures are national. See Zhu Yuanzheng, *Zhonggong caiqing zhengce xin dongxiang* (New trends in Chinese Communist fiscal and economic policies) (Hong Kong: Ziyou chuban she, 1953), *shang ce*, 35–40.

[97] *RMRB*, March 3, 1954.

[98] *SHGSZL* 3, no. 29 (1952): 1939.

[99] These Shanghai cases are reported in *DGB* (Tianjin), June 3, 1954.

[100] *Guojia jingji jianshe gongzhai*; *XWRB*, September 17, 1955.

[101] The foreign cases, many of which came early, are the best documented. *SN*, December 7, 1952, carries a notice of the Shanghai and Hongkew Wharf Co. to its shareholders, recommending "transfer to either a government or a privately operated enterprise of all assets." The

STAGES AND VARIETIES OF EXPROPRIATION

Well before the 1956 Transition to Socialism, the government wanted a monopoly on wholesale trading of four specific commodities. These four were salt (an old state monopoly), lumber (a multi-use product that is bulky and easy to monitor), and grain and cooking oil (the most important agricultural products, first rationed in 1954). The Party therefore "initiated labor-capital consultations" and "carried out the socialist transformation of whole trades" in these commodities. As a result, 80 percent of the relevant firms "suspended business," 16 percent switched to retail trade, and 3 percent moved into other fields. Only 2 percent continued—as institutional parts of state wholesale monopolies.[102] These changes gave a few officials great power in the commerce of four basic commodities.

Market access opportunities, as well as political struggle, thus gave entrepreneurs big incentives for converting to "joint" status, especially by 1954–55. This was a change from 1952. Under the 1954 ration system, many firms could get no supplies to process or sell legally, unless they became agents of companies such as the Municipal Food Bureau.[103] Many had to become branches (*fen dian*) of large state corporations. But in most small firms, it was difficult for the Party to mobilize effective shop-assistant criticisms of petty businessmen, because the shop helpers were members of the same families.

It was often easier to control small firms' supplies of goods or raw materials. In earlier years, the government had been a major buyer in trades like metal processing and in some large-firm industries such as textiles. After 1954, when cloth rations were introduced, the monopoly on cotton supplies and monopsony of legal textile sales brought more official influence to Shanghai's huge industry for weaving and dyeing. Entrepreneurs who did not cooperate with the state found themselves without markets or inputs; this was no way to make a profit.[104]

By the beginning of 1955, different degrees of socialist transformation typified different parts of Shanghai's retail economy. Cloth, sugar, and tobacco shops were tied to state companies by official control of wholesale

---

same journal on December 13 reported closure of the Sassoon enterprises, and the issues of September 3 and 6 carry news about other companies.

[102] *NCNA*, May 14, 1955. Two hundred and twenty firms were involved (ibid.).

[103] *DGB* (Tianjin), March 8, 1954.

[104] An official report by Pan Hannian about this situation is in *JFRB*, February 12, 1955. For other relevant articles see *NCNA*, May 24, 1952, March 31, October 22, 1953, January 11, 1955; *XWRB*, July 1, 1955.

supplies. There was even more state control of the drug, paper, and hard-ware industries, which were then still selling through more than two thousand retailers in Shanghai—but had to buy materials from state companies and "basically" had to sell at state-fixed prices. Other goods at this medium level of control, which were retailed in smaller stores, included wines, soaps, and porcelains. Restriction was greater over a third category of goods, which was subject to tight state deliveries and pricing: rice, wool, wheat flour, coal, cooking oil, and soy sauce. Shops selling these products had hung out signs by 1955 saying they were branches of state corporations. That did not ensure their new official monitors would do anything for them, but it legitimated them politically.

OVERVIEW OF SOCIALIZATION

When labeled "agents of capital holding positions in closed-down shops" were willing to undergo political study for reemployment in other state firms, some were allowed to do so.[105] The Party sorely needed their accounting and managerial skills, even if their unofficial social prestige made them politically dubious and the supplies of goods in which they had traded could now be controlled to make profits difficult on a private basis.

The rate of Shanghai's industrial nationalization was steadier than the particular campaigns for it might suggest. Although a fear of violence instilled by these movements accumulated slowly, it was crucial to the process even in relatively calm times. Data were published on the declining percentage of output in Shanghai's private sector (see table 1).

Heavy industry was increasingly important in this development because of state investment in metals factories that provided a few good jobs, were often easy to monitor, and made high-priority products (see table 2). Its rate of increase as a portion of Shanghai's output accelerated through the Great Leap Forward (and again after 1962). Part of this acceleration resulted from Stalinist policies that gave heavy industrial products high prices. But most of the change resulted from unusual rates of capital investment.

In commerce, the transformation was slower than in industry. In 1953, after the middle of the long period covered by this chapter, over three-quarters of Shanghai's retail trade was still private (see table 3).

These rather steady trends obscure the different times at which different kinds of companies were affected in the nationalization process. Socialism

---

[105] *NCNA*, January 12, 1955.

TABLE 1
Private Sector Industry, 1949–1958
(Percentages of Industrial Gross Value in Shanghai)

Year	Percentage
1949	83
1952	67
1953	67
1954	45
1955	35
1956	0

Sources: Dili zhishi (Geographic knowledge) 7 (July 6, 1959); *NCNA* (Shanghai), February 2, 1955; and *Jiefang ribao* (Liberation daily), September 25, 1954.

TABLE 2
Kinds of Industry, 1949–1958
(Percentages of Industrial Gross Value in Shanghai)

	Heavy Industry (90)	Textiles (90)	Other Light Industry (90)
1949	14	62	24
1952	23	52	25
1958	46	32	22

Source: Constructed from information in *Peking Review* June 9, 1959, pp. 10–12.

came in three stages. During the first, large enterprises that were important for defense, particularly those affected by the GMD blockade (especially in textiles) or confiscated from refugees, became joint state-private. Their previous directors often remained crucial in management.

The second stage arose largely from the ration system introduced in 1954. The state amalgamated myriad small commercial outlets under large municipal companies, each dealing with just a few major commodities. Most of the firms affected at this stage were formally abolished, but the change was often symbolic—a matter of posting new signs in front of old shops, to show them as branches of one or another large state corporation, even though the old managers usually remained on site.

The final stage was the 1956 Transition to Socialism, in which the aim was to baptize all remaining private firms as "joint." The private enterprises that lasted to 1956 generally dealt with goods that were hard to monitor in production or trade, were miscellaneous, or were not vital to supply downstream industries the government already controlled.

Although most scholarly attention has focused on the early Three Anti and late Transition to Socialism stages of this change, the middle stage of rationing in 1954–55 almost surely affected the livelihoods and political standings of a greater number of urban people. From the viewpoint of a great many capitalist families running small shops selling goods under the 1954 rations, that year was more important than any other. Types of changes that took place in six trades (cloth, native cloth, sundries, sugar, coal, and tobacco) are noted in table 4. In grain, an even larger number of shops established wholesale relations with state companies. Joint enterprise status became unavoidable for most Shanghai entrepreneurs.

This move toward "state capitalism" in 1954–55 came from increased official capacity to tap sources of information. Control of materials flowing

TABLE 3

Private, State, and Joint Firms' Output, 1953
(Percentages of Gross Value in Shanghai Industry
and Commerce)

	Private (90)	State (90)	Joint (90)
Industrial output	67	27	6
Commercial output	77	15	8

Source: Jiefang ribao (Liberation daily), September 25, 1954

TABLE 4

Decisions by Shanghai Firms
Selling Nongrain Wholesale Rationed Products, 1954

	Percentage of Total	Number
Closed business	69	496
Changed trade to nonrationed goods	14	102
Became branch of state company/or co-op	13	92
Continued business	3	22
Did not report	1	8
Total	100	720

Source: NCNA, January 12, 1955 (percentages computed).

through Shanghai's port was important to the state, in part because the bureaucracy needed tax revenues from these flows. The Harbor Control Bureau in 1954 increased its official say in matters that ranged from fuel supply for boats to prices of fish to the provision of land-based housing (and even bicycles!) for boat people.[106] By the end of 1955, the government claimed that Shanghai's private river shipping was entirely socialized.[107] The state meant more to more residents after this time.

In many light industries, municipal bureaus organized "small groups" to check product quality and to gather other business information.[108] By no means, however, did all family stores last into the socialist era and become branches of state corporations. Traditionally, stores selling the same kinds of goods were often established on the same part of a single street, even in different entrances to the same building. But during the Transition to Socialism, when such stores became state-owned, side-by-side shops were consolidated to become single branches of the relevant municipal company. Frequently, new employees were brought in, to shake up the shops. Some shifting of personnel among the new stores was also common, and this further facilitated more central control.[109] Organizational changes in themselves could serve to increase the CCP's influence.

A 1955 RECESSION ADDS NEW MEANING
TO THE STATE CONTROLS

The weather gave the state bad luck in efforts to ration grain. Floods ravaged the lower Yangtze valley in 1954, and a grain supply crisis developed in the following year.[110] In 1955, the new official companies could not make deliveries of good-quality food or clothing—within a year of the time they had taken charge of shops for these rationed goods.

Other difficulties affected the production of medicines, lumber, glassware, stationery, and porcelain. Many small capitalists deeply distrusted the socialization effort, even though they could make no profit without cooperating. They could think of the plan as dubious economics, because it de-

---

[106] *XWRB*, December 14, 1956; *NCNA* (Beijing), October 30, 1956; *GRRB*, October 30, 1956.

[107] *NCNA*, December 13, 1955.

[108] *XWRB*, September 8, 1955.

[109] Interview, Hong Kong, with an ex-businessman from Shanghai whose firm underwent these changes.

[110] See Thomas P. Bernstein, "Cadre and Peasant Behavior under Conditions of Insecurity and Deprivation: The Grain Supply Crisis of the Spring of 1955," in *Chinese Communist Politics in Action*, pp. 365–99.

pressed output in their sectors. Shanghai's official Shopkeepers' Union thus had to summon its activists to meetings in August 1955, according to their lines of trade, urging them "to mobilize capitalists to sell commodities that the country needed to sell . . . to sell actively the goods that few people wanted."[111] Illegal firms (*weifa hu*) sprang up in industries ranging from metals and undergarments to brush making.[112] Capitalists in lawful firms were accused of causing "slow-downs."[113] But the factories that performed worst economically during 1955 were those that had just been made joint enterprises, including many in textiles and cigarettes.[114]

This crisis spurred a reorganization of the city's industrial trade guilds "to serve the needs of state transformation. . . . Existing trade guilds cannot meet the demands made on them."[115] Even firms that had long been governed by state plans, such as Rong Yiren's Shenxin Textile Company (which in the early 1950s was still under a capitalist board of directors, two-thirds of whom were surnamed Rong)[116] were reorganized in 1955 and merged with smaller plants, so that the capitalists took more nominal roles in administration.[117] The cotton supply crisis helped merge fifty-five textile mills into nineteen larger, state-private companies that year. This involved closing some plants and "repairing the roofs and walls of others."[118] Shi Ying, who chaired the Shanghai Light Industry Bureau, urged capitalists to "make good use of the time for establishing joint enterprises as soon as possible [and for] clearing property and fixing shares."[119]

The mid-1950s fate of managers in Shanghai's woolen clothing industry also gives an indication of what happened in large plants. Most owners were retired, not retained (see table 5). Although high bureaucrats continued in 1955 to say they hoped to keep capitalists in important roles,[120] there were disagreements in the Party about the extent to which the "national bourgeoisie" could be trusted. In large firms especially, many managers retired earlier than they had planned.

---

[111] *XWRB*, August 26, 1955; the Shopkeepers' Union is the Dianyuan Gonghui. The frankness of this article (p. 4) is typical of the reporting in this newspaper, which was not a Party organ and was published for Shanghai's many "small capitalists."

[112] *XWRB*, September 23, 1955.

[113] *DGB* (Tianjin), October 29, 1955.

[114] *GRRB*, September 20, 1955, indicated that state plans were not being fulfilled in fifteen out of twenty spinning and weaving mills at this time.

[115] *NCNA*, November 21, 1955.

[116] *DGB* (Hong Kong), June 21, 1952.

[117] *NCNA*, August 16, 1955, and *XWRB*, September 3, 1955.

[118] *XWRB*, September 4, 1955.

[119] "Qingchan dinggu"; *XWRB*, August 27, 1955.

[120] *NCNA*, November 25, 1955.

TABLE 5

Employment of Ex-Owners of Shanghai Woolen Textile Firms after Their Socialist Transition in 1955

	Percentage	Number
Not rehired (retired on dividends?)	60	91
Given posts in joint enterprises	40	61
As managers	1	2
As deputy managers	4	6
As factory directors or vice-directors	30	45
As engineers	5	8
Total	100	152

Source: Computed from partial figures in *NCNA* (Shanghai), January 9, 1956.

PARTY RECRUITMENT AND CCP DISAGREEMENTS ON SOCIALIZATION

This book is not designed to cover the politics of the top CCP leaders, or even of the few highest officials in Shanghai.[121] But the purges of East China's main Party secretary Rao Shushi in 1954, and of Shanghai's deputy mayor (and Chen Yi's main political ally) Pan Hannian the next year, clearly related to the issue of how to treat capitalists.[122] Rao's involvement in Beijing politics was important, but the experiences of large groups play an often-neglected role in top-level purges (as changes in 1966 and 1978 also suggest).

The Party's main urban question in the mid-1950s was how hard to press the "national capitalists." The Soviet example, as well as explicit Soviet advice during that period, recommended an attack on the bourgeoisie until it ceased to exist.[123] "The unscrupulous capitalists of Shanghai"[124] had been a topic of speeches by doctrinaire Communists since the early fifties. There

---

[121] For more, see Lynn White, "Leadership in Shanghai, 1955–69" in *Elites in the People's Republic of China*, ed. Robert A. Scalapino (Seattle: University of Washington Press, 1972), pp. 302–77.

[122] According to a cadre in Shanghai, Pan's purge was justified by his communication with Wang Jingwei's authorities during the Japanese occupation. This high official informant also said that Chen Yi was close to Pan.

[123] Rozman, *A Mirror for Socialism*, p. 176, quotes V. I. Lazarev, *Klassovaia bor'ba v KNR* (Class conflict in the PRC) (Moscow: Polititizdat, 1981): "The initiators of the 'cultural revolution' were many times more favorably inclined to the national bourgeoisie than to the working class, the peasantry, and the intelligentsia." The present book largely supports Lazarev's view, although it also finds other "initiators" among proletarians trying to preserve their privileges.

[124] This term is from an article in *NCNA*, March 31, 1952.

had long been tension between Party members who specialized in liaison with managers and intellectuals in the "white" areas before 1949 and those whose work had been in the "red" areas of Communist rural bases.[125] But for many years, differences in policy toward bourgeois-labeled people had to be swept under the Party's rug. The CCP did not know exactly what to do with capitalist managers, because many of its top members realized they could not yet easily do without them.

Not until 1954, when the Party began to have enough information about businesses, could leftist members give serious thought to implementing full socialization. Chen Yun, a high Party politician who has long favored markets along with state control,[126] espoused the "commodity circulation tax" of 1953, which replaced private merchants' taxes and probably slowed the socialization of industry.[127] Economists debated, in early 1954, whether state-run enterprises should follow Marx's advice about "buying the capitalists out." Lenin's New Economic Policy had also "paid the capitalists well" (before Stalin's forceful approach transformed them more quickly). The less expensive alternative—apparently—was to use campaigns and fear to squeeze bourgeois firms out of business.[128]

During the Cultural Revolution long after Rao's downfall, he was accused of having failed to insist on the quick transformation of capitalists. "He advocated distribution of raw materials to state and private enterprises without discrimination."[129] The 1955 Party resolution condemning Rao also said he had "a rightist policy of surrender to the capitalists."[130]

Rao's purge was not made fully public for more than a year after he left the city, so that knowledge of it would not encourage Shanghai capitalists to resist socialization. Even after he was purged, differences within the local CCP on how to treat the bourgeoisie were still evident. A Municipal Party Committee meeting in May 1954 declared itself "basically united," but it admitted some "defects in unity" because of "liberal and bourgeois individ-

---

[125] Examples abound in the Five Anti Campaign. On the purge of Li Jianhua, who joined the Party in 1934 and "worked for long periods in the underground," see *JFRB*, March 11, 1952.

[126] See David M. Bachman, *Chen Yun and the Chinese Political System* (Berkeley: University of California Center for Chinese Studies, 1985).

[127] A critical evaluation of Chen Yun is in *Caimao hongqi* (Finance and trade Red Flag) (Beijing), February 15, 1967.

[128] Meng Xianzhang took the softer line in his *Course in Democratic Economy*, but Yao Pengzhang criticized him severely in *WHB*, January 7, 1954. See Arthur A. Cohen, *The Communism of Mao Tse-tung* (Chicago: University of Chicago Press, 1964), pp. 110–19.

[129] *Current Background* 874 (March 1968): 25, quoting a Cultural Revolution pamphlet, *Thirty-three Leading Counter-revolutionary Revisionists*.

[130] Quoted in Peter S. H. Tang, "Power Struggle in the Chinese Communist Party: The Kao-Jao Purge," *Problems of Communism*, November–December, 1955, p. 19.

ualist tendencies."[131] In the next month, Pan Hannian was in charge of a conference to "examine Party work in Shanghai."[132] In July, large meetings were called, urging businessmen to cooperate with state plans for reorganization.[133]

Recruitment to the ranks of Shanghai's Communist Party had been slow until Rao's fall. In 1953, the growth in local CCP membership was low, despite high-level efforts to raise it. In one urban district whose residents numbered several hundred thousand, precisely eight new CCP members were inducted in the third quarter of 1953 (even though there had been specific preparations in the second quarter for inducting more members).[134] During these three months, the Shanghai Party as a whole admitted only twenty-five hundred members. Over three-quarters were industrial workers, and only 2.4 percent were shop employees. The large number of intellectuals and capitalist-background loyalists who had long been in the Party still formed a majority of its originally Shanghainese membership. Many other members had moved to the metropolis after Liberation.

There was plenty of willingness to admit proletarians to the ranks of the intellectuals, managers, and demobilized soldiers who comprised most of Shanghai's CCP at this time; but there were apparently too few good prospects from that vanguard class. The actual family backgrounds of some admitted as "workers" were also suspect. By the mid-1950s, numerous factory workers had bourgeois backgrounds. "Peasants" who were actually ex-army officers, educated in the hard management school of a civil war, provided as many proletarian candidates—even in this nonpeasant city. Many of these were given good jobs in socialized companies, and their army experience made them prime candidates for CCP membership. The Party established special programs for demobilized servicemen in which they learned "how to issue invoices, how to use the abacus, how to stock inventories, how to fill out forms."[135]

The terms "worker" and "proletarian" referred to official labels rather than any classes that might be properly defined by common relations to the means of production. One of the causes of resentment among disadvantaged status groups lay in the inconsistent (and non-Marxist) bases of the classification. It was already evident that leading members with better class labels—especially cadres and soldiers among the proletarians, and intellec-

---

[131] *NCNA*, May 28, 1954.

[132] *NCNA*, June 27, 1954.

[133] One Shanghai meeting is reported in *DGB* (Tianjin), June 16, 1954.

[134] *JFRB*, December 20, 1953.

[135] *NCNA*, May 18, 1955.

tuals among the bourgeois—were more important politically than the larger labeled groups they led.[136]

The whole year 1954 was a time of radical politics in the industrial departments that later led the Transition to Socialism.[137] But many managers wished to avoid production losses as state power increased. Although Shanghai's local Party probably included more worker-origin members than any other in China, it also contained many intellectuals of capitalist backgrounds—and practically all the workers had been members for less than five years.[138] From 1949 to the end of 1953, just before Rao's purge, the Shanghai CCP admitted only thirty thousand members. This increment was less than a tenth of the usual ratio of Party members to total population; so even though 63 percent of the new members were in industrial jobs, their recruitment was insufficient to change the basic mix of backgrounds among Shanghai Communists.[139]

In the first three-quarters of 1954, about twelve thousand more people became Party members. For the last three months of that year, the admissions figure was almost thirty thousand—of whom 80 percent were workers, more than one-third in private factories.[140] Even after this crash program to admit workers, a clear majority of Shanghai's Communists were still not of proletarian background. The proportion of Party members in the urban population was well below the 4 or 5 percent norm.[141] Shanghai's Party was not really proletarian and it was badly understaffed.

---

[136] The term "status group" is from Max Weber: "In contrast to classes, *status groups* are normally communities. They are, however, often of an amorphous kind. In contrast to the purely economically determined 'class situation,' we wish to designate as 'status situation' every component of the life fate of men that is determined by a specific, positive or negative, social estimation of *honor*, [so] that a specific *style of life* can be expected from all those who wish to belong to the circle" (*From Max Weber: Essays in Sociology*, trans. and ed. H. H. Gerth and C. Wright Mills [New York: Oxford University Press, 1958], pp. 186–87; Weber's italics). He continues, "Property as such is not always recognized as a status qualification, but in the long run it is, and with extraordinary regularity." The Soviets I. F. Federov and V. G. Zubakov criticize Mao for dividing society into classes based on property rather than on links to the means of production—and they have a point. See Rozman, *A Mirror for Socialism*, p. 195.

[137] Representative meetings during the fall are reported in *JFRB*, October 7, 1954.

[138] Rozman, *A Mirror for Socialism*, quotes a Soviet source that in May 1949, only 3 percent of CCP members were workers, and 61 percent were illiterate, with another 13 percent barely literate. The vast majority were of peasant, landlord, and petty bourgeois backgrounds, because many families in these groups had acquired reasons to oppose Japan or the GMD.

[139] *JFRB*, December 20, 21, 1953.

[140] *JFRB*, January 1, 1955. See also *JFRB*, February 18, 1955.

[141] Computed from figures in the text above, while considering Franz Schurmann's estimate of 150,000 CCP members in Shanghai in mid-1956 (*Ideology and Organization in Communist China* [Berkeley and Los Angeles: University of California Press, 1966], pp. 137–38).

Pan Hannian inherited from Rao Shushi the unenviable job of carrying out a Beijing-conceived program in Shanghai that most of the population *and* much of the local Party leadership did not want. Pan was a high-ranking intellectual who also happened to be a long-term Communist.[142] He joined the CCP in 1925, working for many years thereafter in "white" areas.[143] As early as 1935, Pan was friendly with GMD general Zhang Xueliang in Shanghai (before the latter kidnapped Chiang Kai-shek in the Xi'an Incident).[144] He had so many pre-1949 contacts with Shanghai capitalists and intellectuals that his critics would later claim he had been a GMD member.[145] By 1955, Pan enjoyed such close connections with so many important people in Shanghai capitalist and Party circles that many expected him to be appointed mayor.[146] He also spent much time personally cajoling Shanghai capitalists, in an effort to make them put their enterprises under state control.[147] In an early 1955 speech about the treatment of bourgeois, Pan still deplored "cases of the lack of striking a proper medium between severity and magnanimity; and this to some extent affects industrial production."[148] Yet the Party lacked sufficient personnel to replace capitalists, so there was no way to complete Shanghai's socialization without hurting output figures. By July, Pan and his colleague Yang Fan were arrested, and the men who replaced them were less sensitive to the talents of non-CCP local leaders.[149]

---

[142] Interview in Hong Kong with a man who had been in Shanghai and claimed some knowledge of Pan.

[143] See *NCNA* (Beijing), February 28, 1983, which reports Pan's posthumous rehabilitation. Pan was jailed in 1955, was later convicted and sentenced (apparently after a secret trial), and died in Changsha on April 14, 1977. Yang Fan was still alive for Pan's 1983 rehabilitation ceremony, at which he made a speech. Hu Lijiao, second secretary of the Shanghai CCP committee then, praised Pan for "his ability to unite with other comrades and with non-Party personnel to work in full cooperation." This ability was less valued in the 1950s, a period when local elites used inflexible labels to compete with each other, than in the 1980s, when most local leaders thought they could cooperate.

[144] Kai-yu Hsu, *Chou En-lai: China's Grey Eminence* (Garden City, N.Y.: Doubleday, 1968), pp. 131–32.

[145] *Zhongnan diqu hongqi* (Red Flag of the Central South District) (Canton), 3 (March 1968).

[146] Loh, *Escape*, p. 149.

[147] See Sima, *Douzheng shiba nian*, pp. 183ff.

[148] *JFRB*, February 12, 1955.

[149] Pan and Yang later found a patron in the form of Luo Ruiqing, minister of public security, until his purge very early in the Cultural Revolution. This was confirmed both in a Hong Kong interview and in a source that detested all three, *Guangdong wenyi zhanbao* (Guangdong arts war bulletin), n.d. (probably August 1967). Dr. David Chambers of the University of Bristol is now working on a life of Pan Hannian.

CONCLUSION: COSTS OF COMMUNIZATION

By mid-1955, the government had drawn dividing lines between broad categories of Shanghai people. These distinctions were not based on economic classes proper, even though the names of the groups they defined implied they were. Many in Shanghai's Communist Party supported these divisions—and the struggle they foreboded—with considerable hesitancy. Even the CCP's own membership was diverse in background.

This categorization of people was closely linked to a program of economic nationalization. The Party had to recruit staff, or socialist goals might go unfulfilled. The CCP was severely short of experts whom it trusted. Positive labels and promises of patronage could recruit more, and threats of violence could somewhat reduce the need for them.

A totalitarian or monolithic "takeover" model of what happened in Shanghai during the early 1950s neglects the extent of work the socialists had to do, to monitor the urban economy before even attempting to control it. This process was gradual. The main effect of the campaigns at this time derived not from their violent suppression of a few leaders from previous elites. Instead, their main effect was to increase the willingness among far larger groups of local leaders to comply with CCP policies.

For hard-line ideologues in the Party, the whole city was apparently suspect. A decision was taken, about May 1955, that Shanghai enterprises in trades with distant markets or inputs would receive no new capital funds.[150] The amount of investment in Shanghai's 1955 economy was less than the value of depreciation.[151] New capital was less than wear and tear then. Disinvestment is a rare phenomenon over so large an economy, and many plants ran at half capacity or less. Such problems partly resulted from deficiencies in agricultural supply, but they also resulted from severe pressure on capitalists to transfer management of their companies to the state.

Communization of so bourgeois a place as Shanghai would not prove easy. The introduction of urban labeling, the heightening of bossism, and the legitimation of campaigns seemed policies strong enough to do the socializing job. But Shanghai's Party itself was divided between leaders of local families and incoming ex-army cadres. The city's CCP was tiny in compari-

---

[150] A large group of state and joint tobacco, paper, drug, food, and oil-processing factories curtailed their capital construction plans by two-thirds in 1955 (see *NCNA*, June 7, 1955).

[151] Kang Chao, "Policies and Performance in Industry," in *Economic Trends in Communist China* ed. Alexander Eckstein, Walter Galenson, and Ta-chung Liu (Chicago: Aldine, 1968), pp. 558–59.

son with an urban economy that still accounted for more than a fifth of China's industry. Only by using a complex set of threats against capitalists, and only by sacrificing production to politics, could new local leaders over a period of many years begin to assume control of this place. The cost of the policy has received little scholarly attention, because Communist states are generally assumed to be well-unified, efficient at least in their totalism. The greatest cost, not obvious in the 1950s, lay in the long-term effects of dividing talents against each other. Chinese would later waste energies in struggle for local supremacy rather than for their whole community.

CHAPTER 3

Students and Residents:
Policing vs. Patriotism, 1949–1956

Confucius said: "Lead the people by laws and regulate them
by penalties, and the people will try to keep out of jail, but will
have no sense of shame. Lead the people by virtue and restrain
them by the rules of decorum, and the people will have a sense
of shame, and moreover will become good."
—*Analects* 2.3

Values nurtured by families, neighborhoods, schools, and religions affect the
ways people act, as surely as economic and material factors do. Residents
and intellectuals were important, along with workers and managers, in creating conditions for the chaos of 1966–68. Such groups overlap each other,
of course. Administrators and employees are all residents too. The leaders
of local urban groups are often intellectuals in the sense that they have some
education, and many of them have cadre or managerial posts. But a particular analysis of the roles of residents and students can throw new light on
the origins of the Cultural Revolution, because this event affected and
sprang from people's life-styles, not just their work.

An outline history of Shanghai from 1949 to 1956, written in terms of
workers and managers, is available in the last chapter; so a brief treatment
of Shanghai's socializers and symbol makers will serve the purpose here. It
will be clearest to begin with the most important period of residential labeling, which came during the height of patriotic enthusiasm during the Korean
War, and only later show the traditional precedents to this campaign.

EARLY COMMUNIST RESIDENTIAL LABELING

At the end of 1950 and in 1951—the same war period that was crucial
for other kinds of social change—Shanghai launched a "Democratic Reform
Movement" (*minzhu gaige yundong*), in which the population was first divided systematically into "classes" that slowly became groups among residents. Many families with politically dubious backgrounds tried to obtain
favorable, "low-class" labels. In the beginning, the main concerns raised

among badly classed urbanites were indirect. Landlord status had obviously hurt rural families to which it was applied during the land reform. So city folk feared that capitalist status might prove damaging too, even though there was little clear basis for such worries at the time. Classification was not closely linked, at first, to any policy that seriously constrained people. So most capitalist families did not seriously question the files that street committees kept on them.

In July 1951, the Ministry of Public Security issued regulations about these procedures, but they were not applied to everybody in Shanghai until about mid-1955. This system was supposed to pertain to the city's whole population, but it could be implemented quickly only on a voluntary basis.[1] The census of 1953 was a major occasion for a comprehensive creation of files. But precisely because Party leaders knew that social background labels were sensitive, the 1953 census gathered information in only four categories: name, birth date, sex, and nationality.[2] The census would have elicited less compliance had it asked for class status. The 1951 Democratic Reform Movement thus began labeling; but only later in 1954 and 1955—with rationing and more personnel—did the government try to check its notes on each Shanghai person's class label.

A "household registration book" (*huji bu*) was kept for each family, with a page for each person. The head of the family had one copy, and the local police station had the other. Much information was included—name, address, sex, birth date, nationality, marital status, years of schooling, the place of the family's ancestral origin, family origin, *and* class status—although some spaces in many of the completed forms were left blank.[3]

The head of household, practically always the father, was assigned a "family origin" (*jiating chushen*). This entry could be an item in the Marxist list of classes: "worker," "capitalist," "landlord," "rich peasant," "middle peasant," "lower-middle peasant," or "poor peasant." It might alternatively be a phrase like "revolutionary cadre," "revolutionary soldier," "state employee," "free professional," or "small proprietor."[4] The entry on this line

---

[1.] John F. Aird, "Population Growth," in *Economic Trends in Communist China*, ed. Alexander Eckstein, Walter Galenson, and Ta-chung Liu (Chicago: Aldine, 1968), pp. 220–21.

[2] Leo Orleans, *Every Fifth Child: The Population of China* (Stanford, Calif.: Stanford University Press, 1972), p. 15.

[3] One interviewee said that data on unemployed people, especially the elderly, might be so fragmentary as not to include a full name. A "granny" living in the house of a husband Wang and a wife Chen, for example, might just be entered as "Mme. Wang Chen" (Wang Chen shi). Information on children also tended to be scanty.

[4] In order: *gongren, zichan jieji, dizhu, funong, zhongnong, xiazhongnong, pingnong, geming ganbu, geming junren, zhiyuan, ziyou zhiye, xiaoye ju*. This information comes mainly from interviews.

of the book depended on the source of income of the household head just before Liberation. It was the same for each person in the household, but when a person moved into a new family (for example, by marriage), her (practically never his) origin remained unchanged. Thus labeling was legitimated. Everybody received a categorical, bureaucratically assigned name.

The household book also recorded an "individual status" (*geren chengfen*) for each member. This could be one of the categories used for family origin, but usually it was a type of current occupation. As a mid-1950s article explained:

> For example, if an individual's family origin is "landlord," but he is a teacher and teaching provides his main source of income, his individual status is "education worker." If he separates from his family and joins revolutionary work or becomes a staff member in an organ of the people's government, his individual status will refer to that office work. If he is not separated from his family and has no independent work, [his individual status] would be landlord.[5]

The household registers also listed any honorific titles such as "soldier's or martyr's family member."[6] Children under eighteen were not supposed to have any "individual status" yet, though in fact many were recorded as "students."

This system assumed that all people were in debt to their parents for nurture in time of youth, and that such a heavy debt would naturally shape later attitudes. The CCP's household system (even more than the GMD's individual cards, which preceded it) shared some familistic premises with Confucianism. But the Chinese state was by the middle of the twentieth century much stronger than ever before. The tradition of residential control was in principle familiar; but under long-term forceful policies, backed by resources, it assumed an untraditional intensity in ordinary lives.

There was not much controversy about this labeling process during the Democratic Reform Movement in 1951. Most of the labels, no matter when they were gathered, were self-reported. Because the CCP lacked enthusiasts in many areas, it was not yet clear that labels could easily be checked by police or activists. Even in later years, it was possible to request changes in one's registration by having a school or work unit complete the necessary application form (which was not always approved by the police). But on receiving a bad classification, as an ex-cadre put it, "It was very difficult for a man or a whole family to evade being identified in an enemy class. Even if

5 *ZW,* July 7, 1956.
6 *YB,* January 25, 1952.

one could hide it in the beginning, the fact would eventually be discovered through rechecking that took place in later stages of this [Democratic Reform] movement or in later, different campaigns."[7]

The main early use of this system was, however, not to control regular residents of the city, but to check transients who might be refugees from the rural land reform. In the early 1950s, any new arrival to Shanghai was supposed to ask the police for "moved" (*qianru*) or "Overseas Chinese" (*waiqiao*) status.[8] Even if a visitor spent just one night, a family head was supposed to report the "temporary household" (*linshi hukou*) to security officers of the local residents' committee. Interviewees say this rule was honored in the breach, except in families that were under surveillance or had an activist member. Later, higher Party officials admitted "violations of law and discipline in street work." Furthermore: "The street offices that were set up by the people's governments in various sections of the city are not sufficiently sound in organization."[9] It was some time before the Party had sufficient staff to apply the system of labeling in a way that affected residents' lives greatly. The gradualness of this system's introduction, for most parts of the city, made it seem an ordinary policy—not a prelude to later repressions and campaigns. Another reason for the lack of widespread resistance to these procedures in the early 1950s was the fact that previous Chinese governments had imposed somewhat similar residential policies. Registration and constraint of categories of people living in urban areas have been very common in most East Asian countries, in all of Eastern Europe, historically in central Europe, and in other contexts that range from South Africa to the West Bank. Because most Western readers are unaware of the importance of such traditions, however, it is useful to show how the precedents made such policies seem natural and acceptable in China, even though they later combined with policies of guided violence to repress ordinary urban people.

PRE-1949 RESIDENTS AND STUDENTS

Most Shanghai residents came to the city from nearby areas of East China, and they brought their residential styles with them from rural

---

[7] Interview, Hong Kong, with an ex-CCP economic manager.
[8] *SHGSZL* 2, no. 36 (1951): 1303.
[9] *JFRB*, December 17, 1954.

places.[10] A traditional neighborhood in East China ideally contained about
five households, which might cooperate to supply labor or credit for a big
project such as a house raising. This was a ritual unit, less central than a
lineage but sometimes important. When a baby became one month old, for
example, its mother would take it to receive praises at neighborhood
houses.[11]

Modern governments have preferred to regard urban residents mainly as
means to create an industrial tax base, despite the obvious interests of city
folk in the ways they live.[12] The Guomindang, for example, treated Shanghai
residents as essentially a problem in control. It saw urban living and thinking
as largely irrelevant to its main interests, or sometimes as hindering them.
After the Japanese army left the city in 1945, the GMD government conducted a census and divided Shanghai into thirty-two districts, mainly according to the location of police stations. A layered precinct system (the *baojia* system) assigned groups of about ten households to units called *jia* and
put these into larger groups called *bao*, for mutual surveillance. At the large
urban district level, the GMD held conferences every three months, to discuss
schools, local construction projects, the price of rice, epidemic diseases, and
especially public security.[13] These sessions were mainly designed to convey
official intentions to residents, however, not to solicit information from
them that could change government decisions. Residents and students were
to be objects of policy, not in any sense creators of it.

The main concern of the GMD during the Civil War was political dissent.

---

[10] Some of the best research on this topic has been linguistic. Michael Sherrard found that
Shanghai dialect is based, more closely than earlier writings suggested, on the language of peasants in proximate suburban areas, and less than had been thought on the dialects of more
distant areas in East China (*A Lexical Survey of the Shanghai Dialect* [Tokyo: Institute of Asian
and African Languages and Cultures, 1982]). Historian Emily Honig, *Sisters and Strangers*
(Stanford, Calif.: Stanford University Press, 1985), shows there have been major social and
cultural tensions among subethnic groups, notably between northern Jiangsu "Subei" people
and mainstream "Jiangnan" people from south of the Yangzi River. The subject is one that
deserves much further research. This subethnic distinction has received little attention either in
official print media or informal interviews, but it reinforces and overlaps categories of people
defined by policy norms such as are described here.

[11] W. R. Geddes, *Peasant Life in Communist China* (Ithaca: Cornell Society for Applied
Anthropology, 1963), p. 31, and interviews; the traditional unit in rural areas was apparently
called a *xianglin* (if urban, a *linshe*).

[12] The main statement on this for the Communist period is still in Franz Schurmann's *Ideology and Organization in Communist China* (Berkeley and Los Angeles: University of California Press, 1966).

[13] *Shanghai chunqiu* (Shanghai spring and autumn) (Hong Kong: Zhongguo Tushu Bianyi
Guan, 1968), *zhong*, pp. 23–24. Note the similarity between the GMD-run district conferences
and similar meetings called in later years by the CCP.

Cultural institutions such as universities and newspapers came under strict control. In mid-1947, the police closed three liberal Shanghai papers, *Wenhui bao*, *Xinmin bao*, and *Lianhe ribao*.[14] Political activities that year caused the GMD to expel hundreds of Shanghai university and middle-school students, including many who had been elected to class offices, sending them back to their homes. The youths responded with political unrest, "support-the-students badges" on lapels, and "hunger parades" in the streets.[15] These demonstrations continued in 1948, when a major basis for anti-GMD organization among students was patriotic: Chiang Kai-shek had links to the United States, and students then saw America as helping Japan. Harsh Japanese occupation troops had left Shanghai just three years earlier, and the United States–Japan connection became a political disadvantage to Chiang among many Chinese, especially bourgeois families. When the GMD met the student demonstrations with force, anti-GMD campaigns protested the arrests, beatings, and "unreasonable dismissals" by Chiang's police.

Jiaotong University's Student Union particularly objected to a GMD habit of pasting political labels on its opponents. These students—practically all from bourgeois backgrounds—objected to being called Communists. They said they should not be made to wear "red hats" (*hong maozi*),[16] claiming the applicable label was "patriot."

The CCP before 1949 had more success developing a constituency among bourgeois students and teachers than it had among other groups in schools. The main basis of such organization was nationalist, unrelated to social class distinctions. The goal of one of the main student campaigns was to encourage purchases of "national goods" (*guohuo*) from Chinese companies.[17] Many urban students also felt that, in order to serve their country, they should learn how most Chinese live. On a voluntary basis, student groups headed to inland Southwest China and to villages in Zhejiang, where they taught classes for rural children and propagandized against the GMD by writing Communist slogans on paper money that the rampant inflation had rendered worthless.[18] The pre-1949 government tried to establish its rule both among students and among ordinary city people, but with modest success.

---

[14] *Guancha* (Observer), May 31, 1947, p. 5. The reporter was Chu Anping, who in 1957 was prominently criticized as a "rightist."

[15] *Ji'e youxing* and *zhuxue zhang*; *Qunzhong* (Masses) (Shanghai), 31 (August 28, 1947), p. 14, and ibid. 36 (October 2, 1947), p. 18. Another Chu Anping article is in *Guancha*, May 31, 1947, p. 3. For much more, see Suzanne Pepper, *Civil War in China: The Political Struggle, 1945–1949* (Berkeley and Los Angeles: University of California Press, 1978).

[16] ZW, May 29, 1948, p. 8. The similarity to later CCP political labeling may be too obvious to note in the text above.

[17] *Qunzhong* 32 (September 4, 1947): 14.

[18] *Qunzhong* 31 (August 28, 1947): 20.

POLICE AND RESIDENCE ASPECTS OF LIBERATION

The *baojia* system of residence control had been severely denounced by the Communist Party before 1949, and the system was decreed out of existence as soon as the Red Army arrived. The Communist military nonetheless also decreed that Shanghai's myriad *baojia* workers were not to be criticized for their previous actions. The 38 *bao* and 957 *jia* in one area near the center of town were reorganized as early as July 1949 into ten "administrative offices." These were soon followed by "street committees," organized on the same basis—and often using the same personnel.[19] The official interest in monitoring survived 1949 distinctly alive and well.

At Liberation in May, there were 103 police stations (*paichusuo*) in Shanghai; but before 1949 ended, the Communists increased this number to 146.[20] Most GMD policemen continued at their posts. Many middle- or high-ranking officers retired or went into schoolteaching or other professions. At lower levels, a campaign soon began to recruit reliable police. An interviewee said, "Criticism of people whom the regime disliked was a major means of social mobility in Shanghai. . . . People could get police and other jobs by criticizing."[21] But the new recruits were by no means just from worker families or proletarian residential areas. Many were petit bourgeois. In later years, thousands of ex-shopkeepers joined the People's Police, and others got clerical jobs in the Public Security Bureau.[22] Families that were formally capitalist were distributed through many parts of the city. They could fend well enough in large organizations and often were deemed reliable enough by police recruiters. Official concern for well-monitored control still overcame most qualms in the Party about using people from groups with dubious labels.

The first major campaign was the Suppression of Counterrevolutionaries, which began to affect a few of Shanghai's residents severely in September 1950.[23] The first stages of this movement were directed against very few residents, whom the Party knew to be dissidents. The police arrested and sentenced them, before announcing such actions to the public. This campaign did not require large numbers of personnel. It was a matter of secret

---

[19] *Xingzheng bangong shi, jiedao weiyuanhui*; *JFRB*, July 21, 1949.

[20] See *1949 nian shouce* (1949 handbook) (Hong Kong: Huashang Bao Chuban she, 1950), sec. A, p. 6. Even this increased number of stations left an average of 6,850 households per precinct (based on calculations from figures in the same source).

[21] Interview in Hong Kong with an ex-student at Soochow University College of Law, then located in Shanghai.

[22] *LDB*, September 16, 1950.

[23] The best description is Ezra F. Vogel's *Canton under Communism: Programs and Politics in a Provincial Capital, 1949–1968* (Cambridge: Harvard University Press, 1969), chap. 2.

seizures and punishments, publicized only later. The Suppression of Counterrevolutionaries police action against GMD dissidents preceded the Party's efforts in the much larger tasks of organizing unions, cleansing business practices in the Five Anti Campaign, and purging some cadres in the Three Anti Campaign.

By the beginning of 1951, all persons who had any connection with the GMD were supposed to register with their work units. Some were designated "spy elements," even though nothing was done against them immediately.[24] Then on the night of April 28, sirens were heard in the streets of Shanghai as most ex-GMD officers were arrested by the security police. They were taken to public buildings, such as schools, that became makeshift prisons.[25] Over the next four months, thirty-eight thousand "counterrevolutionaries" were tried and sentenced in Shanghai.[26] Firing squads began their work almost immediately, as newspapers reported: "The Government will no longer show boundless magnanimity to dissidents."[27] Only a small percentage of the arrestees received capital punishment, but six public execution grounds were established nonetheless. No one could miss the fact that the newly arrived regime was willing to use its power violently against categories of people thought to oppose it.

Even some anti-Communist reports indicate, however, that many persons tried in 1951 were nonpolitical criminals.[28] Most residents were not directly affected, though acquaintances of the "counterrevolutionaries" had to write long reports. There was widespread concern among residents about the intentions of the new government, even though the climate of the Korean War also made people want to support it.

Prominent Communist leaders, notably Mayor-General Chen Yi whose Third Field Army liberated Shanghai, sometimes issued decrees about the illegitimacy of Shanghai as a whole. At one point, Mayor Chen said squarely, "We must evacuate the population of the city systematically and

---

[24] *Tewu fenzi*; LDB, February 3, 1951.

[25] Robert Loh, *Escape from Red China* (New York: Coward-McCann, 1962), pp. 65–70.

[26] *JFRB*, August 29, 1951. It had not yet been a quarter century since the wee hours of April 12, 1927, when Chiang Kai-shek had treated Shanghai's Communist Party with similar police violence.

[27] *XWRB*, May 1, 1951.

[28] Loh, *Escape*. A Taiwan source says that more than 200,000 people lost their lives in Shanghai during the first five years of CCP rule there, and another 640,000 went to jail or labor camps. These figures seem high and are difficult to prove, even though the fear they imply was real. See the luridly titled *Junmo luanwu de Shanghai shih* (Shanghai, where demons dance in confusion) (Taipei: GMD Central Committee Sixth Section, 1954), p. 8.

transfer factories to the interior whenever possible."[29] Yet the Communists lacked enough personnel to implement these residential ideals. For the most part, they concentrated on improving neighborhood discipline by finding reliable activists, monitors, or bosses in as many urban areas as they could.

Rules at this time were strict, and high officials encouraged basic-level governments to enforce them stringently. When a neighborhood committee ordered that the iron gate of its lane be locked at 9:00 P.M. each evening, the "arrangement constrained the people's freedom and caused mass discontent." The district government heard about this and called a "representative meeting," at which such complaints were aired. Then the lane committee "held a meeting and corrected its former mistakes, to the great satisfaction of the masses."[30] State control was not strong in many residential areas.

Street committees could be officious, but they were closer to ordinary citizens than any other government agencies in Shanghai.[31] Organizing them was a CCP project in 1951, when eighteen hundred were established, nominally to cover more than 80 percent of the city's residents.[32] Each of them was supposed to have subcommittees for welfare, recreation, and sweeping the street, as well as a security subcommittee to report any unusual neighborhood events to the precinct-level police station.[33] In the early fifties, these street and police organizations concentrated on controlling political dissidents, not members of other labeled groups.

Patriotism in the Korean War and opposition to U.S. "rearming of Japan"[34] were immensely useful at this time for the CCP's constituency-building efforts. In the wartime atmosphere, the Party could count on practically all citizens to help clean up the city—to clean it politically and eco-

---

[29] Rhoads Murphey, *Shanghai: Key to Modern China* (Cambridge: Harvard University Press, 1953), p. 27.

[30] *JFRB*, September 13, 1951.

[31] An interviewee said that street offices in Shanghai were "more important administrative units than in most Chinese cities," though they were on average also somewhat larger there.

[32] *DGB* (Hong Kong), November 5, 1951.

[33] Ibid., and two interviews with ex-residents of Shanghai. The stations contained a chief and deputy, usually a "materials room" (*ziliao shi*) for files, a "public order group" (*zhian zu*), a "household registration group" (*puji zu*), and a "patrol group" (*xunluo zu*), among other administrative and operational units.

[34] *SN*, March 13, 1951, reports a conference of Shanghai missionary school representatives opposed to U.S. provision of arms to Japan. The American occupation of Japan was not ended by this time, and MacArthur's headquarters in 1950 had agreed to the establishment of a Japanese "National Police Reserve" of seventy thousand men, who were to be armed as infantry soldiers (despite Article 9 of the American-written Japanese Constitution, which prohibits Japan from declaring war). See Richard Storry, *A History of Modern Japan* (Harmondsworth, Eng.: Penguin, 1960), p. 244.

nomically, but also physically. Streets were swept, ditches drained, rats caught, mosquitoes swatted, and the pond at the old Temple of the City God was dredged.[35] Shanghai's brothels were slowly closed, although that process was not entirely complete as late as November 1951.[36] The Suppression of Counterrevolutionaries movement took action against "local bullies" not identified with the GMD.[37] A mass inoculation campaign had success against smallpox. Propagandists urged policies for categories of urban residential groups ranging from waifs and juvenile delinquents (who were supposed to depart Shanghai) to retired people (for whom New China promised provisions later, when prosperity was to come).[38] There were so many label categories for residents then, the emphasis was still on monitoring the new system more than on using it.

Most of the early-1950s programs that affected residents and students, as distinct from businessmen, did not discriminate against people with capitalist backgrounds. Some programs, beginning with the August 1949 effort to "evacuate" 400,000 people who had come to Shanghai because of flooding in East China, affected poor people who were really proletarians.[39] Programs such as the effort to control inflation, which lasted into 1952, especially benefited people who had money to spend or were not in heavy debt.[40] Many of those beneficiaries were really bourgeois.

Most Shanghai families' reactions to the mix of early-1950s policies were also mixed: they supported some aspects of the new regime, and they feared others. Roman Catholics, for example, were put in a difficult position when their bishop was arrested as a traitor, even though many Catholic families

[35] See *SN*, June 10, July 11, 1952, and Lynn White, "Changing Concepts of Corruption in Communist China," in *Changes and Continuities in Chinese Communism: The Economy, Society, and Technology*, ed. Yu-ming Shaw (Boulder, Colo.: Westview, 1988).

[36] *JFRB*, November 25, 1951. At the beginning of that month, there were at least 180 prostitutes still working in Shanghai (ibid.).

[37] Shanghai shehui kexue yuan, jingji yanjiu suo, Chengshih jingji zu (Shanghai Academy of Social Sciences, Economic Research Institute, Urban Economy Group), *Shanghai penghu qu de bianqian* (The transformation of Shanghai's shack districts) (Shanghai: Renmin Chuban She, 1965), pp. 57ff. gives some striking examples.

[38] See *JFRB*, October 12, 1954, and *NCNA*, August 13, 1956.

[39] *LDB*, December 17, 1949, estimates that after this "evacuation" as many as 40 percent of the sent-down people returned in September and October. Many were shipped out again.

[40] The blockade kept momentum in Shanghai's inflation long after 1949. The consumer price index averaged about fifteen times higher in 1950 than it had been in 1949, and it deflated nominally from that peak in 1951 and 1952 because of severe government action to lower first food prices, then the cost of housing, clothing, and other items. For data, see Ch'en Nai-ruenn, ed., *Chinese Economic Statistics: A Handbook for Mainland China* (Chicago: Aldine, 1967), p. 422.

hoped to support the new government and prove their patriotism in a time of war.[41] Religion laid a continuing claim on many Shanghai residents, even though its institutions were strikingly different in the extent to which they were organized. The Communist Party, supporting a belief system of its own, clearly took first place in that respect, even while it faced other systems organized as diffusely as Taoism or as tightly as Roman Catholicism.[42] Shanghai Protestants gave the Party less cause for concern, partly because the millenarian sects found many sympathetic echoes in Communism.[43] Not for many years after 1949 were family and religious life-styles communized, and even then the change was incomplete, subject to continuing tension and uncertainty.

Change in educational institutions was more abrupt than in most other kinds of institutions during the early 1950s. At the university level, the main reform was a reduction in the number of institutions. Shanghai had forty-three universities in June 1950, but these were reduced to twenty-one by the end of that year. By 1955, there were fourteen, and only eleven in 1961.[44] Most of the change came in 1950–51, when many large firms were also re-formed. The garnering of personnel and enthusiasm for those reforms was clearly linked to patriotic fervor in the Korean War, and the war was really the first big popular campaign for most residents of PRC cities.

All six of Shanghai's private universities were closed at this time, although the main interdisciplinary public ones (Fudan, Jiaotong, and Tongji) absorbed many of the others' best departments and professors. The whole system was centralized, and many of the institutions that survived were in-

---

[41] This is not the place to detail everything that the CCP charged against Bishop Kong Pinmei and his colleagues; arms, confidential documents, stolen state papers, illegal radio equipment, a private prison in a women's seminary, tax evasion, intelligence about airfields and tanks, the militant Legion of Mary (Shengmu Jun)—and much else—all figured here. Suffice it to say that Communists did not believe the church rendered properly unto Caesar, and the Catholic hierarchy did not believe the CCP's aims were just political. See *RMRB*, December 10, 1955, and many other articles.

[42] Catholic church history in Shanghai goes back four hundred years. The important residential Siccawei (Xuhui) District was dominated by St. Ignatius Cathedral until the CCP built the Shanghai Stadium nearby. More on Shanghai Catholicism is available in many sources, including Stanford University China Project, *East China*, HRAF 29, Stanford 3 (New Haven: Human Relations Area Files, 1956), pp. 370–75. See SHNL, August 30, 1966.

[43] By far the most comprehensive work is Philip Wickeri's "Seeking the Common Ground" (Ph.D. diss., Princeton Theological Seminary, 1984). On spy charges against Ni Xisheng of the Shanghai Protestant Assembly Hall, see *WHB*, February 1, 1956.

[44] See Education Minister Ma Xulun's report in *RMRB*, June 14, 1950; see also *GMRB*, June 19, 1955, and Chi Wang, *Mainland China Organizations of Higher Learning in Science and Technology and their Publications* (Washington, D.C.: Library of Congress, 1961).

creased in size. Enrollment at the Shanghai Finance and Economics College, for example, rose from 600 to 2,250 students. Its curriculum abolished elective subjects, eliminated English in favor of Russian, and included "practical work" internships.[45] Courses were also shortened in engineering and science colleges.[46]

The comprehensive universities in 1951 were thrown open to much larger groups of admittees. This reform meant that despite official emphasis on engineering and applied science, the number of students in humanities and natural sciences also rose.[47] Generalism was still highly popular. Admissions policies showed some favoritism to the offspring of proletarian families, but the stress on academic scores at this time meant most Shanghai students were still from bourgeois families.

The city's school system at lower levels also expanded rapidly. Three-quarters of the primary schools in late 1952 were still private.[48] Public schools tended to be larger, and they were more important than private schools at the postprimary level. But there is little evidence to show the Party had full control of Shanghai's educational expansion in 1952, which was officially declared "too fast . . . an extremely blind advance."[49] Schools, like businesses, took several years to communize. Totalism did not come suddenly in 1949, because then (and for more years afterward than Party leaders realized) the resources for it did not exist. The revolution in education, as in other fields, took much longer and was never so complete as newspaper editorials suggested. Society had more power than the state pretended. Policies could irk people, as well as constrain them.

Despite the expansion in secondary schools, there were in these early years more university vacancies than senior-middle-school graduates to fill them. China as a whole in 1953 had only 54,698 senior-middle-school graduates, of whom 34 percent were from Shanghai.[50] But for each of these, China's universities had planned 1.30 vacancies. This ratio rose to 1.54 in 1954. It reversed during the next few years (and by the antirightist summer of 1957 it was down to .55, showing that selectivity in universities was then

[45] *JFRB*, December 31, 1951.

[46] *SN*, February 5, 1952.

[47] *GMRB*, June 19, 1955, and *JFRB*, February 12, 1955, which compares numbers of graduates from technical schools with those from regular middle schools.

[48] *LDB*, October 4, 1952, indicates Shanghai then had over 300 public primary schools, over 900 private primary schools, and more than 400 children's evening classes.

[49] *WHB*, September 14, 1953.

[50] Ibid., and national figures from *RMRB*, April 25, 1957. The percentage here and the numbers that follow have been computed.

linked to control of their size). The Shanghai government clearly wished to cut its education budget in the mid-1950s, but it had difficulty doing so because of popular pressure from ordinary urbanites to support schooling.

REDUCTION OF FAMILY LIVING SPACE

The most important change of life-style for many Shanghai families after 1949 came when the Party, working through street committees, induced families with more than average living space to lease part of it at low rents. This method of creating new dwellings allowed the city to get by with very low expenditures for new construction.

Eventually, families with space also came under pressure to sell the rented parts of their quarters to the city's Real Estate Management Bureau. The low sale prices made sense only because of stringent rent control. This change did not result from a specific campaign in a limited time, and it has therefore been largely ignored in the academic literature.[51] To the extent the policy was effective, it relied on propaganda by street committees and "housewives' unions."[52] It also relied on a spirit of sacrifice during the Korean War and on terrifying experiences that some households were concurrently having because of the Five Anti Campaign in businesses. This change depended on campaigns, especially the Transition to Socialism; and (like the Cultural Revolution much later) its extensiveness shows their increasing synergism, as they become usual for many official purposes.

Sometimes street committees' efforts were unavailing, so that families refused to move from any of their space. In these cases, the committees would generally wait until the next large campaign, in whatever field, and then would try again.[53] The slowly growing, unspecific effectiveness of the campaign habit as a means of garnering compliance for difficult administrative mandates is obvious in changes of housing ownership. Campaigns were often more important for what they did after they ended, together with threatening movements affecting other groups in other areas, than for ac-

[51] Chinese newspapers in the 1950s did not stress this policy. Western economists' books and articles on housing tend to emphasize new investments and averages per capita. Urban planners and architects stress aesthetics and costs of new construction. Other social scientists have emphasized recent or campaign sources of information. The neglect of this topic tells much about the China field, in light of the importance of what happened to millions of city dwellers.

[52] *Jiating fulian*; LDB, June 1, 1950.

[53] Interviews with Shanghai ex-residents.

complishments toward their specific or ostensible goals. Their main effect was to save costs in implementing any major programs.

MID-1950s RATIONING

At the Central Committee meeting of February 6, 1954, Zhou Enlai announced policies for rationing "to ensure the steady supply of foodstuffs and the stability of commodity prices, to overcome spontaneous tendencies toward capitalism among the peasants and to counter opposition against restrictions on the part of the capitalist class."[54] This came after the "good year" of 1953, when rations were fairly large and compliance with the system was not burdensome. Coupons were issued to families by state grain companies, against the presentation of household registers. In September, a similar system was extended to woven cotton and clothing. Household registers also came to be used for identification in school admissions, job recruitment, and a host of other services for residents.

Counterfeiters soon emerged, printing fake residential certificates and ration coupons.[55] The grain supply crisis of 1955 meant smaller amounts issued against the coupons,[56] and "family food consumption plans" were mandated by officials.[57] Such restraints were supposed to affect all households in Shanghai, irrespective of family labels. But some groups—soldiers' and martyrs' families, high cadres, and Overseas Chinese—had subsidies or other means of obtaining goods beyond the rations.[58] Just as administrative policies making people into compliant objects sprang from a shortage of loyalists in relation to goals, so also the implementation of these policies affected people's daily lives increasingly as material shortages became worse.

These changes coincided with a general economic slowdown and with slightly more competition for places in senior middle schools and universities. As a mid-1955 article in a local newspaper said,

In Shanghai, some of the junior middle school and primary graduates are not admitted to schools for higher study, and they cannot take part in

---

[54] Peter Cheng, *A Chronology of the People's Republic of China* (Totowa, N.J.: Littlefield Adams, 1972), p. 30.

[55] *RMRB*, June 28, 1955.

[56] *RMRB*, September 5, 1955.

[57] *Jiating yongliang jihua*; *XWRB*, July 5, 1955.

[58] Interviews. Such subsidies began even earlier; see *YB*, January 25, 1952.

productive labor. They join self-study small groups [*zixue xiaozu*] in various districts. On ordinary days, they listen to broadcast discussions from the Education Bureau over the People's Radio. Sometimes they attend youth discussions for literature and art, run by the Democratic Youth League [parallel to the Communist Youth League, but for nonproletarians]. The condition of their literary entertainment and physical exercise are good. The Shanghai West Sports Ground provides them with all sorts of equipment.[59]

But these youths wanted schooling, and they might have gotten jobs if the economy had been healthier.

By 1955–56, foreign war no longer provided the Party with a patriotic claim on non-Communists. In the mid-fifties, many technicians and some students—mostly of bourgeois backgrounds—still went to rural areas for specific jobs and limited times.[60] But the inequality between peasants' and urbanites' real consumption rose between 1952 and 1956, from a ratio of 1:2.10 to 1:2.22.[61] Moralistic campaigns and rural send-downs (*xiaxiang* or *xiafang*) could not completely gainsay this trend toward increasingly less attractive rural life. It was partly a result of household registration's effect in dampening country-to-city migration, thus preventing peasants from finding urban jobs and sending part of their high urban wages to rural families. In the cities, it was part of a syndrome that justified more and more monitoring of urban populations.

From April through October of 1955, over half a million immigrant "peasants" were sent out of Shanghai "to join agricultural production."[62] Force was used in this campaign. In one area of town, 74 percent of the residents during 1955 were compelled to change their legal homes.[63] In the first quarter of 1956 there was a sharp increase in the number of middle-school graduates going to work elsewhere, largely as teachers.[64]

---

[59] *XWRB*, July 3, 1955.

[60] See Lynn White, "The Road to Urumchi: Approved Institutions in Search of Attainable Goals," *China Quarterly* 79 (October 1979): 481–510.

[61] *QNB*, February 26, 1957, gives the average annual consumption of "employees and workers" (*zhigong*) and "peasants" (*nongmin*) for 1936, 1952, and 1956. The ratios can be computed. The article contains interesting apologies for publishing these results.

[62] *NCNA*, November 16, 1955, gives the number 558,000.

[63] Christopher Howe, *Urban Employment and Economic Growth in Communist China, 1949–1957* (Cambridge: Cambridge University Press, 1971), p. 66.

[64] *NCNA*, April 1, 1956, reports that twelve thousand graduates went, many to Northwest China. See also *WHB*, February 22, 1956.

CONCLUSION: CONSTITUENCIES
FOR REVOLUTION AND MODERATION

Such drastic measures were accompanied by an intense new Elimination of Counterrevolutionaries Campaign, directed against dissidents in general and a writer named Hu Feng in particular.[65] This movement involved conscious political engineering. Even the Party members who most supported it were aware it used political categories for purposes that went beyond current public opinion's views of what should be politically permissible—and beyond the task of countering any serious or immediate danger to the government in 1955.

Deputy Mayor Pan Hannian, it seems, had been dismissed because he could not easily implement such policies. He was too well connected with too wide a spectrum of Shanghai society to have acted convincingly against the likes of Hu Feng.[66] In more general terms, the early 1950s was a period in which Shanghai people were divided into categories. From 1951 to 1955 the Party cultivated a staff to be set above society, but this group was not large enough to command it fully.

Pre-Liberation leading status groups were delegitimated only slowly and incompletely, and important CCP members were connected with many of them. Almost any measure of Shanghai's cultural styles in the 1950s can show how much time was needed for puritanical manners to become widespread. In 1952, only 43 percent of all Shanghai's newspapers had a clear Party or worker orientation, and 57 percent were still bourgeois.[67] A report that the official *People's Daily* reached only 37 percent even of its targeted circulation in Shanghai shows much about public attitudes in the early

[65] Just as this book does not much discuss elite politicians, it also leaves to others the job of discussing high intellectuals. On Hu Feng, see Merle Goldman, *Literary Dissent in Communist China* (Cambridge: Harvard University Press, 1967). Mass *sufan* (Elimination of counterrevolutionaries) meetings are reported in *XWRB*, July 12, 14, 1955, and *NCNA*, July 19, 1955.

[66] Two separate interviewees emphasized that Pan had good relations with leftist writers in groups such as the Ant Society (Mayi She) as well as with capitalists of the sort whom Hu Feng also tried to organize. The immediate cause of Pan's dismissal, according to one cadre who had been in a position to hear such rumors, was Pan's aid to a man who escaped to Hong Kong and who had "saved" Pan on an occasion before 1949. This story is a metaphor for the kinds of conflicting loyalties that permeated Shanghai by the mid-1950s. See also the explicit linking of Pan and Hu in *XWRB*, July 18, 1955. Hu Feng's name was rehabilitated in 1985.

[67] Calculated from figures in *SN*, June 4, 1952. *JFRB*, January 18, 1953, lists the target readerships of Shanghai's main papers: *JFRB* for CCP and other governmentalist readers, *LDB* for the unionists, *XWRB* for "reporting Shanghai's economic construction to rally and educate" a general readership, *WHB* for teachers and students, and *XMWB* on "cultural recreations, athletics, health and social activities" especially among young general readers.

1950s: "It is not only department heads who do not read the *People's Daily*, even the bureau directors seldom read it. To read the *Liberation Daily* [the local Party organ] is considered fairly good. Many important cadres 'do not have the time.' "[68] The Shanghai circulations of papers published explicitly for non-Communist readers—*Wenhui bao*, *Xinwen ribao*, and *Xinmin wan-bao*—all exceeded those of the Party's national and local organs (*People's Daily* and *Liberation Daily*).

Shanghai's old local leaderships were deeply shaken by changes at this time, and the CCP's increasing use of labels, monitors, and violence surely challenged them. But careful Party members in 1956–57 still tried to recruit residents and intellectuals whose talents the new regime needed. Family units remained important at all stages in China's modern change, and larger residential environments also remained crucial in ordinary people's lives. The categorizations, controls, and campaigns that eventually set the city's status groups against each other were all presaged in the early 1950s. If these policies had been reversed rather than intensified in later years, the social war between such groups and types of individuals could have been prevented.

[68] *JFRB*, December 28, 1951.

CHAPTER 4

Workers and Managers: The Transition to Socialism, 1956–1957

Governing a large state is like cooking a small fish; it should
not be overdone.
—LAO ZI

The most important watershed in Chinese political history between 1949 and 1966 was certainly 1957. The Cultural Revolution would have been a different phenomenon without the public reaction to policies that were normalized then. Labeling was intensified by calls, late that year, to "take class struggle as the key link." Monitoring was stressed in slogans to "strengthen the leadership of the Party." The Antirightist Campaign was the most extensive effort (before 1966) by new local leaders to discredit the intellectuals and managers who had seemed essential to the job of running China.

Persecuting "rightists" ended any ambiguity that the Party might treat non-Communist managers noncoercively, even if it acknowledged some truth in what critics said during the 1956–57 Hundred Flowers period. The physical relocation of cadres in late 1957 created an administrative infrastructure for the Great Leap Forward. Since most rightists were intellectuals from capitalist class backgrounds, the leaders from two important groups—the educated and the bourgeois—were all tainted at least indirectly in 1957. After the seemingly definitive split between local elites then, it took more than two decades of struggle before they realized they had to live with one another. But the prelude to 1957 should be described first.

SHANGHAI'S SOCIALIZATION

The official violence of 1955, though directed against relatively few of Shanghai's people, created an atmosphere in which the 1956 Transition to Socialism came easily. This campaign was led by Ke Qingshi, the city's new top Party secretary, who became Shanghai's most important politician in the decade before the Cultural Revolution. Ke had been a member of the Socialist Youth League even before the Party was founded in 1921, and he had long known Mao Zedong.[1] Mao liked a 1955 report by Ke on rural policies, and the Chairman championed Ke's quick rise in China's hierarchy.[2] Shanghai received, in Ke, a policymaker more radical than Pan Hannian, but the difference was a matter of degree. High-level CCP officials disagreed about the effectiveness of pressure policies in particular situations, not about their legitimacy in principle; all used such policies on some occasions. Resource constraints and low-level, unofficial leaders—not just high-level intentions and leaders—continued to determine major outcomes in Shanghai.

Previous campaigns, monitoring, and labeling had given planners means to support the 1956 Transition to Socialism, because these policies had garnered political and financial benefits for the state. The Party had obtained more clout in markets and more centralized trade unions. State control of private wholesalers was "basically completed" in 1955. This meant the state was in a position, late that year, to favor some companies which voluntarily became "joint state-private firms," even before the final campaign to impose that status on all Shanghai's businesses. Dividends for a few early-volunteering firms soared in 1955 (in some cases, to three times the 1954 figures[3]), and this performance, coming at a time of materials shortage, inspired other capitalists to follow suit.

These policies still had not provided enough personnel to manage most retail markets effectively.[4] They had a public éclat and political effect that overstated their actual help to a Party that wanted to follow up its moves toward socialism more comprehensively.

The 1955 supply crisis gave many entrepreneurs incentives to quit their businesses. The shortages also meant that the available union-trained accountants—few though they were—could become high-level socialist businessmen by helping to conduct "austerity campaigns."[5] Trade unions were increasingly organized in hierarchical levels. While this discouraged worker spontaneity, it let the Party use unions to create new structures of manage-

---

[1] By November 1958, Ke became mayor of Shanghai. After leadership stints in the cities of Shijiazhuang and Nanjing, Ke became de facto governor of Jiangsu. For more on him, see Donald W. Klein and Anne B. Clark, *Biographic Dictionary of Chinese Communism* (Cambridge: Harvard University Press, 1971), 1:440–42. Interviewees say that Ke and Mao were in the same Party small group at Yenan for a long time.

[2] Interview with a person who had been a high Shanghai cadre in this period. Ke's 1955 report claimed that the grain shortage of that year in Jiangsu had been overstated by people who wanted to slow collectivization, and Mao viewed this document very favorably. The source also said that Mao was the person who nominated Ke for Politburo membership in 1958.

[3] *NCNA*, July 24, 1956.

[4] *NCNA* (Beijing), January 1, 1956.

[5] For an example in a tractor factory, see *XWRB*, September 6, 1955.

ment. [6] But the pressure policies were less effective at building a new infra-structure of economic personnel and firms than they were at undermining earlier ones.

The campaigns before 1956 greatly discouraged resistance to the Transition to Socialism, which in its turn further regularized the system of social labels (especially for capitalists) and raised the status of Party bosses in all large businesses. From late October 1955, official pronouncements about a "universal investigation of private merchants" instilled fear that the Suppression of Counterrevolutionaries Campaign might expand.[7] Rumors predicted secret leadership meetings to plan this violent movement. Criminal cases, especially involving capitalists, received much publicity then in the press.[8]

At the end of 1955, more than half of Shanghai's industrial production was still private or joint, as were 98 percent of the city's industrial firms (including nearly all small businesses). Deputy Mayor Xu Jianguo then predicted that *all* industry and commerce, even small peddlers, would be brought under public or joint management "within two years."[9] The Municipal Party Committee passed his speech as a resolution,[10] but his estimate was far too conservative. Just three weeks later, on January 9, 1956, Deputy Mayor Liu Xuzhou said more than four-fifths of Shanghai's private industrial output would be produced in joint enterprises "by the end of this year."[11] The plan was then speeded still further, and the changes at least of nominal ownership were completed within two weeks after Liu's prediction. The Party was able to move faster than its own high leaders said it would, because open resistance from capitalists had been so effectively muted by earlier campaigns.[12]

---

[6] An example is in trucking, where the Shanghai Teamsters' Committee (Kache Gongzuo Weiyuan Hui) was part of the Shanghai Transport Union (Banyun Gonghui), itself part of the larger Shanghai Federation of Trade Unions (Zong Gong Hui); see *XWRB*, September 13, 1955.

[7] *NCNA*, October 21, 1955, and *RMRB*, October 25, 1955.

[8] Criminality in Mao's China varied with political campaigns, even when the crimes were nonpolitical. For statistics on numbers of ordinary criminal cases on Shanghai's Huangpu District docks in the mid-1950s, see *XWRB*, August 31, 1957, which suggests a decrease of criminality in early 1957, after a peak in 1956. See also *ZGQNB*, November 15, 1955, which reports a Shanghai court sentencing a capitalist to ten years for maltreatment of an apprentice.

[9] *NCNA*, December 17, 1955, speech of Xu Jianguo.

[10] *NCNA*, December 24, 1955.

[11] *NCNA*, January 9, 1956.

[12] This quick change of expectations echoes the best description of a campaign in English—the chapter by Ezra Vogel on land reform in his *Canton under Communism* (Cambridge: Harvard University Press, 1969), pp. 91–124.

PROCEDURES FOR THE TRANSITION TO SOCIALISM

In December 1955, Mao Zedong had come to Shanghai "to hear the views of the national capitalist friends"—or at least to hear the richest, if not the most typical, entrepreneurs. Capitalists at these meetings dutifully spoke of the need to reduce the period of Transition from the expected twenty years to just a few years.[13]

Socialism was then achieved by blank check: Capitalists were asked to apply for joint status before anyone could fully know what that meant—except failure to apply meant social and political ostracism. Trade guilds within the Shanghai Federation of Industry and Commerce were supposed to compete with one another, to see which could achieve a 100-percent application rate first. Whenever a guild's members had all applied for joint status, it held a parade to celebrate. The guild leader would present the mayor with a large red envelope, symbolizing his group's acquiescence in socialism.[14] "Long lines of shining motor cars, decorated with portraits of Mao" brought the capitalists to such rendezvous, which were punctuated with "explosions of firecrackers."[15] Policies of categorization, monitoring, and threat had obviously been important in making this change peaceful, even if they did not assure the Party enough resources to keep its new commitments or assure that the capitalists would always remain so complaisant toward their new situation.

By January 18, the municipal government reported the application of the last group of capitalists. So "the factories and shops of Shanghai decorated their premises for celebration. . . . Thirteen thousand dependents of private shop and factory owners met this afternoon to welcome the Socialist Transformation."[16] One manager in Shanghai reported knowing only one owner (an elderly paper manufacturer) who resisted this process, was bankrupted

[13] Robert Loh's *Escape from Red China* (New York: Coward-McCann, 1962), pp. 178ff., contains highly interesting material from the viewpoint of a capitalist. Mao was effective in small groups of non-Communists, and he met several of them in the Sino-Soviet Friendship Hall. A picture of one session is reproduced in Richard H. Solomon's *Mao's Revolution and the Chinese Political Culture* (Berkeley and Los Angeles: University of California Press, 1971), p. 321.

[14] Red envelopes (*hongbao*, usually containing money) are traditionally presented to superiors during the Chinese New Year. The traditional merchant guild (*hang*) leaders made such presents to Confucian mandarins, who were supposed to preserve social harmony rather than deal with mundane particular interests; so the symbolism of the 1956 ceremonies had echoes in China's past.

[15] *NCNA*, January 20, 1956.

[16] *NCNA*, January 18, 1956.

within two months by workers' lawsuits, and was sentenced to labor re-form.[17] Shanghai became socialist by official decree on January 21, 1956.[18]

Sign makers had a booming business at this time. No fewer than 165,000 firms in the city soon posted placards showing they were branches of larger state corporations. More than half a year passed, and a majority of these still had no further information about what that meant. The state lacked personnel with both the economic expertise and the political trustworthiness to deal with all its new acquisitions rapidly.

In many large firms, the previous owner became the deputy director. The main local questions were the identity and personality of the new Communist director (often a demobilized soldier), the new boss representing the public majority of shares. The Party did not have nearly enough loyalists to cover small businesses, however; so previous owners frequently became directors of their firms, which were at first just nominally dubbed branches of state companies. In any case, the capitalists were promised "four fixed" provisions:[19]

1. Fixed shares in the new companies
2. Fixed dividends (5 percent on their shares annually)
3. Fixed positions at work
4. Fixed salaries

Reorganization took at least two forms: A joint enterprise might consist of several previously independent firms, put under unified management, so that shares were pooled and administration was joint. In other cases, factories were physically closed, dismantled, or merged.[20] In either case, there were immediate impacts on the incomes and jobs of both capitalists and their new rivals, the socialist managers (when the latter could be found).

The Party had an explicit policy of "lenient treatment for early settlement." Details of specific ownership changes had seldom been finalized at the time of Transition. The policies of pressure had been far more effective at instigating action than at coordinating it, and they remained so throughout the next several years, even when they continued to obtain quick surface results.

The government had to underassess the capitalists' shares at bargain-basement prices to finance this takeover. "Shock attack" teams were ap-

---

[17] Loh, *Escape*, pp. 183–87, which also gives a colorful picture of the celebrations.

[18] *NCNA*, January 21, 1956, and *ZW*, January 28, 1956.

[19] *RMRB*, January 31, 1957; these were the *siding* provisions.

[20] See *Xuexi* (*Study*) (Beijing), no. 4 (April 2, 1956); article by Yao Chongwen in *ECMM* 37 (1956): 20.

pointed, mostly composed of activist proletarians, to finish the Socialist Transition of a few very large firms within just six days of mid-January. The procedures for assessment had been announced and tested in select textile mills during the previous year, and they involved six steps:[21] First, the Municipal People's Committee would give a new company permission to reform as a joint enterprise. Second, an "inventory team," comprising outsiders, members of the local union, and capitalist representatives, would count and list the firm's assets. The third step made nonsense of most of the rest, because it involved joint meetings to set the official value of these assets, which a capitalist report estimated at about one-fifth of their real worth in most cases.[22] Fourth, the shares of various owners were "fixed" on this basis. Fifth, the relevant Party committee would appoint personnel to posts in the new enterprise (considering, naturally, earlier cooperation or resistance at the assessment stage). Sixth and finally, the higher-level state corporation would issue a certificate that the process had been completed.

The appraisals were arbitrarily low. In a textile mill, for example, the sale of an electric motor for 60,000 yuan had been approved by the mill's Party secretary. But this sale was stopped when assets were frozen for the assessment. The inventory team then valued the motor at one-twentieth of that price, or 3,000 yuan. An electrician on the team (who had previously estimated its worth as 70,000 yuan) went along with this, but a manager objected, pointing out that the Tax Bureau had assessed it for property tax purposes at 325,000 yuan. In such cases, the Party preferred that capitalists control each other; so the owner of the plant called in the protesting manager and told him to go along with the 3,000-yuan assessment. A final irony is that the Party had such a shortage of skilled personnel, even for this very large factory, that both capitalists (the owner and the manager) got high posts in the socialized firm.[23]

People with bad labels were down, but there was no way they could be put out. Socialism takes infrastructure, not just will. The Party was not sure what to do with its rival leaders at the local level in Shanghai, but everyone knew it could not do without them. This situation is best documented for the city's largest plants, but it affected much larger numbers of people in small shops and neighborhood factories. The tensions between label groups and within the new organizations created at this time came back to haunt the city's politics for more than a decade.

---

[21] *XWRB*, September 3, 1955.

[22] Loh, *Escape*, p. 188.

[23] Ibid., pp. 193–200. The manager in this case was Loh himself.

SOCIAL STATUS AND MONEY

In most cases, it was planned that a "fixed interest" would be paid to capitalists, at a rate of 5 percent for at least seven years. A textile magnate, Li Kangnian, complained this plan left the bourgeoisie in a formally "exploitative" position, because capitalists would still garner income from property. Li also noted that if payments stopped after seven years, capitalists would have received only 35 percent of the value of their holdings (because of the low assessments). Li thus proposed a scheme of "deposit certificates," whereby the government would "buy out 100 percent of the assessed capital, over twenty years."[24]

Because Li's proposal became well known in Shanghai, local newspapers published data about changes of the income sources for Shanghai capitalists since 1950 in an effort to show that the compensation had been fair.[25] From these figures, it is easy to show that the city's bourgeoisie became considerably less well off as a whole. For the period 1950–55, Shanghai capitalists' total income was 830,420,000 yuan, of which 76 percent was from salaries and 24 percent was from interest and dividends. For 1956, however, the salary component dropped to 55 percent, and the interest/and dividend component rose to 45 percent. By 1956, their total income was only 123,680,000 yuan. Shanghai capitalists' income had thus dropped at an annual rate of 11 percent over the previous six years—but 21 percent less of this came from salary, and 21 percent more came from capital.

Socialism reduced capitalists' incomes, but this only added injury to insult. They were affected more by the continuation of their bad labels, which more clearly than before represented an official effort to encourage social disrespect for them. Their political impotence was obvious because of the assessments, which were generally known to be unfair. The Transition made them, in terms of income sources, more fully capitalist—even while it further

---

[24] NCNA, May 15, June 17, 1957; XWRB, June 22, August 11, 1957; ZW, August 17, 1957, p. 12. Li had promoted "national products" (*guohuo*) before 1949, and in the Antirightist Campaign he was accused of trying to gain power beyond his post in the China Native Products Company. This plan and its author came under severe attack, because it would have allowed the bourgeoisie to doff the "nonexploitative" label.

[25] These data do not distinguish between rich capitalists and ordinary ones, but they suggest that the very richest ones (among those who did not leave for points abroad) suffered less than poorer bourgeois. See XWRB, June 18, 1957, from whose data the following percentages are calculated, as is the 1956 income figure. (These calculations take account of the change in yuan denomination, though not of inflation.) It is also possible, from figures in this article, to make a calculation showing that all private capital in the city had been undervalued; but the uncertainty of some brave premises necessary for this exercise disallow a really accurate answer. Anecdotal materials give that picture as well and more credibly.

delegitimated that social status. Government effort could not fully remove the local prestige of some entrepreneurs, and the tension between informal and official evaluations of labels was exacerbated rather than solved at this time. If the Chinese revolution had destroyed alternative local elites more completely in the mid-1950s, both the Cultural Revolution and recent elite pluralism in China would probably not have been so prominent.

The dispossessed groups and individuals were nonetheless still Chinese, and policies toward them could not be consistent because they were so clearly needed in economic life. They could, officially, redeem their pasts by cooperating with their new overseers. Large capitalists were expected to use part of their compensation to buy government bonds. But Shanghai's richest bourgeois were less disadvantaged in the Socialist Transition than was Shanghai's middle class. State ownership at least ended campaigns to use company funds for buying government bonds.[26]

Some large plants of the richest capitalists had attracted Party planners' attention in earlier years. Overseas Chinese capitalists, who were outside the government's control but might help finance its goals, also received relatively good treatment. A Shanghai Overseas Chinese Investment Company was founded in 1956 to attract money from Hong Kong Shanghainese especially, and these people were entertained well when they returned to inspect their holdings.[27] The Party pampered some of this city's wealthiest bourgeois, while repressing most of the others.

Small shopkeepers and entrepreneurs in street factories, who make up the vast majority of Shanghai's capitalists, were hurt by the change of 1956 even though they were seldom dislodged from their jobs by it. According to one estimate, 80 percent of Shanghai's firms were assessed at less than 2,000 yuan (then about U.S. $800).[28] Especially when the Party could not follow up by sending the socialized firms new resources or loyalist managers, this important class was bothered without being replaced. In one case,

[t]he owner's personal possessions, down to his pots and pans and the baby's crib, were not only included [in the assessment] but were taken away when the State assumed control of his enterprise. . . . Thus the position of about 80 percent of Shanghai's businessmen was nearly hopeless,

[26] *XWRB*, February 23, 1957.

[27] See, for example, *China News Service* (Shanghai), January 17, 1960. Shanghai CCP interest in attracting capital back from Shanghai exiles in Hong Kong remained strong in the late 1980s, and it is partly responsible for the importance of Shanghai Communists in the bodies planning for the future of that gem of the south after 1997.

[28] Loh, *Escape*, p. 190.

and a new wave of suicides began. . . . The small businessman fared ill under the new order, but the big capitalists found that they were not too badly off.[29]

The bitterness of small entrepreneurs after the Transition to Socialism was often intense. It was directed both against incompetent or uncaring Party bosses and against rich capitalists who seemed to be in league with the Party. As a family entrepreneur complained in 1957,

> I am only from an upper middle class family, and not from one of those big families [*da hu*]. I agree with Li Kangnian about fixing the rate for twenty years. . . . The members of my family are skilled workers, and the foundation of our business is firm. We used to talk and laugh without any care. But since the government representative has come, we have to be careful when we talk. . . . Because the government representative is jealous and fears that the private side will get "face," and because the cadres of the Federation of Industry and Commerce are really workers from the proletariat, the difficulties of the private side are always slighted.[30]

The financial security of most capitalists, especially the hundreds of thousands of small shopkeepers, was ended in 1956. Even when their incomes did not drop sharply, this was painful material reinforcement of their negative label.

JOBS IN THE JOINT ENTERPRISES

Because of all the mergers, the Transition to Socialism in Shanghai's light industries increased the number of joint firms in 1956 by only 48 percent.[31] But it changed the meaning of joint status, even for companies that had been semisocialized in previous years. The main concern of entrepreneurs, now, was to prevent their companies from being abolished and to maintain their own jobs—not to prevent socialization.

The number of demobilized soldiers in Shanghai's economy rose about 10 percent in the first four months of 1956, and their positions in management rose much faster.[32] A few ordinary workers were also dubbed "leading

[29] Ibid., pp. 190–92.
[30] *XWRB*, June 18, 1957.
[31] *LDB*, July 4, 1956.
[32] *NCNA*, May 14, 1956; see also May 13.

cadres."[33] These promotions often brought fresh blood into firms, but they also often brought in people who had scant education, including some illiterates. One administrative office was proud to report that 90 percent of its "illiterate clerks" had enrolled in a new "spare-time culture school."[34] It is unclear what the other 10 percent were doing.

This reflected the Party's lack of reds who were expert. No quick political change could solve this administrative quandary, which long remained the main reason behind policies for labels, bosses, and campaigns. Secretary Cao Diqiu of the Municipal CCP Committee complained openly, "Due to lack of experience, there are still many problems in leadership and management in the joint enterprises." He candidly admitted, "Public representatives are absent in many enterprises."[35]

When the Party could find new cadres to send, their days were full of pressure and self-sacrifice, not just new power. Local newspapers publicized the hard lives led by scarce Party loyalists, especially young ones (not retired from the army on sinecures). Some were said never to get to sleep before 11:00 P.M. (late even for urban China). A survey of Party branch secretaries in Huangpu District revealed that one-fifth had "family problems" because of their hard work. In Zhabei District, 28 percent of the public representatives in joint factories were also said to have housing problems. When the father of one of these new cadres became sick, his son could not borrow money for medicine from the factory, lest there be an appearance of corruption. In Changning District, not all the plants had been told they would now have to pay the public representatives' salaries; they had understandably thought the government would pay.[36] New officials at local levels after 1956 were often no happier than the rivals they had partially displaced. Both groups, albeit from different perspectives, shared some resentment of the change, some collective pride, and a sense that the system owed them more than it was giving.

If either one of these loose collections of leaders had been able more surely to win over the other, this mixture of resentments would have been less explosive for the long term. The bourgeoisie's delegitimation in Shanghai was half-baked and only partial. "Joint" nonetheless meant public, in principle for all firms and in practice for all large ones. Enterprises, like the

---

[33] *LDB*, June 4, 1956, gives a case of thirty-two ordinary longshoremen who became leading cadres (*lingdao ganbu*).

[34] *Yeyu wenhua xuexiao*; *Shanghai tiedao* (Shanghai railways), March 6, 1956. The school rather than the culture was spare-time, but the ambiguity of the name applies in either language.

[35] *NCNA*, November 24, 1956.

[36] These sympathies for new public representatives are in *XWRB*, November 21, 1956.

corporations directing them, were formally line items in state economic plans; and they were legally bound to follow the purchase and supply directives in those plans. At the same time, there was no way yet to staff most firms or branches with Communists able to enforce this system into which the urban economy had been scared.

Large firms often benefited from the state's guarantee of their supplies. The manager of Wing On Department Store said in late 1956 that before socialist transformation occurred he had doubts about it. But the change allowed his company's inventories to become five times larger. And he still got to chair the meetings, even though real decisions were now made by "the public side."[37] An ex-Communist planner agreed fully:

> It was not that the state bought out 50 percent or 51 percent of the shares of an enterprise—indeed, it compensated the capitalists for all their capital, however underassessed that may have been. But it was now an ownership system of a joint state-private sort, led by the collective ownership system. The main administrative authority was in the hands of the public side.[38]

The largest group to change career plans because of socialism consisted of capitalist youths. Most managers who were fairly close to retirement quit their jobs in 1956. If they were middle-aged, they were often appointed to deputy or technical positions in their previous firms, or to branch headships if they were shopkeepers. But the Party itself seems to have been divided about "the problem of youth leaving the commercial circles."[39] In the Wing On Company, for example, 928 employees were retained after the Transition to Socialism, but only 36 of them were less than twenty-eight years old. The *People's Daily* lamented in an article about Shanghai: "The pride of tradesmen who know their businesses and their customers is a dying thing. . . . Their work has received no public recognition or propaganda in the 'corridor of glory' of the People's Garden, devoted to publicizing labor models. . . . They are also underpaid."[40] This problem was perceived—not just by the Party newspaper—but little was done about it. When a Shanghai Industry and Commerce Circle's Political School was established to certify the

---

[37] *NCNA*, December 22, 1956.

[38] Interview in Hong Kong. This source's statement that the government fully compensated the capitalists may be subject to challenge, but his statement that the valuations were too low was somewhat unusual from a Communist before recent years.

[39] *RMRB*, August 26, 1956.

[40] Ibid.

loyalty of managers whom the economy needed, less than 18 percent of the students were thirty years old or less, and more than 81 percent were ages thirty-one to sixty.[41] Youths who were more seriously encouraged, in this new order, were members of the Young Communist League.[42] The Transition applied labels to senior managers, old and new; but the labels it gave their children were to prove even more important in later years.

In the reshuffle of 1956, some private managers whose old jobs had been eliminated in January did not receive new ones in other organizations until November (if they received new work at all).[43] The circulation of local elites was extensive at this time, but the old leading status group in the city was neither eliminated nor uniformly urged to keep working. In all of Shanghai's district-level department stores together, 48 percent of the managers were "private representatives" after the Transition. Only 27 percent were new managers, "appointed by the state." The remaining 25 percent were "promoted from among workers."[44] Local capitalists clearly remained crucial to the running of state companies. But as this system became regularized, there was competition for perks among leaders with different labels.

Complaints arose that chiefs of business enterprise groups (*yingye zuzhang*), who were often proletarian-origin overseers, usually had expense accounts. But chiefs of finance groups (*caiwu zuzhang*), who were often bourgeois, tended to have no expense accounts.[45] The conflict between "red professionals" and "bourgeois experts" was not unique to China's experiment in socialism,[46] but it bedeviled many urbanites for a long time after 1956.

WAGES AND WORKERS IN THE TRANSITION TO SOCIALISM

The change of 1956 affected workers as well as cadres. Before that year, socialized enterprises paid their employees according to various rank systems. The 1956 reform standardized union workers' wage scales. Because the Party's relations with middle-income Shanghai families deteriorated

[41] *SHGS* 15 (August 5, 1956): 6.
[42] *ZGQNB*, March 27, 1956.
[43] *XWRB*, November 6, 1956.
[44] Ibid.; the percentages are computed.
[45] *XMBWK*, May 8, 1957.
[46] See Jeremy Azrael, *Managerial Power and Soviet Politics* (Cambridge: Harvard University Press, 1966).

sharply in the mid-1950s, it needed to strengthen a new mass constituency in the proletariat, and the easiest way to do this was to raise their pay somewhat.

This policy reinforced the good label that workers obtained under communism. But it was tempered by a need to save money on the total wage bill in China's most expensive city.[47] At a time when capitalists were obviously giving things up, it was possible to ask workers to make some sacrifices also. Since the Transition came at a Chinese New Year, after food supplies had increased from the shortages of 1955, one way for the government to save money was to eliminate the traditional New Year bonuses. These were decried as decadant practices, and workers at many plants "volunteered" to do without them.[48] Many workers felt, however, that there was a trade-off between the abolition of bonuses and the increase of regular wages.

Other "wage revisions" were expected at this time, but they were slow to evolve (many were delayed for more than two decades). The emphasis of 1956 policy was on standardization and incentives. Before that year, workers' payment in state-run enterprises had been set in terms of eight grades, each receiving a fixed number of "wage points." To determine actual pay, these points were multiplied by an index based on the price of five staples, which cost more in Shanghai than elsewhere.[49] In 1956, this scheme was extended to many new firms, but it was also changed. There were still eight grades for workers,[50] but one-fifth of the wage budget in many firms was set aside for incentives. Bonuses were budgeted for quota overfulfillment and for moving out of Shanghai to work in other cities, usually on a temporary basis. Completing the details of this wage reform took many months, even in large and important Shanghai firms.[51] Overall, it benefited workers. But cadres, not workers, were the officially labeled group that gained most from the Transition.

Many new workers hired in new firms during the Transition[52] came from capitalist class backgrounds. Shanghai's population included many capitalists, and good recruits were plentiful from such families.[53] The change of

[47] The tendency seems to have been somewhat less strong in Shanghai than in other Chinese cities, however. See Vogel, *Canton under Communism*, p. 186.

[48] For example, Loh, *Escape*, pp. 201ff.

[49] Charles Hoffman, *Work Incentive Practices and Policies in the People's Republic of China, 1953–1965* (Albany: State University of New York Press, 1967), pp. 18–22, 28. This system was taken over from the Soviet Union.

[50] For administrative and government workers, a similar system involved twenty-six grades. Technical workers were on a scale of sixteen grades.

[51] *XWRB*, November 1, 1956, indicates the revision was by no means finished on that date.

[52] Examples from the textile and dyeing industries can be found in *LDB*, August 6, 1956.

[53] It has proven difficult to obtain comprehensive figures on the percentage of bourgeois-

1956 raised wages, but it also increased stratification. "New workers" (*xin gongren*), identified as such publicly, received worse treatment and compensation than others.[54] Officials called for trade unions to do more political education, so as to placate these bourgeois-youths-become-workers. The situation was especially complex because other new workers came from the families of new cadres and had good background labels.

Many employers still hired workers on previous terms, often as moonlighters, even though this practice became illegal after the Transition. Underground factories (*dixia gongchang*) recruited workers to make goods whose prices and inputs were unregulated, often at night using the same premises as small joint factories that had earlier been owned by their private-side representatives. Such managers paid workers far more—for example, half again as much per hour—for their moonlighting as for their legal labor.[55] These plants were common in Shanghai during the late 1950s,[56] and they provided jobs both to registered urban residents and to large numbers of peasants arriving from outside.

In many trades, labor recruitment was still often determined by family links with particular rural locations. Even in the mid-1960s, practically all Shanghai pedicab drivers were still "Subei" people from North Jiangsu.[57] This pattern was certainly not eliminated before the Cultural Revolution, although economic reorganization in 1956 and in the 1964–65 period often put new people in charge of hiring.

Some 1957 directives against employing further rural labor were inspired not only by the desire to reduce Shanghai's population, but also by the will to centralize control over the engagement of new workers.[58] The proletariat, and especially its new ex-bourgeois members, became more dependent on

---

labeled people in the city (although some statistics on the percentage in schools are presented below). The meaning of such data would be subject to doubt anyway, because of capitalist-background persons who were able to obtain labels such as "cadre" or "worker" on the basis of post-1949 activities.

[54] *XWRB*, November 24, 25, 1956.

[55] An example in a leather ball factory is in *QNB*, January 22, 1957.

[56] For more, see Lynn White, "Low Power: Small Enterprises in Shanghai," *China Quarterly* 73 (March 1978): 45–76.

[57] The interviewee who described this spoke of the "joint managed" (*lianying*) pedicab companies and reorganized unions in 1956, as well as the establishment of a Pedicab Union Club and the designation of pedicab stopping places then. Emily Honig is engaged in pioneering research on the emergence of a "Subei" underclass in Shanghai since the middle of the nineteenth century. On this and other topics, see her *Sisters and Strangers: Women in the Cotton Mills of Shanghai, 1919–1949* (Stanford, Calif.: Stanford University Press, 1986), and undoubtedly her forthcoming publications.

[58] An example is in *QNB*, January 22, 1957.

Party leaders within units that could hire them under rules laid down in 1956. A deputy mayor complained,

> Some enterprises recruit workers from other places at will, and the concerned departments do not work according to the household system [*hukou zhidu*]. . . . This is most serious in the construction industry. The number of spontaneous factories [*zifa gongchang*] and stall hawkers continues to rise, and they attract large numbers of workers from other places.[59]

High Party leaders' preferred solution was to ship people out of Shanghai.[60] In early 1957, the Municipal Council blithely resolved that the number of Shanghai workers should be 30 percent fewer.[61] This was impractical, as speeches by the council's own members show; but it was set forward as an ideal in any case. This policy would have put the Party in conflict with most workers, had it been enforced. Such radical speculation was fashionable in the Shanghai CCP before it permeated the whole country by 1958. The city's Population Office (Renkou Bangong Shi) estimated that 120,000 people "returned to their villages for production" in the first ten months of 1957.[62] The statistic does not indicate how many of these departures were temporary, to help with harvests and transplantation. It is nonetheless clear that dissonance was increasing between efforts by officials to reform Shanghai and the limited resources to accomplish that renaissance.

TECHNICAL CHANGE AND WORKERS IN THE TRANSITION TO SOCIALISM

Shanghai's Great Leap Forward began, in all but name, during 1956. Extreme hopefulness about what the CCP might accomplish is obvious in the city's 1956 plans for organization and investment. By May, the Party made major decisions to expand capital supplies to the now-legitimate urban economy.[63] Although much of this money was put into large plants that could not begin producing for about two years (by which time the Great Leap Forward was declared), the Transition to Socialism meant a marked

[59] *XWRB*, July 23, 1957.
[60] See Mayor Chen Yi's statement on this point in chapter 2, above.
[61] *XWRB*, January 17, 1957.
[62] *LDB*, November 23, 1957.
[63] *NCNA*, May 27, 1956.

change from Shanghai's net disinvestment of 1955.[64] The advantages of high capital regeneration rates in Shanghai were evident, and light industries were now complemented by more investments in heavy industries such as metals, laths, and electrical machines.[65] The resources available to new monitors in the city were thus greatly increased. At the same time, these new cadres began to face increasing pressures for performance from their superiors in the Party.

By February 1957, many municipal economic organs were merged. Cadres released from them were transferred to middle and low levels. This geographic shift of administrators, which intensified during the Antirightist movement, helped create the infrastructure for a political empowerment of mid-level offices in the Leap.[66] The start of this "decentralization of power" (*quanli xiafang*) can be dated in Shanghai from 1956.[67] Real leaps take lead time. Also, they spring not just from the whims of political leaders, but from an infrastructure of administrators who have specifiable labels and new powers over subordinates.

The experience of a store may be typical: Its monthly business rose by half after joint status, because more goods were provided by state-run wholesalers. The labor force was reduced slightly, but working capital rose to 230 percent of its previous level, about a year after socialization.[68] The manager and two private-side assistants retained their posts, but a new deputy manager (who was also in charge of the local union branch) represented the public side and apparently made all sensitive decisions.

In larger firms, especially in the state sector, the regular unionized work force sometimes decreased. Hierarchy and stratification of workers, however, often increased. In the Shanghai Dockyard, for example, the employment of nontechnical workers rose less than 2 percent between 1952 and

---

[64] See chapter 2 above concerning this net disinvestment. For comparisons with the national situation, especially by 1958, see David Bachman, *Leaps and Retreats in the Chinese Political Economy*, forthcoming.

[65] Christopher Howe, "Industrialization under Conditions of Long-Term Population Stability: Shanghai's Achievement and Prospects," in *Shanghai: Revolution and Development in an Asian Metropolis*, ed. Christopher Howe (Cambridge: Cambridge University Press, 1981), 175.

[66] Franz Schurmann, *Ideology and Organization in Communist China* (Berkeley and Los Angeles: University of California Press, 1966). See also *DGB*, February 27, 1957, and *WHB*, same date, as well as *XWRB*, February 16, 1957.

[67] This was the opinion of an interviewee with management experience in Shanghai at that time.

[68] *XWRB*, June 24, 1957. The store hired fewer than twenty people (ibid.). All percentages are computed.

1954, and then it declined 2 percent between 1954 and October 1957.[69] Yet the work of this dockyard increased in these times; its number of technicians rose 31 percent in the first period, and another 24 percent in the second. Employment of temporary workers increased during and after 1956–57 (though some official discouragement of this practice meant that exact data were not available even to the government). The Transition provided enterprise Party leaders with more resources, and it also increased their power over employees by making high-paying, unionized, "iron rice bowl" jobs more scarce and precious than before.

Technical changes at this time, financed by the new capital, were very often labor-intensive. The union proletariat was better-paid, more restricted in size, more dependent on new Party bosses, and often asked to work hard. Dual campaigns of late 1956 spread "advanced experiences" in industry and encouraged "advanced producers."[70] A newspaper complained that the Advanced Producers' Movement "paid attention only to materialistic prizes and neglected the strengthening of political education."[71] A survey of over five hundred innovations, as reported in a workers' newspaper, averred that only 30 percent should be classed as real advances.[72] In the Shanghai Machine Tool Factory (which later became a hotbed of the Cultural Revolution), a worker in the Axle Casing Shop, after making a useless part, asked a friend to share responsibility for the dud so that his bonus as an "advanced worker" would not be reduced. Another in the Refining Shop hid his defective goods, keeping the raw materials for later use. The prize system was blamed for "hurting discipline," and it was plainly unpopular among unionized workers. The city government intensified it anyway, because it raised production. During the Transition to Socialism and later, the rising power of local Party bosses constrained not just capitalists, but also proletarians.

OPPOSITION TO THE NEW DEPENDENCE

One way to beat the new system was to leave it, and many small entrepreneurs did so. Illegal clandestine businesses, increasingly called "violating firms" (*weifa hu*) rather than "spontaneous firms" (*zifa hu*), were so numerous that in one Shanghai area alone, the local police found 589 of them in

---

[69] Percentages are computed from absolute figures in *XWRB*, November 29, 1957.

[70] *Xianjin jingyan* and *xianjin shengchan zhe*.

[71] *XWRB*, November 8, 1956.

[72] *DGB*, October 27, 1956.

two months.[73] Throughout the city as a whole during the third quarter of 1956, a municipal bureau officially estimated that nearly three thousand "handicraft workshops have been established and not registered" (though its data were admittedly incomplete). Their existence was attributed to "the demand due to a period of brisk business." The workers were housewives and "peasants who have infiltrated from other areas . . . provided with bed and board, paid only four or five mao daily."[74] This phenomenon not only undercut the household registration system, it also led to defections from legal work. One article described a leather-belt factory in which 150 of the 180 workers in its legal, daytime organization also participated illegally:

The big profits in spontaneous handicraft firms have influenced co-opera-tive members to ask for withdrawal from the co-ops so they can operate as individuals. . . . Some work in the co-op by day and in the spontaneous firm at night. . . . Members of handicraft and agricultural co-ops outside Shanghai have been attracted to the city by big profits, and they have come in large numbers—including many who had formerly returned [from Shanghai] to their home villages for production.[75]

Often the new entrepreneurs were Communists. People with good labels and new powers tended to use these for their own families, groups, and net-works of clients. The trade union chairman in a screw factory set up an underground branch on his own. Because he also headed the legitimate firm during the day, he was able "to intimidate the others into silence."[76] A pri-vate-side representative "ran to Canton with his machines and tools, to es-tablish an underground factory." The deputy chief of a police substation collaborated "with a counterrevolutionary, surveillance over whom had just been lifted," to run an underground factory. When a Party member in an enamel factory was asked to invest in an illegal firm, he "wanted to invest, but before he had a chance to complete the transaction, the case became known to the Party branch. . . . He withdrew his shares."[77] Shanghai's top Party secretary, Ke Qingshi himself, admitted this large informal economy showed "resistance from capitalists" and "reluctance and skepticism from workers" about socialization.[78]

[73] RMRB, October 13, 1957.
[74] Ibid. A mao is a dime, a tenth of a yuan.
[75] NCNA, November 13, 1956.
[76] XWRB, December 23, 1957.
[77] XWRB, April 26, July 20, August 18, December 23, 1957.
[78] NCNA, September 20, 1956.

Party leaders finally got a sense that the Transition had been too easy. It obviously was much-resented. They were understandably curious about the amount of disaffection, and they increasingly suggested a need for some liberal tolerance of dissent.[79] The result was the Hundred Flowers period. This was a quasi-liberal movement to recruit bourgeois talents that the state needed.[80] At the height of this famous campaign, especially in the first half of May 1957, a broader range of informative views about China were published in the regular press than during any more recent year. Private-side entrepreneurs, called into forums to air their grievances, expressed themselves clearly—and their frustrations were published.

"I am in my office to decorate it," said one manager.[81] Another suggested, "Only the public-side representatives should be 'managers' of joint companies, since they decide everything anyway."[82] A third protested that public representatives make too many mistakes; in his plant, they vetoed the cheapest method to make a repair simply because it had been proposed by a capitalist. This became a pattern of "real suggestions but false discussion."[83] Another entrepreneur said technicians were treated better than administrators on the private side, even though the whole system "made contradictions between capitalists and the government, capitalists and workers, and government and workers."[84] The official labels did not accurately represent different people's abilities, and they made for tension rather than peace between groups.

A technician-scientist objected that many new cadres interfered in the minute details of scientific work instead of confining themselves to general

---

[79] This book need not, for example, detail the various versions of Mao Zedong's "Hundred Flowers" speech—mostly because that job and other relevant elite factors are covered in Roderick MacFarquhar, *Contradictions among the People, 1956–1957*, vol. 1 of *The Origins of the Cultural Revolution* (New York: Columbia University Press, 1974).

[80] Many Western treatments of the origins of the Hundred Flowers overstate the extent to which it began because of initiatives from Beijing (whether ideals, intended deceptions, or power struggles there) rather than because of needs to mobilize local urban staff among dispossessed capitalists after the Transition to Socialism. Mao's 1956 speech on contradictions among the people nonetheless became, in its various later versions, the symbol of Party policy. The best account of this campaign in Beijing (MacFarquhar, *The Origins*, esp. pp. 187, 199) contains good information on the reaction of a Shanghai businessman, but it still concludes that "Liu sought solutions principally through altering the relations between men and goods, while Mao, though fully aware of the importance of economics, was more concerned to alter the relations between men and men." The latter relations have economic implications too, because they affect people's incentives to work; and Mao apparently knew this.

[81] *XWRB*, May 18, 1957.

[82] *XWRB*, May 19, 1957.

[83] *XWRB*, May 11, 1957.

[84] Ibid.

policy matters.[85] A worker in a traditional handicraft firm chastised cadres in the economic bureau above him by saying, "They know nothing about art." The head of an artists' union (who was a retired soldier, not an artist) frankly told a porcelain maker who was his subordinate, "I know only how to fight."[86] Policy had made him the official monitor of affairs he did not even claim to understand.

Other critics stressed the hidden costs of tight 1956 rules on the security of business information. Yet others dwelt on the amount of talent wasted during rural send-down movements.[87] Many complained of overcentralization, which put administrative power in the hands of people who had no idea how to process the facts needed for good decisions. An egregious case was in the Shanghai Municipal Foreign Trade Bureau, where only one-seventh of the public representatives could read the foreign telegrams on which most of the bureau's work depended.[88]

The mergers of 1956 also produced unexpected costs. Joined toy and match factories were run by the Party secretary of the toy plant, and "this leads to a loss in the match work." Centralization created losses for lawful plants, because more work went to illegal firms that did not need to bother with the red tape.[89]

Even street peddlers appeared at the criticism forums. Some hawkers said they were not averse to being members of the new joint companies. But they were very bitter about not being able to join trade unions, which would give them access to union benefits. Many peddlers pointed out that their peers were ignoring the rules and selling better goods at lower prices than were legal. The peddlers who cooperated with the government got scant business.[90]

Other businessmen expressed similar views, saying they did not mind socialization, but the state should keep its end of the bargain and provide resources. They decried "the negative ideology of waiting for the public representative to arrive."[91] A car wrecker who had applied for joint status in 1956 still waited in mid-May 1957 for notice that his firm's new status was finally approved. A mortician said, "In our line of business, there is no joint corporation yet," so that all the morticians were deprived of the official pa-

---

[85] *XWRB*, May 4, 1957.
[86] *XWRB*, May 17, 1957.
[87] *XWRB*, May 18, 1957.
[88] *XWRB*, May 15, 1957.
[89] Ibid.
[90] *XWRB*, June 18, 1957.
[91] *NCNA*, January 28, 1956, is an early expression of such views.

tronage that had become necessary for getting along, both politically and financially. He complained that he had received no dividends, because his capital had not been assessed. "This is similar to confiscation."[92]

Officials had to ignore many firms, because the Party still lacked adequate staff to take charge of Shanghai's economy. This situation inspired some of the most furious statements at the forums. Campaign policies had led to official unresponsiveness, as surely as to any other result, because the bureaucracy had bitten off more than it could chew. As one angry speaker said about cadres in general, "They do not listen, and they do not ask."[93]

Shanghai's previous low- and mid-level leaders said they had been deprived of self-respect, just as they had been deprived of their previous salaries. They complained that many public representatives had dual jobs and double salaries. "This leads to unstable emotions among some of the staff."[94] They felt that a "manager" should not just be head of the clerks,[95] and that a capitalist should be able to get rid of his bad label, or "doff his hat" (*zhai maozi*).[96]

CONTINUING THE FORUMS: THE ANTIRIGHTIST MOVEMENT

Tables were turned at these meetings in May 1957. The forums continued smoothly, with the same invitees, but now with an opposite purpose: to lambaste the Party's critics as "rightists." The Antirightist movement became the most crucial labeling campaign before the Cultural Revolution. A majority of its victims were intellectuals, rather than businessmen. The very word "intellectual" acquired new and sharply negative political meanings after this campaign.

A high portion of Shanghai's talented people came from families that had both capitalist and intellectual labels, even though only a small portion of them, including some Party members, were dubbed rightists. The movement had many aspects, and a minor immediate one, showing its partial similarity to earlier campaigns, was its budgetary effect. In the ten months after the Antirightist Campaign began, Shanghai industrialists bought 25 percent

[92] *XWRB*, May 18, 1957.
[93] *Buwen, buwen*; *XWRB*, May 18, 1957.
[94] *XWRB*, May 24, 1957.
[95] *XWRB*, May 15, 1957.
[96] *XWRB*, May 24, 1957.

more government bonds than the government had earlier planned to ask of them.[97]

The Shanghai Industry and Commerce Circle's Political School, where the Party had hoped to woo managers, turned out to include more than two hundred rightists. In Shanghai district people's congresses, seventy-three deputies—all of whom had passed muster sufficiently to be put on ballots shortly before—were also named as rightists.[98] A large part of Shanghai's local leadership alternative to the CCP was castigated with this label.

But the Party itself also had searing experiences in 1957. The specific deficiencies highlighted by its critics were far too numerous and cogent to ignore. The first need was to assure Party members, especially in unions, that administrative faults would be corrected at high levels before low ones, and that "solidarity" with the Party's main proletarian constituency remained a paramount policy.[99]

Some CCP members had joined the critics (in a style to be replicated ten years later, on a larger scale). In a movie studio, a deputy Party secretary challenged the main secretary directly; he accused his boss of restricting his freedom to marry and his participation in some campaigns.[100] Many criticisms concerned the campaigns against counterrevolutionaries and the limited access for many Party members to secret dossiers.[101] Others claimed that the arrogance of cadres led to violence,[102] as in the case of a CCP cadre and her mother-in-law (the latter had committed suicide).[103] In the vast majority of cases, the Party after May explicitly backed its secretaries against their attackers.[104] But the whole experience also led to a serious movement for cadre "reeducation."

Cadres' embarrassment about Hundred Flowers criticisms gave the main impulse to a send-down movement of both rightist critics and (for brief periods) CCP loyalists. This in turn created the administrative infrastructure for mid-level decentralization during the Great Leap Forward of 1958. Campaigns for administrative retrenchment and simplification (*jingjian*) had

[97] *XWRB*, March 26, 1958.

[98] *WHB*, January 6, 1958.

[99] *XWRB*, May 24, 1957, reprinted speeches by high Party leaders to a meeting of thirteen thousand Shanghai union members the previous day. See also *XWRB*, June 6, 10, and July 25, 1957, which are all about meetings for workers. One on June 5, for eleven thousand of them, was addressed by Lai Ruoyu, chairman of the All-China Federation of Trade Unions.

[100] *XWRB*, July 25, 1957.

[101] Two examples are in *XWRB*, September 14, 29, 1957.

[102] Examples are in *XWRB*, July 21 and August 7, 1957.

[103] *NCNA*, November 25, 1956.

[104] *XWRB*, August 31, 1957.

been intensively publicized since late 1955.[105] Top officialdom evidently hoped Party loyalists could be most effectively used if they were scattered geographically among small cities, towns, and low-level offices. The difficulty, of course, was that CCP cadres did not ordinarily like to be seconded to the boondocks. At local levels, they had plenty of prestige to resist making this Beijing initiative a widespread reality—until 1957. Campaign policies, after the Hundred Flowers, commonly threatened monitors as well as unofficial people. This set a pattern that reached its peak ten years later.

An Austerity Campaign in Shanghai offices was enforced during the Hundred Flowers bombardment with a send-down (*xiafang*) of cadres from the prestigious "organ school" (*jiguan xuexiao*) of the Municipal Council itself.[106] As early as April, when Hundred Flowers critics were blasting cadres into embarrassing situations, the Shanghai First Heavy Industry Bureau sent down one-sixth of its leaders "to basic units." This type of administrative reform took place all over China on a much larger scale less than a year later.[107] It was the main operational meaning of the Leap, and it would hardly have been accepted among cadres without the Hundred Flowers.

The main period for decentralization, administrative streamlining, and cadre reeducation did not come until late November and December. After the Antirightist movement began in May, Party members could argue against retreating under fire. By the autumn, they were too busy criticizing rightists. Local newspaper articles, opining that "the division of labor is poor and many jobs are redundant" in city offices, nonetheless finally led to an expanded Administrative Streamlining Campaign.[108] By the end of November, the Municipal Council resolved to correct the fact that "about 60 percent of the 470,000 cadres now in municipal administrative, industrial, and commercial units have never undergone class struggle and lack labor training." It assured any doubters that "voluntary transfer and transfer under unified arrangements should go hand-in-hand."[109] A plan was announced to reassign 140,000 cadres—beginning with high officials, but soon to include many others—before the end of February 1958.[110] When a district

[105] See Kau Ying-mao, "Governmental Bureaucracy and Cadres in Urban China under Communist Rule, 1949–65" (Ph.D. diss., Department of Political Science, Cornell University, 1968), p. 288, and also Harry Harding, Jr., *Organizing China: The Problem of Bureaucracy, 1949–76* (Stanford, Calif.: Stanford University Press, 1981), pp. 164–65.

[106] *QNB*, March 22, 1957. See also *XWRB*, February 6, 1957.

[107] *XMBWK*, April 3, 1957.

[108] *XWRB*, November 26, 1957.

[109] *WHB*, December 1, 1956.

[110] *LDB* and *XWRB*, both November 30, 1957.

Party committee announced its own send-down plan a few days later, it listed high officials and spoke of their having made "their individual plans for reform" in a nearly explicit reference to the sins uncovered before May.[111]

The portion of cadres who "went down," at least temporarily, reached over 90 percent in many Shanghai government units.[112] They left central offices for just short periods if they had only to show a willingness to participate in labor. But many left for longer times, because they were seconded to the lower-level offices for real administrative work. One-quarter or more of the cadres sent down were CCP members, at least in certain units.[113] Technicians were affected by this campaign less often than administrative staff.[114]

There was a difference between the send-down of rightists and that of cadres, because the latter went to independent positions at low administrative levels and might conceivably advance their careers there. The rightists often lost their household registrations, knew their families were disgraced because of their labels, and expected to stay in their new jobs indefinitely. For them, the send-down was "labor reform" (*laodong gaizao*). As an ex-Party interviewee said,

> Often a cadre and a rightist "went down" together, from the same unit to the same unit. For example, if a university professor was sent to sweep floors in a primary school, he was likely to be accompanied by an educational cadre, who went from the same university to the same primary school for administrative work. In this way, the sometimes strong personalities of the rightists had less influence at the lower levels than they would if they had been sent there alone.[115]

Official sources claimed the rightists deserved such treatment because they had "tried to weaken the solidarity of the people."[116] But what they had done more specifically was to speak out against the fast-increasing power of a bureaucracy of overseers who lacked the resources to manage Shanghai. Those monitors could assure their domination of the lives of most employees

[111] *XWRB*, December 11, 1957.
[112] *XWRB*, December 3, 10, 1957; an example is the West Suburbs District Public Security Bureau, from which 92 percent of the cadres went down at least for a while.
[113] *XWRB*, November 27, 1957; an example is the Municipal Transport Bureau.
[114] Interview with an ex-cadre who had done technical work.
[115] Interview in Hong Kong with a bourgeois who went to university in Shanghai.
[116] *XWRB*, June 26, 1957.

of large and medium-sized urban work units, but they lacked the resources to follow through on their revolutionary promises.

CONFIRMATION OF LABELS, CAMPAIGNS, AND DEPENDENCE IN 1957

At the height of the Hundred Flowers period, an especially harsh critic declared: "The proletariat is selfish; so no class supports the people's government."[117] This was clearly not a position the Party could accept, so the CCP embraced its proletarian constituency more seriously after 1957 than before. A worker (who had joined the Party's critics but had been a CCP member for two years) was not punished as a rightist. On the contrary, he was promoted, brought to the attention of Chairman Mao for having finally risen above his youthful fling with "bourgeois individualist thinking," and held up as an object of study to rally proletarians.[118] All labels acquired more forceful meanings at this time.

Legitimacy in China had a narrower scope after 1957, and the criterion for official prestige became increasingly political and less social. There were popular reactions against this trend, but they flourished mainly in clandestine parts of society. At a low level in a poor section of Shanghai, a millinarian cult of "divine healers" grew in late 1957 as a counterrepresentation of this situation.[119] But revitalization movements could hardly be the capitalists' main reaction. As Franz Schurmann has written, "Personal authority has always been resented in China, particularly among higher social groups."[120] The Party knew, after 1957, that it had to impose patron-monitors on Shanghai's society even more than it had done before. In early 1958, the *People's Daily* editorialized:

> Some bureaucrats hardly visit their factories. . . . When they do, they tend to assume an expressionless look in front of the masses, forbearing even so much as to smile. [But] only 10 percent of our staff at most are guilty of this work style. We must not, therefore, view all our CCP members and government personnel in this light, as did the rightists.[121]

[117] *XWRB*, September 11, 1957.
[118] *WHB*, October 8, 1957.
[119] *WHB*, December 28, 1957. For a sharply drawn rural example, see Ann S. Anagnost's "The Beginning and End of an Emperor: A Counterrepresentation of the State," *Modern China* 2, no. 2 (1985): 147–76.
[120] Schurmann, *Ideology and Organization*, p. 245.
[121] *RMRB*, January 27, 1958.

Policies of pressure had now demoralized many capitalists and subordinates. They had given activists and Communists considerable hubris, as well as more work than they could do. The revolution was so important, and there were so few qualified to make it, the Party used people even if they did not smile.

CHAPTER 5

Students and Residents: Flowers, Coercion, and Minds, 1956–1957

what if a much of a which of a wind
gives the truth to summer's lie. . . .
—e. e. cummings

The experiences of 1956–57 were felt not just in Shanghai's economy, but also in the city's residential and intellectual culture. This was a period of quickly growing immigration to Shanghai. The annual rate of increase in permanent residents, from 1950 through 1957, had averaged less than 4 percent,[1] but the annualized increase from June 1956 to October 1957 was an extraordinary 13 percent.[2] Legal residence changes accounted for more than seven-tenths of this rise, and transients created another quarter of it.[3] The Transition to Socialism revamped Shanghai's labor market, and the Party's new cadres brought in many of their fellow villagers and family members as urban residents. The labeling, monitoring, and campaigning policies empowered upwardly mobile local officials to create a new environment for daily life in Shanghai.

[1] This and the subsequent estimates are based on calculations from data in a speech by Deputy Mayor Xu Jianguo, quoted in *JFRB*, January 7, 1958. This reported a Shanghai population at the beginning of 1958 of 7.2 million, of whom 95 percent (6.86 million) were legal permanent residents. Some were legal transients; a further unknown number must have been nonregistered persons. Legal residents increased by 1.84 million from 1950 to 1957, from a starting level of 5.02 million. The figure of approximately 4 percent is based on these data.

[2] Ibid. Reported a June 1956 registered permanent population of 6.02 million, and then an increase in October 1957 of 840,000. This implies nearly a 10 percent increase per year. Actually, the influx was even greater, because the transient population rose in these seventeen months from 6,000 to 340,000. The total population in June 1956 must have been 6.08 million, and the increase during the year after that, about 791,000. The result is the figure of about 13 percent.

[3] Ibid. Between June 1956 and October 1957, Xu reported a rise of 820,000 in the number of permanent residents. Another part of the speech indicated that the transient increase was 280,000. The natural increase among immigrants was 30,000. The components add to a 1.13 million rise, and the portions are obtained by division.

WHAT SOCIALIZATION MEANT FOR RESIDENTS

Even before 1949, Shanghai was split into districts where residents generally had different social statuses. This geography is worth describing, because it remained more or less permanent, even in later years. The central strip of stores and tall buildings, the middle of town centered on Nanjing Road, lies between Suzhou Creek and the ex–French area and to some extent north of the creek near its confluence with the Huangpu River. Much of the city's best housing is in another east-west strip south of the western sections of this business district, the old "French Concession" of quiet, tree-lined streets. Near the Huangpu River, south of the eastern part of the central business strip, is a "Chinese city," an area of very dense housing easily identifiable on maps because of the circular road that has replaced its defensive walls. Still further south along the the river is a large district of inexpensive buildings, factories, and slums. North of Suzhou Creek lies another large area of dense housing (much of it built in Japanese style during the 1920s). To the northwest is another area of factories and slums. Most buildings in these parts of the city remained unrepaired for half a century after about 1937. The influx of population during 1956–57 strained this scanty housing as never before. Since demand for residential space could be channeled, the scarcity of living space gave more political clout to the city's new local monitors.

After the 1956 socialization, Shanghai incomes became less stratified than in most third world cities, but the state's need to invest in joint enterprises took money away from any construction unrelated to these firms. Thus professionals and managers, including many bourgeois, lived in worse housing than their counterparts in other countries at China's general economic level.[4] Socialization meant building "new towns" (*xin cun*) on the outskirts of Shanghai for the workers and staff of favored enterprises. A model for these developments was Caoyang Village, built earlier for "over 1,000 advanced workers and their families."[5] Such projects were common near factories in the suburbs, but they could accommodate relatively few of the city's workers and cadres—the ones most favored by the post-Transition networks.[6]

[4] Martin King Whyte and William L. Parish, *Urban Life in Contemporary China* (Chicago: University of Chicago Press, 1984), pp. 44, 80.

[5] *NCNA*, July 4, 1952.

[6] See maps in Reginald Yin Wang Kwok's "Trends of Urban Planning and Development in China," in *Urban Development in Modern China*, ed. Laurence J. C. Ma and Edward W. Han-

Socialization also severely rationed access to housing in previously built-up areas. Newly married couples had (and still have) great difficulty finding good space for their families in Shanghai. Mid-1950s policies pressured families with above-average space to lease their "surplus" at low rents. No substantial public money went into upkeep of housing, and private incentives for maintenance also declined. The deterioration in quality of Shanghai's old stock of residential space was therefore sharp. The main effect of these changes was to make individuals more dependent on their work units for any new or better places to live.

The Transition to Socialism also legitimated investment in joint firms, thereby increasing the attraction of Shanghai for job seekers from rural areas. Hiring was now largely controlled by new leaders, including many demobilized soldiers of peasant origin, who liked to appoint workers from their own native areas. On the other hand, young family members of long-time staff and workers were often able to compete for jobs successfully on grounds of expertise. So in some Shanghai units, tension arose between two groups: public representatives having rural backgrounds and more established urban cadres or previous leaders in work units. Such friction would have been important if it had been restricted to workplaces, but the shortage of housing extended it to residential life also. Old and new bosses found themselves in conflict not just over business affairs, but also over resources for the life-styles of their families and associates.

Rural relatives of the new socialist managers often arrived in Shanghai in hopes of obtaining regular urban registration or work. By mid-1956, there was a major influx; the city's population increase temporarily rose to a phenomenal rate of 15 percent per year.[7] Over 70 percent of the immigrants were said to be peasants. High Party leaders of the municipal government were determined to send them back to their homes. In December 1956, the government estimated that about 4 percent of Shanghai's total population consisted of long-term "temporary" residents, and it admitted there were many more in the city who had not registered even on a temporary basis.[8]

This deluge created a need for urban welfare services that the municipal government could not ignore but was also not prepared to fund. The Civil Administration Bureau held a series of conferences on the importance of

---

ten (Boulder, Colo.: Westview, 1981), pp. 147–93; Ka-iu Fung, "The Spatial Development of Shanghai," in *Shanghai: Revolution and Development in an Asian Metropolis*, ed. Christopher Howe (Cambridge: Cambridge University Press, 1981), pp. 269–99.

[7] *LDB*, March 14, 1957. The rate is calculated from data for eight months, beginning in May 1956.

[8] *JFRB*, December 26, 1956.

sending peasants out of Shanghai. It encouraged "social relief through self-help." One of these meetings discussed "how the division of labor among urban areas might be clarified . . . to develop the functions of basic organizations," so the city would be prepared in case of floods or typhoons.[9] The government tried to organize neighborhoods and urge collective units to face locally the obvious urban problems that the city could not afford to solve while meeting high investment quotas. Activists could make names for themselves at this time—and could later get jobs as local monitors—by helping in these welfare efforts.

As in the burgeoning cities of other low-income countries, however, Shanghai's new immigrants did not demand much from officialdom.[10] Their main hope was to remain in the city, finding temporary employment if permanent work was unavailable. Urban services remained minimal in many parts of Shanghai under the prevalent policy of benign neglect. For example, through the end of the 1950s about one-third of the water consumed in the city by industry as well as households was drawn from wells.[11] Many ordinary citizens could still live in Shanghai without household registrations, if they were willing to depend on means of supplying their needs outside the official rations. News media might complain that cloth, for example, was available "at high prices, instead of against coupons." Alternatively, ration coupons could be bought from illegal brokers.[12] The Party did not have enough checkers to close access to such channels, even though most residents depended mainly on the government.

The CCP's strength in low-level Shanghai residential organizations in 1956 was tenuous. Throughout the whole city, during that whole year, only 609 of the 125,000 lane cadres were admitted to the Party.[13] People who had enough political capacity to enter the CCP could pull better jobs in state enterprises than lanes could offer. Being a monitor in a rich organization was usually more interesting than service in a poor one.

Control of residential life was lower on the Party's agenda, because of costs rather than ideals, than control of workplaces. Shanghai people in the 1950s thus still had more alternatives of life-style in their homes than in their

---

[9] *XMBWK*, March 9, 1957.

[10] Wayne Cornelius, "Urbanization and Political Demand-Making," *American Political Science Review* 68 (September 1974): 1125–46, analyzes this comparatively, though not in China.

[11] Based on statistics in *NCNA*, July 18, 1959.

[12] *NCNA*, August 13, 1957. These illegal salesmen were called "yellow oxen" (*huang niu*).

[13] *XWRB*, March 8, 1957. Women comprised over 70 percent of these admitted cadres, and 80 percent of all lane cadres were women.

factories or stores. This was especially clear in the sphere of religion, which Shanghai's Communists did not seriously try to alter, except when organized churches threatened to assume political roles. At Shanghai's Yufo Temple, a two-week festival in May 1956 celebrated the Buddha's arrival in Nirvana. Famous monks from many parts of China provided sermons.[14] Campaigns were not launched against this kind of activity in 1956, because the cadres were so busy with their economic work.

Daoism, at least in its philosophical form, is surely the most anarchic of all religions; but in early 1957,

> Shanghai Daoist circles held a representative meeting. . . . Formerly, these religious elements seldom contacted each other, but now they learn from one another and always keep in touch. . . . In order to run Daoism well [*sic*], and offer further power to the country's socialist construction, the 'Shanghai Daoist Association Preparatory Committee' will be established. It will elect a council, a director, and a vice-director.[15]

"Doing without doing" (*wu wei er wei*), as in the Daoist motto, was not the socialist style. True to form, Daoists did little to object, at least in public, when officials imagined the sect needed a dependent, modern organization.

Secretly, they were more active. A "Purple Bamboo Hall of Divine Healers," for example, had been "smashed by the Shanghai Public Security Bureau in 1951." But in 1957 a shamaness among its leaders was still in the city, connected with a company that imported coffins from other parts of the country. In the home of the head of the coffin firm, she "restored the reactionary Daoist sect . . . claimed to be the avatar of a living buddha, and a fairy princess descended from heaven."[16] The residential culture of this most modern Chinese city was more diverse than official images had it.

Shanghai's small but cohesive community of Chinese Muslims began to organize politically, in the open months of 1956 and early 1957.[17] A Protestant theological seminary opened in Shanghai during late 1956.[18] When Typhoon Wanda damaged a cross on St. Ignatius Cathedral that autumn, workmen were sent not only to repair the cross but also to strengthen the

[14] *NCNA*, May 17, 1956.

[15] *XMBWK*, March 12, 1957.

[16] *WHB*, December 28, 1958.

[17] *XWRB*, August 22, 1957, reported that Muslim leader Jin Youyun wanted to establish a political organization of Shanghai Muslims; so he was called a rightist.

[18] *NCNA*, October 9, 1956.

tower and walls.[19] The religious culture of the time was very mixed, and it provides a measure of the state's limits—or at least its priorities—during the Transition to Socialism.

Youth cultures were also diverse at this time, especially because greater central control of the economy made access to jobs more difficult. From January to October 1956, the city government conducted a roundup of seventeen thousand "vagrants" (*youmin*). Fully 35 percent were given factory jobs in Shanghai. Another 18 percent were sent to their hometowns, mostly in rural areas of the municipality. Half were sent farther away, but some may well have returned.[20] Removal of vagabonds from the city had been on the official agenda for years, but now resources were put into this policy at a time of economic expansion and employment. The effect of these removals (even though many came back) was to strengthen the local monitors who were designated to oversee residences.

Western media have suggested that China's difficulties with juvenile delinquency are new products of the reform period under Deng Xiaoping. But street gangs of unemployed youths were plentiful in the mid-fifties (as were Red Guard bands by the late sixties). In 1957, for example, a gang called the "Ten Brothers," whose leader had been jailed for thieving and fighting, split over how to divide the spoils of a robbery. More than fifty members of one faction appeared for a brawl on an appointed evening, but their opposition failed to show. Instead, the police had been informed, and the gang members were all arrested.[21] Girls, as well as boys, participated in activities of this sort. In one late 1956 case, police sent twenty-five young gang women to a "Female Reform School" that the city maintained for such people.[22]

Young workers also formed bands that tangled with groups of the unemployed, reportedly to "make trouble" (*nao shi*). "Their actions are disadvantageous to the working class, to themselves, and to social construction," according to a newspaper. Some gangs, by 1957, apparently consisted mainly of worker-label youths. Other clubs seem to have been mainly ex-bourgeois. At least, one young activist claimed, "These teddy boys are created by the influence of capitalist thinking."[23] Tighter organization in Shang-

---

[19] *NCNA*, August 5, 1956. Party distrust of the Roman Catholic church surfaced during the Antirightist Campaign. For example, a believer was dubbed a rightist for criticizing cadres who had commandeered a church for a secular meeting at the time of a mass; see *XWRB*, May 4, 1957.

[20] *XWRB*, November 28, 1956.

[21] *XWRB*, September 11, 1957.

[22] *XWRB*, November 19, 1956.

[23] *XWRB*, June 22, 1957.

hai, which the mid-1950s brought, was already creating aversions among youths with different labels.

Discipline in schools was a related problem, since the instructors were overwhelmingly from families with labels that became worse in 1957. Shanghai's Education Bureau reported incidents in which students rebelled against faculty, despite very strong Chinese traditions of respect for teachers. In one case, middle-school students insisted on "turning away from a teacher's lessons and gathering to sing songs." In another, they "bolted the door of the classroom and refused admission to the teacher." In a third, at a primary school, students "propped a waste paper basket on the top of a door, scheming to make it the teacher's headgear."

These incidents resemble some moments in the Cultural Revolution, when campaigns again became a form of play for children (as well as a serious conflict among local elites). In families, children quickly pick up the meaning of their elders' political experiences in campaigns like the Transition to Socialism. The causes of these tensions by late 1956, were considered to be "very complicated. . . . Schools have become large and overcrowded. . . . Some of the teachers have lost enthusiasm." A newspaper ruminated, "Another cause was the neglect of some students, who are loosely labeled 'backward' and who have no clear understanding of their own futures."[24]

Proletarians formed clubs at this time, and these usually had official sponsorship. The Young Communist League managed a shooting range and marksmanship clubs in each district of Shanghai by the beginning of 1957.[25] By the next year, a major program conducted by army instructors certified no fewer than 310,000 Shanghai youths as trained marksmen.[26] This movement presaged extensive army involvement in residential affairs after 1963.

Shanghai's culture remained varied and colorful, in comparison with less prosperous places in China, despite movements to standardize it. Newspapers might rail at "evil tendencies in social dance parties" or "the general fostering of a bourgeois way of life."[27] But the Party lacked the personnel with the informal prestige to change such things quickly. The influence of Shanghai's capitalist years still affected its life-styles deeply. In early 1957, when the newly socialized Shanghai Underwear Company realized it could sell more goods, it "organized two teams to measure the figures of people in different places," and it "investigated the styles, colors, and qualities de-

[24] *NCNA*, November 21, 1956.

[25] *QNB*, January 1, 1957.

[26] *NCNA*, October 6, 1958. See also *QNB*, December 21, 1956, and *XMBWK*, May 5, 1957.

[27] *XWRB*, November 28, 1956.

manded."[28] Even socialist managers could plan to sell underwear in many colors, not just red. Policies of pressure became official precisely because the government lacked more reliable means to exert power out in the city's neighborhoods.

THE EFFECTS OF SOCIALIZATION ON STUDENTS AND INTELLECTUALS

Shanghai's secondary education system, by the 1956 Transition to Socialism, was larger than ever before. Double sessions had started at most schools in 1953, and during the next three years enrollment rose by 350,000 at the middle and primary levels. One tenth of this increment was financed by the double-session policy alone.[29] But this more democratic enrollment, combined with an official will to save money, also meant the schools were more crowded. Teachers worked harder than before. Most of them, however, had long worked in government-monitored institutions; even the mid-1950s mostly hurt higher-level intellectuals. But by 1957, more ordinary teachers were severely overworked too.

The 1955 Elimination of Counterrevolutionaries Campaign, though it purged only a few important writers such as Hu Feng, had been the first major post-1949 police campaign against many highly ranked intellectuals. Some were asked then to compose autobiographies starting with activities at age eight, and their essays were studied in small groups. According to policy, "rightist" deviations found in such narratives were to be treated less harshly than "leftist" deviations that showed excessive zeal in the people's interest.[30] The campaign caused some suicides. Its main effect for high intellectuals was a parallel, in the cultural sphere, to the simultaneous effect on businessmen of increasing government control of markets. It frightened them into complying with further changes during the Transition.

In January 1956 (the month of socialization in business too), 115 private middle schools, 42 tutorial schools, and 606 private primary institutions became public.[31] At first, it may seem surprising that these academies remained

---

[28] *XMBWK*, February 25, 1957. A later report on the scandal of antirightism in this underwear company appears in *XWRB*, March 26, 1957, which lists four nonjudicial sanctions against private-side representatives: dismissal (*chezhi*), demotion (*jiangzhi*), recording mistakes (*jiguo*), or warning (*jinggao*).

[29] *QNB*, January 11, 1957. Of the increment, it can be calculated from raw figures that 24 percent were middle-school students.

[30] Robert Loh, *Escape from Red China* (New York: Coward-McCann, 1962), pp. 165–70.

[31] *NCNA*, January 19, 1956.

outside the public sector for seven years after the Communist victory. But revolution was not a sudden event, created by waving a wand; it required staff and resources over many years. Education was not, after the early reforms that the Korean War made cheap because of bourgeois patriotism, a high priority for the Party cadres. So schools were not nationalized quickly. The first comprehensive plan to unify Shanghai's secondary curriculum in all institutions came in 1956.

Higher education reforms at the time of the Korean War had been extensive and surprisingly easy for the Party; but after that, the CCP concentrated on businesses, which had a higher priority. Funds were scarce for universities. Even the Shanghai Construction Engineering College, for example, had so little dormitory space that some students moved into "grass sheds" (*caopeng*), with walls made of coarse rushes and windows, doors, and mattresses all of straw.[32] Despite this benign neglect, university students complained in mid-1956 that administrators tried to regiment them too much:

> Students in oral exams just recite what the teachers tell them. . . . Everything is fixed with great regularity by the administration; so the students fail to organize and arrange their own living. . . . They obey the national [job] distribution but show no initiative. . . . Our working, sleeping, and eating hours—and all social activities—are fixed by the administration. We are most dissatisfied with this kind of mechanized life [*jixiehua de shenghuo*] and nursery care. . . . This cannot go on.[33]

The complaints centered not just on regimentation, but on the lack of budget for facilities that might have helped sustain a sense of community in schools. All four thousand students at Tongji University had access to a single piano. They had no more than three Ping-Pong tables. The nine hundred women students shared ten showers. In the university clinics, "doctors don't even bother to examine their patients; they just pass out prescriptions." Lighting in classrooms and dorms was poor. At this engineering university, there were no scientific journals "suitable for college students. . . . Some of the students' hair grows gray before their time."[34]

Despite the official indolence and lack of resources that underlay these complaints, the government standardized universities' hiring procedures in the mid-1950s. Instructors were divided into twelve salary grades (*jibie*), three each for full professors, associate professors, lecturers, and assistants.

---

[32] *QNB*, December 21, 1956.
[33] *JFRB*, August 16, 1956.
[34] Ibid.

Hiring any full professor, even in minor institutions, had to be approved by the Ministry of Higher Education in Beijing, and in Shanghai's major national universities, so did hiring at any of the next six ranks down. Copies of the files on all university teachers above the assistant level were kept in Beijing, at the State Council's Bureau on Experts.[35] This gave Party authorities readily available information about many intellectuals.

The government's quid pro quo, in 1956 at least, came in the form of effusive promises that intellectuals would be treated better. Government money was pledged for libraries, museums, conferences, and research assistants, as well as better medical care and housing.[36] Unemployed intellectuals were urged to register and were given work as teachers.[37] Scientists in fields ranging from horticulture to mathematics made twelve-year plans for their research (though these seldom lasted through 1967).[38] Shanghai's learned societies, with more than ten thousand members, held seven hundred seminars in the year after March 1956.[39] "Advancing toward science" was an upbeat slogan to match the change toward socialism.[40]

Academic standards nonetheless still crucially affected decisions in 1956 schools. One technical institute in Shanghai, which had admitted a group of workers and peasants in a previous campaign, flunked two-thirds of them during that relatively liberal period.[41] Jiaotong University, the Shanghai Mechanical Engineering College, and other schools recruited students with "high, precise, sharp" minds (and they were later criticized for this error in the Cultural Revolution).[42]

The liberal era did not guarantee future stability in official attitudes toward intellectuals. In 1956, the portion of high school graduates promoted

---

[35] In 1959, this "Zhuanjia Ju" became the "Science and Technology Committee" (Kexue Jishu Weiyuanhui). The information is from a Hong Kong interviewee, who had attended or taught at universities in Shanghai, Yunnan, and Canton. See also *Zhonghua renmin gongheguo fagui huibian* (Collection of laws and regulations of the People's Republic of China) (January–June 1959), 9:109.

[36] *XWRB*, March 7, 1957, and *NCNA*, March 10, 12, 1956.

[37] *NCNA*, March 17, September 13, 1956; see also *RMRB*, May 23, 1956.

[38] *WHB*, March 9, 1957.

[39] *XWRB*, March 7, 1957.

[40] *Xiang kexue jin jun.*

[41] *HQ* 3 (March 1968): 7–13. The Shanghai Mechanical Engineering Academy flunked twenty-nine of forty-four worker-peasants in one class during 1956 (ibid.).

[42] *Gao, jing, jian*; ibid. *HQ* claimed that Ke Qingshi opposed Chen Peixian on these educational admissions policies throughout the whole period from 1956 to 1966; but there is scant contemporary evidence to prove that hypothesis, and the 1968 source for it could well be biased. The assertion that Chen (but maybe Ke, too) opposed flunking academic failures who were Party members is backed up by some anecdotal statistics.

to colleges rose by one-fifth over 1955.[43] At least 8 percent of university graduates were not expected to find work after receiving their diplomas, however. The number of these graduates hired was not much greater than in earlier years, though now more of them sought jobs.[44] Such problems were soon solved by more government control of promotions. In 1957, the rate of secondary graduates entering universities was about half that of 1956, because of the Antirightist Campaign.

Party admission for intellectuals was another matter. Many pre-Liberation CCP members in the city had a college education, but the rate of new recruitment for really distinguished intellectuals between 1949 and the Transition to Socialism had been low. The Party's Shanghai newspaper admitted in mid-1955 that "during the past few years, only five full professors have become Communists."[45] Rates of Party recruitment among ordinary intellectuals were also surprisingly low. Only seventy-three young lecturers and assistant professors and seventy-eight schoolteachers joined the Shanghai Party in the first half-decade of Communist rule. Few high-level intellectuals were recruited into the Party between Liberation and 1956.

Early in that year, however, the rate went up (though it remained lower than leaders implied in speeches about the importance of intellectuals). Distrust was evident between intellectuals' unofficial leaders in local units and Party monitors who had been sent to oversee them.[46] The Party's status in Shanghai, as a representative of the state but separate from important parts of society, created a situation in which "democratic" and nonaffiliated people could often be most useful to Communist goals if they remained outside the Party, at least publicly. An ex-Communist interviewee said that the CCP would "consider whether their role might be greater if they remained democrats, or would be greater if they entered the Party." Sometimes it was decided "to absorb them into the Party without announcing their identity among democrats; so they can still have a good chance to lead democratic

[43] Figures covering the whole country are given in Jürgen Henze, "Higher Education: The Tension between Quality and Equality," in *Contemporary Chinese Education*, ed. Ruth Hayhoe (Armonk, N.Y.: Sharpe, 1984), p. 116.

[44] Deduced from figures in *GMRB*, June 19, 1955, and *JFRB*, July 5, 1956. The latter source gives many statistics, including data from which it can be calculated that 36 percent of Shanghai's 1950–56 university graduates were in humanities (*wenke*).

[45] *JFRB*, April 25, 1955, did not specify the time; but apparently the whole 1949–55 period was meant.

[46] *GMRB*, March 18, 1956, gives data on a mass admission of eighty-four Communists at Fudan University in February 1956; but apparently just a quarter of these were instructors, and none were full professors.

persons."[47] It is difficult to know, for example, how many of Shanghai's deputy mayors in this period entered the Party secretly (*mimi rudang*). A statistical comparison of the work done by the deputy mayors who were announced Party members and the others shows no significant difference between the groups.[48]

Party recruitment reached a peak in June 1956, when twenty thousand new Shanghai members were admitted. Only one-tenth of 1 percent of the entire membership were "high-level intellectuals," even after this enrollment. Workers now made up over 60 percent of the municipal Party; but some others were educated people who had come in before 1949, and the ranks of "workers" at this time also included some intellectuals.[49] The rush of admissions in 1956 shows that major Party leaders wanted to take on cadres from more diverse Shanghai groups, but their policy was applied unsystematically. Local monitors from nonintellectual backgrounds had no wish to admit rivals.

Other policies supported recruitment to the Communist Youth League and to satellite "democratic parties." The League increased its Shanghai membership by 79 percent from 1955 to 1957, mostly because of a campaign for this purpose in mid-1956.[50] Among some good-label, or favored, youths, the League was a stepping-stone for quick rotation up to the Party. The chairmanship of the CYL in one Shanghai district had eight incumbents in 1956 alone (apparently because of an aversion, later dropped, against having Party members head League units).[51] But the numbers are such that clearly most League members were never admitted to the Party.

The Democratic League, the Revolutionary Committee of the Guomindang, and other specialized "democratic" parties also had major recruitment drives in 1956. Some more than doubled their membership.[52] But in 1956, neither CYL membership nor democratic party membership represented a real dispersion of political power to new social groups. These changes mainly meant more open, regularized, explicit dependence on the CCP. Labels determined which organizations people should join; CCP super-

---

[47] Interview in Hong Kong with an ex-cadre who had been in Shanghai.

[48] Lynn White, "Leadership in Shanghai, 1955–69," in *Elites in the People's Republic of China*, ed. Robert A. Scalapino (Seattle: University of Washington Press, 1972), p. 369.

[49] *LDB*, June 28, 1956.

[50] *QNB*, January 11, 1957, and a related article in the issue of January 1.

[51] *QNB*, January 22, 1957.

[52] *GMRB*, January 21, 1957. The earlier big expansion of "democratic parties" had coincided with the Korean War; cf. *NCNA*, January 28, 1951.

visors were appointed for each of them; and the recruiting came in the form of campaigns.

INTELLECTUALS BLOOM

In the Hundred Flowers period, intellectuals were particularly eloquent in expressing their resentment of this pattern. As a biochemist said,

> There is too much blind obedience in the Party. The cadres who are CCP members have absolute power and are arbitrary. Specialists who are not Party members have offices but no power. . . . This wastes talent and time. . . . Cadres pay no attention to the opinions of others and force people to accept their orders. . . . The twelve-year plan is just another piece of formality. . . . Many Party leaders like others to call them "heads" [*shou-zhang*]. This is the bureaucratic style of the feudal period.[53]

An engineer said, "Many intellectuals are bored, because they have nothing to do."[54] A physiologist complained, "Research institutes need the leadership of real scientists. . . . Those who are interested in scientific work are sent elsewhere. . . . Those who have relatives in Taiwan or America are not allowed to go abroad for further study. These comrades are considered unreliable in politics, second class citizens. Such restrictions are inappropriate for high-rank researchers."[55]

Average intellectuals were almost as scathing in their critiques of excessive labeling and bossing. The city's Education Bureau was said "not to understand the working conditions of the lower levels; as a result, schools become independent kingdoms of the principals."[56] A non-CCP teacher said, "The Party leadership in Caoyang Middle School employs its favorites and promotes cadres without justification. The school is ruled by cliques, and there is no democracy."[57] Another instructor pointed out that "Party members like to say the thinking of scholars and experts is backwards; but this has a great [negative] impact on activeness."[58]

[53] *XWRB*, May 15, 1957.
[54] *XWRB*, May 18, 1957.
[55] *XWRB*, May 16, 1957.
[56] *XWRB*, May 15, 1957.
[57] *XWRB*, July 17, 1957. This non-Party critic praised the Party secretary over the school's principal; their feuds had clearly been the staff's preoccupation for some time.
[58] *XWRB*, May 15, 1957.

THE ANTIRIGHTIST CAMPAIGN
AMONG RESIDENTS AND INTELLECTUALS

The struggle sessions of summer and autumn, 1957, established among intellectuals a strong principle of guilt by association. These meetings expanded the dossiers on intellectuals, and it became clearer than before that friendships alone could justify the damning of "rightists." This practice, once it became customary, extended the system of labels by linking it to an assumption that patron-client links were normal for all interactions, either among state representatives and their underlings, or among others.

Retrospective reports show that, on secret orders from CCP leaders in Shanghai, many urban units were expected to dub 5 percent of their members "rightists." Universities were supposed to label at least 7 percent of their faculty this way, and if possible an equal portion of their students.[59] Often the incriminating nexus assumed in an accusation would be farfetched. A major charge against a Shanghai Democratic League officer, for example, was that he had received letters from a friend of one of the most prominent national rightists in Beijing.[60] A woman physics student was guilty because she had befriended the daughter of a prominent rightist.[61]

Not only did guilty people come in groups; they had done so for years. Long-past deeds were dredged up, to show how original the sins of the accused had been. A rightist professor, who retained his post at Fudan University, was accused of transgressions since the 1930s at least. He had been introduced to the GMD liberal intellectual Hu Shi; then he had been linked to the translators of disapproved books (including one by Chiang Kai-shek). In the 1942 CCP rectification, "under the pretense of helping the Party in reform, he falsely labeled CCP members, aiming to blacken the Party's leaders." In another case, a physicist before 1949 had developed explosives that could be detonated at cold temperatures. So he was accused of rightism for potentially helping the GMD against the Soviet Union.[62] But the actual "crime" of the rightists was current political dissent. They comprised an alternative elite that could have run Shanghai. Understandably, new local monitors after 1956 were wary of them. In the city's most important orga-

---

[59] This information comes from interviews in Hong Kong (from people who could not document the assertions), but also from sources such as Yue Daiyun, *To the Storm* (Berkeley and Los Angeles: University of California Press, 1985), pp. 32, 102.

[60] *XWRB*, July 20, 1957; Peng Wenying received letters from a friend of Luo Longji.

[61] *XWRB*, July 12, 1957; Ma Mingmin was a friend of Wang Zaoshi's daughter.

[62] *ZW*, August 17, 1957, p. 12.

nizations, the rightist label was pinned on whomever that organization's Party patrons distrusted most.

By no means had all the rightists criticized the CCP during the Hundred Flowers period. Some had been chary of that movement all along. One Shanghai movie actor revealed his position with the logically elegant statement, "Only lies are safe."[63] Many did nothing. Others incited younger or braver people to make the criticisms instead and "passively advocated setting fires [that is, criticizing new cadres] to settle old scores."[64]

Whatever the evidence under which people were assigned rightist labels—and often it was not revealed until years later[65]—political resentment against many Communist supervisors assigned to work units was real. One rightist, using phrases that would later become common in the Cultural Revolution, said his Party overseers were "ox ghosts and snake spirits," so that merely a "mild wind and fine rain" would be insufficient to quench the people's anger against them.[66]

At universities, and among nonadmitted youths who wanted to be there, the most important substantive complaint concerned the policy of "promoting excellent students directly without examinations."[67] These officially "excellent students" were mostly from "workers' and peasants' accelerated middle schools" or were cadres seconded for university training. A guidance counselor at Tongji University, writing in the college's regular bulletin, called this policy "sectarian." She said it hurt the quality of education and was "a way to 'sell' students that is just like a wholesale business for goods." Her article apparently struck a responsive chord. By the next day, the walls of the Tongji cafeteria were covered with "signs and cartoons insulting the worker and peasant students. The posters objected that accelerated middle school students are given priority . . . and they should go back to their workposts. When Tongji students from accelerated middle schools entered the canteen, some of the undergraduates shouted at them, telling them to get

---

[63] *XWRB*, November 28, 1957, by which time actor Shi Hui's brother Shi Jing was serving a fifteen-year jail sentence for being less taciturn.

[64] Ibid.; Chen Renbing, a rightist professor at Fudan, was said to "dian huo" to "suan jiu zhang."

[65] Liang Heng and Judith Shapiro, *Son of the Revolution* (New York: Random House, 1983), indicate that the original charge against one of Liang's parents (which caused their divorce and much alienation) was fatuous but secret until 1979. This example is typical.

[66] Ibid. *Niugui sheshen* was the Cultural Revolution's most frequent reptilian label. *Hofeng xiyu* contrasted, by 1967, with "violent wind and torrential rain" (*paofeng zouyu*). These uses in 1957 set important precedents.

[67] *Youxiu sheng mianshi zhisheng.*

out."[68] A group of students, apparently from bourgeois backgrounds, printed newsletters attacking the admission-without-examination policy. These were distributed not only in Shanghai but also in three neighboring provinces, where similar conflicts among youths with different labels also existed.

It was easier to be bold during the Hundred Flowers period than during the Antirightist period, however. Divisions between democrats emerged readily in struggle sessions.[69] The CCP guaranteed immunity to some leaders in democratic parties, but only so they could preside over the rectification of other members. A deputy mayor of Shanghai, in the "Revolutionary Committee of the GMD" satellite party, formed a group of noncritical democrats early in the Antirightist movement. These notables were not persecuted, because they helped the crusade against rightists.[70]

This campaign was uneven not only among different local leaders, but also geographically in Shanghai. In Putuo District, especially in its people's court, the Hundred Flowers period had been lively, and the Antirightist Campaign was therefore severe.[71] In some areas such as Xuhui District (which has a Catholic religious tradition, good residential neighborhoods, and several publishing houses), high ratios of bourgeois-labeled people made 1957 exceptionally turbulent. In other areas (Putuo is an example) concentrations of schools, colleges, factories, and other large institutions where dependence on Party bosses was already advanced brought the same result. The 1957 movements, like other campaigns, arose not just from policy documents, but from social factors whose distribution could be measured in different parts of the city.

Even ordinary Shanghai people, who did not participate in the 1957 politics of criticism and reprisal, were changed that year by the examples they saw around them. These events severely embarrassed both the state (because so many of the criticisms were true) and its enemies (who were finally repressed). The high leadership of the city's Party was able, in this situation, to revive long-standing efforts toward moving many teachers and ordinary office workers away from well-financed institutions to smaller units or toward the countryside. Many intellectuals were rusticated; that label, for

---

[68] *XWRB*, June 25, 1957.

[69] *XWRB*, June 17, 1957, recorded a conflict in the democratic Jiusan Study Society between Secretary General Zhong Mingsheng and member Wang Hengshou.

[70] *XWRB*, July 25, 1957. The deputy mayor may also have been a Communist secretly admitted to the Communist Party (*mimi rudang*).

[71] *XWRB*, September 26, 1957.

many years after 1957, officially meant they had a moral obligation to become peasants.

Jiaotong University, for example, had established a branch at Xian, the historic capital in a poor part of western China. By mid-1957, the effort to ship more of Jiaotong's staff out of Shanghai became increasingly effective.[72] Fudan University also sent down more than one hundred teachers "to work in villages." The rusticates included official monitors as well as older intellectuals; off to the fields went the first secretary of the university's CYL, a member of its Party standing committee, and ten teachers of politics.[73]

Favored cadres generally spent little time away from Shanghai, however, whereas rightists often received rural household registrations that prevented their return. Many monitors went for only a short while. Other youths might be rusticated (*xia xiang*) or sent down to factories (*xia chang*). By late 1957, this was an ordinary part of their education.[74] The Party was insufficiently staffed, however, to allow this kind of training for long spells among its main members. Their ability to command obedience within the city rose, after the weeding out of dissenters; so the lack of alternative leadership in many units increased the dependence of ordinary members on CCP appointees, whether or not the latter went through purification rituals in the countryside.

More dissidence had surfaced in schools than in businesses during early 1957. Toward the end of that year, the Party transferred 250 high-ranking local CCP members from work in economic and financial fields to work in education and culture.[75] The Party learned, during 1957, about the weakness of its base in residential and cultural institutions. The first all-city meeting of lane cadres ever to be held in Shanghai took place in June 1957, after the Antirightist Campaign had begun.[76] Its purpose was to ensure that criticism sessions in work units would result in the long-term absence of rightists and bourgeois-origin students from Shanghai neighborhoods.

The effects of 1957 were to confirm the division between favored and nonfavored labels in the city and to strengthen local units' Party leaders. New controls worked better on ambitious people, who were willing to cooperate with the Party, than on independents who were willing to accept low status. As one rightist said, leaders (especially young activists) became always correct, and nonleaders (especially the old) became constantly

---

[72] *XWRB*, July 13, 1957, and an interview in Hong Kong.

[73] *XWRB*, November 27, 1957.

[74] *LDB*, November 20, 1957.

[75] *XWRB*, November 13, 1957; these 250 Party members were all important enough to be heads of *ju*, *chu*, or *ke* offices.

[76] *XWRB*, June 22, 23, 1957.

wrong.[77] The power of monitors had increased, despite their 1957 embarrassments. They were still relatively few, for such a large and complex city; but their administrative principles—labeling, patronage, and campaigns— were increasingly effective for their short-term goals.

Despite the Transition to Socialism, not all Shanghai people yet thought like socialists. The Party, having assumed at least nominal management of the city's remaining independent institutions in 1956 and having weathered the storms of 1957 with less damage than its enemies sought to inflict, had apparently perfected techniques that could make Shanghai Communist. But the CCP's achievements of this era were more impressive than solid, and years of further struggle would prove necessary to achieve real socialism. The short-term accomplishments of the pressure policies were still more obvious, at this time, than their long-term costs.

[77] *XWRB*, September 8, 1957.

CHAPTER 6

The Great Leap Forward
and Salvation by Work, 1958–1962

They can, in fact, conceal a fifth of their harvest. Certainly the
official size of the harvest goes down, but the actual grain is
still there. That is why I often advise local leaders not to be too
harsh on peasants if they conceal part of their harvest.
—MAO TO POMPIDOU

The Great Leap was no political relaxation; but after the traumas of 1957,
it was at least a change. People who survived the previous campaigns with
their reputations intact could now prove themselves, by exhausting themselves. On this basis, they could hope for respectability in the newly socialist
Shanghai. The Leap was billed as a struggle against nature, against the obstacles that kept China economically backward.[1] It was a social struggle,
too, but of a new and sublimated sort. This huge campaign reflected a continuing conflict between labeled groups, as well as between individuals in
new hierarchies. It was an effort to alter these tensions and channel them to
official ends. Almost everyone (except rightists) had a legitimate opportunity
to work hard in 1958. The Leap was obviously a campaign, but less obviously directed against specific groups than earlier campaigns. Labels and
patronage were important for this period—because they had been applied
earlier, not because they were extended then. The irony is that by 1961 the
Leap's *unintended* economic effects had further sharpened the importance
for individuals of both labeling and patronage by reducing nonofficial resources even more than official ones, even though Leap policies were not
designed to raise coordination so much as to inspire people.

---

[1] If the 1958–61 campaign was a scientific struggle against nature, as much of the literature
at that time described it, then clearly nature won. The Great Leap Forward (*da yuejin*) is also
often called the "Three Red Banners" (*sanmian hongqi*, that is, the general line of building
socialism, the Leap, and the people's communes). Some scholars prefer the latter name because
it identifies the movement as Mao's, but this title also may tend to identify the Leap as an early
attempt to make cultural revolution. One aim of this book is to marshal evidence that Mao was
not the main cause of either of these two huge movements, even though his support of them
was an immediate cause. Another is to show that, despite their historical relationship, these two
events were very different from each other for the vast majority of urban people who lived
through them.

The Leap was a movement for mobilization, not control.[2] This campaign-against-nature had precedents in other countries. Such movements, at least in cities, may be defined most easily as periods of rising state investment;[3] and their archetype is Stalin's "big push" for Soviet industrialization in the 1930s. Even market economies have seen periods of intense, state-sponsored investment.[4] There is nothing specifically Leninist about this practice. The United States from the Civil War to the depression,[5] Germany in its *Grundzeit* under Bismarck, and Japan under the Meiji reformers suggested precedents to Chinese politicians who were interested in industrial leaps. By 1958, the Chinese government was impatient, as these earlier governments had been; and 1957 bequeathed it a decentralized array of cadres to administer a big push.[6]

After an Antirightist Campaign that had been grim for the Party and its opponents alike, more investment made a popular program. Economic planning nonetheless has slower effects than political campaigns, because blueprints and capital construction require time lags. Heavy industrial investment that became important for Shanghai's output by 1958 had been mostly designed in 1956. A "Great Leap Forward" in the political sense was nonetheless first announced for Shanghai at a huge meeting of workers on March 16, 1958—a month and a half before the first commune in Henan province, and half a year before the national push to communize rural areas.[7]

This chapter, and this book, do not deal mainly with China's peasants and countryside. So the interpretation of the Leap here will be from an urban, partial, atypical point of view. Such an approach to the event will show new things about it, and one of the most important is that Shanghai was affected by the production shortfalls of rural communes only with a time

[2] See the most creative book yet published on the PRC, Franz Schurmann's *Ideology and Organization in Communist China* (Berkeley and Los Angeles: University of California Press, 1966).

[3] Analogues to 1958, in the following decade, would be 1963 or 1969, not 1966–67. This can be partly seen in investment rates, as noted by David Bachman, "Leaps and Retreats in the Chinese Political Economy," forthcoming article.

[4] The most suggestive treatment is still Karl Polanyi's *The Great Transformation* (New York: Rinehart, 1944), which shows how the British state sponsored entrepreneurs in some periods.

[5] Read how industrial interests kept power from the Civil War to the New Deal in E. E. Schattschneider's *The Semi-Sovereign People* (New York: Dryden Press, 1960).

[6] Jane Lindsay Lieberthal's "From Cooperative to Commune: An Analysis of Rural Administrative Policy in China, 1955–58" (M.A. thesis, Department of Political Science, Columbia University [ca. 1971]) is still the best analysis of 1955–57 precedents for what happened in the countryside during 1958.

[7] *XWRB*, March 15, 1958.

lag. If this Leap had been an urban phenomenon alone, it would probably have been a more positive experience for many people in the city.

At the beginning of spring in 1958, Shanghai held a "Mass Sports Week." Here a strict construction of the Great Leap policy was in force: One jumper set the national record, with his 4.4-meter pole vault. Officials insisted that "the immediate aim is wide participation rather than setting records."[8] By the end of this week representatives of sports organizations refused to divulge record times, lest mere statistics take the edge off popular involvement. The Mass Sports Week reached its "climax" when several million Shanghai residents exercised, all together, to the rhythms of music broadcast over the city radio. The Great Leap was a movement for discipline, but it did not exclude people on the basis of their class labels or positions in work units.

EFFECTS OF THE LEAP ON MANAGERS

The official cult of exertion and exhaustion was not new in 1958. Early in the previous year, for example, "many doctors [were] already practicing a 24-hour-a-day duty system. They have to attend patients, visit sickrooms, perform emergency treatment, teach, and work in factories."[9] Pressure of this sort during the Leap only continued the expectation, after the liberal period of 1956–57, that capitalist experts would be mobilized. But now, with the rightist label a potential threat even to people with presentable histories, the Party needed to provide no quid pro quo for such efforts on the part of non-CCP local leaders. Positive incentives were also resources for this movement: public praise, activist awards, and medals. Even cadres, by 1958, were widely expected to press themselves to full capacity. They had to join the remaining bourgeois experts in a mutual expiation of what had happened in 1957.

Groups for political work (*zhengzhi gongzuo*) visited factories to assure that both "public" and "private" administrators would spend time in workshops, doing manual labor.[10] They also tried to continue enforcement of the bureaucratic streamlining campaign. They urged firms to reduce the number of offices and incumbents, to simplify rules, and to send more cadres of all kinds for part- or full-time productive labor.[11]

Despite the tensions in this campaign (and despite continued repression

8 *NCNA*, April 3, 1958.
9 *XMBWK*, February 18, 1957.
10 *XWRB*, April 24, 1958.
11 *XWRB*, April 25, 1958.

of rightists), official statements in Shanghai about class warfare were relatively conciliatory in early 1958. As the radical mayor Ke Qingshi said,

> Relations between classes have sometimes been explosive, as during the wild attack of the capitalist rightists. But they can be mild, now that the antirightist struggle is victorious and the class enemy has been forced to retire. . . . Since most capitalists and bourgeois intellectuals, who are neutral, accept socialist transformation and the leadership of the proletariat, we should trust the majority of them . . . and try to win as many as possible to the left wing. . . . Facts have shown that persuasion is the most positive and effective Marxist method.[12]

Ke himself was not always as meek, during the Leap, as this implies. In the summer of 1958, the Antirightist Campaign continued, but on an unpublicized basis, and more against cadres than against ex-bourgeois who lacked cadre status. That summer, Ke arranged to have the "rightist" label put on liberal cadres Zhou Ke and Tan Xisan.[13] The extent of such labeling was less widespread than it had been the previous year, and newspapers reported only a few cases involving these "extreme rightist elements" (*jiyou fenzi*), who tended to work in Communist organizations. The vast majority of people in 1958 could justify themselves by hard work, even though this movement among a few high politicians reinforced memories of the previous year.

The official opening in the Leap to Shanghai's most important downwardly mobile social groups, especially the ex-bourgeoisie, affected CCP recruitment. The percentage of Party members in Shanghai's total population jumped from 2.3 percent in mid-1956 to 3.4 percent by mid-1959 (a rise of nearly half in a period of three years).[14] This trend continued into the new decade, and the admittees included professors and engineers as well as more workers.[15] By May 1960, the Shanghai CCP contained 304,000 members, of

---

[12] *RMRB*, January 25, 1958. The speech was delivered a month earlier but was delayed in publication, presumably to keep up pressure for the rustication campaign.

[13] Interview with a person who had been a high cadre in Shanghai at this time. Zhou Ke was among those who opposed a "reckless advance" (*mao jin*) during the Great Leap. Tan Xisan, a Youth League cadre, was reportedly of the opinion that Ke Qingshi worried too much about cultural purity and wanted, for example, to suppress certain kinds of dancing too strenuously. This summer 1958 movement was sometimes called "implementing antirightism" (*fanyou bukou*).

[14] Kau Ying-mao, "Governmental Bureaucracy and Cadres in Urban China under Communist Rule, 1949–1965" (Ph.D. diss., Department of Political Science, Cornell University, 1968), p. 267.

[15] *NCNA*, July 1, 1960.

whom more than one-quarter (80,000) had joined since the start of 1959.[16] Rewards of this sort were available only to people who threw themselves into work for the Leap's policies, but many did, and they were from various backgrounds. Under Leap norms, anyone could atone for bad-class origins by current contributions.

EFFECTS OF THE LEAP ON WORKERS

Somewhat less pressure of this sort was put on ordinary workers, to whom many Party cadres were grateful for support (or at least silence) during the difficult spring of 1957. Real proletarians and peasants were deeply affected by the economic consequences of the Great Leap after 1958, but they did not need the salvation-through-work ethic that sprang from the mutual embarrassment of China's local urban elites. The proletariat was by definition already saved. The separation of persons by label remained potentially important, but the most crucial people thus separated were local leaders.

Unionized workers were the CCP's main mass constituency in Shanghai. Wage policy is a good index of the Party's need for this popular base; and by 1958, the CCP leaders saw this need as great. During the Leap, in contrast with the Transition to Socialism, official wage policy was sharply anti-piece-rate. Four objections were published against payment-for-product wages at this time: First, these incentives were said to destroy solidarity among workers: "Some piece-rate workers are too proud of their high wages and look down on hourly wage laborers. The others dare not raise their efficiency, lest they be ridiculed for working hard in order to get more money."[17] Second, young workers did better under the piece-rate system than did their elders, because they had more energy. So this system was said to cause tension between generations (and as the published critiques did not mention, younger Shanghai workers by 1958 were disproportionately from nonproletarian backgrounds). Third, piece-rate systems were accused of preventing technical innovations, because workers would allegedly maximize production under established systems rather than attempt to invent better methods. Fourth, "the piece-wage system lent itself to the growth of bourgeois ideas among workers and enlarged contradictions between the state and the workers, between the leadership and the masses."[18] Fifth, piecework systems gave

---

[16] *JFRB*, July 1, 1960.

[17] *Jiaoxue yu yanjiu* (Teaching and research), September 4, 1958.

[18] Ibid.

maintenance engineers more power over production workers (and managers).[19] If a machine broke down, an ordinary laborer under this system had to depend on technicians to fix the problem, before he could begin to earn money again.

Piece rates made it more difficult for a Party patron in a work unit to build a reliable clientele among regular workers. This system forced managers to apply pressure for production on laborers. But success in raising output only led the managers' own superiors to impose higher production quotas. The political problem with this system, from the viewpoint of many cadres who had recently taken charge of factories, was that it reduced their ability to forge tight links of dependency with their proletarian charges. In October 1958, twenty thousand Shanghai workers were thus switched to hourly rates. More than 100,000 were scheduled to make this change soon thereafter.[20]

Politics within work units also spurred a revival of the traditional apprentice system. The increasingly "cellular" structure of the economy, along with a decentralization of budgets, allowed Communist managers to finance new procedures for choosing members of their work forces.[21] This meant "apprentices usually come straight from middle schools. . . . They are supplied with food, clothing, medical care, and other necessities."[22] They naturally developed personal commitments to the managers responsible for hiring them into these choice regular jobs.

Such changes required money. "Economic construction" took only 16 percent of all Shanghai municipal expenditures in 1955, but this increased to 30 percent during the Transition to Socialism in 1956—and it soared to 75 percent in 1958.[23] The Leap funding in that year for all Shanghai industry

---

[19] See Bruce MacFarlane, "Visit to Shanghai," Sydney, Australia (apparently at the University of Sydney), 1968, informal mimeographed travel notes. For comparison, see the classic by Michael Crozier, *The Bureaucratic Phenomenon* (Chicago: University of Chicago Press, 1964).

[20] *XWRB*, October 19, 1958.

[21] See Audrey Donnithorne, "Comment: Centralization and Decentralization in China's Fiscal Management," and Nicholas R. Lardy's differing "Comment," both in *China Quarterly* 66 (June 1976): 238ff. Statistical confirmation of Donnithorne's position in this debate emerges from Thomas Lyons's *Economic Integration and Planning in Maoist China* (New York: Columbia University Press, 1987), and also from Lynn White's "Shanghai," in a mooted volume on economic bureaucracy in Chinese provinces.

[22] *NCNA*, April 9, 1959.

[23] Percentages were calculated from raw figures in Chen Nai-reunn, ed., *Chinese Economic Statistics: A Handbook for Mainland China* (Chicago: Aldine, 1967), p. 450. This money was raised partly by reducing the 1955 delivery to the central government from 28 percent to 8 percent, but also by cutting funds for social services, culture, and education from 26 to 13 percent—and allegedly by cutting administrative costs from 27 percent to 4 percent. ("Other"

was so extensive, it took more money than had been invested during the whole 1949–57 era.[24] Shanghai's chemical industry nearly doubled the value of its fixed assets in 1958, for example, and this trend continued into the next year. In steel, during the first four months of 1959 alone, Shanghai used nine times more capital than it had in 1958.[25] Policies of pressure for expansion, but not for control, were the norm of the Leap.[26]

New capital during the Leap financed mechanization that often displaced unionized labor, rather than absorbing more of it. Top officials kept tabs on innovations that saved high-paying labor, and they sponsored campaigns for the adoption of such gadgets. One plant claimed to have "reduced the portion of manual work from around 55 percent to 25 percent" during a "mechanization campaign." Another claimed to have reduced an index of "labor" contribution "from 95 percent to 11 percent in a little over one month."[27] Whatever these Leap-style, multifold changes meant specifically, they tended to stratify Shanghai's work force. Sometimes they resulted in a reduction of regular workers, though not of contract workers. This made unionized jobs even more precious, and so tied full-time staff more tightly to their patrons. General economic expansion at this time also meant that socialist bosses could hire more clients than ever before.

Favored workers received unprecedented benefits during the Leap, and the state could finance this only because their proportion among all workers was declining. By the hot summer of 1959, when managers could not get enough raw materials from rural areas and thus had to make layoffs, they were nonetheless solicitous toward their main clientele of unionized workers. They tried to make Shanghai's mills less like infernos, at least for the

---

costs decreased from 3 percent to zero.) The 1955 and 1958 totals would thus each add up to 100 percent, if these portions are correct.

[24] *NCNA*, May 23, 1959; this statement measured the funds in nominal yuan, and it could be tricky either to prove or disprove in real terms. The 1956 (low) assessment bases for valuing the early period's capital may have been used; if so, they qualify the meaning of this report. Nonetheless, 1957 investment was considerable; so the rise in 1958 was sharp by any standard.

[25] Ibid., and *WHB*, June 14, 1959.

[26] Schurmann, *Ideology and Organization*, pp. 410ff., elaborates the choice between "exploitation" and "control" with precedents from, respectively, the Ming's *lijia* and the Qing's *baojia* systems, from civil and military traditions, from natural and administrative villages, and from much else. Schurmann may also intend to link this difference to both the choices, respectively, for "human organization" that inspires activity or "technical organization" that coordinates it, and to choices for "pure ideology" that lets a system adapt to its environs or "practical ideology" that makes it a weapon to change its environs. These last two differences (one from Durkheim, the other from Mannheim) are however not the same—and one of Schurmann's many contributions is to make that clear.

[27] *NCNA*, March 8, 1960.

registered proletariat. Swimming pools, air conditioners for union cinemas, iced soft drinks, moonlight boat trips on the Huangpu River—all these assured that Shanghai workers would keep cool in the economic and climatic heat wave of mid-1959, and would more deeply appreciate their overseers.[28]

Satellite cities, sponsored during the Leap, also fostered the segregation of workers into different groups. Minhang, twenty-five kilometers south of Shanghai, became a major center for electrical equipment. About five thousand people had lived in Minhang during the early 1950s, but seventy thousand came by the end of the decade to staff the new industries, occupy new apartment buildings painted in five colors, and use the thirty-one stores, new hospitals, libraries, cultural centers, theaters, and workers' clubs.[29] A hotel was built for visiting businessmen. A four-lane expressway, lined with trees, connected the new town to central Shanghai.[30] Wujing, also on the Huangpu River fifteen kilometers upstream from the city center, was for chemical industries. The main body of Shanghai's work force, back in the city proper, was stratified but without so much physical segregation.

The Leap's economic problems stemmed from inefficient rural marketing and lack of incentive that affected Shanghai's heavy industries only indirectly and slowly.[31] Heavy industry, not much relying on agricultural supplies, was increasingly important as a portion of the city's overall output. For these reasons, the economic depression struck Shanghai after it hit most other parts of China. The city's heavy industry, which was the sector most dominated by state factories, for the first time produced more than half of the city's whole industrial output in 1959: 53 percent, as against 46 percent in 1958.[32] This city could use capital well, and the economic disaster of the Leap did not originate there. When the slump came, it laid a basis for even more official control of urbanites' daily lives—for reasons the planners had never intended.

---

[28] NCNA, July 14, 15, 1959.

[29] Minhang was on many visitors' itineraries by the early 1960s. See Edgar Snow, *The Other Side of the River: Red China Today* (New York: Random House, 1961), pp. 539–40; Frederick Nossal, *Dateline—Peking* (London: Macdonald, 1962), pp. 189–91.

[30] NCNA, September 1, October 10, 1959. See also BR, February 16, 1960, pp. 17–18. Deputy Mayor Cao Diqiu and others were criticized for the extravagance of the Minhang road during the Cultural Revolution.

[31] G. William Skinner, "Marketing and Social Structure in Rural China," *Journal of Asian Studies* 24, nos. 1–3 (1964–65).

[32] JFRB, May 18, 1960. State-fixed prices affect this result; but from 1958 to 1959 textiles decreased from 33 percent to 27 percent, and other light industries, from 22 percent to 21 percent. This source also indicates that Shanghai's total 1959 annual wage bill increased just 7.2 percent, as against 1958.

MANAGERS FACE THE DEPRESSION:
A STRENGTHENING OF PATRONAGE

Agricultural supply problems accelerated the structural change to heavy industry. Those shortages, much more than the capital-intensive Leap plans, eventually decreased the overall availability of work for ordinary citizens. The input dearths began to reverse what had been a clear trend in 1958 toward more semiformal and illegal firms. Underground businesses, as well as collectives associated with low-level residence committees, were not effectively repressed by the police. But they were deprived of raw materials by the failure of the rural Leap during the "bad years" of 1959–61.[33] Depression, not repression, became the main constraint against the twilight economy.

Managers in 1958–59 had a great deal of discretion over the use of funds they received. Once they got a credit line from the People's Bank on the basis of plans, their use of funds was surprisingly free.[34] So long as an enterprise was fulfilling its quotas, especially for production, and so long as unplanned luxury goods were not openly being made, government authorities did not prevent local managers from controlling enterprise monies. Additional loans might be floated for unexpected medical costs, for extra production drives, or even for workers' education expenses or "welfare tours."[35] In general, reforms of the banking system during the Transition to Socialism reduced the central power of planning ministries over managers. Further reforms in the Leap prevented effective control by the People's Bank.[36]

The independence of managers was also increased by a cultural tendency of Chinese organizations that begin with one function to proliferate into others. "Gigantism" of this kind was officially approved during the Leap.[37] It meant that leaders of an organization were supposed to take responsibility for meeting all the needs of their subordinates, without having to rely on supplies obtained from outside the organization. This propensity to legiti-

[33] See Lynn White, "Low Power: Small Enterprises in Shanghai," *China Quarterly* 73 (March 1978): 45–76.

[34] Interview in Hong Kong with an ex-Communist cadre in economic planning.

[35] *Fuli xing de lüyou*; ibid.

[36] See Carl E. Walter, "Party-State Relations in the People's Republic of China: The Role of the People's Bank and the Local Party in Economic Development" (Ph.D. diss., Department of Political Science, Stanford University, 1981).

[37] Franz Schurmann, *Ideology and Organization*, contrasts the Ford Motor Company, which began by producing autos and stuck with that role, with General Motors, which has branched out into many lines of production. He points out that the branching pattern is usual in China.

mate gigantism in multifunction organizations increased the leaders' ability to make their followers dependent for a greater variety of resources.

A steel mill, for example, could set up a popsicle factory,[38] a swimming pool for workers' use in hot summers, an electric bulb factory to provide jobs for the spouses of the workers[39]—or any other project, however unrelated to steel making—so long as its leaders could create a better sense of community among unionized workers by funding such projects. The assumption that organizations can proliferate their roles for the sake of brotherhood makes them more independent of other organizations and increases the power of local leaders over followers.

The physical wall surrounding any large Chinese factory, university, hospital, or other institution symbolizes this same ideal of tight communal organization. Such walls generally have few gates. The compound is protected by watchmen, who may ask for membership cards (or letters of introduction, signed by members) from anyone wishing to enter. Walls of this sort predate 1949 and are commonly found in Taiwan and other Chinese places, where urban space allows them. But the Leap reforms financed even more cellularity. They did more than carry on the tradition; they reinforced it with new policy.

Leninist discipline, as much as any Chinese cultural norm, suggested a need to know who was included in an organization and who was not. This added a modern vector to the traditional cellularity, and the physical construction of new walls around factories and other institutions was obvious in Shanghai especially during the Leap. Chinese propensities to gigantism and exclusive community were given fresh resources by the official guidelines at that time.[40]

"Private representatives" in joint industries were retired or given technical jobs, while administrative work was increasingly controlled by Party secretaries. As an ex-cadre put it, "Especially after 1958 [that is, after the depression began], state representatives assumed more and more responsi-

---

[38] Interviewees say that the Wuhan Iron and Steel Factory, at least, did establish a popsicle factory in the Leap. The Chinese, rather than specifically Communist, meaning of this is underlined by the fact that the Kaohsiung Iron and Steel Factory in Taiwan has a subordinate ice cream plant.

[39] An example, seen by this author and dating from the Leap, was at the Caoyang New Town housing project in Shanghai. The city's Electric Bulb Company subcontracted work to a small factory, which was staffed mainly by wives of employees of the other corporations (including a steel mill) that formed a consortium to finance the housing project.

[40] Schurmann emphasizes the cultural continuity. The present treatment emphasizes that Leap organizational policies strengthened that tradition, which could have been modernized by opposite policies (such as were later supported by reformers after 1978).

bilities."[41] Within a unit, the top Party leaders were generally concerned to maintain unity among themselves, so that higher authorities would not intervene because of political disputes, and so that private representatives would see less chance to regain their lost status through complaints in a time of economic lack. The city Party's elders were able, with official directives and an increasing monopoly of scarce funds, to give their subordinates an incentive structure that optimized the value of cooperation rather than political conflict.

At the Shanghai No. 1 Iron and Steel Plant by 1961, for example: "Leadership cadres are seriously helping basic cadres, such as workshop chiefs, foremen, and group leaders, in improving their ways of thinking and methods of work. A few of the basic-level cadres are . . . liable to adopt rash attitudes and to handle problems in an oversimplified way."[42] "Heart-to-heart talks" and "short-term training classes" were recommended as means by which factory leaders might correct aberrations or signs of local dissidence. Patronage and dependence may be a long-standing tradition in Chinese culture, but the specific new policies of the late Leap were designed to intensify rather than reduce this habit of clientelism.

Subordinate and alternative leaders, if they were dissatisfied with their situations, had just two options: to complain about the depression, or to cooperate with their bosses regardless of the local economic problems. Their information and resources, which might have allowed more choices, were reduced both by policy and by economic scarcity. So they were faced with a "model of adaptive behavior" strongly favoring dependence.[43]

MORE SOLDIERS AND LOYALISTS
BECOME CADRES IN THE LEAP

By 1959, PLA recruits from the large conscription of 1955, having served their four-year stints, returned to the civilian economy. Many now had enough political status to join Party staff in rich enterprises. This group's assumption of nonmilitary jobs affected the relation between the PLA and

[41] Interview, Hong Kong, with an ex-Party member who had long done economic work.
[42] *RMRB*, June 26, 1961.
[43] Herbert Simon contrasts "models of optimization" involving many alternatives and much information with "models of adaptive behavior" involving only two options and imperfect information. See Karl Deutsch, *The Nerves of Government: Models of Political Communication and Control* (Glencoe, N.Y.: Free Press, 1963), p. 42, and Herbert A. Simon, *Models of Man: Social and Rational* (New York: Wiley, 1957).

Shanghai society and furthered a trend that intensified after 1964, in the two years prior to the Cultural Revolution.

Cadre status had been the customary right of demobilized soldiers since 1949, irrespective of their class origins. The CCP in the late Leap needed all the loyal staff it could get, and the influx of ex-1955 conscripts was therefore welcome. As the *Liberation Daily* pointed out, "Several years' training and education in the army have greatly heightened their [the demobilized soldiers'] political and ideological level. While still in the PLA, many of them gloriously joined the Communist Party."[44]

Many of these veterans took jobs in the city's Public Security Bureau, which was reorganized during the second half of 1958 to incorporate civilian "people's police" units. As leaders of these groups, they could assume important roles as security officers of large factories. Other demobilized soldiers tried to become economic managers directly. Because the army had high prestige among most Shanghai groups, these cadres brought some military discipline (or at least language about it) to large Shanghai companies late in the Leap.

Officialdom also grew at this time because of the incorporation of other groups. After some cadres had returned from "rotation send-down" (*lunliu xiafang*) in 1958, a trickle of further returnees continued for many years. Even rightists came back to Shanghai, especially in 1960–61, though many others remained in rural areas where they would pose no danger to local leaders appointed by the Party.

DISCIPLINE IN DEPRESSION:
CONTRACT WORKERS AND BOURGEOIS

The main problem by 1960 was a shortage of rural materials and markets. Factories were encouraged to "compete" with one another to produce more, despite the resource constraints. Factory leaders urged their charges to make communal commitments to high quotas—and then to fulfill these ahead of schedule.[45] By 1960, however, normative campaigns of this sort, combined with managerial freedom to round up resources anywhere, were together insufficient to solve the problem of severe shortages.

When layoffs became necessary, the contract workers were the first sent back to their villages. Some young workers with dubious family back-

[44] *JFRB*, April 19, 1958; cf. *XWRB*, April 17, 1958, and March 28, 1959.
[45] *NCNA*, March 14, 1958, December 17, 1959, and many other dates.

grounds, even if they had been admitted to unions, could also be induced to become farmers in the Shanghai suburbs.[46] The label system had been sufficiently instilled that when serious labor surplus problems arose in the late Leap, factories could round up the usual suspects for rural work. Some of the rustication was supposed to be permanent. By the autumn of 1960, however, short-term send-downs were also organized among regular workers and commercial staff. These unionized employees were asked to help with the harvest; and their stomachs by 1960 gave incentives for this project, because food was what many people wanted in that time of shortage.[47]

The previous emphasis on heavy industry, and the bias against service and light-industrial projects, had affected even slum areas of Shanghai, where poor proletarians live. In Yaushui Lane, 65 percent of the labor force was employed in industry by 1960; but only 37 percent had been industrial in 1949.[48] This switch probably slowed the effects of Leap unemployment in the urban labor market, which thus depended less on rural input supplies (except food) than light industries would have done. But even in 1960, one-quarter of the workers in Yaoshui Lane were unemployed.[49] Independent urban economic sectors were largely shut down by the rural production failures of the communes in 1961.

The depression was dangerous for the CCP, even as its effects gave official monitors a closer monopoly of resources and jobs. Party leaders in many factories were wary of criticisms that bourgeois-labeled persons, who still had many important technical roles, might raise about the economic mismanagement after 1958. When conferences on this topic were held to sound out views, however, the experiences of 1957 were fresh enough that few or no criticisms were actually heard.[50]

Party leaders apparently distrusted this public silence. So the Shanghai branch of the Chinese People's Political Consultative Conference (including both CCP members and democrats) sponsored study sessions for ex-capital-

[46] Interview with an ex-technician for the Shanghai Textile Machines Factory, who reported on the period 1958–64 and who mentioned that some workers with dubious family backgrounds were sent to Chongming Island. This is a county of Shanghai Municipality that is the third-largest island in China, near the mouth of the Yangtze River.

[47] *XMWB*, September 27, 1960, refers explicitly to food incentives.

[48] Shanghai shehui kexueyuan, Jingji yanjiu suo, Chengshi jingji zu (Shanghai Academy of Social Sciences, Economic Research Institute, Urban Economy Group), *Shanghai penghu qu de bianqian* (The transformation of Shanghai's shack districts) (Shanghai renmin chuban she, 1965), p. 65.

[49] Ibid.

[50] An example is the Shanghai conference from May 12 to 30, 1960. See *NCNA*, June 18, 1960.

ists to discuss current affairs: the rebellion in Tibet, the Cuban revolution, China's "technological and cultural revolution," even "construction work." This was all under the watchful eyes of monitors, and the depression was not on the agenda.[51] The Shanghai YMCA sponsored an "old friends' meeting" of retired Christian preachers, business executives, doctors, engineers, headmasters, and other potentially dissident types, providing "light and interesting activities, intimate talks ... visits to factories, theater parties, hikes, holidays, and dinners"—lest they think too much of what they might have done, had they not retired.[52] On Chinese New Year, 1959, the CCP even sponsored a festive "get-together" for former GMD military and administrative officers in Shanghai.[53] This Saturnalia was mainly ritual, and not much criticism emerged from it. Memories of 1957 were still fresh.

The primary late-Leap attitude toward bourgeois, however, was still that China needed them, and that they could be usefully reformed. As a theoretician put it,

> Within the CCP, there are a number of people from bourgeois families, because the Party was built up and grew in a country that had a large petty bourgeoisie. . . . Under certain historical conditions, advanced elements of the petty bourgeoisie can enter the ranks of the political party of the proletariat. The working class has the historical mission of transforming the majority of the petty bourgeoisie, who have joined its rank and file.[54]

Managers were still divided by labels; socialist monitors were strengthened by the unintended effects of the policies for new communes; and the Leap despite its obvious failures was the most massive campaign yet.

CONCLUSION: CADRE DOMINANCE IN ECONOMIC DEPRESSION

The legitimacy of a dominant role for worker-origin cadres had been reasserted, even in a time of economic disaster. The realization among CCP leaders that their policy could fail so badly led them to be even more eager to substitute their own men for holdovers from the old regime. Especially in

---

[51] *JFRB*, December 31, 1959.

[52] *Tianfeng* (Heavenly wind) (Shanghai), nos. 7–8 (August 25, 1962): 20.

[53] *China News Service* (Shanghai), February 7, 1962.

[54] *Heilongjiang ribao* (Heilungkiang Daily) (Harbin), December 17, 1959, in *SCMP* 2208 (1959): 1; this is not a Shanghai source, but its ideas were widespread in this era.

the newest and best-financed state industries, such as steel, the Party badly wanted new superintendents "promoted from the ranks of the workers."[55] Special courses were established in night colleges, to aid the promotion of worker cadres. By 1961, large "spare-time" educational programs were staffed by factory technicians (partly because the lack of raw materials gave workers spare time then).[56] Socialist managers' recommendations were prerequisite for admission to classes that could lead to promotions. By mid-1961, 800,000 workers in Shanghai were studying in spare-time schools. The city fathers attempted to raise the admission rate to 85 percent of the applicants; but a "state of imbalance" arose because many workers were interested in technical rather than ideological education, and because schools "did not treat different [labeled] students differently" and "did not emphasize current production."[57]

For ordinary employees, the main lesson of the post-Leap depression was to confirm the importance of labels, despite less explicit emphasis on them. Especially as the extent of the economic debacle became evident to everyone, the Party organized meetings of workers to show how much worse the pre-1949 situation had been. Poor workers would address "forums recalling the past and making comparisons," to show how good 1961 was.[58] Workers' armed uprisings were commemorated festively—and workers were urged to keep their arms, especially in case of new adversity for the proletariat.[59]

The head of the Shanghai Trade Union Federation made speeches in the late Leap urging everyone to keep the antirightist struggle going.[60] Proletarian pride was not a victim of the Great Leap's failure, because along with the local centralization of power in firms, it underlay the new local authority structure. Even though the Leap began with a de-emphasis on labeling and monitoring, these policies emerged from it stronger, because of its failure. And precisely because this campaign was not designed mainly to pit local elites against each other, they did not realize at its end that none of them could finally defeat all others. A later, more directly conflictive, campaign in the late 1960s would be needed to put those dreams to rest.

---

[55] *NCNA*, November 2, 1959, refers explicitly to Shanghai's iron industry and says that three of the four hundred team leaders, foremen, and superintendents were recruited from among workers. Because the meaning of "worker," here, is not necessarily tied to "family origin" in the registration books, an exact conclusion is hard to draw.

[56] *NCNA*, April 28, 1961; see also *NCNA*, July 23, 1960, and *XMWB*, June 8, 1961.

[57] *GRRB*, May 14, 1961, article on Shanghai.

[58] *RMRB*, February 26, 1961, article from Shanghai.

[59] *NCNA*, March 21, 1962.

[60] *QNB*, December 18, 1959.

CHAPTER 7

Exhaustion in the Leap among Residents and Intellectuals, 1958–1962

Who am I, unlearned and unlettered, to offer an opinion?
—DR. HU SHI

The most similar 1950s analogue and precedent to the Cultural Revolution was the Antirightist Campaign, not the Great Leap Forward. The relative social resources of local Party elites, compared with those of non-Party notables, were still limited throughout the 1950s. At first, the official optimism of 1958 stirred some hope among families like those stigmatized the previous year that their censure might be diminished. Hard work, rather than class struggle, was the state's main theme by 1958. Urban residents of many kinds could win back their sense of decency, if allowed to earn it fairly. The Leap was of course foreshadowed by 1957; but it was basically different, even though its decentralization of power to mid-level Party patrons was possible only because of mutual embarrassment of Communists and their critics after that experience. For urban people, at least, one of the most important failures of the Leap was that it missed healing the 1957 wounds between local leaderships, because Party leaders did not see where their policies of pressure were leading. That setback opened the way to far more conflict between these elites later.

Local officials garnered more resources in the 1960s, when economic depression changed the life-styles of other urbanites even more sharply than it changed those of cadres. But in 1958, food and shelter were not as fully rationed as they later became. The social prestige of non-CCP leaders had been reduced—but not eliminated—during the Party's political victories before 1958. The Leap, because it ended with more acute embarrassment but also more cornered resources for local Communists, finally increased tensions between them and local rivals.

DIFFERENT RUSTICATIONS FOR DIFFERENT GROUPS

As the Antirightist Campaign against intellectuals waned, the government was able to translate fear among many kinds of nonproletarian families into more rustication of capitalist youths. On Christmas Eve, 1957, a huge crowd sent off five thousand Shanghai secondary school graduates to Wuhu, Anhui Province.[1] Three thousand young people with bourgeois labels came to a meeting in late February 1958, and "they pledged themselves to a complete transformation in three years . . . giving up high wages and other privileges, doing physical labor . . . and urging their families to accept socialist transformation."[2] In April, eleven thousand educated youths went to Anhui and Hubei to create fifteen "large-scale farms."[3] The pressure was not directed against intellectuals and Hundred Flowers critics alone, but also against bureaucrats who had been embarrassed at that time.[4] The meaning of this send-down was ambiguous.

On one hand, it was advertised as socially useful education, especially in agricultural skills. Cadres and ex-bourgeois, both from groups that had suffered 1957 criticisms, were vaguely promised they could relegitimate themselves through rustication and labor. A March 1958 conference for sent-down personnel praised their new abilities, declaring they had "already, in just three months, become people who are capable."[5] Some rusticates became special symbols of the high social prestige that officials wanted for rustication. A few send-down volunteers, for example, were members of the famed Academia Sinica.[6] Cadre rusticates, by mid-1958, were assigned leadership roles in small towns and rural areas. They were the administrative infrastructure for mid-level decentralization in the Leap, empowered now in "real" China, which meant the countryside.

On the other hand, this rustication-and-streamlining amounted to punishment, rather than legitimation, for most of its participants. Party members, including those who had been co-opted from capitalist families because the CCP lacked enough experts, were treated better than students (and much better than rightists). The send-down of favored cadres was by rotation, for three to six months only. Other rusticates stayed longer or indefinitely. As an ex-Communist interviewee said of the majority of volunteers, "They knew this was punishment."

Ex-peasant immigrants to Shanghai were also subject to official hounding.

[1] *XWRB*, December 25, 1957.

[2] *NCNA*, February 27, 1958.

[3] *XWRB*, April 12, 1958. This article still refers to "daxing nongchang," not to communes (*renmin gongshe*).

[4] *XWRB*, January 10, 1958.

[5] *Nongwen nongwu de ren*; *XWRB*, March 18, 1958.

[6] *XWRB*, December 23, 1957. Premier Zhou Enlai visited Academia Sinica members working in two agricultural co-ops (*nongye she*) in the West Suburb of Shanghai (ibid.).

Their send-down was ambiguous—sometimes advertised as a glory, sometimes indistinguishable from a penalty. Poor urban immigrants were forced back to their native villages in early 1958, at the same time capitalists volunteered for emigration. The residents' committee that had jurisdiction over Penglai Bus Station, for example, conducted a major roundup of squatters on the station premises. In a period of just two days, most of the denizens of this area, who had been living separately or without official protection, were shipped away. The remaining "households" averaged more than ten persons. Some squatters were almost surely able to stay because of village or family links with local cadre-patrons.[7]

THE AMBIGUOUS VALUE OF CULTURAL DIVERSITY DURING THE LEAP

The Leap's system of decentralized cadre management, psychological tension, and hard work for downwardly mobile groups—along with favoritism for unionized workers—proved productive for a while. This system allowed flexibility in hiring urban contract workers. It also allowed short-term transfers of city residents to rural areas in crash agricultural seasons. It was motivated in the city folk who did unusual things in 1958 only because of the severity of the previous year's campaign.

To harvest the spring rice crop, many Shanghai colleges closed during the middle of June 1958, and their students went to suburban counties.[8] For gathering the second rice harvest in October and for planting winter crops, a "labor army" totaling 120,000 people went to the suburbs. The press reported with much fanfare that high officials led this labor army.[9] Experiences such as rustication were supposed to teach intellectuals how they could move from "neutral" to "left-bourgeois" and finally to "working class" status.[10] The Shanghai branch of the Democratic League vowed to

---

[7] *XWRB*, January 10, 1958. Practically all (84 out of 89) of these "households" sent down contained only one person. Yet the population in this ward coming from villages outside Shanghai before the roundup had been 195, and the send-down reduced it by almost half, to 106. This implies that the average size of the immigrant households allowed to stay in the city was more than ten persons. Despite the small sample size, this is indirect evidence that the ability to stay in Shanghai depended on personal relations, especially with a protecting cadre, and on the labor value of large families. Three other examples of this kind of rustication are reported in *XWRB*, January 18, 1958.

[8] *XWRB*, June 4, 1958.

[9] *XWRB*, November 21, 1958; on the next year, see *XWRB*, November 1, 1959.

[10] *WHB*, December 5, 1957.

transform "85 percent of its basic-level units" to "five-good" status in 1958. This meant they became good at accepting Party leadership, cooperating, fulfilling assigned tasks, executing plans, and studying political theories. These are all virtues of dependence on the CCP.[11]

The label "rightist" was still difficult to remove in 1958, though by the next year reprieves from this worst badge became more available. As an interviewee said,[12]

> It was not easy to take off the rightist label, once it had been pasted on. There never was a time [prior to 1979] when that title could be removed easily. But sometimes Communists advocated "lenient" management of rightists who improved their political ideas or became model workers. If there was ever a placid period for removing this label, it was during the 1959 Tenth Anniversary celebration of the PRC.

Legal removal of the rightist label followed principles that were not constant over the years. Even when a rightist was declared no longer to deserve that bad tag, the records originally justifying it remained in the ex-victim's file. As everyone knew, they might be used again in a later campaign. The Leap was a time of forgiveness, albeit of an ambiguous sort.

Similar ambiguity was evident in Shanghai's newspapers. These media were of two types, for two different readerships resident in the city. Morning newspapers were generally Party organs, whereas afternoon papers usually appealed to "different groups of readers, whose demands are somewhat different." As the limited-circulation journal for reporters, *News Front*, pointed out in mid-1959, "Their basic mission is the same, but they have to present descriptions of facts from different points of view. Should evening papers publish editorials? [They should, but] this is not easy, because it is difficult for them to find writers [for ex-bourgeois readerships] who can compose good editorials or critical articles."[13] The result, at this time, was official support to publish fewer newspapers for Shanghai's extremely large non-Communist readerships. The audiences, which different media were officially supposed to address, were less finely divided during this general mobilization than before or after it.

Popular religion came under far less criticism during the Leap than during most earlier years following Liberation. The government in 1958, spending so much money then on so much else, even funded a thirteen-story pagoda

---

[11] *NCNA*, March 21, 1958.
[12] Interview in Hong Kong with an ex-Communist.
[13] *Xinwen zhanxian* (News front), no. 11 (June 9, 1959): 5–8.

to house the Buddha's Tooth Relic. A monk was allowed to address the Central Committee of the CCP itself, and he reported widespread religious rites. "In Shanghai," he said, "there are so many requests for Buddhist services that the monasteries are unable to satisfy them all."[14]

The Leap was also no Cultural Revolution in fashions or art. A Shanghai women's magazine of late 1958 admitted that some materials for clothes were indeed "expensive and bourgeois." But, "now that our nation is making a Great Leap Forward, . . . we want to raise our cultural and artistic level. So when circumstances permit, our people may gradually look well-dressed."[15] This could seem a well-conceived socialist plan. The 1959 Spring Festival shops in Shanghai advertised "perfumed bed sheets" and "Hawaiian" electric guitars.[16]

Especially as economic shortages became more obvious in the later Leap, there was less need to criticize luxuries (even as there might have been more reason to do so). The life-styles of leading Shanghai capitalists were a major topic of the press by 1961, probably because their luxury could help dispel public perceptions of shortage. They were described wearing well-cut British suits, driving Buicks, smoking "State" cigarettes (Mao also favored this brand, of course), and paying for their wives' expensive coiffures.[17]

By mid-1961, even the tradition of send-down had changed. College students might go to summer resorts, and the Shanghai Educational Workers' Trade Union arranged for three hundred university faculty members to visit scenic spots, including the Hangchow's West Lake and Anhui's Huang-shan.[18] Neon signs, which Party purists still regarded as egregious symbols of capitalist extravagance,[19] appeared in 1961 on the Overseas Chinese Hotel, the Shanghai Museum, and the bourgeois-lining "Great World" Amusement Center.[20]

Maybe the best example of Shanghai ambiguousness about the Leap in residential life was the much-discussed nonestablishment of urban com-

[14] Donald MacInnis, *Religious Policy and Practice in Communist China* (New York: Macmillan, 1972), p. 246.

[15] *Hong Kong Mailer*, no. 161 (December 2, 1958). Thanks to Mr. Loren W. Fessler for this reference.

[16] *NCNA*, February 3, 7, 1959.

[17] *South China Morning Post* (Hong Kong), July 14, 1962.

[18] *NCNA* (Beijing), July 29, 1961.

[19] The Shanghai play *On Guard Beneath the Neon Lights* extols an army unit that resists urban sins; see a positive review in *NCNA*, March 20, 1963.

[20] *South China Morning Post* (Hong Kong), November 23, 1961. These signs came in for special condemnation in *On Guard Beneath the Neon Lights*, a precedent to Cultural Revolution thinking.

munes. Although many Chinese cities launched communes of various sorts, and Shanghai had a few preparatory organizations for them, an official announcement of late 1960 averred that Shanghai's situation was "complex." Urban communes would appear only when "conditions have ripened for their establishment."[21] The main move in the direction of urban communes was the founding of over three thousand large canteens, able to handle meals for about four hundred persons on average.[22] Residence committees were merged into large lane committees in May 1960, "to fulfill the great task of setting up urban people's communes in Shanghai."[23] But no commune was ever formally declared. Many residents had their rations managed through canteens. When food shortages set in, however, even Communist bureaucrats became less eager to extend this kind of dependence.

THE LEAP'S EFFECT ON SCHOOLS: TWO TRACKS

The Leap further institutionalized two types of education and employment for Shanghai local leaders: one for "red" administrators, and the other for "expert" technicians.[24] The red track was officially favored, but the Party's continuing lack of skilled personnel meant that people choosing the expert-vocational route (for which any degree of political loyalty short of dissidence was enough) could still live decently in the city. Legitimate opportunities for experts were necessary in Shanghai's staffing structure.

In 1958, Shanghai founded both "red and expert universities" and "specialized universities." The city also established two types of institutions for work-study students: "spare-time red and expert universities" and "vocational universities."[25]

At lower levels, the Leap was a period for residential and economic units to establish myriad part-time and vocational schools. These were not cen-

---

[21] This arcane and complex topic is mooted in a number of sources, notably the *New York Times*, August 20, 1960, and D.E.T. Luard, "The Urban Communes," *China Quarterly* 3 (July–September 1960): 76–77.

[22] *XMWB*, June 13, 1960.

[23] *JFRB*, May 14, 1960.

[24] Martin King Whyte and William L. Parish, *Urban Life in Contemporary China* (Chicago: University of Chicago Press, 1984), refer to the legitimate opportunity for professional as well as political workers. The general argument is also presented in Michel Oksenberg's "The Institutionalization of the Chinese Communist Revolution: The Ladder of Success on the Eve of the Cultural Revolution," *China Quarterly* 36 (1968): 61–92.

[25] Respectively *hongzhuan daxue, zhuanke daxue, yeyu hongzhuan daxue,* and *zhuanye daxue; XWRB*, October 20, 1958.

trally financed—or controlled. They provided, in the educational sphere, the underpinnings of the stratified, two-track system for channeling people that was an important legacy of the Leap to later years. By October 1958, Shanghai had over one thousand "people-run" schools.[26]

The Transition to Socialism in schools (combined with a demoralization of teachers during the Antirightist Campaign and the post-1956 interest of Party cadres in enterprises richer than schools) had created a context in which government monitoring of the secondary system was surprisingly light. By 1958, the Party lacked staff to implement its educational ideals of 1956. Many Party loyalists concluded that dealing with intellectuals was a potentially dangerous, thankless, unprofitable task. Because education remained a high priority of many Shanghai families, however, the actual 1958 enrollments soared. By the fall of that year, junior-middle-school education was all but universal, and 53 percent of the city's middle and primary schools were "run by the people," not by the government.[27] Enrollments in the government schools were higher, as was the quality of the students because of free tuition. The diversity of Shanghai's educational institutions rose in 1958.

This freedom did not last. The portion of high school graduates entering colleges may be the best index of youths' satisfaction or frustration, and this index fluctuated wildly through the Leap. In 1957, it was only 57 percent, because the Antirightist Campaign removed universities' ability to handle their usual number of students. During the period of relegitimation in 1958, however, the ratio more than doubled to 135 percent (that is, a great many who entered college that year did not come directly from high school). In 1959, the index receded below parity, to 92 percent. By 1960, the reasons for its rise to 112 percent relate more to the lack of alternative employment than to an increased desire for education. But then the promotion index really plummeted in 1961 and 1962, to 29 and 24 percent respectively![28] Hopes for university training among large numbers of school graduates were therefore dashed.

---

[26] *Minban xuexiao*; XWRB, October 12, 1958. These were also called "schools run by lanes" (*lilong ziban de xuexiao*); they included spare-time middle schools, middle vocational schools, and higher vocational schools (*yeyu zhongxue, zhongdeng zhuanye xuexiao, gaodeng zhuanye xuexiao*).

[27] NCNA, October 5, 1958, and XWRB, January 1, 1959.

[28] The statistics are rounded from figures in Jürgen Henze, "Higher Education: The Tension between Equality and Quality," in *Contemporary Chinese Education*, ed. Ruth Hayhoe (Armonk, N.Y.: Sharpe, 1984), p. 116. The index rose slightly in 1963 and 1964, but it has never been higher than 46 percent in all the years since its level of 112 percent in 1960. This late-Leap change was permanent.

All the criteria for selection—political *and* academic—thus became more important in 1961, because competition for the fewer places rose so dramatically then. Since the mid-1950s, there had been disagreements between high Shanghai leaders about the extent to which school admissions should be based on academic tests. Mayor Ke Qingshi identified with affirmative action policies for would-be students of proletarian background, but Municipal Party Secretary Chen Peixian was identified both with an emphasis on academic standards *and* with an emphasis on giving special consideration to applicants who were Party members, regardless of their class backgrounds.[29]

During the Antirightist Campaign, Ke's policy had prevailed. Family origins became more important than before, at least for acceptance to good schools; but because the portion of accepted students among all applicants was then so much higher than it later became, there was no insuperable constraint in 1957 against bourgeois-labeled students. Admissions in the Leap reflected a pragmatic view, favoring somewhat more equal treatment of applicants. The mobilization ethic kept rates of acceptance into schools high; so distinctions between Ke's and Chen's policies then made scant difference. Affirmative action views were less relevant to admissions when many applicants were taken.

Chen's influential views during the Leap nonetheless saved some Party members (not proletarians generally) when they were in danger of academic failure. At the Shanghai Mechanical Engineering College, for instance, two-thirds of the workers and peasants who had entered in 1956 were later forced to leave without their diplomas. They flunked out because they could not handle the work. All the proletarian students who were not Party members had left this class by mid-1959—though practically none who were in the CCP failed. The Party's "pragmatic" bureaucrats and its affirmative action "radicals" may have had some disagreements; but in actual cases, both groups were willing to apply policies that gave Communists special treatment.

Teachers were promoted during the brief 1961–62 era (which bears many resemblances to other campaigns for mobilizing liberal intellectuals in 1956–57 and 1978–79). An exceptionally large number of lecturers were advanced to professorial rank, and even more instructors were promoted to be lecturers.[30] It was later claimed that "bourgeois professors" had a voice,

---

[29] *HQ*, no. 3 (March 1968). This is a CR critique of Chen, but it is probably accurate on this point.

[30] *NCNA*, September 21, 1962.

then, in recommendations on the later careers of students. So they were criticized for having "persecuted outstanding workers' children, as well as teachers of worker or peasant families, by ordering them to leave the universities or sending them to work in rural villages."[31] Children with poor academic records were sometimes sent to the countryside, even if their background was proletarian.[32] These policies represented a brief reversal of the antirightist repressions begun in 1957. A majority of all rightists were intellectuals (they had some college training), and most were also teachers. Several rightist instructors, who had been sent to villages for labor reform in 1957 from a Shanghai primary school, were able to return to their previous jobs in the early 1960s; they even received salary increases.[33] During this brief quasi-liberal period of 1961–62, some rightist teachers even had their labels removed.[34]

NO SCHOOLING AND NO EMPLOYMENT
FOR MOST YOUTHS

The changes in these policies, along with the economic depression, nonetheless meant that most students "could neither gain admission for higher study nor get a job."[35] Even though academic standards were important for school admissions, the promotion ratios were so low that most capitalist-label youths (like their peers with other labels) could not achieve university entrance. Such youths might form "self-study groups," listening to radio broadcasts and joining activities that street offices organized to keep them out of trouble. But these measures were palliative and temporary. The Party reverted to its standard policy whenever urban people became inconvenient. Monitor them; then hold campaigns for sending them to rural areas.

Middle-school graduates were the main targets of this campaign in 1961–62. This period saw unprecedented coordination between schools and street committees, leading to more massive and long-term rustications (a trend

[31] This report, about the Tongji University mathematics department, appeared in *NCNA*, October 29, 1967.

[32] Several interviews; see also Whyte and Parish, *Urban Life in Communist China*, p. 47.

[33] Interview with a Shanghai woman who taught at the Zhongxing Road Primary School of Zhabei District in 1962–63, URI, Hong Kong.

[34] A superbly documented example is the case of Yue Daiyun, author (with Carolyn Wakeman) of *To the Storm: The Odyssey of a Revolutionary Chinese Woman* (Berkeley and Los Angeles: University of California Press, 1985).

[35] *RMRB*, June 5, 1962, referring to 120 "self-study students" (*zixue sheng*) on Kunming Road, Yangpu District, Shanghai.

that continued sporadically until 1968, when the send-down was nearly universalized for youths).[36] Teachers, parents, and youths who had temporarily returned from country stints spoke at "pledge conferences" for new graduates who were asked to go.[37] Pledges to rusticate were easier to obtain than actual emigration, especially from graduates who had technical skills. But economic depression reduced the number of jobs *not* controlled by the state, even more than it reduced state factories' ability to channel the hiring of new or temporary workers.

Class labels were very important in determining who would have to go. As one ex-CCP interviewee said bluntly,

> There was a greater tendency to send graduates of bourgeois, landlord, and rich peasant backgrounds on rural send-down than to send graduates of other family backgrounds. . . . The general policy, after all, was that people were morally deficient if they had no experience working hard with their hands. For their own good, they should be the first to go to the farms.[38]

As a capitalist-background volunteer reported, "Some peasants called the transferred youths 'landlords.' "[39]

Once in the rural areas, sent-down students often found themselves near other rusticated city folk, both rightists and cadres. Peasants tended to lump these three urban groups together, blaming them indiscriminately for unsuitable marketing and incentive policies during the "three bad years" of 1959–61. Rusticated students had career interests in avoiding close association with rightists. Yet many of those who later returned to the city carried back memories of a countryside understaffed by Party experts but containing significant numbers of subdued or feisty rightists.

Many urbanites found ways to avoid the agricultural work that was supposed to transform them:

[36] See Lynn White, "The Road to Urumchi: Approved Institutions in Search of Attainable Goals during Pre-1968 Rustication," *China Quarterly* 79 (September 1979): 481–510, and Thomas P. Bernstein, *Up to the Mountains and Down to the Villages: The Transfer of Youth from Urban to Rural China* (New Haven: Yale University Press, 1977).

[37] *GRRB*, August 8, 1961, dispatch from Shanghai.

[38] Interview in Hong Kong with a middle-aged man who had not been a rusticated youth but knew many.

[39] Interview with a Teochiu student, of bourgeois family background. He was not from Shanghai but reported about Shanghai people whom he had known as fellow Red Guards during the Cultural Revolution.

We had to take part in physical labor. . . . But some of my class were very clever. They suggested that we could . . . put our money together and run a chicken farm. . . . We used some property belonging to one of us in Shanghai, and together we contributed five thousand yuan. . . . We paid servants to do all the work, except when the Communists were coming to inspect the farm; and then we worked very hard for them to see. Normally we only went there for a few hours, three days a week, and spent the time drinking tea and talking. The Communists were apparently very satisfied and praised the old man who suggested the chicken farm.[40]

This send-down campaign may have communized the views of a few rusticates. But the more certain thing it did was to concentrate them in country spots, where they learned from each other. A major unintended effect was to normalize a cynical routine of claiming official policies as sanctions for personal advancements. In the Cultural Revolution, this habit was further decentralized.

THE LEAP'S EFFECT ON DEMOCRATS AND INTELLECTUALS

For many of Shanghai's older educated people who were not tagged as rightists, the period between 1956 and 1961 meant many meetings. In the Transition to Socialism, highly ranked intellectuals had to attend study groups on Marxist theory. If they were not already members of united front parties, they were urged to participate. When asked "Why did you decide to join," one of them responded, "It was really for the sake of my work. . . . If you don't join, the government will not give you any [job] to do."[41] In the Hundred Flowers Movement and then the Antirightist Campaign, such people again had to attend forums. By 1958, Leap policies convened yet more frequent meetings.

Those whose main work remained in the city met to learn that "Shanghai's intelligentsia should not fail the heroic age."[42] Professors and scientists drew up individual plans for becoming both red and expert.[43] The city's branch of the Political Consultative Conference in late 1958 established a

---

[40] Ibid.

[41] *Current Scene* 1, no. 6 (1961): 4–7.

[42] *WHB*, February 22, 1958. This is the title of an article that was run in two major Shanghai papers.

[43] *NCNA*, February 24, 1958.

"Shanghai Socialist Institute" at a commune in Jiading County. It sent three thousand "democratic personalities" on a two-year "training by rotation . . . to establish their labor viewpoint."[44] Thus many educated people without rightist labels nonetheless received temporary punishment for being what they were: local alternative leaders who could have run Shanghai, if Party members were not doing so.

As economic problems set in, the Party had to handle these potential leaders more carefully. A prominent CCP deputy mayor, in October 1959, called for the "blooming of one hundred flowers" as if recent history had vanished:

> Everyone is equal. Anyone may state his views according to the results of research. . . . Imperialists, reactionaries, and revisionists spread rumors and slanders about the Party's policy, saying that "the line of letting diverse schools of thought contend is fake." "It was taken back, as soon as the situation turned unfavorable." "There is no freedom for academic circles in China." But all this has been disproved by various activities.[45]

But such speeches ignited scant debate. Polite, stereotyped "big criticism movements" among intellectuals at this time show mainly that the Leap involved far less open political struggle between local elites than the earlier blooming had. These movements, beginning in 1958 and continuing in the next three years, were not liberal but were also not as confrontational as the 1957 events had been. They showed two local elites passing like ships in the night. These local leaderships remained somewhat separate, because neither had the resources fully to displace the other.

By 1961, when the economic situation was worse, the Party convened "meetings of immortals" and required academics to attend. The shortages were then too serious for direct discussion, however—even by labeled immortals. Shanghai economists met to verify that agriculture was the "root" of Chinese growth and that productive forces have a "dual character." They proved that the U.S. economy was about to collapse.[46] Rostow's stages of economic development were examined as a slander of socialism and of the Soviet Union.[47] Shanghai social scientists were sent to farms for further research, so that they could refute the rumors of economic trouble.[48]

Shanghai engineers met to receive "complete directions" on their work,

[44] *WHB*, October 12, 1958.
[45] Shi Ximin's speech is in *GMRB*, October 8, 1959.
[46] *NCNA*, March 13, 1961.
[47] *GMRB*, March 28, 1961.
[48] *GMRB*, March 10, 1961.

and they reportedly were made to realize the "tremendous achievements in scientific research and design during the past three years."[49] For intellectuals whose specialities had less obvious relevance to the depression, forums were nonetheless held to discuss strictly delimited topics: Historians mooted the role of the late Han's General Cao Cao and of the late Ming's Li Zicheng.[50] Shanghai geneticists argued for the more pluralist of two theories in their field.[51] The Shanghai Law Society changed its name, to become the Shanghai Society of Politics and Law, though the revision showed more hope than substance.[52]

The famous writer Ba Jin, addressing a 1962 Shanghai Congress of Writers and Artists, was one of the very few intellectuals to speak at this time in a language that was not completely allusive.

> Who is not afraid of correction? Who wants to receive a rain of heavy blows, just because he has published a piece of writing? Many are forced to be cautious in speaking and literature. They would rather say what others had said before them, and talk in as general terms as possible. Even when they are discussing small matters, they want to add high-sounding introductions and conclusions. . . . They do not care whether their writing is useful or not; they only want to be left in peace. . . . Though people rarely hear the fears of individuals mentioned at public gatherings, yet when I have private talks with other authors, we all agree that the presence of such fear obstructs creative writing.[53]

Most intellectuals had understood since 1957 that the results of differing from official views could be painful. Fear had become a main motive for compliance with policies, even more important than it usually is in all societies. Novelist Ba Jin, whose art requires seeing the links between social contexts and personalities, was better equipped to understand all this than were the social planners who liked policies of pressure for their short-term effects.

It made little difference that there were doubts about the wisdom of these

[49] *GMRB*, May 16, 1961.

[50] The participation of important national political figures such as Wu Han and Guo Moruo in this discussion was important, because some of the statements were indirect critiques of Mao Zedong and defenses of Peng Dehuai. Interviewees help on this, though the press does too: *WHB*, May 28, 1961, and *GMRB*, February 25, 1961, are examples.

[51] *RMRB*, April 23, 1961.

[52] *Zhengfa yanjiu* (Research on politics and law) (Shanghai), no. 1 (1962): 44.

[53] Adapted from *SCMM*, no. 323 (May 5, 1962), translating *Shanghai wenxue* (Shanghai literature), no. 5 (May 5, 1962).

policies of pressure by 1962 even within Shanghai's Party.[54] The rules of comradeship there made it ungentlemanly for the doubters to go public with their qualms. Even Party members who had reservations about excessive labeling and campaigns were constrained by the norm that vanguard monitors should stick together.

THE LEAP IN STREET ORGANIZATIONS

Ordinary citizens were under much less surveillance than potential leaders during the Leap. Shanghai's low-level urban committees had long been sparsely staffed. In 1957, Beijing had two and a half times more street-level cadres than Shanghai. In 1959, Wuhan's density of such cadres was three times that of Shanghai.[55] The ten large districts in this huge East China metropolis averaged 250 residence committees each.[56] Span-of-control problems badgered the whole residential system, and the most qualified state cadres preferred to work in economic firms.

The number of people to be monitored also rose during the Leap, because of immigration. An ex-cadre reported,

> By the second half of 1958, at the high tide of the Great Leap Forward, the drifting population in Shanghai and other cities became very large. Every cadre was busy purchasing construction materials, and people were blinded by the false surface and slackened their public security work; so in a short while, the applications for household registrations became many. Management became lax. In some streets, newcomers only had to notify an activist or a residential group leader by word of mouth, and that would be counted as the legal procedure for establishing residence. Peasants from nearby blindly flooded into the city [*mangmu liuru chengshi*] and later became black persons and black households [*hei hukou*].[57]

[54] According to a Party interviewee, the ex-mayor of Shanghai Chen Yi and the current mayor Ke Qingshi attended a conference in Guangzhou in 1962, at which Chen said he wanted a "ceremony to remove hats" (*jaimao li*) for intellectuals who had been given capitalist labels. Ke disagreed. In Shanghai, too, some leaders at many levels approved positions like Chen Yi's, and some took positions like Ke Qingshi's.

[55] Calculated from Kau Ying-mao, "Governmental Bureaucracy and Power in Urban China under Communist Rule, 1949–1965" (Ph.D. diss., Department of Political Science, Cornell University, 1968), pp. 261, 264.

[56] Calculated from *WHB*, May 8, 1959. A "district" is a *qu*.

[57] Interview with a cadre who had done economic work in Shanghai.

When asked why so many rural people swarmed into Shanghai at this time, another source replied, "They are all looking for odd jobs. They know they can't be regularly employed unless they have a permanent address ... but it's fairly easy for them to get temporary jobs."[58]

Few Party cadres had a personal interest in stemming this flood of immigrants. Various sources suggest the newcomers were often in the same families as officials. They came because they knew they had patrons in Shanghai. The government could not easily control its own minions in such a personal matter, although a hopeful 1958 newspaper reported, "Many cadres and employees urged their relatives to return to their home villages."[59] The immigration, which flourished in 1958–59, was later reduced not just by state controls but by urban food shortages.

Edgar Snow, visiting Shanghai in 1960, reported cases of beriberi, pellagra, and calcium deficiency—as well as frank opinions from workers that the amount of available rice was insufficient.[60] News articles advertised: "Staff in the canteens know exactly the tastes of everyone. ... In order to understand and satisfy the needs of the people, they ask for opinions."[61]

Urban districts also organized their lane cadres to enforce food rations by "raising political awareness and policy standards."[62] But the stores had "practically nothing to sell."[63] A major difficulty of introducing canteens was that they had to compete with families for supplies of food and coal.[64] By 1962, there were reports of classic rice riots on the outskirts of Shanghai, where peasants on several occasions overpowered guards and looted government granaries.[65]

As the rural economy slowly improved in 1962, Shanghai newspapers headlined what in other years would have been unremarkable: "It is now the season for vegetables."[66] The suburbs even exported vegetables in cold-storage railway cars to Shandong and Heilongjiang.[67] Longhua Temple held a completely traditional fair for three days in April, at which a variety of

---

[58] *Current Scene* 1, no. 6 (1961): 3–4.

[59] *XWRB*, January 10, 1958.

[60] Edgar Snow, *The Other Side of the River: Red China Today* (New York: Random House, 1961), p. 538.

[61] *XMWB*, April 6, 1960.

[62] *XMWB*, June 16, 1961.

[63] *Standard* (Hong Kong), January 16, 1962.

[64] *China Mail* (Hong Kong), March 28, 1962, based on a letter from a German businessman residing in Shanghai.

[65] *Standard* (Hong Kong), October 31, 1962. This particular refugee report was unconfirmed, but it was not PRC policy to issue press releases on rice riots.

[66] *XMWB*, April 11, 1962.

[67] *XMWB*, April 14, 1962.

food and other goods was sold, as long as the supplies lasted.[68] The Leap brought some change to Shanghai's residential patterns, but not what the government had planned. Economic shortage made rations more equal temporarily, while also raising the value to residents of whatever resources the official monitors could control.

THE LEAP'S LEGACY

Massive mobilization in the Leap was at first a relief from the repression of the Antirightist Campaign. But economic failure led to a more two-track urban society than had existed before. The sectors of life about which the Party cared most (especially the industrial economy) were more tightly organized in large institutions by the end of the Leap. Policy toward other sectors was largely a matter of quick exhortation and benign neglect; and this was viable, because the depression made other sectors relatively poorer. When the policies of pressure returned in full force later, they were more effective than ever before because residents had fewer alternatives to compliance.

Reforms in criminal justice can summarize this change from 1958 to 1962. In the first euphoria of the Leap, the apparent intention was to suspend crime for the duration. "A mass movement was launched, urging everyone to be law-abiding. . . . Alley residents and people's police marched with gongs and drums to submit their security pledges in advance. They proposed to make it thoroughly difficult for bad people to exist."[69] Judges were largely sent to farm work, or they were retired.[70] They tended to be borderline liberal types; and in a uniform leaping society, who would need them?

Shanghai's prisons still had plenty of business, though, by the early 1960s. Edgar Snow then visited a jail containing twenty-five hundred inmates. He was told many more offenders were at a labor reform camp run by Shanghai in northern Jiangsu.[71] Other camps accommodated Shanghai rightists in Anhui, Heilongjiang, Xinjiang, on Changxing and Chongming

---

[68] SHNL, April 30, 1962. Monks were not in evidence at this fair, and reporting on religion throughout the Leap is rather scanty. But see *JFRB*, September 24, 1958, and *NCNA*, May 6, 1960. The Party's approach at this time was to emphasize the alternative, secular faith rather than to spend scarce resources repressing older religions.

[69] *NCNA*, March 9, 1958.

[70] *JFRB*, November 9, 1958.

[71] Snow, *The Other Side*, pp. 547–48.

islands in the Yangzi River, and on Fuxing Island in the Huangpu River.[72] This "gulag" was extensive, and it was largely (though not wholly) maintained for political prisoners. If the Leap's hopes for economic expansion had not been dashed by mainly rural failures, local Party leaders might have retained their prestige, so that deportation of their rivals would have been less necessary.

Many more people, less outspoken or unlucky than the convicts but with similar ideas, held still necessary jobs in Shanghai. The values of the time were so incoherent that common activities like attending school or volunteering for work were an indistinguishable mixture of glory and punishment, initiative and expiation.[73] Party cadres, emerging from the 1959–61 trauma with their local rivals relatively weaker than before, saw no reason to abandon the administrative means of categories, controls, and campaigns that had brought quick results before the Leap experiment. Now they had even more resources to make those policies stick.

[72] Interview with a Malay Overseas Chinese who was arrested by the Public Security Bureau of Huangpu District in 1961 for some unstated immorality, and who served as a convict in the Fuxing Island Labor Reform Camp, 1962, URI.

[73] For a promise that "there are many outlets for school graduates," see *Shishi shouce* (Current events handbook) 11 (June 6, 1962); and for a 1961 report about a worker cadre who was able to bring his daughter back from rustication in Shandong, see *WHB*, May 25, 1968.

CHAPTER 8

Tightening Control over the Economy, 1962–1966

Return, faithless Israel, for I am merciful,
says the Lord; I will not be angry for ever.
—JEREMIAH 3:12

During the prelude to the Cultural Revolution, the state ruled the society in China more thoroughly than during any other equivalent length of time. Economic depression after the Leap built socialist institutions more surely than purposeful campaigns had done, because it shut down nonstate enterprises. Underground and semiofficial factories could glean few raw materials in the early 1960s, and they sold to stricken markets. So most unofficial companies went out of business or had to merge with government-controlled firms.[1] Job seekers became more dependent than ever before on official hiring. The depression by 1961 consummated what the laws of 1956 merely began. The stage was set for unprecedented government guidance in the lives of both managers and workers.

POST-1961 REVIVAL OF DEPENDENT LABOR

"Labor service stations" (*laodong fuwu zhan*) had been established by Shanghai's authorities during the blockade of the early 1950s. But for the rest of that decade, individuals seeking jobs could most effectively approach firms directly or through relatives. During the three bad years of 1959–61, labor service stations became less important, because the firms they represented had few jobs to offer. The economic recovery of 1962, however, was immediately preceded by a sharp decline of the portion of secondary graduates allowed into universities and by an official revival of the send-down campaign. In this context, the government pushed to guide labor markets more completely.

As one ex-cadre put it, "Now everyone had to go on the recommenda-

---

[1] See Lynn White, "Low Power: Small Enterprises in Shanghai," *China Quarterly* 73 (March 1978): 45–76.

tions made by labor service stations." This caused "quarrels and confrontations" between the stations and job seekers they were supposed to serve—especially when officials decided that a recent graduate should be sent down to the countryside. Because Party cadres in early 1962 hoped many of the 200,000 workers hired during the Leap could be sent out of Shanghai,[2] the pressure on labor stations to rusticate their clients was enormous. Problems also arose when station officers tried to govern hiring that managers (with their own networks) had hoped to control.[3]

A local station might recommend send-down, rather than any urban job, for months after an unemployed person first applied. Unless he was a political "bad element," however, the labor station would eventually relent and arrange at least an undesirable job in Shanghai. The labor stations often would line up only temporary (*linshi*) jobs for people who refused to go to the countryside. As an "intellectual youth" said, "The service station would not assist some kinds of people. Protesters against the send-down campaign, and especially youths with 'bad' family backgrounds, seldom received jobs through them. These groups sometimes had intense feelings about the labor stations."[4] Much of the available work was in construction and was physically difficult. The station negotiated wages and deducted a service fee (*fuwu fei*). If one job ended, a youth linked to a service station might remain on the books in hopes of landing another. This pattern gave station cadres more opportunities to urge jobs in the countryside instead, and it allowed them to keep track of youths. But it was a humiliating system for their clients, because the patronage that labor stations offered was typically undesirable, impermanent, and nonunionized. Such employment was for people who became, in effect, Shanghai's second-class citizens. Labor stations and their staffs became common targets of attack during the Cultural Revolution.

The temporary labor system nonetheless met the policy needs of CCP planners, because it was inexpensive to run. At least it must have seemed so, in the short run. Deputy Mayor Cao Diqiu, who was Shanghai's top speechmaker for economic affairs during the decade before the Cultural Revolution, did not mince words. "Factories and enterprises must employ fewer workers who are permanent. More workers should be temporary. . . . Employees should be chosen flexibly, from among the peasants. In this way, the

---

[2] Interview with a person who was a high Shanghai cadre in 1962. Apparently this 200,000 figure was a desired quota, rather than an accomplishment.

[3] Interview in Hong Kong with a centrally minded ex-cadre who had been attacked during the Cultural Revolution.

[4] "Intellectual youth" (*zhishi qingnian*) means a middle-school graduate; this one, who had received labor station work, was interviewed in Hong Kong.

latent power of labor can be tapped. The relationship of town and country, and the worker-peasant alliance can thus be strengthened."[5] Cao had the idea that peasants might work on the land at busy times in the crop cycle, and in factories during slack agricultural seasons. But the reality was that peasants preferred higher-paying industrial jobs on a permanent basis, and unionized Shanghai workers preferred not to have them in the city at all. This system, in which the hirelings could be "both workers and peasants" (*yigong yinong*), lowered costs for managers; and it raised the relative status of well-established union members. But it repressed most others.

As the economy recovered, the state enforced new restrictions on employing labor. It was more effective than ever before in attempts "to subject the administration of wage funds to constant supervision and inspection."[6] The labor stations, working under district-level governments, tried to centralize control over this most important managerial activity. Newly hired personnel, especially for state factories, were supposed increasingly to be qualified school graduates, approved by labor market monitors in municipal agencies and in schools. Apprenticeship still existed, but many factories would consider only school graduates even for posts as apprentices.[7]

The salary differences between apprentices and union workers (as between contract workers and regular ones) remained very great. In a truck repair factory at this time, first-year apprentices received only 14 yuan per month, whereas most workers received 50 yuan, technicians got about 85 yuan, and the salaries of leading cadres could range up to 130 yuan.[8] So there was a great deal of salary stratification among probationary and regular workers, as well as competition to get into the state employment system.

The strength of this system arose from the effects of the post-Leap depression, more than it came from post-1962 labor laws, because shortages had driven many nonstate firms bankrupt. Even enterprises run by lane committees, under nominal "collective" ownership, were often ruined. Others avoided this fate only by merging with larger, better-authorized, and more official firms. New hiring had now to be approved by the Party monitors in those larger companies.

---

[5] *WHB*, September 26, 1964. Cao spoke at the First Session of the Fifth Shanghai People's Congress. For another perspective on this, see the pioneering article by John Wilson Lewis, "Commerce, Education, and Political Development in Tangshan, 1956–69," in *The City in Communist China*, ed. J. W. Lewis (Stanford, Calif.: Stanford University Press, 1971), pp. 153–73.

[6] *LDB*, August 18, 1962.

[7] This point is overstated in the *South China Morning Post* for April 11, 1964.

[8] Interview with ex-worker for the Car Repair Plant of the Shanghai Public Utility Bureau, reporting on the period 1963–65, URI, Hong Kong.

The state's ability to channel raw materials, as the economy revived after 1962, meant its enterprises prospered, though many independent ones died. In this context, capitalist-origin individuals often wanted to obtain "worker" status. Promotions for ex-bourgeois laborers depended inversely on the extent to which campaigns in the mid-1960s emphasized the importance of family backgrounds. For them and for proletarian-labeled workers alike, promotions and wage increases were rare.

EDUCATION, JOB, AND CAPITAL
ALLOCATIONS STRATIFY WORKERS

"Employees' spare-time schools," which hinted at advancement for their students, appeared in large numbers during 1963 and 1964.[9] According to an ex-manager, state factories could make (and arrange higher approval for) all basic decisions on whether to establish a school, whether to make it full-, part-, or spare-time, whether to make it technical or comprehensive, what the students should learn, and who was to instruct them. Attendance at these schools varied considerably, [10] but many workers received diplomas.

The problem was what to do with them afterward. By 1963, Shanghai had seven times as many technicians as in 1957, though a majority of these experts still lacked worker family labels.[11] At some plants such as the Shanghai Machine Tool Factory (which became a bastion of radicalism in the Cultural Revolution), upwardly mobile "expert" workers increased in number by 1963. These new-minted engineers were active in suggesting technical innovations.[12] By the following year, the media were full of articles about the Technical Reform Movement.[13] The message of this propaganda was ambiguous: It stressed the importance of more efficiency for both capital and labor, irrespective of the effects of innovations on the work environment. This aspect of the Technical Reform Movement served classic capitalist purposes (as its critics pointed out during the Cultural Revolution). It honored anyone who made such an innovation, regardless of the innovator's class label. But another sometime message of this campaign was that only

[9] *Zhigong yeyu xuexiao*; XMWB, July 3, September 23, 1964.

[10] An ex-cadre spoke of "ratios of participation" (*canjia bili*), which is happy officialese for a bad problem.

[11] NCNA, June 21, 1963, refers to 48 percent of technicians in Shanghai light industry as "workers," but this almost surely included some relabeled ex-bourgeois.

[12] NCNA, July 18, 1963.

[13] *Jishu gexin yundong*; XMWB, August 4, 1964.

persons with years of work experience—and that meant innovators from proletarian families[14]—were capable of making really good decisions about techniques.

By 1965, the campaign more often alleged that proletarians knew best how to innovate.[15] Employees responded with literally thousands of good and bad technical proposals. Capital was required to put most of these into practice, and that seldom happened. But the Technical Reform Movement stirred personal ambitions among many Shanghai factory workers. By mid-1965, Party spokesmen tempered their praise of the movement with warnings that the aims of an innovation should be "clear and well-defined."[16] Not just any change would do. This was sensible, but it was not the interpretation of the Technical Reform Movement that many labeled workers had endorsed. An official routine of judging everything by political categories of people had been on the upswing for a decade and a half, and not even scientific topics could be considered separately from that habit.

National capital allocations at this time favored "Third Front" inland investments in heavy industry.[17] From 1964 to 1971, about two-thirds of the state's industrial investment went for such projects, which in objective terms were the main economic policy of the Cultural Revolution. These inefficient undertakings were justified by military dangers (from the Soviets in the north and the Americans in the south), though they also served the provinces from which many top CCP leaders hailed. They represented a new industrial strategy for China, albeit one that showed scant confidence in cities and urban managers. Taxes and extractions from Shanghai largely paid for it.[18] The patrons of the metropolis had to save costs, and they did so by reducing the number of their clients rather than by weakening the ties that bound dependents to them. Resources, not just intentions, crucially determined policies.

Welfare for unionized workers therefore increased during 1962–65, but

[14] *NCNA*, July 9, 1963.

[15] *XMWB*, March 1, 1965.

[16] *RMRB*, June 10, 1965, article about Shanghai.

[17] *Da san xian*. This relies on pathbreaking work by Barry Naughton, to be published in *New Perspectives on the Cultural Revolution*, ed. William Joseph, Christine Wong, and David Zweig (Cambridge: Harvard University Press, forthcoming). Naughton's periodization of CR economic policy, for which he has investment figures and in which 1966 is *not* a watershed, is just the kind of eye-opener the China field needs.

[18] Nicholas R. Lardy, for example in *Economic Growth and Distribution in China* (Cambridge: Cambridge University Press, 1978), chap. 4, began the job of showing much redistribution of wealth from coastal cities to inland provinces, even in the early 1960s for which data have been scarce. Exact figures on this topic are very moot (see esp. Audrey Donnithorne's "Comment," *China Quarterly* 66 [June 1976]: 328–39); but it is clear that Shanghai was taxed.

cost-conscious managers tried to limit the groups receiving such benefits. Medical staff for the important cotton textile industry was increased in this era.[19] Retirement or death benefits, as well as other items of social insurance (enacted in the early 1950s), were applied more consistently in the mid-1960s.[20] Some factories provided their regular workers with major amenities. The Yangshupu Power Plant by 1963 accommodated its unionized employees with a large dining room, a clinic, a library, table tennis facilities, lounges, spare-time primary, middle, and college-level schools, and generous pensions of 50 to 70 percent of wages on retirement.[21]

Such benefits were available only to regular staff in the plant. New recruits, who had to serve as apprentices before attaining regular status, were excluded—and they complained. Many of them, hired in the new era, were rather well educated. They were criticized for "thinking the factory work too dirty, strenuous, and hard." They "thought their apprenticeship was a waste of their talents" acquired in middle schools. "To overcome these attitudes, the leading organizations of the plant began mass education, contrasted the old society with the new, and invited veteran workers to explain their own experiences," showing the apprentices why they should put up with second-class status.[22]

To contain costs without reducing workers' benefits or rates of new investment, it became necessary to restrain the hiring of regular workers and to lay off temporary workers. Shanghai's steel industry received so much capital during the Leap that by 1964 it supplied 70 percent of local needs, compared with only 30 percent in 1957. But the state did not want to squander money on workers.[23] In one steel factory:

As the plant became more and more mechanized, a considerable number of the workers taken on in 1958 were found to be redundant. . . . The [1966] labor force has been cut by roughly one-third since 1960. Those

[19] *NCNA*, July 11, 1963.

[20] For background, see Charles Hoffman's *Work Incentive Practices and Policies in the People's Republic of China, 1953–1965* (Albany: State University of New York Press, 1967), pp. 35–42. See also Joyce K. Kallgren's "Social Welfare and China's Industrial Workers," in *Chinese Communist Politics in Action*, ed. Doak Barnett (Seattle: University of Washington Press, 1969), and her nicely titled "Public Policy and Life in China," in *The People's Republic of China after Thirty Years: An Overview*, ed. Joyce K. Kallgren (Berkeley: University of California Center for Chinese Studies, 1979), pp. 95–122.

[21] *NCNA*, June 19, 1963. Before 1949, this plant had been American-run, and in 1948 it supplied four-fifths of Shanghai's electricity. The CCP was strong among its workers then, so that it could claim to be a "Red Fort."

[22] *GRRB*, April 4, 1963.

[23] *NCNA*, October 12, 1964.

displaced have been transferred to new industries that have grown up in Shanghai, or they have helped to pioneer the development of steel works in other parts of the country.[24]

Although layoffs in Chinese industry have not received much attention, the capitalization and high labor benefit costs of the Leap led to mass job dismissals by the mid-1960s.

Further examples of industries affected by this pattern can be found along Shanghai's waterfront: in cargo handling, shipping, and fishing. The Shanghai harbor was extensively modernized in the late 1950s. Installation of new equipment allowed the harbor to handle 40 percent more cargo in 1959 than in the previous year. This was done entirely by mechanization, "without adding a single worker."[25] In the next few years, with economic problems, managers' incentives to hire stevedores declined sharply. When markets revived under government control, there was plenty of money to continue the mechanization program, and the rate of new hiring remained low. Hierarchy, control, and stratification rose sharply among Shanghai dockhands.[26]

Each industry is somewhat different, but the Leap's aftermath also caused problems in shipping and fishing. During 1958, several hundred sailors from the Shanghai Sea Transport Bureau were taken into a program that trained them to be pilots and engineers. These people were mostly of "sailor and stoker origins." But by 1962, they were told they did not qualify as technicians—even after their training—so they had to remain at their previous jobs.[27] Frustration was extensive in such groups.

In fishing, mechanized trawlers were increasingly important, and they required fewer hands to operate than the older boats. With electronic sensors to detect schools of fish, machines to haul the nets, radios, and boat accommodations designed for sailing without full families, modern trawlers cut into the sales of traditional fishing folk, who continued the life-style of "boat

[24] *NCNA*, August 23, 1966.

[25] *NCNA*, January 18, 1960. See also Chen Gang [pseud.], *Shanghai gang matou de bianqian* (Change on the Shanghai docks) (Shanghai: Shanghai renmin chuban she, 1966), esp. pp. 79–87.

[26] For more on stratification among Shanghai's stevedores, and its results, see Raymond F. Wylie, "Shanghai Dockers in the Cultural Revolution," in *Shanghai: Revolution and Development in an Asian Metropolis*, ed. Christopher Howe (Cambridge: Cambridge University Press, 1981), pp. 94–95.

[27] *NCNA*, August 10, 1968. This Cultural Revolution source indicates that one of these trainees, by 1968 promoted to captain, sailed a ten-thousand-ton freighter from Shanghai to Qingdao with the guidance of the Great Helmsman's "little red book," rather than with the help of a pilot. On that trip, at least, he did not run aground; and clearly he enjoyed being master of the ship.

people."[28] Other families that ran river barges were forced into dependence on the state, whose agents monopolized new and powerful tugboats, pulling trains of barges thus compelled to stay together.

Monitoring was a syndrome that fed itself. After the recovery from depression, the staff available to the Party, while still insufficient for all its goals, became larger than before. When state organizations with more agents were able to reduce their subordinates' alternatives to compliance, especially among youths seeking promotions, state manpower increased further. More loyalists were available, especially in economic work, to oversee the revived resource exchanges after 1962. This represented a change of degree from the 1950s. So long as official control of the boom after 1962 could be maintained, the state system garnered new raw materials that allowed still further recruitment of talent for monitoring—and thus encouraged still further dependence.

THE ECONOMIC BASES
OF WORKER STRATIFICATION

In many industries and shops, new capital and restrictive labor policies during the mid-1960s created tensions that helped shape the factions of the Cultural Revolution. In plants or units where there had been slight chance of promotion, frustrated workers were inclined to rebel against their cadres. Even within the same factory, differences of this sort could be obvious between workshops. In the Shanghai Machine Tool Factory, for example, the Press Shop in the early 1960s included about two hundred workers on two shifts, mostly young, tough, and from villages. But the Electric Shop had only thirty workers on a single shift, with education, expertise, and higher salaries. The three hundred workers in the Molding Shop all labored on one shift in the morning, because the job was physically difficult. The assembly, transport, and other shops also had distinctive traits related to their tasks.[29] This diverse, highly stratified and divided machine tool plant became one of the most famous sites of struggle in Shanghai's Cultural Revolution a few years later. Not surprisingly, political factions in the plant followed the divisions between shops.

When workers in the Shanghai Glass Machines Plant chose sides in 1966, three-quarters of the technicians allied with "Scarlet Guards" (Chiwei Dui)

[28] *NCNA*, March 30, 1963.
[29] Interview with ex-worker for the Shanghai Machine Tool Factory, reporting on the period 1960–63, URI, Hong Kong.

in supporting most of the old cadres; and half of the production leaders joined them. But three-fifths of those in the Molding Shop entered the opposing group, along with three-quarters of the Casting Shop.[30] Stratification in wages often arises from differences in types of work, but the control policies in mid-1960s Shanghai factories exaggerated these divisions and created strains that became obvious in the Cultural Revolution.

Other important differences existed between whole factories. The plants about which Party officials cared most, especially in heavy industry, were unlike the great majority of enterprises, to which CCP leaders gave minimal aid. Factories in the steel-eating sector were almost always run directly by the state at municipal or district levels; these were large and well financed. The dependence of their employees on local CCP leaders was requited with resources. Many of their workers were from families with proletarian labels, hired especially after the major influx of capital to this sector during the Leap.

The rest of the economy had firms of widely varying sizes. When a firm was large, the managers tended to be Party members who could have trouble retaining autonomy unless they remitted good profits and other money to higher authorities. Commercial stores, many of which were long-established in Shanghai and stable in their personnel despite differences in size, often received less attention from high officials.[31] Large and old textile plants could be more cheaply controlled because their raw materials, few in number and bulky, were easy to monitor. Ordinary employees in both the favored and nonfavored sectors generally became more dependent on their bosses in the mid-1960s than before. But all these differences in firms' sectors, sizes, and backgrounds affected the speed with which this dependence increased.

Worker stratification was also great because of the prosperity of Shanghai's official sector, when compared with China as a whole. Wages in unionized Shanghai jobs were generous; this place had the highest industrial compensation rates in the country.[32] Especially for regular workers, who often received twice as much money as contract helpers in the same factories, prudence dictated obedience to factory heads, no matter what their policies or

[30] *RMRB*, January 23, 1967. The technicians in this plant were few, and they were said to be "corrupted cadres sent there by the Party after Liberation."

[31] Confucius and Marx both had prejudices against commerce, and this is a major respect in which old Chinese ideas survived the revolution. Marx once held that "[a]ll expenses of circulation . . . do not add any value to a commodity"; see *Capital* (Chicago: Charles Kerr, 1924), 2:169. Confucius placed scholars and peasants above merchants, in his ideal social order.

[32] Barry Richman, *Industrial Society in Communist China* (New York: Random House, 1969), pp. 686–87.

personal styles. Otherwise, one might find oneself out of a job, and bad references could make finding a new one difficult. Prospects outside the city were less attractive. Unionized Shanghai workers thus had personal incentives to throw themselves into any campaign their bosses wished to conduct. They benefited greatly from the system of the mid-1960s, and they were generally willing to support it.

Contract workers were dependent in another way, because they could easily be removed from a factory where they protested. They gained little from the prevailing system, and they had reasons to protest; but they would not last long if they did. Especially when labor station cadres were encouraging send-downs to the countryside (where incomes were roughly one-third of general urban levels[33]), contract workers' usual reaction in the mid-1960s was to hold their peace and swallow their resentment.

Low wages were a particular complaint of many who later "rebelled" in the Cultural Revolution. As one worker said plainly, even before that drama began, "There has been no change in wages during the past few years; the wages are too low. After working for several years, graduates from secondary vocational schools are still paid 48 yuan; but that cannot buy much. How could they have enthusiasm?"[34] The stratification of wages by categories of people meant that some workers were not under much compulsion to produce. Observers on the street saw "pedicab drivers snoozing in the seats of their cabs; they don't have much work to do."[35] The atmosphere inside factories could be lackadaisical.[36] But all three policies of pressure kept order in Shanghai, through 1965 at least, and gave local bureaucrats great power over workers.

DEPENDENCE AMONG MANAGERS

Managers of small enterprises and commercial businesses were subject to sporadic and unpredictable constraints on their work. Teams were sent ir-

[33] Exact, comprehensive work on the agricultural/nonagricultural income gap is difficult to find or to believe; but this relies on an estimate of approximately one decade later in Martin King Whyte and William L. Parish, *Urban Life in Contemporary China* (Chicago: University of Chicago Press, 1984), p. 54.

[34] From an early 1960s industrial survey quoted in a Red Guard source hostile to these viewpoints, in *SCMM*, no. 640 (January 13, 1969): 21.

[35] Sophia Knight, *Window on Shanghai: Letters from China*, 1965–67 (London: Deutsch, 1967), p. 47.

[36] Summaries of many reports, not all relating to the mid-1960s, are in Richman, *Industrial Society*, and William L. Parish, "The View from the Factory," in *The China Difference*, ed. Ross Terrill (New York: Harper and Row, 1972), pp. 185–98.

regularly to check inventories in more than three thousand Shanghai firms, to increase state control of new resources during the economic revival of 1962–63. These teams could certify the records of holdings or could recommend further inspection. Managers in medium-sized businesses had more and more difficulty obtaining inputs unless they were tightly linked to larger state organizations.[37] In smaller enterprises, by 1964, district-level finance and trade departments ran a "Socialist Good Shop Movement" with the same aim of increasing state checks on inventories.[38]

Tax cadres were supposed to be important enforcers of economic legality, but their main purpose was to collect revenue rather than ensure compliance with all the laws. Throughout 1964 and 1965, tax departments "systematically expanded financial audits of enterprises" and conducted random checks on many firms. They found violations in drug companies, bathhouses, and many other businesses. "Some tax collectors went with [workers] to the warehouses and assisted the supply and marketing departments of enterprises in auditing their accounts and drawing up inventories. This resulted in the discovery of 250,000 kilos of various raw materials."[39] On one hand, these cases show the continued importance of non-Party managers who were not entirely tied to the state system—that is, the continuing importance of local leaders who were not Communists. On the other hand, they also show the Party's determination to realize the ideals of the Transition to Socialism. As a cadre said in an interview, "It was intolerable to have such a large illegal sector of the economy. The tax offices, having a different task from the productive organs, logically and actually became the main enforcement agencies for observance of the law."[40]

Different Shanghai firms had different degrees of financial autonomy, depending on their size and the tight or loose relations they had with higher state offices. The Shanghai Truck Factory, for example, had practically no separate factory management in the mid-1960s; all of its major decisions were made by the municipal Bureau of Communications and Transport. But the Shanghai Steel Company had managers who could take out major loans on their own approval.[41] The more centralized style of rule led to more pro-

[37] *DGB* (Beijing), June 9, 1962, article about Shanghai.

[38] *XMWB*, May 9, 1964. The issue of May 11 reports a meeting with speeches by Chen Yi, Cao Diqiu, and Li Yanwu (later a member of the Revolutionary Committee, then the head of the Shanghai Municipal Finance and Trade Political Department of the Shanghai Party Committee). Not until June did a meeting in Beijing declare the Department of Finance and Trade there to be "political" too.

[39] Articles about Shanghai in *DGB* (Beijing), November 4, 1965, and January 3, 1964.

[40] Interview with an ex-cadre mainly in economic work.

[41] Richman, *Industrial Society*, pp. 481–82.

duction pressure—which was protested during the Cultural Revolution as a policy of Liu Shaoqi:

> The "trusts" [vertically organized groups of firms] demanded improvements of quality and quantity of production and lower production costs in a short period of time. To achieve all this in Shanghai, they advocated a policy of "six unified": unified supply, marketing, transport, storage, procurement, and accounting. They substituted quality and profit for the propagation of Mao Zedong thought. . . . They emphasized "perpendicular leadership." This was an attempt to place the trusts above the leadership of the local [*sic*] Party and government, and to turn them into independent kingdoms. A high degree of centralization in the trusts is actually the decentralization of the power of the Party center and of Chairman Mao.[42]

The economic cadres whose power increased most during the brief 1962–64 period were "public-side representatives" and Party bosses, appointed during the Transition to Socialism and the Leap. High officials and disempowered workers alike acquired an interest, by 1964, in having some agency to oversee these overseers. Their preferred solution, first developed in the army, was "political departments." These offices, staffed in many work units by demobilized soldiers, restrained the earlier socialist managers—and tended further to divide local elites.[43]

During April and June 1964, "political departments" took over the CCP Central Committee's economic offices. By 1965, many small government offices had "political bureaus," and even handicraft co-ops and street factories might sometimes have "political counselors" to advise on their work.[44] As more such entities assumed authority in factories such as the Shanghai Silk Mill, the powers of local branch secretaries were limited. Other Communists obtained greater rights to express their views. This began a rebellion against dependence among managers that escalated sharply in the next few years. By 1966, local Party branch secretaries had to be re-

[42] *WHB*, April 29, 1967. On types of decentralization, see also Franz Schurmann, *Ideology and Organization in Communist China* (Berkeley and Los Angeles: University of California Press, 1966), whose concepts this article echoes.

[43] See Xi Guang [Yang Xiaokai], "Zhungguo wenhua tageming de shehuizhuyi zhidu de tu po" (The Cultural Revolution's disruption of the socialist system), *Zhishi fenzi* (The Chinese intellectual), no. 7 (Spring 1986): 13.

[44] *Zhengzhi pu; zhengzhi chu; zhengzhi zhidao yuan*; interview in Hong Kong, and personal communication from Donald Klein. Political departments, like Party committees, exercised "piece leadership" (*kuaikuai lingdao*) within units. They could suspend, at least temporarily, instructions coming down vertically in the form of "string leadership" (*tiaotiao lingdao*).

minded to "exchange ideas with members before meetings, so that everybody can come prepared . . . and the members can tell each other their opinions. . . . The Party Branch Secretary should also take the lead in doing group
labor."[45] By the time of the Cultural Revolution, heads and deputy heads of
many units found themselves in opposite factions. The latter often resented
past bossing by the former, even if they had similar family labels.

LABELS FOR CADRES AND WORKERS
IN THE MID-1960s

The Socialist Education Campaign, first announced in 1962, was a movement to reemphasize the importance of class labels. This initiative, whose
official line changed through many political twists and turns, revived the
threats of 1957 against local leaders; and it was an important prelude to the
Cultural Revolution, especially in rural areas.[46] Part of this long-lasting campaign was the Four Cleans movement, which formally referred to the importance of checking on accounts, granaries, materials, and work points. In
practice, it was mainly an effort to increase class struggle.[47]

The habit of keeping files on individuals, containing information that
they had no effective chance to rebut, was established in CCP organizations
well before 1949.[48] The gradual reduction of social alternatives through the
1950s and early 1960s, as the Party's staff slowly increased, made the secret
dossiers more important to larger numbers of people. Several cities held
campaigns during the post-Leap depression to gather intelligence about
Party and non-Party cadres alike. Security departments in big firms kept data
on the family background, individual status, overseas connections, and

---

[45] *RMRB*, April 14, 1966.

[46] *Shehuizhuyi jiaoyu yundong*. Richard Baum, *Prelude to Revolution: Mao, the Party, and
the Peasant Question, 1962–66* (New York: Columbia University Press, 1975), covers these
matters nicely and somewhat reduces the ground the present book must cover. Baum emphasizes Mao and rural issues somewhat more than the interpretation here. *Prelude to Revolution*
and his work with Frederick Teiwes (n. 47 below) are indispensable to study of the Cultural
Revolution.

[47] Richard Baum and Frederik C. Teiwes, *Ssu-ch'ing: The Socialist Education Movement
of 1962–66* (Berkeley: University of California Center for Chinese Studies, 1968), p. 15.

[48] Patricia E. Griffin, *The Chinese Communist Treatment of Counter-Revolutionaries,
1924–1949* (Princeton: Princeton University Press, 1976), e.g. p. 102, contrasts harsh norms in
the Jiangxi period with a greater frequency of remitted sentences in the Yanan and Civil War
periods, and such punishments must have required the keeping of legal dossiers in relatively
stable base areas.

other characteristics of each worker.[49] A police examiner later claimed that "internal purification forms" were secretly filed on many local leaders, and he thought they should have been used more vigorously to prevent their abuses of power.

> The problems of cadres who were "purified" were not seriously studied. They were just listed and put in the file. Therefore some who were transferred [to other jobs] were discriminated against, and when mistakes were made, these errors hindered not only the activeness of the people involved, but also the next generation.[50]

The files apparently contained standard data about leaders, including questionnaires about their "thoughts": "Has he or she raised any suggestions, even within limits? What was the content of these suggestions?"[51] Another page concerned opinions of Party members in the cadre's unit and at higher levels. Further information was supposed to be included about the cadre's spouse, the class origins of various members of the family, and any "mutual relations and correspondence" with others, especially overseas. This was an opportunity for Party leaders in units to gossip officially (but secretly) about their subordinates and each other. They put information in files that could deeply affect careers and whole families.

These dossiers posed open dangers to the human rights of their subjects, because they were designed for use in campaigns. This fact can obscure their more subtle effects at other times. Knowledge of the existence of secret files encouraged dependence, even in the absence of a campaign. Not just a cadre's own career but also the fortunes of relatives depended on the good will of anyone who could publicize or ignore reports in files. The file monitors were local Party loyalists, especially demobilized soldiers by 1964, who had a tendency to support each other.

Earlier socialist cadres also banded together (sometimes with pre-1949 managers who had worked with them since 1956) to preserve the local sta-

---

[49] The Jiangnan Dockyard, for example, had a complement of thirty-five guards (*baowei*), headed in 1964 by a demobilized soldier from Shandong. The public security section of the yard, which kept files on everybody, oversaw personnel decisions, sent offspring of "bad" classes off to the countryside, and was a major organ of management (interview, URI, Hong Kong).

[50] According to *Fan Peng, Luo heixian* (Against the Peng [Dehuai], Luo [Ruiqing] black line) (Canton), May 1968, an "internal purification form" (*nei qing biao*) was completed on large numbers of cadres. Most of the information in this article concerns Canton, but the purification form apparently followed national standards and was used in other cities too.

[51] Ibid.

tus quo. It was much easier for Party members to do this than for others, but the Socialist Education Campaign and Four Cleans Campaign were relevant to non-Party notables too, if only because they tended to split the ranks of the Communists. At high levels in Shanghai, a "Tuesday dinner party" of CCP "people at the core of industrial and commercial circles" gathered regularly. "For external consumption, the aim was political study; but actually, this was a place for fellow members of industrial and commercial circles to exchange views and study strategies for dealing with the [political departments in] government."[52] There were two main clubs for high cadres in Shanghai. The "Culture Club" (Wenhua Julebu), for a small minority of the highest officials, was located in the Shanghai Mansions Hotel. Another club for Communists was maintained in the Peace Hotel during the mid-1960s.

But the managers who formed the most coherent CCP groups were ex-soldiers. In a 1965 survey by a foreigner of top factories, 33 percent of the managers and 45 percent of the Party secretaries claimed poor peasant origins. [53] It is safe to say that practically all these managers obtained their jobs after demobilization, as did other managers who claimed "worker" origins. Fissures began to appear in the local leaderships of many Shanghai firms, on the basis both of politically labeled groups and of patron-subpatron tensions.

CAMPAIGNS FOR PROLETARIAN PRIDE

The Socialist Education Campaign and its slogan, "Never forget class struggle," tended to legitimate the jobs of people with proletarian labels—and to delegitimate high position, education, or promotion for people who had other labels. This movement has not been much studied for cities, though a literature is available about it both in rural areas and as a topic of dispute among Beijing leaders.[54] The roots of this campaign in Shanghai can be traced to 1957 and before—and more immediately back to early 1960, when the local garrison called a meeting of Shanghai "Scarlet Guards," workers, and soldiers who were veterans of many periods in Shanghai's rev-

[52] *RMRB*, July 27, 1969. The source is hostile to its subject and calls this group a "Petöfi Club," but similarities to the "Friday Club" convened by presidents of twenty-seven Mitsubishi companies each month in Tokyo, and to similar sessions in many societies for the management of relations among powers, suggests ample justification for the group to meet.

[53] Richman, *Industrial Society*, p. 296.

[54] See especially Baum and Teiwes, *Ssu-ch'ing*; and Baum, *Prelude to Revolution*.

olution dating back to 1925–27 militias.[55] These were joined by Young Pioneers and current PLA officers. By 1963, unions and district-level militias trained "backbone elements" to encourage the study of Mao Zedong thought, with the support of the military.[56] Trade unions in 1963 were also active in propagandizing the army model hero Lei Feng,[57] the Four Good Company of Nanjing Road, and other exemplars of disciplined resistance to bourgeois culture.

The year 1964, especially its summer, was a high point for this army-led proletarian campaign. Factory workers gathered for sports meets.[58] "Military summer camps" in the suburbs and neighboring provinces were organized among students and workers by the Shanghai Garrison District in conjunction with local unions and the Education Bureau. More than 300,000 Shanghai militiamen participated in these rural excursions.[59] Back in the city, steel factory militias did physical exercises between their furnaces and slag hills. A drama troupe called the "Brotherhood Soldiers," composed of PLA members with proletarian labels, gave skits about class struggle to all travelers passing through the Shanghai North Railway Station.[60] Similar campaigns were continued during the winter of 1964–65, with additional suburban camps and activities inside the city.[61]

A "Socialization Campaign" (*shehui hua yundong*) was publicized in 1964. But only in early 1965, when military work teams and political departments were entering factories more freely than before, did Cao Diqiu call on cadres to "organize a climax of industrial production" and begin a new "production and austerity campaign."[62] The Socialist Education Campaign, unlike its quasi-rival the Socialization Campaign, emphasized class education rather than economic production. It was not much introduced to urban areas until January 1965, even though it had been important in the countryside for three years before that. As part of the Socialist Education Campaign, government and Party committees at all levels were supposed to have "Four Clean" offices charged with "class education." This occasion for increased class struggle spurred further competition between local leaders with different labels.

---

[55] *XMWB*, March 31, 1960.
[56] *GRRB*, October 8, 1963, article about Shanghai.
[57] *NCNA*, March 7, 1963.
[58] *XMWB*, May 24, 1964.
[59] *Junshi xialing ying, jingpei qu*; *XMWB*, July 9, 1964.
[60] *Zidi bing*; *XMWB*, August 1, 1964.
[61] *XMWB*, December 29, 1964, describes a "winter military camp" (*dongji junshi yeying*) at Yushan, near Shanghai.
[62] *Shengchan jieyue yundong*; *XMWB*, February 19, 1965.

Tensions between various kinds of local Communists were now as obvious as tensions between any of them and ex-bourgeois leaders. Over thirty people from the Four Cleans work team of the Shanghai Municipal Party Committee were sent to the Shanghai Tobacco Company. On arriving at the factory, this group took over the functions of the manager (the ex-owner), the deputy manager (who had previously made most decisions), the Party secretary and second secretary, as well as other leaders. The movement did not yet affect a great many people directly, but it involved much writing in secret files and further labeling of managers who were found to be historically deficient—or disliked by worker-origin leaders in the factory.[63]

In the Car Repair Plant of the Shanghai Public Utilities Bureau, six cadres ran seriously afoul of the Four Cleans work team. Three had hidden overseas connections, including relatives in Taiwan; the other three were from landlord families, but had managed to cook their household registrations to indicate they were from poor peasant families. Of these cadres, half were soon sent down to rural work, and the other half remained in the factory under surveillance. No fewer than forty-five other workers at this plant were found guilty of misdemeanors, such as dealing on black markets and "spreading rumors." Another six (including three in the Finance Department) were charged with embezzlement. All told, six CCP members were dismissed. But four activists in the campaign were admitted to the Party, and about forty to the Youth League. Above all, the Four Cleans Campaign made clear that an ambitious person might make a career by criticizing others.[64]

This campaign, while catching some cadres who had abused their authority, did not affect small economic units in Shanghai. It showed how information in dossiers could be used against people, and it aimed to increase the official legitimacy of castigating people on the basis of labels. The journal for Party members, *Branch Life*, was filled at this time with material about the need for proletarian solidarity. A worker-reporter told his own story concerning "how I became a writer, after being a half-illiterate worker, with the help of this paper. . . . My self-confidence increased. . . . Now I really understand the truth of class and class struggle. I will try my best to help reform the brothers and sisters of our class and to make advancement together."[65] The head of the Shanghai Party Propaganda Department, a re-

[63] Interview with ex-manager of the Shanghai Tobacco Company, URI, Hong Kong.

[64] Interview with ex-worker for the Car Repair Plant of the Shanghai Public Utilities Bureau, who reported on the period 1963–65, URI, Hong Kong. A similar interview with an ex-worker for the Shanghai Nanyang Brothers Tobacco Company, who reported on the period 1959–65, turned up a similar team that found misdemeanors in politics, work-style, and economic dealings. Several cadres were rusticated and one received a five-year prison sentence.

[65] *Zhibu Shenghuo; WHB*, July 6, 1964.

porter named Zhang Chunqiao, stressed the need for all media to let workers know the debt they owed the Party. He also stressed the link between their interests and those of the army.[66] The main point is not that the PLA and a few propagandists like Zhang revived the habit of emphasizing class labels. More interesting is that many small urban communities had been deeply split by many such policies for many years; so the appeal from the radicals fell on some ears that wanted to hear it.

MID-1960s CONFLICT BETWEEN LOCAL ELITES

One purpose of the urban Socialist Education Campaign, like many others before it, had been to gather information about people. This movement meshed with efforts at greater control. But now the campaign was directed not just in the Party's interests. It now had the potential to hurt many CCP cadres who had gained authority during the previous decade.

Local leaders promoted from among the workers were supposed to take charge of campaigns in this period. During the few years before 1965, about a thousand plants in Shanghai had been put under directors who had worker labels. In the spring of that year, 13,600 further workers were proposed for posts as engineers or technicians.[67] Propaganda under the auspices of local unions and militias continued to stress in 1966 that workers could become "specialists."[68] This idea encouraged careerism on the part of many—and frustration among those who could not claim labor class origins. The proletarian criterion for advancement was called the "blood doctrine" (*xuetong lun*) by the beginning of the Cultural Revolution. Those against whom it discriminated of course resisted it bitterly; and they had the resources to do this, because many still had informal social prestige.

The proletarian ethic was by no means fully realized in Shanghai's economy, or even in Party admissions, because older socialist managers were also threatened by the new cadres who promoted it. Some Shanghai leaders were explicit, in the mid-1960s, that people should be judged according to their potential contributions, not according to their past histories. As the Party leader of a heavily urbanized Shanghai county put it, "When leaders think they are marching ahead, they are behind. When they realize they are behind—then they make real progress. . . . Never adopt the attitude that things

[66] Zhang Chunqiao later led the Shanghai Revolutionary Committee. He was personally of bourgeois and intellectual, not proletarian, background. See also *XMWB*, for example July 5, 1964.

[67] *NCNA*, April 29, 1965.

[68] *NCNA*, July 16, 1966.

are all right, and now much better than in the past. The future is where standards must be set."[69]

Shanghai did not practice what the Socialist Education Campaign preached. Old experts retained many positions of authority, as well as control of much wealth, during the mid-1960s. A Western professor of business administration, surveying Shanghai factories in 1966, found that the efficiency of management in various firms did not correlate with the amount of capital the state provided for new equipment. But good management did vary with high salaries for the managers.[70] In other words, sharply inconsistent values underlay cadre policy by the mid-1960s.

This was most obvious in recruitment policies of the Party and Youth League. In 1965, many young people of ex-bourgeois background in Shanghai were allowed publicly to criticize the League as having "a glass door, through which they can see but cannot pass." Such complaints brought an official response.[71] A national League meeting in the spring of that year declared its aim of "uniting with and organizing the absolute majority of youths." In a tolerant spirit, this meeting recognized that "over 95 percent of the youths, including the great majority of the sons and daughters of the exploiting classes, are demanding progress and have an active revolutionary spirit."[72]

League cadres, for example at the Shanghai No. 9 Cotton Mill, were criticized for wanting to

> impose a large number of "additional qualifications" on the applicants. They think youths who have not undergone prolonged tests or have not been commended by their organizations, or apprentices or temporary workers who have not become regular workers, or youths who have yet to master difficult production techniques, or even youths who are diminutive physically are not qualified to join.[73]

Proletarian cadres in this mill, who "had called a halt to recruiting new League members," were chastised. The size of the mill's League branch rose from about 200 members (more than 60 percent of whom had been overage) to more than 450 members (among whom only 8 percent were overage).

[69] Speech of Mo Dungao of Jiading County, in *RMRB*, November 11, 1965.

[70] Richman, *Industrial Society*, p. 824.

[71] *ZGQN* 21 (November 1965), in *SCMM*, no. 504 (November 1, 1965): 7.

[72] From the League's Ninth Plenum Communiqué, in *ZGQN* 10 (May 16, 1965), quoted in James R. Townsend, *The Revolutionization of Chinese Youth: A Study of Chung-kuo Ch'ing-nien* (Berkeley: University of California Center for Chinese Studies, 1967), p. 65.

[73] See note 71 above.

Capitalists were participating in droves. Throughout Shanghai, 200,000 youths had some participation in the CYL during 1965.[74] Activist workers in the No. 9 Cotton Mill decided, however, not to join the League that year, apparently because they felt it had been taken over by capitalist class enemies.

Official norms for political action at this time were ambiguous, to say the least. In China as a whole, 8.5 million new members were recruited into the League, according to one report, during 1964 and 1965—and there was not much vetting of class backgrounds in this process.[75] But this political semienfranchisement of nonproletarian people came while the Socialist Education Campaign was still continuing. Official signals to people at this time were very confused.

Recruitment to the Party also increased in 1965. The number of new Shanghai CCP members that year was 29,800, including shop assistants, teachers, and students as well as workers and peasants. Despite the concurrent propaganda for proletarianism, a statement about Party recruitment indicated that "as to family background, class status, and social relations, we must carry out the Party's class policy of giving importance to performance. We must proceed with concrete analysis in matter-of-fact ways, and we must distinguish circumstances and deal with each case on its merits."[76] Although in mid-1966 the Party admitted more "ordinary workers," who would be able to "apply Mao Zedong thought in solving many problems they encounter during production,"[77] even the Party in Shanghai had new representatives with many labels.

There was still, in 1966, a severe inconsistency between the ethic of discrimination against nonproletarians and the fact that many competent people had capitalist backgrounds. The Socialist Education Campaign stressed the evilness of families with such labels, even though many people with bad tags were still needed to make the urban economy run. The post-Leap depression increased the dependence of individuals on bosses, even though the Party in many local units was not agreed on who should be the top patron. Very local elites were now thoroughly fragmented, and the stage for Cultural Revolution was fully set.

---

[74] *WHB*, May 5, 1966. An ex-CYL Shanghai official, who had been criticized during the Cultural Revolution, nonetheless doubted that all these youths had actually joined the League. There is conflict between the available reports on this point.

[75] Interview with an ex–Red Guard, in Princeton, 1986.

[76] *JFRB*, February 20, 1966.

[77] *NCNA*, June 20, 1966.

CHAPTER 9

A Standardized System for Urban Statuses, 1962–1966

Refrain from exalting the worthy, so that people will not
scheme and be corrupted. . . . It was when the Great Dao declined, that there appeared humanity and righteousness.
—DAODE JING

Famine after the Leap left China's Communists with big doubts about the
strength of their political constituency. In 1962, for example, basic-level
elections should have been held, according to the state Constitution; but in
a time of such severe general shortages, they were omitted.[1] The Party was
less sure of its popular base during the depression than ever before. The
recovery between 1962 and 1966, however, was a time when Party leaders
could again tighten guidance over students and residents.

These attempts were made possible by a slowly increasing loyal staff at
the Party's disposal. More fear of control created more incentives to CCP
allegiance, and more loyal cadres caused more fear of control. This syndrome became strong in the half decade before the Cultural Revolution, and
it meant the three policies of pressure were unprecedentedly effective then.
As an administrative system, this synergy worked to save short-run costs for
the government in its coordination and control functions. As a long-run policy, it built up resentment that exploded by 1966.

COLLEGE ADMISSIONS:
ACADEMIC TO POLITICAL, WORKER TO CADRE

By 1961–62, Shanghai had followed a national trend to reduce rates of
university admission sharply, and to base acceptance on academic exams.[2]

---

[1] The announcement did not, of course, blame economic problems for the cancellation of
the vote; but interviewees leave no doubt about this reason. Biennial elections were held in
1954, 1956, 1958, and 1960, as well as 1964 and 1966 (*Union Research Service* 43, no. 17
[1966]: 141ff.).

[2] On the lowering of promotion ratios, see chapter 7, above. The stress on academic criteria
was later identified with leaders like Liu Shaoqi and Deng Xiaoping. See *HQ*, no. 3 (March

Shanghai Party secretary Chen Peixian was later said to have "encouraged bourgeois intellectuals" and to have "opposed the transfer of politically advanced worker-peasants into scientific research," forcing some proletarian youths to "go back where they came from."[3] Because of sharply increased competition for university admissions, and because students of bourgeois backgrounds often did better on the tests, this policy reduced the number of worker youths entering colleges. But it had far less effect on the number of *cadres'* offspring receiving admissions. Proletarian labels were no longer enough to assure good treatment, at this time when general shortages were just beginning to lessen. A bourgeois label was a partial disadvantage then, even though many capitalist-family students were still admitted to colleges. The best family labels at this time were—more clearly than ever before— "cadre" or "Party member."

Educational policies changed so quickly in 1960–62 (and municipal Party leaders were so obviously divided on them) that school officials were unusually free of nonacademic supervision.[4] But by mid-1963, the brief quasi-liberal period had ended, and low-level school administrators no longer had as many options. Higher-level admissions policies became less ambiguous and more stable. Family background criteria, for the first time, became the most significant touchstone for school entrance. University places remained scarce, but now they were awarded on the basis of labeled status more than on academic achievement. Only 31 percent of the secondary graduates were accepted nationally. For the first time, a student had to be both bright *and* well-labeled (at least on the household register, if not in historical fact), to receive higher education.

This combination of a low quota for university admissions and a strong emphasis on class background was unprecedented. It created intense competition. Entrance policies for lower-level schools were not severely restrictive; but higher secondary schools and universities, especially prestigious ones, became very difficult to enter. Life chances for ambitious and hard-working youths are important in any society, and CCP admissions policies by 1963 surprised and discouraged many residents. Students of capitalist class backgrounds, including many who could have looked forward to university in previous years—even those with a chance to clear the academic

---

1968) for Shanghai examples; for the national picture, see Byung-joon Ahn, *Chinese Politics and the Cultural Revolution: Dynamics of Policy Processes* (Seattle: University of Washington Press, 1976), pp. 61–64. Interviewees have confirmed the importance of this change and of the subsequent emphasis on class criteria in 1963.

[3] *HQ*, no. 3 (March 1968).

[4] Part of this is indebted to an oral presentation by Joel Glassman.

hurdles that had applied before 1963—now were forced to lower their expectations. They could not go to college.

The families that benefited most from the 1963 policies were those of soldiers, high cadres, and Party members. Shanghai Specialized Teachers College, for instance, draws all its students from the city with the largest nonproletarian population in China. But by 1963, only 15 percent of the restricted quota of admits were nonproletarian.[5] Ex-bourgeois-background cadres were sometimes able to have their offspring categorized favorably; so it is difficult to be sure about the real proportions of university students by social background in the mid-1960s.[6] But the trend was clear, and it favored new and official local leaders and their families at the expense of older and nongovernmental elites.

District-level officials, who were often demobilized soldiers, enforced the affirmative action policy with verve. For example, the head of Zhabei District's Education Bureau in 1963 was an old guerrilla leader from northern Jiangsu. The head of his personnel section, which kept files on teachers and decided which instructors and school administrators to rusticate, was from a similar background.[7] Many important Party patrons in the educational system were from peasant, not worker, backgrounds; and many were not from Shanghai. But they were cadres; so it is hardly surprising that official rather than class labels became crucial for admission at this time.

These changes of 1963 did not mean, however, that students with dubious family labels were weeded out, if they were already admitted to universities. The class that entered in 1962 was not scheduled to graduate until 1966. It included many academically excellent students, of whom some (though not all) had "bad" labels. Interviewees have estimated that in good Shanghai senior middle schools, even during the two or three years before the Cultural Revolution, most students came from households that originally had bourgeois tags (although some were now relabeled as "cadres"). Even in universities, a majority were still from capitalist backgrounds.[8]

---

[5] Interview with a Shanghai person who studied at the college and reports on the period up to 1964, URI, Hong Kong.

[6] James R. Townsend, *The Revolutionization of Chinese Youth: A Study of Chung-kuo Ch'ing-nien* (Berkeley: University of California Center for Chinese Studies, 1967), pp. 67–68, gives national figures showing the worker-peasant portions of university students at 20 percent in 1953, 48 percent in 1958, and 66 percent in 1965.

[7] Interview with an ex-teacher at the Zhabei First Middle School, who was also an ex-employee of the Shanghai Education Bureau, reporting on the period from the mid-1950s to 1963, URI, Hong Kong.

[8] A Party official, who had been in school during the early 1960s, guessed in an interview that 80 percent of good senior-middle-school students and 60 percent of university students in Shanghai at that time were originally bourgeois. These proportions are higher than suggested by the figures for earlier years in Robert Taylor's *China's Intellectual Dilemma: Politics and*

Teachers in the mid-1960s were struck by "the great variety in the levels of intelligence" among students. "Some have far quicker reactions than others. . . . How immensely difficult is this task of making them use their own judgment."[9]

Officially, new recruits through education to Shanghai's elite were supposed to be "both red and expert" (*you hong you zhuan*), not just one or the other. Indeed, the number of admissions was so restricted during this era, only youths with many virtues passed all the hurdles to higher education. But informally, among pre-1963 admits in particular, it was understood that some youths could have respectable careers on a "white expert road" (*bai zhuan daolu*).[10] Professionals in Shanghai, who were largely from capitalist-labeled families, tended with their wives and children to create household incomes at least as high as those earned by administrative cadres.[11]

The emphasis here on university admissions rather than those at lower levels is appropriate. Colleges had become far more competitive than schools, and the many articulate leaders of important youth groups in the Cultural Revolution went through the university admissions process. Admission to secondary schools only required approval at the urban district level in Shanghai.[12] Primary education was, by this time, universal in the city. The youths who made the Cultural Revolution were mainly "college-bound."[13] Fully one-quarter of Shanghai's whole population in 1963 consisted of students.[14] The experiences of these youths during the years just before the Cultural Revolution were crucial to their later attitudes as Red Guards.

University Enrolment, 1949–1978 (Vancouver: University of British Columbia Press, 1981), p. 106; but Taylor's statistics may omit relabelings that could change the picture considerably.

[9] Sophia Knight, *Window on Shanghai: Letters from China, 1965–67* (London: Deutsch, 1967), pp. 43, 68, reporting on classes at the Shanghai College of Foreign Languages. These comments are poignant, coming from a young British socialist with high ideals.

[10] Interview with a student educated during the 1960s.

[11] See evidence suggesting this in Martin King Whyte and William L. Parish's *Urban Life in Contemporary China* (Chicago: University of Chicago Press, 1984), pp. 93–94.

[12] *XMWB*, July 2, 1964, and *NCNA*, October 12, 1963.

[13] See the best article yet published about the Cultural Revolution: Anita Chan, Stanley Rosen, and Jonathan Unger's "Students and Class Warfare: The Social Roots of the Red Guard Conflict in Guangzhou (Canton)," *China Quarterly* 83 (September 1980): 397–446. This article emphasizes demographic factors (the young industrial work force of the early 1960s and an early-1950s "baby boom") more than the present book, which stresses unintended results of policy (e.g., the business employment effects of the depression) for which the statistical indexes changed more quickly. But the Chan-Rosen-Unger essay has got to be required reading for anyone interested in the topic of this book.

[14] *NCNA*, October 12, 1963, estimates 2,400,000 students in the city, "one student for every four people."

WHAT THE REJECTS DID

The 1963 change left many talented middle-school graduates in need of jobs. Because they were bright, Shanghai factory managements were more interested in them as employees (despite their sometimes-dubious labels) than they had been in rejects from admissions rounds in earlier years. Thus many unofficial-background youths joined the industrial work force—and brought into it severe grievances against bureaucrats.

Because these youths and their families remained eager for education, the 1963 university admissions policies also spurred a growth of factory schools. New workers of questionable class backgrounds enrolled in large numbers.[15] These schools also admitted many students from worker and peasant backgrounds, and often their "educational standards [were] comparatively low."[16] But the best of the university rejects did very well in these schools. They would also have been candidates for promotions in factories, if not for their labels. These youths, if they could get regular unionized jobs, naturally stirred the envy of worker-origin leaders. So the same mid-1960s admissions policies that increased tensions between labeled groups in schools also had an identical effect in factories.

Restrictive education and labor policies after the economic depression created youths who were unwilling to accept the Party's work assignments after graduation from middle schools. These people were called "social youths" (*shehui qingnian,* a bureaucratic euphemism). Sometimes neighborhood committees established local academies of learning for these people, "to absorb street youths."[17] The teachers were mostly graduates of senior middle schools, themselves often university rejects; and the students were rejects from lower levels. Students in these academies, often not among Shanghai's most ambitious youths, resented the personnel bureaucrats less than the young teachers did. The teachers often shared the same hopes as students in competitive institutions, because they knew they were able to handle high-status jobs.[18] Policies of labeling and personnel-monitoring kept them from those positions.

---

[15] Interview with an economic cadre, who specifically equated the rise in 1964 of nonregular schools "led by different factories and different industrial bureaus" with "Liu Shaoqi's line" in education.

[16] *XMWB,* October 7, 1964; see also *RMRB,* September 3, 1964, article about Shanghai's part-time schools.

[17] *XMWB,* January 11, 1966, gives a report about East Changzhi Road, which organized a night school.

[18] This relies on the author's interviews, as well as those reported in Susan Shirk's *Competitive Comrades: Career Incentives and Student Strategies in China* (Berkeley and Los An-

Local Party leaders tried to channel the increasing urban resources after 1963 through their own hands. They succeeded imperfectly, but monitoring rose faster than in any previous era. By the middle of the decade, as the urban economy became somewhat more prosperous, school graduates could get part-time jobs more easily than before.[19] But the ability of monitors to control Shanghai's economy grew almost as fast as the supply of resources, and this meant unprecedented official control. For example, city residents had long posted handbills on telephone poles to sell various items or services. Such ads offered to exchange residences, do odd jobs, tutor school-children, give music or language lessons, repair radios and gadgets, fix plumbing, or do other spare-time tasks. Some even advertised private stencil cutting and duplicating. These telephone-pole ads gave residents services that were not officially monitored. In 1963, local overseers in Shanghai launched an effective campaign for the removal of such notices.[20]

RESIDENCE COMMITTEES AND MILITARY DISCIPLINE IN 1964–1965

Even as the Party was sponsoring urban "class struggle" on a scale that would have been impossible in the early 1950s, it tried to replicate the policies of that earlier time, on which many local Communists and non-Communists alike looked back with relative satisfaction. The most effective claim that Shanghai's CCP ever laid on capitalists was during the Korean War, and its grounds were patriotic. The PLA, assuming a much greater role in local Shanghai affairs in 1964, naturally chose this model from the past.

Urban face lifting had been high on the agenda in 1951; so it was prominently emphasized in 1964–65 too.[21] Many of the busiest streets, including Nanking, Huaihai, Tianmu, and Tibet roads, were then scheduled for repaving. Parks were to be "greened" (*lühua*).[22] As in the early 1950s, there was

---

geles: University of California Press, 1982). See also the superbly differentiated treatment of various kinds of schools and geographic areas in Canton at this time, in Stanley Rosen's *Red Guard Factionalism and the Cultural Revolution in Guangzhou (Canton)* (Boulder, Colo.: Westview, 1982).

[19] Interviewee's report, confirmed by *SN*, October 26, 1965.

[20] *SN* article, May 30, 1963, written by a White Russian then still resident in Shanghai and teaching language there.

[21] *XMWB*, June 21, 1964; this policy of *zhengdun shirong* was later attacked during the Cultural Revolution.

[22] *XMWB*, April 3, 1965.

a movement against mice and rats.[23] A "Public Health Sudden Attack Campaign"[24] fought diseases and insects, using institutions almost identical to those of the earlier time. [25] Neon signs, which were especially repugnant to puritan cadres, were not taken down in the mid-1960's, but their messages were changed. The "Great World" amusement center now sported a gay neon sign saying, "One Hundred Flowers Bloom; One Hundred Schools of Thought Contend."[26]

Differences by 1964 made the Party's ideological claim on most Shanghai residents less compelling than it once had been. The presence of American soldiers in Vietnam provided some basis for general loyalty, as previously in Korea. But now, Chinese troops were not massively involved. U.S. "advisers" in South Vietnam were farther away then Korea, not yet numerous, and not actually fighting Chinese. Despite this, much was made of them in Shanghai demonstrations. Workers' groups organized by the army paraded often against the U.S. buildup, especially in 1965 after it increased.[27] In a Nanshi District primary school,[28]

> portraits of Chiang Kai-shek and the Americans are hung under a grape arbor, and now these are full of holes from the people shooting them with airguns. On the playground, there is a military physical exercise game about resisting Americans and aiding Vietnamese. The pupils make drawings of imaginary single-plank bridges, rugged roads, wire nets; and they destroy the enemy with hand grenades. In the story room, teachers tell stories of struggle and war.

Retired servicemen and the Shanghai dependents of fallen soldiers, many of whom had died in Korea, were recruited as propagandists to the residential population of the city.[29] But memories of 1957 and 1961 made this new foreign war a less sure basis than the Korean case for Party cadres to claim allegiance from non-Party people.

Although there was no land reform campaign to occupy bourgeois youths in the 1960s, the restrictive admissions policies for schools and jobs placed new emphasis on rural send-down. By the second half of 1963, many university graduates were sent to the countryside for at least six months of man-

[23] *XMWB*, March 20, 1965.
[24] *Weisheng tuji yundong*; *XMWB*, April 22, 1965.
[25] See also "Shanghai—a Clean City," *NCNA*, November 23, 1965.
[26] *Standard* (Hong Kong), February 6, 1963.
[27] *XMWB*, August 8, 10, 1964, for example.
[28] *Kang Mei yuan Yue*; *XMWB*, July 5, 1965.
[29] *XMWB*, July 30, 1964.

ual labor.[30] School acceptance was sought not just for education or urban careers, but also because it meant a delay (at least) of rustication. The 1963 admissions quotas frustrated non-Party-family applicants for that reason especially. A few relatively idealistic cadres, who thought special treatment for their children was unfair, had to take definite steps to counteract an assumption among personnel monitors that officials' offspring should not be treated like other youths.[31] The vast majority of cadres, however, accepted this benefit for their families as a matter of course and a natural benefit for the revolutionary cause. To keep and increase its scarce personnel resources, the Party in effect established a norm of affirmative action for the powerful.

The 1963 rustication goals were high. Personnel officers planned to persuade 100,000 students to go down to the countryside in that year alone.[32] This quota proved unrealistic, and great efforts at propaganda produced only 30,000 applicants from the whole city then—of which half eventually went to rural areas. Nonetheless this effort at send-down was unprecedented in scale, and it set the style for the next few years.

Students with bourgeois family labels were encouraged to stay in the countryside longer than others. As in the fifties, the rustication campaign sometimes created divisions within families, because parents tended to oppose their children's departure from Shanghai, even when their progeny were willing to take up such adventures (or at least, to take the gamble that rural work would help their later urban careers). Youths were sometimes publicized for refusing to fill in applications for school entrance exams, despite efforts by their parents to "implore, coax, command, threaten, and beat" them into asking for more education.[33]

This kind of youthful idealism arose not just from abstract motives, but also from the decreasing legitimate alternatives (in terms of either jobs or schooling) that many adolescents faced. Partly to encourage more real volunteers, the bureaucracy created "short-term" rustication programs for students before their graduation, to accustom them to rural work in the suburbs. From Caoyang Middle School in a workers' housing project, third-year students went to help in rice paddies near Shanghai, but they were back

---

[30] Interview with an ex-cadre who thought this policy was good, since intellectuals had "detached themselves from labor."

[31] See Thomas P. Bernstein, *Up to the Mountains and Down to the Villages: The Transfer of Youth from Urban to Rural China* (New Haven: Yale University Press, 1977), p. 109.

[32] Interview with a person who was a high official in Shanghai in 1963 and was directly involved with youth work.

[33] *ZGQN* 21 (November 1, 1964): 24–26; the main example here is from Nanking.

in the city a few days later.[34] Campaigns were old-hat by this time. They still frightened people, but youths and their elders alike had developed ways of riding these waves without toppling. Enthusiasm is always part of a political movement; but increasingly it was a surface phenomenon, because individuals learned how to adapt campaigns to their personal interests.[35]

PROLETARIAN AND CADRE JUSTIFICATION IN SCHOOLS

The Socialist Education movements of this period promoted solidarity among good-label students. Proletarian middle schoolers, in a residential area closely connected with several large state enterprises, were organized in groups to visit selected parents and "to discover the history of oppression and exploitation experienced by their families."[36] The school administration organized exhibits and show-and-tell sessions, at which students summarized the childhood hardships of their ancestors. Students told of their parents' difficult apprenticeships, growing up separated from grandparents, and other ancestral sufferings. This propaganda campaign relied on traditional Chinese familism, but it intensified and used familistic mores in ways that are unrecognizable in traditional terms.

The Four Cleans Campaign in Shanghai schools advertised the dubious origins of many teachers. In the Shanghai Music Conservatory, for example, each cadre, instructor, and student had to write an autobiography beginning at age nine. "Thought inspection meetings" (*sixiang jiancha hui*) met weekly during the conservatory's campaign, to discuss these essays.[37] But the Four Cleans were generally less severe in schools than in factories, because this movement revealed few scandals that had not been previously known. Shanghai teachers in general had backgrounds that obviously made them bourgeois, and very few had seriously tried to hide their family origins. A fecund source of Four Cleans scandal in factories was embezzlement. But in schools there was less to oversee, since they had low budgets and little money.

Pedagogical ideals were nonetheless publicly important as symbols. The cadres needed to justify school recruitment on nonacademic grounds and to legitimate educating conformists who would submit to monitoring. A major

[34] *XMWB*, August 18, 1966.

[35] For much more on these patterns, see Shirk, *Competitive Comrades*.

[36] *RMRB*, February 4, 1963, article about Kongjiang Middle School.

[37] Interview with a Cambodian Overseas Chinese, who studied at the Shanghai Music Conservatory before 1965, URI, Hong Kong.

example of this legitimation effort emphasized traditional doubts about written exams. Long ago, neo-Confucianists like the famous philosopher Zhu Xi had pointed out that tests promote careerism, inspiring students to oppose one another for social position, and that exams may encourage memorizing rather than thinking.[38] Such philosophers thus advocated recruitment by recommendations, not tests. Aspects of the 1963 reforms coincided with these old Chinese traditions. But the role of tests, not only for integrating the bureaucracy but also for finding competent recruits, was also a Chinese habit that harmonized well with modern needs. Cultural traditions, in this case and others, were broad enough to provide a variety of options for current use.

Exams in schools were objects of criticism in a 1965 campaign. Collective education (*jiti jiaoyu*) and group exams, which encouraged students to depend on each other, were advocated as being more ethical and socially constructive than tests of individuals. The legitimacy of collective testing was linked not just with ideals of teaching, but also with the premise that new members certified in an elite should accept the naturalness of their dependence on other members.[39] Originality was not the goal. Monitoring and conformity are supportable in an ethical system that assumes overseers can be wise.

This type of education also assumes proper recruitment by motives rather than by accomplishments. Since individuals' aims are often hard to assess, recruitment came down to selecting people on the basis of their labels, families, or connections. One observer has written that "beneath the surface of compliance lay an informal society which did not conform with the Maoist vision," and subverted its formal ideals by encouraging people to manipulate each other.[40] The result was an emphasis on differentiating labels and individual alienation, instead of community.

The Party accused teachers (still overwhelmingly bourgeois) of giving proletarian students too much work. As a local paper explained,

> The Education Bureau organized specialists to study this problem. They found that students are busy all day, doing schoolwork and preparing for

---

[38] Donald J. Munro, "Egalitarian Ideal and Educational Fact in Communist China," in *China: The Management of a Revolutionary Society*, ed. John Lindbeck (Seattle: University of Washington Press, 1971), p. 294; and esp. David Nivison, "The Criteria of Excellence," in *The Chinese Civil Service: Career Open to Talent?*, ed. Johanna M. Menzel (Boston: Heath, 1963), pp. 92–106.

[39] For descriptions of the open book exams, see *WHB*, July 23, 1965.

[40] Shirk, *Competitive Comrades*, p. 3. This book is the main analysis of urban China's school cultures.

exams. In order to pass the tests, they have to memorize whole books. Schoolwork also weakens education in political thought and productive labor, and this happens because teachers do not understand the education policy of the Party.

Even this radical text suggested a fly in the ointment: "Activities that reduce schoolwork also create problems; an example is the issue of how to spur the students' eagerness in study."[41] Because secondary schools were split into classes of about fifty students, who took all classes together and were headed by chosen monitors, activism was promoted in campaigns for *either* academic study or political rectitude. [42]

The vast majority of teachers had come to their posts under a different system. Admissions policies of 1963 institutionalized an ideal of stratification on the basis of labeled status groups. Proletarian movements of the 1950s (even the Antirightist Campaign) had been unable fully to break the legitimacy of old curricula. Just as the recovery from the depression was the period in which socialist economic decrees of 1956 first became real, so also it was the time when Party loyalists first gained academic control in schools. In both the economic and educational cases, the mid-1960s institutions had to be restricted in size of membership, to make supervision feasible for the Party's still-limited bevy of activists.

TENSIONS BETWEEN TEACHERS AND STUDENTS WITH DIFFERENT LABELS

Teachers, however, still wanted students to be like themselves. As a Shanghai paper put it in 1965,

> Some like students who have learned well, even though they do not pay attention to political study or to labor. They are interested in quiz games and in creative writing, rather than in going to Xinjiang. . . . Some like students who are polite and obedient. . . . Should one be polite to an imperialist? Or obedient to a capitalist?[43]

The Party generally had personnel enough to staff admissions offices, but not to staff classrooms. Since many new students were from different back-

---

[41] *XMWB*, April 7, 1964.
[42] See Shirk, *Competitive Comrades*, p. 36.
[43] *WHB*, February 20, 1965.

grounds than their older teachers, generational conflicts within schools became severe (as did divisions among students over the virtues or faults of
particular instructors). Campaigns to educate faculty on the need for radical
reform were attempted,[44] but there was no agreement between teachers and
students on the goals of education at this time. By 1966, after three years of
status-based admission and a decay of academic accomplishment, the en-
trants of 1963 were about to begin their senior year. Some dropped out to
join the army.[45] Most stayed, but they held a Cultural Revolution instead.

Both proletarians and capitalist students could express their views openly
by 1965. The few working-class teachers protested "discrimination against
the children of workers and peasants" by their colleagues, most of whom
were said to have "blind faith in books and the traditional dignity of teachers."[46] Instances of poor students disobeying school rules were subjects of
complaint, as were instances of ex-bourgeois teachers' failure to understand
financial and educational poverty.[47]

Especially by September 1965, some Shanghai officials were protesting
that schools "called too many meetings." They emphasized that students
should have a chance to go home and study, and that "interference" in their
extracurricular lives by Youth League or other officials was unwarranted.[48]

AMBIGUITY IN CULTS DURING THE MID-1960s

The policies of pressure, applied extensively in the Socialist Education
Campaign, failed to unify China's cultural symbols among increasingly diverse groups. Just as Communist radicals conflicted in high politics with
Communist managers, and just as local capitalist-label elites in cities never
completely lost their social status, so also many inconsistent symbols retained their social legitimacy throughout the 1962–66 period—despite the
campaign to homogenize them.

When the Buddha's birthday happened to fall on a May Day, the week-
long festival to honor that occasion was traditional, not socialist. The Ven-
erable Wei Fang led several hundred monks in a service at Yufo Temple, and

---

[44] *Shanghai jiaoyu* (Shanghai education), April 12, 1965.

[45] *XMWB*, August 6, 1966.

[46] *GMRB*, February 5, 1965, article by a teacher of politics at the Shanghai Xiangming
Middle School. For a later view see *Shanghai jiaoyu*, March 12, 1966.

[47] Both are mentioned in *WHB*, February 2, 1965.

[48] *ZGQNB*, September 7, 1965, article by the CYL committee of Yucai Middle School,
Shanghai.

the reviving economy provided goods for over two thousand booths at the accompanying traditional temple fair (*miao hui*).[49] Rural hawkers were not so numerous as in previous years, and the police tried to control prices.[50] But one interviewee claimed that planners allowed free markets at times when Ke Qingshi (who disapproved) was in Beijing, and stricter rules applied when the puritan Mayor Ke returned to Shanghai.

Chinese traditional religion was anathema to the Socialist Education Movement's emphasis on labeling, because the cult of ancestors based on clan registers was "used by the ruling classes to cover up the sharp contradictions between them and subject classes." So by late 1963, many old habits came under explicit attack. The main label any person carries is a name, and traditionally the personal names of a generation within a family share the same first Chinese character. This habit came in for particular scorn in 1963.[51] By the lunar New Year of 1964, school children were mobilized to respect the "proletarian family tree," rather than lineages. They were asked to discourage their families from holding parties, burning incense, or spending money at this Spring Festival.[52]

The clearest symbolic precedent for the Cultural Revolution came one year later, in February 1965, when antitraditional activities increased sharply. The Temple of the City God, Yufo Temple, Baoan Temple, and others were blockaded by school youths on the Spring Festival day. Only old people could enter without being harassed. Shops selling joss sticks were forcibly closed. Children kept monks away from public places.[53] School youths were told not to tolerate traditional New Year's slogans, such as "congratulations and prosperity," since "these are only the thoughts of feudalism and capitalism."[54] Eating the traditional New Year's Eve dinner was discouraged, and distant family members were not supposed to come home to Shanghai for this observance.[55] Firecrackers were not supposed to be lit.

---

[49] *NCNA*, May 1, 1963. The author saw fairs near both Yufo and Longhua temples on the Buddha's birthday in 1987, too.

[50] "Shanghai Letter," *South China Morning Post* (Hong Kong), May 18, 1963, about the same fair as the previous reference.

[51] *ZGQNB*, October 26, 1963. According to custom, the disyllabic personal names of a family's offspring in a particular generation all begin with the same character, taken from a poem. The next generation uses the next word in the verse. But many names chosen in the mid-1960s are distinctive for containing characters that suggest socialist enthusiasm, such as those for "red" or "defend." These most individual labels, not just group ones, became subject to politics then.

[52] Total bank savings were said to be higher at the 1964 New Year than one month earlier; see *NCNA*, February 27, 1964.

[53] Detailed in sl, February 16, 1965.

[54] *Gongxi facai*; *XMWB*, January 23, 1965.

[55] *Nianye fan*; *XMWB*, January 27, 1965. See also *XMWB*, January 11, 1965.

Ceremonies of patronage were traditionally prominent at New Year, and they required that celebrants bring "red envelopes" (*hongbao*) containing money to the homes of their superiors. But an activist Party secretary of several small factories reversed the custom by gathering together their managers—and visiting the workers' homes instead, to pay respects (not cash).[56] This was a Saturnalia, a purely ritual reversal of roles that actually confirmed their hierarchy, because the status differences between the visitors and the workers remained clear.

Modern uses for tradition, in either its ordinary or obverse forms, were obvious. A four-day holiday for factory and administrative workers was held in 1965 throughout Shanghai, and respects were paid to elders by their offspring.[57] Lunar New Year remained the most important festival for the city's people, even in the mid-1960s and even though its observance formalized many of the tensions that were soon to explode. By 1966, New Year was still celebrated in something like the usual style; but the Qingming Festival to clean ancestral graves was officially converted into a national memorial day for revolutionary heroes. No holiday was given then to employees, although representatives of the city, the army, factories, and schools visited official graves. At this edgy time, just before the onset of the Cultural Revolution, old customs of respect to ancestors and burning paper money had "almost disappeared completely," at least in public.[58] The campaign against them had driven them underground.

MILITARY STYLES IN CIVILIAN LIFE

Socialist Education was carried to ordinary Shanghai citizens not just through schools and Party activists' campaigns against tradition, but also by the police. China's public security forces are part of the army. The police are formally coordinate with the land, sea, and air forces. Any policeman with a post in a street office or above has a regular military rank. This bureaucracy is also subject to the Ministry of Public Security, but the minister has always been one of the PLA's most important officers. Shanghai's police force in the mid-1960s was an important means for broadcasting ideas to urban residents, and its patrolmen by 1964 were participating very actively in local politics.

Policemen's "love the people months" (*aimin yue*) began in 1955 as tem-

[56] *XMWB*, February 3, 1965.

[57] "Shanghai Letter," *South China Morning Post* (Hong Kong), February 9, 1965, gives a balanced report.

[58] "Shanghai Letter," *South China Morning Post* (Hong Kong), April 15, 1966.

porary campaigns to have officers on the beat "perform good deeds for the masses," in the best style of Boy Scouts. As an ex-cadre said,

> "Love the people" months were not so successful when they involved just the public security forces as when they involved the whole PLA, because some police had bad behavior and were popularly avoided—as is traditional in China. . . . If the families being visited were questionable, they would worry that serious problems might arise after conversations with police; so they would not be frank. So the month's propaganda value was great, but it did not specifically fill the need for which it was intended.[59]

Army Day on August 1 was always another occasion for this type of campaign. Soldiers on that day in 1964 came to residential areas and repaired roads, treated sick people, pushed carts, transported coal balls, and gave free haircuts.[60] Yet everyone knew that the police force remained a potential instrument of state coercion. That was its mandate, whatever else it did; and efforts to obscure that role were inherently ambiguous, at a time of intense pressures designed to shape the lives of officially labeled groups.

TRAINING MANY KINDS OF YOUTHS
IN MEANS OF VIOLENCE

Further campaigns to raise the public involvement of the army in 1964 included quasi-military awards to civilians. Activist public security cadres, in particular, were called to conferences and declared "five-good warriors." Whole groups of them might be dubbed "four-good companies."[61] They were supposed "to lift high the red flag of Mao Zedong thought and study the writings of Chairman Mao." By early 1965, they joined other urban activists in "inspection teams," sent out from district offices to make sure that streets and factories carried out the policy of "supporting the army and giving preferential treatment to military dependents."[62] At the Shanghai Children's Palace, extracurricular counselors with military experience were imported to organize "military games" for the red-scarved Young Pioneers.[63]

---

[59] Hong Kong interview with an ex-cadre.
[60] *XMWB*, July 28, 1964.
[61] *Wuhao zhanshi, sihao liandui; XMWB*, March 31, 1964.
[62] *XMWB*, January 23, 1965.
[63] The "Shanghai Shaonian Gong" is a children's palace on Soviet models in an ex-capitalist

The army thus sponsored campaigns on behalf of a general style of life. Rural send-down was the most important residential movement by 1964, and it was politically and organizationally military. In Shanghai, it was partly run by the Xinjiang Production and Construction Corps, a part of the PLA.[64] For proletarian youths especially, the army staffed short-term camps in the Shanghai suburbs. At one such bivouac, the youths got up at 5:00 A.M., studied weapons and practiced firing them for six hours each morning, and also had PLA officers help them "learn Chairman Mao's works."[65]

The garrison of the East Sea Fleet, headquartered in Shanghai, set up military training camps for carefully selected students.[66] At its 1964 military camps, students learned "the capability and construction of all kinds of weapons, as well as how to throw grenades and to shoot with live bullets."[67] In the summer of the next year alone, more than ten thousand Shanghai university students each spent more than a week at military camps. The number of students from 140 Shanghai middle schools to have such experiences, in that single summer, exceeded fifty thousand.[68] Drill in the use of violence was no mere social theory for Shanghai youths by the mid-1960s. It was concrete as well as practical for them, because it dealt explicitly with the defense of labeled groups in potential campaigns. Soon they found new chances to use this military knowledge.

The army also founded "national defense athletic clubs" to liaise with civilians. Some of these leagues received subsidies from military budgets, and they set up branches to offer classes in primary and middle schools. "The most important instruction was in shooting and communications."[69] Rifle clubs, radio clubs, navigation clubs, electrical engineering clubs, ship machinery clubs, flag signal clubs, and parachuting clubs—all of which were established in Shanghai at this time—involved more military than athletic exercise. In the same period, however, district education departments funded soccer camps during the winter of 1964–65.[70] A year later, the officials found a novel way to celebrate New Year, and they organized thirteen

---

mansion. The "brigade counselors" were *dadui fudao yuan*, and the "military games" were *junshi youju*; *XMWB*, August 4, 1964.

[64] See Lynn White, "The Road to Urumchi," *China Quarterly* 79 (September 1979): 481–510.

[65] *XMWB*, July 20, 1964.

[66] *XMWB*, July 15, 1964. Some interviewees claim that Jiang Qing's radicals were even more important in Shanghai naval units than in the army.

[67] *Shidan sheji*; *XMWB*, August 3, 1964.

[68] *WHB*, August 27, 1965.

[69] *XMWB*, January 26, 1965.

[70] *XMWB*, January 25, 1965.

thousand people to participate in "mass long-distance running events."[71] These Shanghai marathons suggest a taste for travel and personal movement that soon became a hallmark of life for young urban Chinese. Campaigns were brought to the personal level in this era, so that much larger numbers of participants became adept at them.

THE LOWER TRACK FOR "SOCIAL YOUTHS"

Not all youths wanted to participate in such activities or were encouraged to do so. "Social youths" had urban household registrations—but also un-proletarian class backgrounds and no links to bureaucratic patrons. Social youths still depended on labor stations and small collective enterprises, or their families, for their livelihoods in the mid-1960s. The authorized solution was still to move them out of town. In the spring of 1964, all officially labeled social youths were invited to a mass "farewell party for those who are going to Xinjiang." This fete was held at Culture Square in the center of the city. A designated representative of the social youths gave a speech, urging his fellows to join the volunteers and leave Shanghai.[72]

In that summer, street committees gave "parties to enjoy the cool evening breeze" (*naliang wanhui*), so that adolescents might "carry out emulation activities." Private tutors, of whom Shanghai now had many because good students with unsavory class labels could not enter colleges, were asked to try their skills in rural schools instead.[73] Youths who had joined the Red Cross or had studied some botany, for example, were told how much more they could do with their talents if they would move to the countryside.[74]

Street committees coordinated such activities, and in July 1964 there was a campaign to organize "education work groups for youths and children," staffed by volunteers in lanes.[75] Each group was headed by the director of the very local lane committee, aided by representatives of the local Youth League, the Women's Federation, the culture and education department of the supervising street committee, the principals of any local schools, lane cadres in youth work, and representatives of the people's police. Each street

[71] "Shanghai Letter," *South China Morning Post* (Hong Kong), January 13, 1966.
[72] *XMWB*, May 17, 1964, carries Wang Shihua's speech.
[73] *XMWB*, July 18, 1964.
[74] *XMWB*, July 17, 1964.
[75] *Qingshaonian jiaoyu gongzuo zu*; *XMWB*, July 4, 1964, gives an example from Ping-liang Street, Yangpu District.

was supposed to have a "summer work plan," designed to habituate its youths to the idea of rural labor.[76]

In 1965–66, a schoolchild's first experience at work in the country still consisted of an ordinarily brief stint in the Shanghai suburbs. Even senior-middle-school students were usually sent just a few miles out of town, for "double struggle labor" at harvest time.[77] Alluvial Yangzi River islands within Shanghai's municipal borders were expanded in area by youths sent there for reclamation projects. Top Shanghai officials "gave the flag" in July 1964 to a group headed for nearby Changxing Island, during elaborate ceremonies at that group's "pledge meeting" before its departure.[78]

But the Party leaders' highest priority for Shanghai youths was more distant rustication, especially to West China. In 1963–64, no fewer than sixteen thousand Shanghai "intellectual youths" went to Xinjiang.[79] In the latter year, a special agency called the "Shanghai Youth Alliance" was formed to propagate this send-down to central Asia, three thousand miles away.[80] High officials of both the city and the Xinjiang Production and Construction Corps appeared at mass rituals to send off contingents of graduates. Factories organized "half work–half study laborers," mostly young and labeled bourgeois, to leave for Xinjiang.[81] Residential street committees, however, kept the main responsibility for send-down recruitment—and vulnerable street cadres also received the brunt of resentment in later years.

By 1966, newspapers made clear that "applications to go to Xinjiang" were "accepted" in categories formed by districts and streets.[82] This was a geographic quota system. Youths from different areas were instructed to present their applications on specific days. The residential cadres had allotments to meet, and the youths affected were often bitter. As a Shanghai emigrant reported, "If you get crossed up with a lane cadre, you've had it, for in the lane they are the law. There is no other law under which they must operate."[83] A 1970s survey suggests that three-fifths of ward security officers were disliked by local residents, whereas only one-tenth had "medium" relations with them. The 30 percent who had "good" links with their charges

---

[76] *Shuqi gongzuo jihua.*

[77] *Shuangqiang laodong.* Some examples are in *XMWB,* July 29, August 4, 1966.

[78] *XMWB,* July 14, 1964.

[79] NCNA, February 18, 1965.

[80] Shanghai Shi Qingnian Lianhe Hui; *XMWB,* May 21, 1964.

[81] *XMWB,* June 12, 1966. This issue reports such developments in district-level factories for scientific instruments, weaving, thermos bottles, dolls, raincoats, wristwatches, and metals.

[82] *XMWB,* May 31, 1966. This gives a total number of applicants for one street and an application schedule for others.

[83] Quoted from an interview in Whyte and Parish, *Urban Life ,* p. 287.

may well have gained these by winking at minor offenses. The send-down movement increased the power of official monitors in residential units by the mid-1960s, just as politically selective hiring and education policies did so in factories and schools.

CONCLUSION: DECLINING UTILITY OF THE POLICIES OF PRESSURE

In this time of expanding state influence over individual lives, many Shanghai residents' main interest was to make sure of their connections with cadres. The Socialist Education Campaign was a general effort to guarantee that government agencies would distribute jobs, school admissions, and other benefits. The proletariat was supposed to gain from this plan; but that group contained so many, they could not all be helped. So the people most advantaged by these movements of the mid-1960s were in the proletariat's vanguard—local leaders of Party branches and activists in Socialist Education struggles. Many workers received no new benefits at all. This dissonance of theory and resources discomfited two groups: noncadre proletarians, and Party members who lacked proletarian backgrounds (or who lacked links to the Four Cleans work teams or political departments). Affirmative action plans were scant help to those they were supposed to succor, and they trivialized the hopes of Shanghai's older elites. Labeling, monitoring, and campaigning clearly had declining returns from their further use as administrative techniques by the mid-1960s. All three kinds of pressure were applied intensively at this time, but their unintended consequences began to nullify the effects for which they were designed.

These policy failures could not be officially recognized, because by the mid-1960s even the Party's expanded staff was inadequate to achieve all its goals. Its response was to create unprecedented numbers of loyalists among unionized workers by means of a family-like religion for proletarians. The main national newspaper for workers ran propaganda from the political department in Shanghai's "Good Eighth Company of Nanking Road," which was an army unit. These soldiers, mostly of peasant background, visited factories to talk about class struggle. The company maintained an "honor room," almost like a clan temple, in which the "family treasures" of written stories about old Party members were read aloud to inspire audiences.[84] The Good Eighth Company "often sent cadres to various government offices,

---

[84] *GRRB*, May 10, 1963.

people's organizations, factories, and schools to make reports." This army propaganda unit sent out inspirational teams for several years, and its special mandate was to help people with good labels. But much of Shanghai's informal elite still lacked these labels. No one was safe, not even cadres, if Four Cleans teams could promote their members by activism in purification campaigns.

As the government's economic resources increased after the depression, specific rules in many bureaucracies mandated more help for workers, soldiers, veterans, and dependents of revolutionary martyrs (who were largely casualties in Korea). These groups received preference for jobs and school admissions. At New Year's time, police helped clean the homes of families of soldiers who had died in battle.[85] District Party committees organized conferences for lane cadre activists, and they discussed "how to use the idea of class struggle to deal with disputes in neighborhoods."[86] "Neighborhood unity" was held up as a goal, but only if it accorded with "revolutionary principles" and benefits for good-label groups.

Street committees organized storytellers to narrate past class conflicts.[87] Middle-aged women formed choirs to sing revolutionary songs.[88] Such activities affected most residents, and they were contemporary with the use of Shanghai as a base for national radicals who propagated new kinds of "revolutionary opera."[89] With army help, Mao's wife Jiang Qing organized conferences on artistic topics in the city. By early 1966, a "Spring in Shanghai" music festival premiered the cantata *Forward, Glorious Workers of Shanghai*. A laborer from the Shanghai Solvents Plant sang the aria, "A Veteran Worker Studies Chairman Mao's Writings." An octet of five-good fighters from the local air force contributed another song. Dancers from the primary school of the Shanghai Normal University performed a ballet entitled *We Want to be Farmers When We Grow Up*.[90] Campaigns at this time protested too much.

[85] *Huji jing*; XMWB, January 22, 1965.

[86] XMWB, December 28, 1964. Neighborhood unity (*linli tuanjie*) was a qualified ideal, here.

[87] *Jiedao gushi yuan*; XMWB, March 13, 1964.

[88] The Christian influence on this Shanghai activity is evident. The main choir (*geyong dui*) was in Hongkou District. See WHB, November 24, 1965, and XMWB, July 8, 1966.

[89] This propaganda is already better-documented in English than the view from the street. Jiang Qing directed a production of Shanghai's Academy of Peking Opera in mid-1964. The academy's singing troupe lived with a PLA unit for three months in 1964–65 to find inspiration for new styles of performance (XMWB, February 21, 1965). See also Lynn White, "Leadership in Shanghai, 1956–69," in *Elites in the People's Republic of China*, ed. Robert A. Scalapino (Seattle: University of Washington Press, 1972), pp. 340–41.

[90] WHB, May 15, 1966.

The most publicized contribution of the era was the revolutionization of a traditional Shanghai opera, *The Red Lantern*. As a critic explained, one of the main allurements of the traditional version of the opera lay in the close, warm relations among members of a family who had "flesh and blood" links and "deep love." The new version tried to retain these features, while "making the sentiments proletarian."[91] Familism and patronage were just fine, in the right family.

The Chairman of the Republic, Liu Shaoqi, summarized the status system among students and residents when he reportedly said that "high-level youths" enter universities, those from "middle-level" families get work in urban factories, and "low-level" youths go to the countryside.[92] This was something like a class analysis, and it was increasingly accurate; but its categories were not conventional. They defined status groups, imposed politically. The top stratum comprised mostly families of cadres and soldiers, whose actual family origins were mixed. The large middle group included practically all real workers (many of whom by the mid-1960s had capitalist labels). The third group comprised people ranging from vagabonds to educated dissidents, without official patrons. Because government policy excluded so many informal local leaders from the favored group, and because pressures to conform among that group's members had become difficult to bear, the situation created by the Party's main administrative policies of the previous fifteen years had now become highly explosive.

[91] *WHB*, July 13, 1965.

[92] Liu's three terms were *shangdeng*, *zhongdeng*, and *xiadeng*, quoted in Bernstein, *Up to the Mountains*, p. 279.

CHAPTER 10

Maoists Try to Remake Management, 1966–1968

The future is bright;
the road is tortuous.
—A CCP Constitution

The aim of this book is not to give a general report on Shanghai's Cultural Revolution, but only to show how its violence and ostracism began. For this purpose, it is enough to follow events through the period of greatest chaos in 1966–68. The task of these chapters on the time of tumult is more complex than that of earlier sections. They must show how social reactions to labels, monitors, and campaigns caused the brutality, but they must also show how other precipitating factors (related to Mao's initiatives and divisions in national and municipal elites) broke the dam to loose the flood of widespread frustrations that the policies of pressure had stored, as in a reservoir, for many years. Those three policies were the central causes of violence in this movement. They channeled broad cultural and personality options that might otherwise (and usually do) create order rather than chaos. These policy variables can now be linked both to immediate triggering factors and to underlying cultural and personality options, in an array of explanatory levels sufficient to account for this historical outbreak of mayhem.

There would be, at this point, several possible ways to proceed with the presentation. One choice is to divide the 1966–68 data into three parts (on labels, monitors, and campaigns); but this would structure the argument heavily in advance, to the exclusion of other variables that could emerge as important in a less-confined narrative. So a better alternative is to retain the previous form of presentation, dividing the 1966–68 material into sections on workers and managers, then residents and intellectuals (because substructure and superstructure, economy and symbols, are *not* the main explanatory means in this book). This allows a continuation of the most obvious kind of analysis (also not central here, except through the idea of accumulation): the straightforward narrative by time.

This approach, in which the categories of presentation are basically different from those of explanation, should be a rough kind of test for the main thesis, which is centered on policies. The method requires that the three topics of labeled groups, clientelist links, and legitimated violence arise in chapters or paragraphs organized otherwise (by the economic/symbolic difference, or by time). It also may allow a more lively telling of the story—and Shanghai's Cultural Revolution is full of obviously dramatic events. Most important, this approach should encourage readers to stand outside the main argument and observe the extent to which it applies—and the extent to which other factors may explain some aspects of the Cultural Revolution, especially those different from its turmoil.

ARMY-PROLETARIAT FAMILISM IN 1966 AND THE "BLOOD PEDIGREE"

In June 1966, over twenty thousand unionized workers in Shanghai joined the Communist Party.[1] Political department cadres encouraged the formation of clubs of youths from the "five red types" (*hong wu lei*; that is, workers, poor and lower-middle-class peasants, revolutionary cadres, revolutionary soldiers, and dependents of revolutionary martyrs). It is worth noting that three of these five red types are not social classes in any proper Marxist sense. The "blood pedigree theory" (*xuetong lun*) was summed up in a quasi-traditional couplet:

If the father's a hero, the son's a good chap;
If the father's a reactionary, the son's a bad egg.[2]

These ideas were understandably popular among some workers, and especially among cadres. The main guarantee of the political importance of such notions lay in the power of armed factory militias.

These military forces, which had been well funded since 1964, were di-

---

[1] *NCNA*, June 31, 1966.

[2] An interviewee quoted this couplet by Tan Lifu: *Laozi yingxiong er hao han; / laozi fandong er hundan*. This sort of saying was a *duilian*, displayed on either side of a door; on the lintel, the horizontal (*hengpi*) slogan was *Dangran ru ci* ("Of course it's so!"). But Jiang Qing, much of whose constituency was actually ex-bourgeois, did not like Tan's poem, so she proposed one of her own: *Laozi yingxiong er jieban; / laozi fandong er beipan* ("If the father is a hero, the son is in the successor generation; / if the father is a reactionary, the son betrays him [becoming acceptable]"). Her *hengpi* was "It should be so!" (*Yinggai ru ci*). See also Gordon White, *The Politics of Class and Class Origin: The Case of the Cultural Revolution* (Canberra: Australian National University Contemporary China Centre, 1976), p. 29. This was also called the "origin only theory" (*wei chushen lun*). Both terms originated with opponents of the doctrine, in the summer of 1966.

vided into contingents averaging ten reservists each.[3] Demobilized soldiers in political departments tended to take charge of these armed units. The soldiers were mostly, though not entirely, of proletarian origin. Such militias were not easy to join. As an ex-cadre explained,

> Anyone who wants to join the people's militia must make a formal application, which is then approved or denied by Party officials at the level above the unit whose militia he would enter. Approval is not automatic. Ordinary reservists have much less access to arms than core militia [*jigan minbing*]. Workers whom their cadres consider fit for recruiting are asked to apply, and it is definitely good for their careers if they are activists in militia work. Militias are not formed among street residents, but only in places of labor or study. Ammunition for exercises is supplied by the Municipal People's Armed Forces Department [Wuzhuang Bu] and the Public Security Bureau, with all the important arms coming from the former. The guns of core militiamen are better than those of others, who often practice without real guns.[4]

These units were the basis for many proletarian conflict groups throughout 1966 and 1967.

The Socialist Education Movement's emphasis on class struggle meant to favored groups that their virtue came by ascription, not achievement. That movement's political departments had, in effect, created two kinds of cadres: demobilized soldiers and political department staff, on one hand, and people who had been managing work units before 1964, on the other.[5] In many units, these two groups were alternative leaderships. Monitoring, as well as labels, thus created political bands. Implicit and explicit violence defined the boundaries of these groups with increasing clarity in public, as the movement progressed.

Political clannishness was not limited to the masses; it also permeated the elite. The Party was the most important "family," the top patronage network in Shanghai, unifying leaders of the city with each other and with national politicians. This fraternity held together tightly in the 1960s—far better than descriptions from the CR aver. Mayor Ke Qingshi presided over this club in Shanghai. Ke's main deputy mayor and successor Cao Diqiu was his

---

[3] *XMWB*, January 18, 1966; the groups were called *minbing ban*.

[4] Interview with an ex–Party member who had much experience in various kinds of urban work, in Shanghai as well as elsewhere.

[5] See Xi Guang [Yang Xiaokai], "Zhongguo wenhua da geming dui shehuizhuyi zhidu de tupo" (The Cultural Revolution's disruption of the socialist system), *Zhishi fenzi* (The Chinese intellectual) (New York), no. 7 (Spring 1986): 13.

"old friend."[6] Ke had been in the same Party study group as Mao Zedong at Yenan, and he also had fine relations with Liu Shaoqi.[7] Ke was in networks that involved most of the national leaders—not just Mao and Liu Shaoqi, but also Lin Biao. The defense minister's daughter, Lin Doudou, called Ke "uncle," and she wrote passionate revolutionary letters to the mayor's son, Ke Liuliu.[8] Ke kept calligraphy by Mao under the glass atop his desk. It was possible for him to preside over inconsistent, potentially conflicting policies in Shanghai, because the label of high Party cadre created the strongest family of all, and because the CCP's patronage by the mid-1960s became peerless.

Family ties can lead to bitter feuds, however; and Ke had also been central to these in Shanghai. During 1963, Ke demoted the more bureaucratic Shi Ximin and promoted the more radical Zhang Chunqiao in the municipal propaganda apparatus.[9] But the mayor was an important patron, and economic bureaucrats like Cao continued to work prominently and harmoniously with Ke, even though Cao and Shi apparently had no clash (and were both later purged in the Cultural Revolution). Not just at this high municipal level, but also in many smaller units, personal dependencies like that of Cao on Ke often overrode other interests.[10]

---

[6] Cao was toppled in the Cultural Revolution and Ke's memory was greatly honored then; so it was notable to hear these interview reports from two separate ex-cadres concerning good relations between Ke and Cao.

[7] Liu Shaoqi was chosen for the honorific but important role of head of the funeral committee when Ke Qingshi died on April 9, 1965 (*XMWB*, April 10, 1965).

[8] *CNA*, July 2, 1965, p. 7.

[9] *1969 Zhong Gong nianbao* (1969 Communist China yearbook) (Taipei: Zhong Gong Yanjiu Cazhi She, 1969), 5:41.

[10] It is possible to find lapses of loyalty between Shanghai cadres who suffered together in the Cultural Revolution, and it is also possible to find disharmony between politicians who gained together in this movement. For example, Shi Ximin complained bitterly about maltreatment by his superior in the Party, Qian Junrui, though they were both toppled in 1967. Persistent rumors referred to tension between the Shanghai Garrison (and Lin Biao) and the leaders of the Shanghai Revolutionary Committee (and Jiang Qing). Indeed, a few years later Lin Biao fell and the radicals did not. Interviews place the following Shanghai leaders in the "Lin family": garrison commander Liao Zhengguo, fleet commander Gao Zhirong, air commander Ji Yingwu, and public security head Li Binshan. Jiang Qing's "family" reportedly included surviving municipal Party leader Feng Guozhu, finance and trade czar Li Yanwu, high Party secretaries Chen Linhu and Lu Wencai, and trade union ideologue Xu Jingxian, as well as the main Revolutionary Committee leaders. The point is not that these speculations are wrong (they were probably right) but that personal ties rather than policy ideas long kept these two groups from conflicting and unified each of them internally after they did conflict. Shi Ximin's "confession" is in *Weidong* (Defend the East) (Tianjin), June 15, 1967. On the high-political "families," see *XDRB*, October 11, 1968, and *Wanren cazhi* (Magazine for the millions) (Hong Kong), no. 50 (1968): 6; and earlier, *Shanghai zhengquan douzheng* (Shanghai power struggle) (Taipei: n.p.,

Political solidarity of this clannish sort made other forms of social bond less important. State economic planning tended to increase clientelism. Campaigns, based on the idea that pressures for social goals would be either violent or ineffective, made people narrow the range of colleagues they trusted. General, rather than functionally specific, ties between people became crucially important. Labels also induced familism. By mid-1966, cadres of political departments, soldiers in the army, and workers from pre-1949 proletarian backgrounds made up Shanghai's official legitimate family. Some other local leaders had prestige, but the policies of the state had been aimed for seventeen years at reducing it.

HIGH AND LOCAL ELITES AT THE SLOW START OF VIOLENCE IN 1966

Mao Zedong was an inspiration to diverse urban Chinese, especially at three times in 1966. First: On May 16, his Central Committee issued a circular establishing a "Central Cultural Revolution Small Group." The May 16 document also countermanded a February report by "moderate" Beijing mayor Peng Zhen, and it roused radicals throughout China. Second and most important: On August 8 the Central Committee passed a resolution (reportedly written by Mao himself) warning against indiscriminate persecution and—above all—rescinding the police's usual authority to prevent political groups from forming outside the Party. Third: On August 18, Mao appeared at a Beijing rally of one million Red Guards, accepting their armband. Mao's public support for the "Cultural Revolution" (a term that still meant different things to different people) led many to take up politics.

"Cultural Revolution" had been a propaganda theme in high politics for some time. It at first had scant effect on managers and workers, except insofar as it filled their newspapers. Mao and his wife Jiang Qing had used Shanghai as a base for critiques of their rivals in Beijing.[11] This was commonly known and rumored; but it did not bear directly on most people's lives. Some Communist leaders' infatuation with the idea of holding a "cul-

---

1967). On patronage in general, see John Wilson Lewis, *Political Networks and the Chinese Policy Process* (Stanford, Calif.: Northeast Asia–United States Forum, 1986).

[11] A Shanghai critic, Yao Wenyuan, published a famous attack on a drama by a Beijing deputy mayor in *Wenhui bao* on November 10, 1965—at Mao Zedong's behest, since the play criticized the Chairman for his repression of Defense Minister Peng Dehuai's objections to Mao's Great Leap policies. Three months later, Jiang Qing chaired a "Conference on Literature and Art in the Armed Forces," also held at Shanghai. *NCNA*, May 18, 1967, gives a good description.

tural revolution" went back much further—at least to the Soviet attempt at a movement by that name in the late 1920s.[12] In Shanghai, efforts to convert such notions into attacks on institutions began in the publishing industry. The head of Zhonghua Bookstore, Li Junmin, was assailed in June 1966.[13] A local newspaper complained that Li "borrowed old things to satirize new."[14] The slogans and name of this movement were not new, however. Clearly some important politicians, including Mao, were interested in it; but for most people in Shanghai's economy, this at first seemed to be just another campaign.

Mayor Cao Diqiu on June 11 read a "mobilization report" for the Cultural Revolution to a mass rally of ten thousand at People's Square in the center of town, encouraging "all Party members, Youth League members, the masses of peasants and workers, and revolutionary cadres and intellectuals to carry the Great Proletarian Cultural Revolution through to the end."[15] In July, Mayor Cao chaired a meeting to celebrate the forty-fifth anniversary of the founding of the CCP in Shanghai, and he spoke on the same podium with a diverse group of his later rivals: a representative of the Shanghai Garrison, a textile union chief (who was later on the Revolutionary Committee), and a student leader from Fudan University (later the most militant of Shanghai's schools).[16] The clientelist norm, now well established, had two opposite effects: First, it made everyone interested in the views of that father of fathers, Chairman Mao, who refrained from commenting in public about Shanghai's leaders Cao and Chen (with whom he may have hoped to get along). But second, it also gave those local patrons more claim to rule in Shanghai. Mayor Cao Diqiu and Municipal First CCP Secretary

---

[12] See William G. Rosenberg's *Bolshevik Visions: The First Phase of the Cultural Revolution in Soviet Russia* (Ann Arbor, Mich.: Ardis, 1984), and works cited in its footnotes.

[13] Four years earlier, Li Junmin had published a novel (*Du Fu hui jia* [Du Fu returns home]) about a poet's brave petitions to a Tang emperor on behalf of the common people, and about how the poet was purged at the hands of a bad emperor. This tale strongly resembled a drama that Mao's polemicist Yao Wenyuan had criticized. It was another allegory on Mao's mistreatment in 1959 of those who criticized the Chairman and the Leap. See Ding Wang, *Niugui sheshen ji* (Collection of ghosts and monsters) (Hong Kong: Sanjia Dian Shuwu, 1967), p. 106; *1967 feiqing nianbao* (1967 Chinese Communist yearbook) (Taipei: Feiqing Cazhi She, 1967), pp. 345, 583; and *XMWB*, June 26, July 12, 1966.

[14] *Jie gu feng jin.* Li could counterattack with another phrase, saying Yao had "sold off his friends to seek glory" (*mai you qiu rong*). But Li had, not long before, been a colleague of Yao's in the radical post-1963 CCP Municipal Propaganda Department. As with many such cases, it is hard to verify CR assertions that leaders who became rivals in 1966–68 had always been so. Earlier evidence suggests they had often cooperated, under patrons like Mayor Ke.

[15] *XMWB*, June 11, 1966.

[16] *XMWB*, July 1, 1966.

Chen Peixian were the designated satraps, and most Shanghai people expected their word to be authoritative.

Neither Cao nor Chen ever spoke in public against the Cultural Revolution. All high leaders tried to manipulate political action in Shanghai during 1966—but neither the "moderate" nor the "radical" camp had overwhelming resources or clear identities. Mayor Cao and Secretary Chen supported a version of the CR, even after it made their work more difficult in late August—indeed, even after it purged them in January. They were revolutionary patrons; they had fine high-cadre labels. They knew from experience that bold association with ever-changing campaigns can be a necessary course for an administrator, in a context of policies that are unstable to raise compliance. In the hot summer of 1966, even as political department cadres organized struggle meetings in some cultural institutions, and as suicides among the first bourgeois victims began, the leaders of the Shanghai Party supported this movement.[17]

The "Sixteen Point Decision" of August 8, from Mao's Central Committee, was the most important specific spark for Cultural Revolution that ever came from Beijing, because it forbade the public security apparatus from suppressing new political groups. These began forming almost immediately. According to one source, participation was now explicitly open to people from the "seven black categories" (*hei qi lei*: landlords, rich peasants, counterrevolutionaries, bad elements, rightists, bourgeois, and reactionary intellectuals).[18] Political organizing, even violent action, was now a course that any common-label or common-rival group might take.

This directive of Mao's was not encumbered with consistency. It warned against indiscriminate persecution of people, but it also let unprecedented kinds of groups organize to vent their frustrations—which were intense enough to start exactly that kind of persecution. Mao's donning of a Red Guard armband (when most Red Guards were still good proletarians) was ambiguous in meaning, because no one could know what direction the youth movement would take, now that millions who had suffered discrimination could join it.

Some interpretations of the Cultural Revolution make much of Mao's

[17] On the suicides, see the *Star* (Hong Kong), December 12, 1966, and Sophia Knight, *A Window on Shanghai* (London: Deutsch, 1967), who also reported the start of the movement at the Shanghai Foreign Languages Institute, where she was teaching (pp. 228ff). It is tragic that, later and elsewhere, Ms. Knight also died similarly.

[18] Xi, "Zhongguo wenhua," p. 12. The author of this article has confirmed this information in an interview, although another interviewee emphasizes that "black category" members who were able to join Red Guard groups did not advertise their backgrounds.

intentions, but it would be hard to say these were always clear to the Chairman himself. He had a generalized liking for struggle and chaos. As he said after a fracas at a school in the summer of 1966, "There is one good thing about our era: the left-wingers get beaten up by the right-wingers, and this toughens up the left-wingers."[19] He did not always seem concerned, however, about which constituencies or policies might motivate such violence: "Some of the students did not have terribly good family backgrounds, but were our own family backgrounds all that good?"[20] The legitimacy of label categories, of avuncular advice, and of social violence was more constant, from Mao, than were the aims to which any of these habits might be put. Mao often took no stands on specific goals.[21] So he often decentralized fights over real resources until local winners were obvious.

In August and September, Mao took an inspection tour in the best imperial fashion, declaring that China's counterrevolutionary enemies were to be found on the "ultra left," not just the right. By September 15, he came out for patronage by warning: "Our cause will come to a stop, unless youth can respect experienced Party cadres."[22] And on September 20, his "latest directive" found "no reason whatever that the ranks of the workers' party be split into two big factions, bitterly opposed to each other."[23] By that time, however, his reduction of police controls—just one month earlier—had loosed on Chinese urban society local dynamics that were already quite beyond his span of control. Mao did not rule in the Cultural Revolution; he mainly reigned during it.

THE GLOSS OF ORDER: A ROLE FOR THE ARMY

The PLA, as soon as late summer, was everyone's insurance that China would hold together despite the new politics and disorder. The military had

---

[19] Stuart R. Schram, ed., *Chairman Mao Talks to the People* (New York: Pantheon, 1974), p. 258.

[20] Ibid., p. 268.

[21] This habit of Mao's, in more peaceful times than the Cultural Revolution, is suggested by Michel Oksenberg, "Chinese Policy Process and the Public Health Issue: An Arena Approach," *Comparative Studies of Communism* (April 1974): 375–412. This beautifully structured essay distinguishes the expression of vague values in "Mao's arena" from a "policy-specifying arena" showing more consistency, as well as "bureaucratic," "campaign," and local "community" arenas involving various kinds of administrative implementation. Different sorts of politics, defined along several dimensions, are shown to be typical in each of the five arenas. These strong patterns apply even to the CR.

[22] *WHB*, September 15, 1967.

[23] *WHB*, September 20, 1967.

connections in factories that made it independent not only of radicals but also of Party cadres. Many officers wanted to support their fellow cadres, but this impulse was countered by vague orders from Mao to support "rebels." The army was confused and somewhat neutralized during early stages of the CR. The Sixteen Points, which exempted soldiers from the jurisdiction of the Central Cultural Revolution Small Group, were "ardently hailed" by Shanghai "factories of the navy," as well as by the "sons and daughters of peasants and workers" at a university.[24] But the military was also supposed to "support the left"; and the most radical people were those most frustrated by the policies of pressure and manipulation by officials. Such "rebel" factions emerged in August to oppose a monopoly of politics by people with "good" proletarian labels. Even then, a "reporting group" of the Shanghai Garrison joined "revolutionary" staff from a shoe factory, students from a teacher's college that enrolled proletarians, policemen, and a "Red Thunder" youth group to make cultural revolution.[25] Shanghai air force units were especially active that August in "supporting" Red Guards who were offspring of cadres and officers.[26] In the same month, Secretary Chen Peixian called a meeting of service cadres in the West Suburb Park, to ask that naval and air force propaganda teams visit hotels where Beijing Red Guards were staying in Shanghai, to persuade them not to attack the Municipal Party Committee. Chen reportedly said, "You soldiers have to be well-prepared to take over the work of the city.... And if the [unofficial-background] Red Guards attack the Municipal Committee, you are going to stop them."[27]

Garrison commander Liao Zhengguo sent soldiers to keep order at the Municipal Committee building, which a group of Beijing Red Guards occupied on September 4.[28] In later months, the acting commander of the East Sea Fleet, Rao Shoukun, and the local deputy head of the air force, Wu Jun, were able safely to claim they had honored too many of Chen Peixian's establishmentarian requests, though they had meant all along to "support the

---

[24] *XMWB*, August 14, 1966.

[25] The Chinese name of the "Red Thunder" group, Hong Lei, has a punning *lei* that makes it sound like either "red thunder" or "red types." This group was in the Synthetic Fiber Research Institute and received special praise from the media; see *NCNA*, September 2, 1966, and *SHWB*, August 30, 1966.

[26] *SHWB*, August 27, 1966.

[27] *Da pipan tongxun* (Great criticism bulletin) (Guangzhou), October 5, 1967, reporting on a late August 1966 meeting. Chen asked that more than two hundred sailors go to the Hengshan Hotel, and that the air force send its men to the Yanan and Heping hotels. The source is hostile to Chen.

[28] The author was able to interview one of the main organizers of this student seizure of CCP headquarters, who stressed that Beijing had many more (maybe five or six times as many) university-level students as Shanghai had, so that worker-leaders were relatively more important in the East China metropolis.

left."[29] The armed forces served to hold China's political system together, because revolutionary policies had disrupted civilian economics and politics.[30] "Campaigns" were originally a military concept; but when overuse made their cost far exceed their benefit in civil society, the army stepped in reactively, to moderate the damage.

On October 1, 1966, Cao Diqiu celebrated National Day in style. Reportedly, "the Red Guards did not mind the removal of their big character posters to put up portraits of Mao or placards of quotations for the celebration."[31] Cao invited six hundred top officials to review a parade of 800,000, receive a twenty-eight-gun salute, and hear a speech by the mayor on the "excellent situation of the Cultural Revolution in Shanghai" and on the need for more "propagation of Mao Zedong thought." Cao saluted the Red Guards and asked Shanghai people to be gracious to visitors. Only in early November was Cao's public openness modified. Because of the Sixteen Points, he could not rely on police to control Shanghai as thoroughly as before (although at low levels, some patrolmen continued their previous repressive habits as late as mid-December).[32]

The main organization opposed to Cao and Chen called itself the "Shanghai Workers' Revolutionary Rebel General Headquarters," and it contained many people with bourgeois labels. This was the center of a loose federation of fifteen groups called the "Shanghai Workers' Revolutionary Rebels." The crucial Liaison Department in the federation contained cadres who remained amenable to the Municipal Committee longer than the federation's radical "Headquarters," which was its main political leadership.[33] Only in December were these establishmentarians in the Liaison Department removed, although conflict flared between the Party committee and the Headquarters long before then. The impulse for real change in Shanghai was now coming from people not previously labeled to make it, and cadre-proletari-

[29] *Da pipan tongxun* (Guangzhou) October 5, 1967. Also, the author has interviewed the organizer of the temporary takeover of the committee building, who by 1986 was no longer a Red Guard but a reformer sojourning in Princeton, N.J.

[30] Kau Ying-mao, *The People's Liberation Army and China's Nation-Building* (White Plains, N.Y.: International Arts and Sciences Press, 1973), refers to Morris Janowitz's "reactive militarism," which is very different from a "praetorian" coup. See also Lynn White, "The Liberation Army and the Chinese People," *Armed Forces and Society* 1, no. 3 (1975): 364–83. Campaign policies can lead to unintended coups.

[31] "Shanghai Letters," *South China Morning Post* (Hong Kong), October 21, 1966.

[32] See *SHWB*, December 17, 1966, for a story about incidents at the lane level in Jing'an District.

[33] Respectively, the *Shanghai gongren geming zaofan zong siling bu* and the *Shanghai gongren geming zaofan pai*; a liaison department is a *lianluo bu*; *SHWB*, January 16, 1967.

ans were now obstructionists. So the discontents chose new labels, like "revolutionary" and "rebel."

In early November, the Headquarters asked for a meeting with the mayor for support and recognition. Cao sent representatives to meet its leaders and to "make investigations," (as one report says, to "gather black materials" against them).[34] These emissaries were later accused of "carrying out espionage activities in the revolutionary mass movement."[35] The extent to which there would be a political break between the Party's cadres and discontented groups that now could form under radical leaders was uncertain to all of them, through the autumn of 1966. Campaign attacks had long been legitimate, and their extension to struggles against particular cadres had become normal in the Socialist Education era. But could this principle be further extended to justify assaults against large groups that were really (not just allegedly) well organized, with some chance to protect themselves? This was a new question in the PRC.

The Cultural Revolution spread in Shanghai's economy largely because cadres in political departments wanted to encourage a version of it that emphasized class struggle among labeled groups. Some Shanghai workers expressed indignation after the September incursion of Red Guards into local Party offices.[36] But the "young pathbreakers" had prestige as students, and many in contact with them enjoyed "the tumultuous spirit of Shanghai" at this time.[37]

The densely populated, half-rural "suburbs" of Shanghai—an expanse of territory under the city's jurisdiction, extending for a radius of about fifty kilometers around it—also received news of the movement.[38] Unhappy con-

---

[34] *Hongwei zhanbao* (Red Guard combat news) (Shanghai), January 8, 1967. Cao's emissaries were Liu Kuanying and Yang Huijie, head of the Party committee's Socialist Education Office. Yang's office was in charge of liaison to the Headquarters and had some authority even in the Liaison Department of the rebel federation. Yang reported to two high Party secretaries named Wang Shaoyong and Ma Tianshui (who, despite their roles at this time, later became the most important rehabilitated cadres on the Shanghai Revolutionary Committee). Ma was also later accused of trying "to collect materials on how the Workers' Revolutionary Rebel Headquarters established an illegal court, beat up others, and arrested people without authorization—but he failed to find any such material" (ibid.).

[35] Ibid.

[36] *China Topics* (Hong Kong), October 25, 1966, p. 4, on *Pravda*'s article about Shanghai of September 16.

[37] See Raymond F. Wylie, "Red Guards Rebound," *Far Eastern Economic Review*, September 7, 1967, p. 462.

[38] For much more on the suburbs, see Lynn White, "Shanghai-Suburb Relations, 1949–1966," in *Shanghai: Revolution and Development in an Asian Metropolis*, ed. Christopher Howe (Cambridge: Cambridge University Press, 1981), pp. 241–68.

tract workers, with jobs in the central metropolis, often spent weekends there; and they lived in the suburbs between stints in city factories. Large suburban market towns had disproportionate numbers of "social youths," ready to storm the center of the metropolis and demand proper urban registrations and unionized jobs.[39] Many groups were waiting in the wings, to claim their due against monitoring bureaucrats who had tightened control over them for decades. These groups could interpret the Sixteen Points in essentially the opposite way approved-background workers interpreted them.

The proletarian purists, however, were still better organized. Political departments had sometimes relied on capable bourgeois-background new workers, to help fight their conflicts with managers who had run factories without interference from 1956 to 1963–64. These mostly still retained their posts as directors or high secretaries, because the Socialist Education offices had personnel enough for hit-and-run work teams to irk them, but not enough to replace them permanently. A large firm affected in November by such tensions was the Shanghai No. 17 Cotton Mill, in which six CCP members pasted their "first revolutionary big character poster" against the factory's Party secretary. The protesters claimed they "all had family histories full of blood and tears in the old society."[40] Their complaint was against a "revisionist cadre line of recruiting deserters and turncoats." Urban factory jobs are plums in China, and previous policies had created a situation in which patronage networks could easily split people according to labels. By late 1966, rival local leaderships could now legitimately use threats of force to vie with each other for control of job allocations and economic goods.

The upwelling of frustrated interests that the Sixteen Points let loose created confusion among many leaders in Shanghai. Many understood that important masses and local elites had been repressed; so the new situation presented opportunities for advancement—but for whom? A vague consensual theme at this time was the importance of classes, and in November 1966 Shanghai people attended a large "class education exhibit" of items that Red Guards had taken from rich people's houses: a portrait of Chiang Kai-shek hidden behind a landscape painting, a copy of his book *China's Destiny*, some U.S. dollars, gold ingots, pearls, gems, fur coats, whiskey, even binoculars.[41] One ex-capitalist was caught with 137 bottles of Vaseline Hair Tonic. Against this, all could unite.

---

[39] A March 1966 campaign in five county seats near Shanghai attempted to concentrate the "social youths" on a single commune, but there is no evidence it effectively rounded them up. See *XMWB*, March 29, 1966.

[40] *NCNA*, June 3, 1969, reporting events that came to a head in November 1966.

[41] Knight, *Window on Shanghai*, pp. 230–35.

Such aesthetics became so important, even ex-capitalists could claim that "revolutionary" was the only important label now. This tag made for superficial unity, even when its meaning was not firmly established. Many scandals were now unearthed by Red Guards who came from "bad" families—and who thus had more reason than proletarians to show the ardor of their revolutionary faith.

POLITICAL EXPRESSION FOR NEW DEMANDS

The city fathers reacted in different ways to this upsurge of political participation, but none of them had the organizational resources to channel it. Zhang Chunqiao, the most important antiestablishment figure on the Municipal Party Committee, announced in early November: "We have planned to make revolution in factories at the next stage."[42] But in fact, no one whosoever had control of such developments. Regardless of any plans by Zhang or by fellow committeemen who soon became his rivals, some factories were already affected by the movement, either because of student visits, or political departments' class struggles, or contract workers' demands for better wages. The main force for change in 1966 came from small collectivities, not from top politicians of any stripe.

When groups discontent with their treatment under the policies of pressure came to express their grievances, the city fathers did not know what to do. Members of the "Workers' General Headquarters" appeared on November 8 at the Municipal Party Committee's central office, demanding recognition and an audience with Mayor Cao. He demurred, apparently because the petitioners' agenda involved wage and job-category demands. Disparate small groups cooperated to arrange the first rally and parade of "rebels"; they petitioned the Municipal Committee on November 9, and twenty thousand people attended. But by no means did all fifteen organizations within the rebel federation directly challenge the authority of Cao and other Party secretaries. On the contrary, many later said they thought they were presenting petitions whose legitimacy the Party would have to take seriously.

The Municipal Committee instructed its minions not to recognize or support the new federation. Groups of establishmentarian workers (called "gangs of hoodlums" by the rebels, probably because these gangs were factory militias) appeared for a counterdemonstration. The paraders nonetheless proceeded to the committee offices and continued to insist on seeing

---

[42] *Collection of Speeches by Central Leaders* (Beijing: Beijing Film Studio, December 1966), p. 4.

Mayor Cao. They were told to go to another place, where they waited until 2:00 the next morning, when a group of them resolved to present their petition in Beijing.[43] About twenty-five hundred commandeered a train, with the help of employees at the railway station in Zhabei. Irregular rail schedules had already become normal, because students had been boarding trains for some weeks without tickets, claiming a right since August to "make revolution" anywhere in China. The railway employees and police, formally under the army, loyally tried to obey the August rules and "support the left." Some "revolutionary tourists" were workers, either with bad political labels or with other reasons for discontent. When it came to commandeering trains, these were more welcome to the railwaymen than students had been.

When a small band of the petitioners reached Anting East, halfway to Suzhou, their train was directed to a siding and stopped. The Shanghai Party Committee leadership expressed concern about the Headquarters' independence; so it sent colleagues and relatives of the petitioners (members of the same patronage networks) to urge their return to Shanghai. More than half did go back.[44] Other petitioners telephoned Beijing; and on November 11, Zhang Chunqiao flew with air force help to Anting. He joined the emissaries of the Party committee—of which he was a member—trying to persuade the workers to return for discussion of their grievances in Shanghai. But five hundred of them, under a Party member named Geng Jinzhang, would hear none of it and went further to Suzhou. Zhang reversed himself and said he would endorse the demands if he could escort this "Suzhou Brigade" back to Shanghai. Once there, he had to sign their petition at a rally on Culture Square. The only hitch was that other leaders on the committee did not agree with his actions. Zhang had no consistent policy, and the leadership's disarray was evident soon after the signing, when Zhang went to the committee offices and met Cao in an effort (which was unsuccessful) to explain himself.[45] Many mass groups and discontented individuals were now autono-

---

[43] This chapter owes much to Neale Hunter, *Shanghai Journal: An Eyewitness Account of the Cultural Revolution* (New York: Praeger, 1969), and Andrew G. Walder, *Chang Ch'un-ch'iao and Shanghai's January Revolution* (Ann Arbor: Center for Chinese Studies at the University of Michigan, 1978). These differ from each other in their interpretation of events, but both are highly useful. Also useful are Gerald Tannebaum, "The 1967 Shanghai January Revolution Recounted," *Eastern Horizon* 7, no. 3 (1968): 7–25, and Evelyn Anderson, "Shanghai: The Masses Unleashed," *Problems of Communism* 27, no. 1 (1968): 12–21. The author has seen some but not all of the Red Guard tabloids that Hunter collected. Walder is currently also at work on Red Guard materials. The question of the relative importance of high- and low-level initiatives, in causing the Cultural Revolution, is a major interest for both Hunter and Walder (despite their differences), as it is here also.

[44] *Hongwei zhanbao* (Shanghai), January 8, 1967.

[45] Hunter, *Shanghai Journal*, pp. 140–42, citing *Hongwei zhanbao*, January 8, 1967 (this

mous, driven by their own interests that had grown as side effects of years of official pressure. But they were no longer effectively contained by such policies.

SPLINTERED CONSTITUENCIES AND UNCERTAIN LEADERS

High leaders' opportunism was matched at this time by a similar chaos in lower elites. Nobody knew whether the Party's committees were still authoritative; the prestige of all managers was thrown in doubt. Zhang had signed the rebel document as a member of the Party's Central Cultural Revolution Small Group (even though its chair, Mao's secretary, had a policy on the specific issue in Shanghai like that of the Municipal Committee).[46] Within two weeks after this, Zhang's office was ransacked, and he was attacked on wall posters.[47] Campaigns were still the rage in Shanghai, but they were no longer any single group's monopoly.

By December, even the *People's Daily* favored more leeway for the free expression of old grievances. It advocated

letting the masses elect Cultural Revolution groups. . . . Members of these organizations must not be appointed by superiors, nor is behind-the-scenes manipulation to be allowed. A system of general elections must be instituted in accord with the principles of the Paris Commune. . . . In the Cultural Revolution, no leaders of industrial and mining enterprises should strike at and retaliate against workers who have made criticisms or disclosed facts, nor are they allowed to reduce the wages of these workers, discharge these workers from their posts, or for the same reasons discharge contract workers. . . . Revolutionary workers who have been fired and

---

newspaper has been an important source for many researchers of this topic). Mayor Cao reportedly retorted to Zhang, "What you're saying is that all of us, all the members of the Municipal Committee, are in the wrong on this matter!" At another point, speaking to someone else, the mayor was quoted thus: "Chunqiao signs and catches us all with our pants down!" (ibid.).

[46] Ibid. The head of the Cultural Revolution Small Group in Beijing, Chen Boda, who was nominally Zhang's superior in that group, had sent a telegram to the Anting workers supporting the Municipal Committee's position that they ought to return to Shanghai. After Chen supported Zhang's action, a committee secretary telephoned Chen to ask, "Why the devil didn't you discuss it with us first?" The lame response was that Zhang had general authority. In practical terms, no one exercised such authority.

[47] Interview in Hong Kong with an ex–Red Guard who saw the posters and heard about the office ransacking.

forced to leave their factories must be allowed to return, to participate in production. They must be given wages that have been withheld.[48]

Contract workers or ex-rightists, some unionized individuals who disliked their bosses, and transformed or radicalized capitalist youths tended to join together in supporting this call for vaguely defined "revolution" as a justification for airing their grievances. Even Party cadres or managers with established client networks were inclined to go along with the new demand for money, whenever it suggested they could be openhanded with money and expand their patronage. "Radical" politicians supported such popular claims in late 1966, but within months they were repressing lower leaders who articulated these demands.[49] Different kinds of people could use this movement for opposite ends.

Small face-to-face groups gave the Cultural Revolution its fearsome force. A tremendous variety of them organized during November and December. Clubs of temporary and contract workers, rusticates from communes, army veterans' groups, and many other kinds of clubs freely participated.[50] When yet another band of workers headed off with their own demands toward Beijing, Zhang and Cao agreed they should be stopped; so this group, too, got no farther than Suzhou. After bargaining, Zhang persuaded Cao to sign the group's requests. Soon, however, the editor of the Party newspaper *Liberation Daily* rallied other, more establishmentarian "rebels" through the *Wenhui bao*, indicating that most committee members felt Zhang's policy was wrong—though obviously there was not yet a full break between Zhang and his colleagues on the committee, since Cao had also endorsed the latest demands.[51] At both high and low levels, there was continuing ambiguity about the extent to which groups let loose in August could ultimately cooperate with each other.

At 1:00 A.M. on November 30, a rebel student group occupied the offices of the Party newspaper.[52] These students, unwilling or unable to join Red Guard cliques closer to political departments, came from many back-

[48] *RMRB*, December 26, 1966.

[49] For this emphasis on Zhang's level, see Walder, *Chang Ch'un-ch'iao.*

[50] See Wylie, "Red Guards Rebound," p. 462.

[51] This editor's speech inspired Rebel ire against the Party paper (despite the fact that *Liberation Daily* had followed instructions to "support" the Rebels by allowing them to print their main tabloid on its presses). The editor, Ma Da, now heads *Wenhui bao*; he spent a night in the author's house at Princeton in late 1985. See also *WHB*, November 17, 1965, and Hunter, *Shanghai Journal*, pp. 143–44.

[52] The occupying group was the "Revolutionary Committee of Red Guards from Shanghai Schools and Universities," also known as the "Red Revolutionaries."

grounds. On December 2, they allowed a considerable force of workers—but not all with originally proletarian labels—into the newspaper offices. The occupiers repulsed a fierce attack from a group of good-background workers, some of whom managed to get into the building through an open window. The Party paper's absence from newsstands the next day disrupted habitual routine in many offices, and cadres were upset. By December 4, antirebel groups tried to retake the *Liberation Daily* building, using fire engines with hooks and ladders (apparently made available to them by police-linked groups). The attackers were driven off, but with many injuries to the defenders. As one of them said, "We rebels have been trying for six months to get this kind of chaos. We've had little success before this, but now at last we've made it!"[53] Unofficial campaigns could now take place.

On December 5 after intense negotiations, two secretaries of the Municipal Committee signed the demands of the rebel group, guaranteeing that an issue of the faction's *Red Guard War Report* would be sent to the whole mailing list of the *Liberation Daily*, assuring that the newspaper staff would make self-criticisms, and suggesting that the class labels of the rebels would not become subjects of struggle in their units: "When the workers return to their jobs, Party authorities and work teams must not make life difficult for them. They must not be harassed or forced to debate."[54]

Militia federations of true-red proletarian workers were now unsure where their Municipal Party Committee stood. Presumably they were pleased it had not ratified the promises that two of its secretaries had made to dubious-background youths. But some workers and militias joined together, on December 6, to form the "Scarlet Guards" (*chiwei dui*). These laid siege, in their turn, to the *Liberation Daily* offices, and by December 9 they had taken the building. At a rally, they denounced the previous occupants, the rebels, not just as rightists but as "fascists." Outside the newspaper offices, they sang a rousing chorus of "Never Forget Class Bitterness."[55]

Favored-label people felt their government was welshing on its commitment to affirmative action on their behalf, and they would not recognize that it lacked the resources to support that policy fully. As late as December 10, Cao's attempt finally to direct short-term policy toward groups with the means to sustain it stably—that is, to mollify the discontented who were now more powerful than before—seemed parallel with Zhang's. Cao announced that the Municipal Party Committee

[53] Hunter, *Shanghai Journal*, p. 165, trans. from *Hongwei zhanbao*, December 30, 1966.
[54] Hunter, *Shanghai Journal*, pp. 166–68.
[55] Ibid., p. 172.

publicly admits that the *Liberation Daily* incident . . . was caused by its [the committee's] bourgeois reactionary line. . . . But the Committee looks on the actions of the Rebel [not all proletarian-label] workers during the *Liberation Daily* incident as proletarian and revolutionary. Working hours lost by the Rebels are to be considered holiday time. Mayor Cao Diqiu will personally apologize to the wounded and their families, and the Committee will be responsible for all medical expenses. The Committee is in favor of the Red Revolutionaries' uniting with workers in the factories and joining them in the Cultural Revolution.[56]

These leaders were still in office, not yet in struggle sessions. They were trying to be loyal to the Party's central policies, even in December long after the chaos started. Yet the conflicting social forces created by measures they had sponsored for a decade and a half were now beyond their control. The Party's leaders, nearly irrelevant except as symbols, found themselves in charge of little more than their desks. They soon acquiesced, when people supporting or detesting the policies of pressure wanted to sit in their chairs instead.

The Shanghai Party Committee did not divide into two factions; it crumbled into many. First Secretary Chen Peixian knew that cadres in the education and rustication systems would never be forgiven by social groups now able to articulate political interests; so Chen at mid-December meetings said criticisms of these bureaucrats had to be allowed.[57] Different committee members supported different groups—and sometimes a single member supported conflicting groups, while claiming loyalty to the committee even as some of these groups were attacking it. Campaigning as an abstract work-style had overwhelmed any substantive campaign aims.

PARTY UNCERTAINTY AND "ECONOMISM"

The Committee often did not defend itself and pursued contradictory or vacillating policies.[58] On December 23, when 100,000 Scarlet Guards held

[56] Ibid., pp. 173–74, trans. from *Hongwei zhanbao*, December 30, 1966.

[57] The top officials involved were Chang Xiping, against whom Beijing radical Nie Yuanzi had made particular attacks since August, and Yang Xiguang.

[58] Secretary Ma Tianshui apologized for having discouraged the publication of the *Red Guard War Report*, which was sharply opposed to Party leaders like himself. Also, the committee could apparently do nothing to influence a violent conflict at the *Shanghai Evening News*, which had long published tabloids from proletarian workers' groups but was on December 22 occupied by "Rebels." The committee was more reactive, and closer to splintering into more than two subgroups, than it is often depicted in later literature.

a rally against the committee, both Mayor Cao and Secretary Chen appeared. Cao acceded to a list of demands from these good-label workers, just as he had earlier to opposite petitions from bad-label workers. Chen at first refused to sign (though he is usually depicted as Cao's staunch ally). But later, he was persuaded to go along. The next day, Chen denied that he had consented.[59] On behalf of the committee, he was again reacting to nonproletarian "Rebel" opinions, just as Cao had reacted to the interests of established workers.

"Economism" became a major issue in December, but even months earlier in the chaos of the Cultural Revolution, workers had been able to revise some rules in their own favor. Economism was mostly a matter of workers coercing cadres to approve demands for higher pay and other privileges.[60] In textile mills using shifts, the reduction of work points for bad cloth production was abolished as a "capitalist" means of management.[61] Hiring rules were of greatest interest, however, especially to nonunion workers and the unemployed. A large number of suburban rusticates and social youths, encouraged by mixed signs of tolerance on the Party Committee, especially from Zhang Chunqiao, joined other Rebels at a nonviolent sit-in near the center of Shanghai on December 27. The mayor also appeared at this meeting, even though it was threatened by a counterdemonstration of Scarlet Guards.[62]

The position of temporary and contract workers was always precarious, because they had grievances against bosses who could hurt them. But on December 26, a *People's Daily* editorial told managers they must not be fired. Even nonunion workers were eligible for back pay, if they had been suspended in the melee between different kinds of workers during that month.[63] Zhang Chunqiao wanted at this time to recruit support from nonunion contract workers and social youths, especially because many unionized workers then opposed him.[64] Some factory managers outside political departments almost surely saw chances of increasing their own patronage among such people by easing the discrimination against bad-label workers. As a proletarian tabloid hostile to this "Party capitalist" coalition at one factory put it, "They vigorously instigate second-grade workers to demand

[59] *Zuguo* (Fatherland) (Hong Kong), November 1968, p. 35.

[60] For further definition, and an amusing instance of Shanghai dockworkers beseiging a cadre for seven hours in a toilet until he approved their demands, see Raymond F. Wylie, "Shanghai Dockers in the Cultural Revolution," in *Shanghai*, ed. C. Howe, pp. 112–14.

[61] *JFRB*, September 16, 1966.

[62] Hunter, *Shanghai Journal*, p. 205.

[63] Ibid., and *Current Scene*, March 15, 1968, pp. 8–9.

[64] See Lynn White, "Workers Politics in Shanghai," *Journal of Asian Studies* 26, no. 1 (1976): 99–116.

promotions, young apprentices to demand additional wages, women workers to demand welfare benefits, and cooks to demand subsidies. They even incite masses to 'rebel' against their working clothes, rubber or leather shoes, and collective dormitories."[65]

The main wave of "economism" began in late December. Managers offered extra money to workers in order to maintain clientelist support at a time that was politically tough for bosses. Piecework systems were abandoned, on the ground that different shops did different kinds of work, which were not comparable. Disparate shops in many factories formed factions that opposed each other. Many managers gave "economistic" bonuses only to regular unionized workers; others gave them also to contract or temporary types. These actions increased "contradictions between different kinds of workers."[66] More to the point, they reflected the rising cost of keeping monitors in power, now that so many of these patrons were so deeply resented by such large portions of their designated clienteles.

Economism was a policy initiated at low and middle levels during a time of factious politics to pay for habits that were now more expensive. It was not a plot by top politicians. Many workers had long felt undercompensated: In early 1966, the Shanghai Federation of Trade Unions administered pensions for only 130,000—a small portion of the city's labor force.[67] Hard jobs with low pay still went disproportionately to North Jiangsu coolies. Stratification in Shanghai's proletariat had almost surely increased, not decreased, since 1960; and the favored groups wanted this to continue as much as the others wanted it to change.

STRESSES BETWEEN DIFFERENT KINDS OF WORKERS AND PATRONS

Tensions between managers who had gained their posts during the Socialist Education Movement and those who had joined their units earlier

---

[65] *RMRB*, January 16, 1967; this plant was not in Shanghai, however. Kitchen budgets, referred to here, are a perennial topic in Chinese units. Managers increase their patronage by providing meals for employees; but cooks do the shopping, and avoiding embezzlement is a widespread source of tension. This is not high politics; but the pattern of conventional minor rake-offs by cooks is so common, the total amount of such payments in China as a whole must be enormous.

[66] See Anderson, "Shanghai," pp. 12–28. On Lenin's definition of economism as bourgeois union policy, see his "What Is to be Done."

[67] *NCNA*, March 12, 1966. A percentage of the total work force is not calculated here because some pension schemes may not have been included in the numerator. The coverage of Shanghai's workers was far from complete, however.

affected Shanghai's Cultural Revolution in factories.[68] Many Rebels resented the Party committee's and some managers' efforts to accommodate unionized labor in this period. As one radical tabloid put it, after the mayor signed a unionists' petition: "No doubt Cao Diqiu was only too glad to agree to the demands. The revolutionary people of Shanghai, on the other hand, do *not* agree to them. As far as the Rebels are concerned, the Lord Mayor's signature is not worth a fart!"[69]

When unionized workers became angry in their turn, they could readily capture attention by calling strikes. The propriety of such actions has always been a theoretical riddle for Communist governments. By 1967 in Shanghai, that problem was beside the point: no authority was strong enough to stop strikes. The Party committee's sometime support of contract laborers brought from unionists a "three stop" (*san ting*): of work, electricity, and water supplies. Power generation did not cease totally, though, because the small, well-established work force at Yangshupu Electric Plant was induced to "declare proudly that electricity supplies would not be interrupted, so long as they were at the furnaces."[70] The water stoppage was also incomplete.

Rail service and much other work temporarily ended, however. At 5:00 A.M. on December 30, someone at the Shanghai Station in Zhabei turned off the current supplying all stop/go beacons along the main lines to Nanjing and Hangzhou.[71] Within an hour, unionized workers in the suburb of Wusong (apparently including pilots who guide ships up the Huangpu River to Shanghai docks) also left their jobs. Some postal and telecommunications workers disappeared too.[72] That day and the next, over sixty thousand Scarlet Guards boarded trucks for Beijing. They were stopped at Kunshan by a much larger number of Rebels (almost surely transported there with army help, but also involving rural or sent-down youths without urban household registrations). After violent battles for the control of transport lines, lasting at least through January 4, most of the Scarlet Guards had to return to Shanghai. Establishmentarian loyalty among some regular workers had

---

[68] This discussion draws on many sources. See *RMRB*, December 26, 1966, trans. in *SCMP* 3852 (1966): 1, and Bruce MacFarlane, *Visit to Shanghai* (n.p. [apparently University of Sydney], 1968), entry of April 21, 1968.

[69] From *Hongwei zhanbao*, January 4, 1967, trans. in Hunter, *Shanghai Journal*, p. 189. Cao and Chen tried to serve two basically different kinds of groups, both the previously favored and the previously unfavored sectors of Shanghai's work force—as the principles of August implied they should. Eventually, they lost the support of both.

[70] *NCNA*, January 16, 1967.

[71] *NCNA*, February 9, 1967.

[72] *GMRB*, January 25, 1967.

weakened their co-unionists' strike. But politicians had to respect factory militias and to acknowledge the strength of previously favored workers.

Rebels also wanted to travel and express themselves. Two days later, a group of them got one of five trains that were stranded at the Shanghai Station to move, "even though the ordinary railroad workers were absent, [and the Rebels] didn't know much about running locomotives. But they were full of love for Chairman Mao."[73] Ten hours behind schedule, the train arrived at Changzhou, halfway to Nanjing, where the amateur engineers were advised that a train ahead of them did not have its lights on, and that none of the signals were working. So they stopped.[74]

On January 9, a "Shanghai Workers' Revolutionary Rebel General Headquarters Railway Liaison Command" moved into the offices of the local railway administration. Two days later, the trains were running again.[75] The railroad stoppage was later officially blamed on a minister in Beijing who had run the railway system for years.[76] But this leader was not in Shanghai and had not controlled access to trains for several months. The stoppage came mainly from anonymous low-level worker-leaders and ex-soldiers in Shanghai. It was not a general strike, because many Shanghai workers (especially in commerce) were of nonproletarian class backgrounds and had no sympathy for the Scarlet Guards. The Municipal Committee's loyalty to central directives favoring Rebels had nonetheless created a situation in which crucial aspects of the economy stopped—despite the intelligible intentions of either the committee or of the radicals writing those directives.

THE "JANUARY REVOLUTION" AND UNRULY CONSTITUENCIES

On January 7, the first serious struggle meeting against Mayor Cao, Secretary Chen, and their main associates was televised throughout the city. Chen, especially, was accused of having created "two separate systems of education," apparently for people from different backgrounds. He was also

[73] *RMRB*, January 20, 1967.

[74] Ibid. After a wait, and after army assistance, this Express No. 14 finally reached Beijing.

[75] *RMRB*, January 15, 1967.

[76] The two offending officials were Lü Zhengcao and Xiao Wangdong, neither of whom appears much in Shanghai reports; see *Jinjun bao* (Attack report) (Beijing), January 28, 1967. A wall poster implicated the mayor of Nanjing and important central leader Tao Zhu; see Tokyo cable in *Ming bao* (Hong Kong), January 10, 1967. One local leader, identified only as "Zhang," is mentioned in *Gongren zaofan bao* (Workers' rebel news) (Shanghai) January 10, 1967.

chastised for promoting "a lot of new cadres."[77] The struggle meeting against Cao and Chen did less to restore order, however, than did promulgation of new police rules on January 7. These new regulations rescinded the August restraints on patrolmen, though by this time the police had become ineffective. An "Urgent Notice" of January 9 was also designed to freeze all units' savings accounts, revoke all permission for people to leave Shanghai for "exchanging revolutionary experiences," and order all factions occupying public buildings to leave.[78] Such brave decrees were little more than wishful thinking, in that January, except insofar as the army might help enforce them.

Zhang Chunqiao tried to rebuild a cohesive constituency for Shanghai government at this time. The main worker groups that had sometimes allied with Zhang were the First, Second, and Third regiments, loosely federated with each other and owing loyalty to worker-leader Geng Jinzhang. Especially after the large Scarlet Guard rally on December 23, Zhang had insisted that the regiments put themselves under his control. As late as January 6, however, when Zhang repeated this demand in a telephone call to Geng, the latter reportedly said, "Zhang Chunqiao is against our independence. I have put it to the men that they should join the Workers' Headquarters. They say they would rather stay in the Regiments. Can I help it if we have the power and the Workers' Headquarters is a cipher?"[79]

Another independent group was the Workers' Third Headquarters, led by Chen Hongkang. This group was willing to accept members with backgrounds as dubious as that of its head; Chen's father had been a GMD policeman. The Red Guard Army was another nonstudent group, which included many demobilized soldiers and was linked to a national network of veterans' associations. None of these were Scarlet Guards, but each eventually opposed the Municipal Committee as well as its sometime member Zhang Chunqiao. They were also separate from each other.

Army links to Scarlet Guard militias provided Zhang's main hope of ending the strike and developing support for himself. His plan was, apparently,

[77] Chen's past differences with the deceased Mayor Ke Qingshi received much attention in the CR, even though there is scant public evidence for these from the 1950s and early 1960s. An interviewee who was a high cadre in Shanghai for most of the late 1950s and early 1960s said that Mayor Ke and Secretary Chen had disagreed then; but they managed to keep these divisions secret, and to run the city effectively together, throughout that period. This interviewee also suggested that Ke's differences with Cao Diqiu in the same long period were much less. Red Guard tabloids tended to overstate the split between Ke and Cao.

[78] *WHB*, and *JFRB*, January 9, 1967; reprinted in *RMRB*, January 12, 1967.

[79] *Gongren zaofan bao* (Workers' rebel news) (Shanghai), March 13, 1967, trans. in Hunter, *Shanghai Journal*, p. 227.

to use soldiers in Scarlet Guard units to attract "middle-level cadres who are hoodwinked," and thus "welcome repentant Scarlet Guards." Zhang advocated "pointing the spearhead at the upper level" within the Scarlet Guards organization, arresting or demoting leaders from the top down until cooperative ones could be found.[80] He was not in a position to be very choosy about the previous labels of prospective allies, or to worry about their previous statuses as high or medium monitors, or to obtain sure compliance by threats. These administrative techniques had become less useful, because they had been pushed so far that people now knew how to deal with them. At least for a while, Zhang had to politick seriously for support, promising much to everyone and not bothering with consistency among his own principles.

LINKS BETWEEN LABELS
AND CONFLICT GROUPS

The variety of interest groups active by mid-January was unprecedented. It would be impossible to give a list of all such organizations, because they combined with each other in both policy federations and patron-client networks. Their members did not always agree with each other. It is nonetheless possible to list major categories that apply not only in Shanghai, but also in other cities.

First came the formation of student groups, of both "good class" and "rebel" kinds. These all called themselves Red Guards (*hong weibing*). Then workers organized, usually as Revolutionary Rebel factions (*geming zaofan pai*). Temporary or contract workers tended to call themselves Red Laborers (*hong laogong*). Housemaids and servants dubbed themselves Red Warriors (*hong zhanshi*). Unionized workers from proletarian backgrounds were sometimes Scarlet Guards (*chi weidui*). Demobilized soldiers and political department cadres often joined federations called the Red Flag Army (*hongqi jun*) or Red Guard Army (*hongwei jun*).[81]

In many cities during the course of 1967–68, such diverse groups joined two loose coalitions. The first consisted of "conservative factions" (*baoshou pai* or *baohuang pai*, as their enemies called them) mainly recruited from the families of political department cadres, activists who had proletarian family

---

[80] This policy is outlined, circumspectly but clearly, in *WHB*, January 20, and *GMRB*, January 25, 1967.

[81] See *China News Summary* (Hong Kong), 153 (January 12, 1967): 3; and Xi, "Zhongguo wenhua," p. 14.

backgrounds before 1949, unionized workers, most kinds of demobilized soldiers,[82] policemen, and students who had entered prestigious schools through affirmative action.

A second broad coalition, which was often called the "rebel faction" (*zaofan pai*), contained some pre-1964 managers, many temporary and contract workers, youths who had been rusticated but were now back in the city, Party civilians who had specialized in "united front" or "white area" work, students whose families contained members with bad political labels, and other activists whose families had income from land or capital before 1949 and needed to live down their dubious class labels.

In Shanghai, at least until late February 1967, the most powerful coteries representing the "conservative" position included worker-militiamen and Scarlet Guards. Their main rivals were called Revolutionary Rebels. In Guangzhou, these two federations came to be called, respectively, East Winds and Red Flags. In Wuhan, the establishmentarians dubbed themselves the Million Heroes, and the more radical moiety was the Workers' General Headquarters. In Wuzhou, where the Cultural Revolution became especially violent, these were respectively the Alliance Command and the Revolutionary Rebel Grand Army. In Beijing, the more conservative coalition was called the "Heaven Faction" (because of participants from the Aviation Institute), whereas the more radical group was the "Earth Faction" (because it was partly led from the Institute of Geology).[83]

It would be possible to list ten or twenty Shanghai organizations in each of the two coalitions at any particular time in 1967, but the most important group for any individual tended to be much smaller. The total of patronage networks and interest circles in each of the large urban moieties was huge. Personal ties between leaders and followers are difficult in big groups. Within a single workshop (for example, No. 3 at the No. 2 Shanghai Steel Factory), at least four organizations had formed by January, with the colorful names "Red Daggers," "Scaling Perilous Peaks," "Tough-Bone Lu Xun," and "Iron Brooms." Furthermore, each band "stressed its special fea-

---

[82] Many demobilized soldiers had been in Socialist Education Campaign work teams and political departments, but others had been frustrated by this movement, either because they did not advance as fast as their more activist comrades, or else because they had been recruited for foreign wars on patriotic grounds from dubious class backgrounds. This latter group disliked "class struggle." Others, who could end up as "rebels" rather than "conservatives," had run afoul of the Socialist Education Campaign because their application of military discipline in civilian monitoring roles had made them unpopular.

[83] Hong Yung Lee, *The Politics of the Chinese Cultural Revolution: A Case Study* (Berkeley and Los Angeles: University of California Press, 1978), pp. 217, 233, gives this argument in detail for Beijing and Guangzhou.

tures and was unwilling to join with others."[84] Different workshops in the same steel plant had further cliques, which might temporarily oppose or ally with any others or with factions throughout the city.

As the Rebels well knew, the end of the old Party did not by itself stop the policies of pressure they resented. One of their tabloids warned, "Up to now, some comrades think that everything is solved because the Shanghai Municipal Committee has been overthrown. They think the revolution has been 'thorough.' But they fail to see what the reactionaries transmit to factories through the work of bureaus, departments, and corporations of the Center."[85] Local organizations were thus told to seize the "black name books" (*heiming ce*) that Central organizations kept in Shanghai. Rebels also gathered information on cadres who had been cleared as "good" or "reformed" in the Socialist Education Movement, but who might not actually be so.[86] They wanted more flexible labels in the future.

CONTINUING IMPORTANCE OF OLD LABELS AS THE STATE REORGANIZES

The strike and Kunshan battles were only the most obvious examples of general chaos. Just as important, by January, was a widespread voluntary withdrawal by managers and professionals with dubious old labels. Doctors stopped showing up at their hospitals in January. At the beginning of the next month, a special decree ordered them to appear and treat the sick.[87] With established managements weaker, labor organizations in many units became stronger. The local Party newspaper thus launched a campaign against the "guild mentality" in people who "organize their ranks according to occupations and branches of work."[88] In other words, they became harder to control when they coalesced according to current substructural categories, rather than according to administratively labeled status groups.

Contract workers assigned to tough jobs, however, made a more solid Marxist analysis, by pointing out in a tabloid that their group was like a real class (and an exploited one, by the mid-1960s, even though some of its members had old official labels such as landlord or bourgeois):

[84] *RMRB*, January 31, 1967.

[85] *Jidian zhanbao*, February 19, 1967.

[86] Ibid. This paper was in Zhang's organization, and it used localist rationales for obtaining materials that might later denigrate cadres in Center-led units if they refused to cooperate with Zhang.

[87] *CNA*, April 7, 1967.

[88] *JFRB*, March 15, 1967.

> The system of temporary workers and contract workers implies capitalist relations of production between employer and employee. . . . The purpose of hiring temporary workers and contract workers is to make maximum profit with minimum investment. This involves exploitation of the labor and surplus value of temporary workers and contract workers, [who] are kept out of such organizations as the Party, the League, and the militia.[89]

Accordingly, on January 6, workers employed on a temporary (*linshi*) or out-contract (*waibao*) basis held a mass rally in People's Square. They vowed to Chairman Mao that they would "abolish the irrational system of temporary and contract labor," which "prevents workers from making revolution."[90] They had real complaints, they were mostly real proletarians, and some of their leaders became important in Rebel efforts to reorganize the city.

By this time, it was somewhat easier for people with bad labels to participate in the Cultural Revolution. A "Red Guard Army," composed mostly of demobilized soldiers, admitted some members with dubious backgrounds. This caused its rivals to call it "a gathering place for labor reform criminals."[91] Youths whose parents had been tagged with labels like "rightist" had strong interests in justifying themselves, especially when the municipal state again changed course and began to reorganize against them.

Zhang Chunqiao reversed himself in January and tried to ally with previously favored groups, rather than with the discontented factions whose support he had curried only a few weeks earlier. By January 14 the newspapers under his control praised new "revolutionary production committees" in "teams, workshops, and sections."[92] These appear to have been new agencies staffed by old leaders. Central "radicals" showed the limits of their radicalism by backing the attempted return to establishmentarianism. On January 15, one of them called for more monitors, castigating the naive for having "allowed the management of all matters to be taken over by the revolutionary faction [*sic*!]. They have concealed themselves in the background and are allowing social discipline to deteriorate, so as to make us a laughing stock. Consequently, it will be much more effective to adopt a policy of su-

---

[89] *Honggong zhanbao* (Red workers' war report) (Shanghai), February 6, 1967.

[90] *WHB*, January 6, 1967.

[91] *Geming lou* (Revolutionary tower) (Shanghai), March 10, 1967. This tabloid was apparently one of Zhang Chunqiao's.

[92] *RMRB*, January 14, 1967, reprinted from *JFRB*. These were in the Shanghai Glassmaking Machinery Factory.

pervision."[93] At the same meeting, Zhou Enlai said, "We should not promote the work style of laborers taking over management, as they have done in Shanghai."

Ex-radical top leaders had insufficient means to implement these ideas, however. The city's economic performance declined sharply, if temporarily, in 1967.[94] Stores, banks, and other commercial institutions in Shanghai were scenes of dispute throughout January (and often for more than a year later). Many firms were easy for discontents to shut down, precisely because they had long been under the thumbs of municipal monitors. Red Guards could control myriad small businesses by invading just a few central offices. For example, pawn shops had been instructed to stop issuing credits; they remained open only to redeem pledges. This was easy to administer, because they were all branches of a single city corporation that Red Guards advised.[95] Banks lost most of their practical supervisory functions after the Great Leap Forward,[96] but the chaos in 1966–68 reduced such control even further. In mid-January 1967, the Party's Central Committee instructed "banks to refuse all payments on behalf of state organs, state-owned enterprises, business units, or collective economic units, if such payments do not conform with state regulations," newly defined in strict terms.[97] To prevent advance payments of bonuses for the Lunar New Year in 1967, PLA members had to be sent into some banks.[98] But accountants, not soldiers, have the skill for such jobs. The new government, like the old, tried to extend monitoring widely, but without much success, because like the previous regime it had a relative shortage of appropriate personnel.

A REVOLUTIONARY ORDER?

The basis for a new order was nonobvious. Shanghai's *Wenhui bao* editorialized: "Rebellion is justified. 'This has gone too far' is the view held by

[93] Chen Boda, Mao's associate and head of the Central Cultural Revolution Small Group, quoted from a report by the *Asahi shimbun* correspondent, dispatch of January 16, 1967, in *China News Summary* 154 (January 19, 1967): A8.

[94] Officially published claims of output increments were lower in the first half of 1967 than in previous years, and actual production may well have declined. See Colina MacDougall, "The Economic Cost," *Far Eastern Economic Review*, July 27, 1967. In the Shanghai No. 2 Camera Factory, less than one-tenth of the month's quota was made during the first half of January (*NCNA*, February 17, 1967).

[95] SHNL, December 24, 1966.

[96] See William Byrd, *China's Financial System: The Changing Role of Banks* (Boulder, Colo.: Westview, 1983), p. 36.

[97] *Dongfang hong* (The East is red) (Beijing), January 22, 1967.

[98] XDRB, January 20, 1967.

those who favor revolution made in comfortable ways. . . . Violent attack is
the only means to destroy all enemies. . . . Either one actively supports the
revolutionary actions of the rebels, or one firmly opposes them. There is no
middle road."[99] The *Red Guard War Report* (as radical a tabloid as anyone
could wish) urged the organization of a new Party Committee for Shanghai.[100] Some wanted to end the chaos. Others felt more free than before.

Many social youths and returned rusticates, as well as their family members, joined political groups hoping they could purge the personnel and
change the policies that had labeled them. Many took direct action to serve
such interests. They moved into Shanghai even if they lacked household registrations. Large old houses, in Jing'an and Xuhui districts particularly, were
occupied by squatters and ex-rusticates, sometimes relatives of the bourgeois
who had long lived there.[101]

Various political coalitions in the city tried to reassemble the crumbled
cake that January left, but usually they could not cooperate.[102] The idea of
a "Paris Commune" was sufficiently ambiguous to garner support, though.
It promised to be at once new and legitimate, revolutionary and orderly. (No
one stressed that the Paris Commune had lasted just ten weeks.) A Shanghai
People's Commune came on the municipal agenda. This idea was so widely
popular, various local leaders claimed to have thought of it first. By February
4, Chen Hongkang made a speech claiming that his Workers' Third Headquarters had originated the idea of the commune, but "because of a few
disagreements with [Zhang's] Workers' Headquarters, they came to oppose
it."[103] At the February 5 rally that inaugurated the commune, its essential
sponsorship by the army was obvious: Garrison Commander Liao Zhengguo spoke "on behalf of all commanders and fighters of the PLA units stationed at Shanghai," vowing "resolutely and ruthlessly to suppress anyone
who dares undermine the Shanghai People's Commune."[104] On February 6,
Zhang's "Temporary Committee" for the People's Commune issued its
"No. 1 Order": "The PLA is the foundation of proletarian dictatorship."[105]

[99] *WHB*, January 6, 1967.

[100] *NCNA*, July 14, 1967, quoting a January dispatch.

[101] *XDRB*, May 28, 1967, reporting about earlier events.

[102] For example, on the last two days of January, Geng Jinzhang's supporters invaded an
office of Rebel workers' organizations in south Shanghai. Geng telephoned Zhang to ask for
the support of the army in this action. When Zhang refused, Geng reportedly shouted into the
phone, "Aha! You sent the army to help your friend Xu Jingxian. He belongs to the revolutionary left wing and I don't—is that it?" (*Gongren zaofan bao*, March 13, 1967, trans. in
Hunter, *Shanghai Journal*, p. 245).

[103] Hunter, *Shanghai Journal*, p. 246.

[104] *Shanghai Radio*, February 5, 1967, in *China News Service*, no. 160 (March 9, 1967).
See also *WHB*, February 7, 1967.

[105] *CNA*, March 31, 1967.

It was to undergird a "Paris Commune of the 'sixties of this century." The spectacle proved to be only a temporary distraction from the split of real interests among groups in Shanghai.

Chairman Mao, iconic patron that he was, made no public decree for the commune. But his name was so closely linked to the liberties of August that some communards sent him a cable presuming his opinion: "You personally supported the creative spirit of the Shanghai revolutionary rebel group and the establishment of this new form of regional state organ of the proletarian dictatorship, the Shanghai People's Commune."[106]

There was much less consensus on Zhang's management of the commune. A group of students, "though they marched with flags to celebrate the founding of the People's Commune, had their spears pointed at" Zhang's organization. "There were even armed struggles and a counter-current."[107] Despite this "February Counter-current" (*eryue niliu*), the army helped advertise the title of commune; and by February 5 newspapers printed the names of supporting organizations.

The institutional vacuum left by the end of the Municipal CCP Committee could not be filled with a mere name, however attractive. The army staged no coup but found itself engaged in "reactive militarism" after the overextension and collapse of civilians' policies: "It is not possible for the PLA to refrain from intervening. Some people use 'non-intervention' as a pretext to suppress the masses. . . . The demand of all genuine proletarian revolutionaries for the army's assistance must be met."[108] In mid-February, Shanghai papers remained full of praise for the commune,[109] but Chairman Mao had second thoughts. He reportedly said, "If the country sets up communes, then the Chinese People's Republic will have to change its name to be the Chinese People's Commune. . . . The Chairman suggests that Shanghai should change a little."[110]

Disorganization, at high levels as well as low, permeated all efforts to reorganize. On February 24, Zhang called a rally to celebrate the establishment of a "Shanghai Revolutionary Committee," which he said had been formed on February 5 (which most citizens had thought was the birthday of

---

[106] Ibid.

[107] *Jidian zhanbao* (Machinery and electricity war report) (Shanghai), February 19, 1967.

[108] See Kau, *The People's Liberation Army*, p. xlviii. The quotation is from *NCNA*, January 25, 1967, rephrasing a *JFRB* editorial. See also Harvey Nelsen, "Military Forces in the Cultural Revolution," *China Quarterly* 51 (July–September 1972): 444–74.

[109] See *JFRB*, February 11, 1967, for example.

[110] Newspapers stopped referring to the commune on February 22. See *China Topics*, no. 511 (January 8, 1969).

the commune).[111] Zhang ate his hat in front of all Shanghai, in a long television speech. He calmly announced there had been no commune. This was symbol-juggling more than management; and a speech did not make a coalition.

As one of Zhang's own newspapers candidly admitted, "The organization of this [Revolutionary Committee] is extremely loose, because there are factions and ambitionists working here. An alliance must be formed. . . . Personnel in the Headquarters must be supplemented with true revolutionaries, recommended by various branches."[112] Geng Jinzhang's group, the demobilized servicemen's Red Guard Army, as well as "right opportunist" factions, were all accused of having bad leaders, though the policy preferences of its followers were the Revolutionary Committee's most important problem. Resentments from years of the three policies of pressure had been expressed but still not thoroughly addressed. The new government's main constituency was the PLA, rather than any wider social base.

MEMORY OF PRESSURE'S RELEASE
LIMITS LABELING AND MONITORING

The Cultural Revolution had given some workers, especially temporary workers, reasons to ally with some bourgeois, including rusticated youths and school graduates who had been denied promotions. Zhang had previously sought support from such groups; but he became wary of them. They might demand he follow costly new policies. He tried to dissolve all groups not based in old institutions, saying that "revolutionary organizations should be confined to their respective trades, professions, and areas. They should avoid recruiting, [so that] people join their own ranks."[113]

Attempts by the police to repress groups articulating old grievances were combined with efforts to dry up their funds. The new regime established a Financial Supervision Team, which was authorized "to liquidate all the property and money of organizations of temporary workers, contract workers, reserve workers, out-contracted workers, and the liaison stations among educated youths from country and mountain areas and youths supporting frontier regions, as well as farm workers."[114] These money monitors were far outnumbered by the people they oversaw, however.

---

[111] *RMRB*, February 28, 1967.
[112] *Hongse zaofan bao* (Red Rebel report), Shanghai, February 28, 1967.
[113] *NCNA*, February 27, 1967.
[114] *WHB*, February 28, 1967.

The Revolutionary Committee averred sadness that many real workers and cadres were still in opposition. It sought, after January, support from old-regime types, more than from radical students with dubious class backgrounds.[115] As the committee resolved melancholically, "An overwhelming majority of red militia detachment members have been deceived."[116] But in fact, they had not been deceived. Zhang was now supporting proletarian policies they liked, of the 1963–65 kind, defined along old parameters that the techniques of pressure had ingrained. They recalled that a few months earlier, he had done just the opposite. They had no reason at all to trust his constancy.

Political support was where one found it, in early 1967. The Revolutionary Committee's newspapers increasingly asked proletarians to "create conditions for revolutionary leading cadres to 'show their color,' and to eliminate ideological obstacles in the way." This meant that workers might accept more ex-capitalist managers.[117] Zhang also emphasized, "No matter what revolution we carry out, we all have to eat. Therefore we must promote production."[118]

To achieve this end, the army arrested leaders who were the new committee's rivals. But decapitation of interest groups does not address their needs, and the lapse of this police function after August 1966 made its reimposition far more difficult. The first act of the Revolutionary Committee, on February 25, was to decree that Shanghai's harbor, airports, post offices, radio station, railways, newspapers, and many factories were under army rule.[119] A Military Control Commission had already been created, probably in January.[120] This organization also supervised the "people's armed forces departments" at municipal, district, and county levels.[121] And it oversaw the police.

The Shanghai Public Security Bureau began, by March, to show there was life after August. It issued an order that some workers' organizations in Wusong be dissolved.[122] Leftist rhetoric from the Revolutionary Committee did not obscure that its connection with the army remained close. When the

---

[115] *WHB*, March 5, 1967, makes this distinction.

[116] *RMRB*, January 20, 1967.

[117] *WHB*, March 7, 1967.

[118] *Ziliao zhuanji* (Special collection of reference materials) (Guangzhou), February 10, 1968.

[119] See Alexandra Close, "Mao Plays His Last Trump," *Far Eastern Economic Review*, March 16, 1967.

[120] This commission was the *junshi guanzhi weiyuanhui; Shanghai Radio*, March 25, 1968.

[121] *Shanghai Radio*, June 27, 1967.

[122] *WHB*, March 1, 1967.

Revolutionary Committee wanted to hold a peasants' rally, it could not round up many peasants; but the PLA sent fully armed troops from the suburbs to guard the site of the conclave.[123] When the Red Flag Army faction became too bothersome, the committee sent police and soldiers to surround two of that group's offices, capture some leaders, and confiscate documents implicating others.[124] These methods did not rely on the persuasiveness of any social ideals in the Cultural Revolution.[125] Organized coercion was a costly means of monitoring, and even the army lacked the resources to use it in many places at once. Nor did it bring all the committee's rivals to heel immediately.

The social interests represented by Geng Jinzhang's coalition did not disappear—even after military pressure caused it to collapse as an organization. The disruption of this post-August group can be traced in stages. First, Geng's allies were weakened. Chen Hongkang's lieutenants deserted, as the GMD connections of Chen's father and the Protestantism of his mother received much publicity. Second, the Red Guard Army of demobilized soldiers, which was also allied with Geng and was particularly strong in the suburbs, received orders from local military units to join no groups outside their workplaces. Third, Geng's rampant proletarianism (bordering on the "blood pedigree theory") and his emphasis on his own Party membership alienated his potential allies in Shanghai's large ex-bourgeoisie. Finally, there were defections among Geng's own units.[126]

The army could splinter a proletarian organization like this, but it had no way to terminate the interests it represented. The most important coteries at this time were increasingly small. For example, many who could no longer participate in Geng's coalition nonetheless remained deeply opposed to the Revolutionary Committee and its "use of our [workers'] name." Often they could still print tabloids, and they gave Zhang Chunqiao the nastiest set of epithets the contemporary dialect provided: "compromiser," "factionalist,"

---

[123] *WHB*, February 2, 1967.

[124] *WHB*, February 19, 1967.

[125] Many analysts have for this reason called Maoist organizations like this committee "fascist." Wang Xizhe, "Mao Zedong and the Cultural Revolution," trans. in Anita Chan, Stanley Rosen, and Jonathan Unger, eds., *On Socialist Democracy and the Chinese Legal System* (Armonk, N.Y.: Sharpe, 1985), pp. 177–260, relates Mao's (or Stalin's) "fascism" to peasant utopian culture. Walder, *Chang Ch'un-ch'iao*, p. 79, avoids this word but shows Zhang was no romantic. Edward Friedman, "After Mao: Maoism and Post-Mao China," *Telos* 65 (Fall 1985): 23–46, uses the phrase too. This always wakes up readers.

[126] *Jidian zhanbao*, February 9, 1967. Interpretation of this period depends on which issues of tabloids one reads. Hunter's superb collection apparently did not include this issue, although he had the April 5 edition of the same paper (by which time it had come fully under Zhang's wing, so he called it "a moderate tabloid of little interest" [*Shanghai Journal*, p. 307]).

"reformist," "small-bandist," "dispersionist," "secessionist," and so forth.[127] In order to woo such people, the Revolutionary Committee had to alternate its constituencies; so for months it sounded proletarian. *Wenhui bao* thus declared, "The fruits of the Four Cleans Movement must be safeguarded."[128] The new regime was all for labels. But bestowing them could no longer garner the political support it once had, because labeling as a policy had proven to be unstable, a cause of public strife and private cynicism.

The old policies were also less effective than before in recruiting talent. The Revolutionary Committee needed cadres; but in some offices, three-fifths or more of them had been under severe fire.[129] They and their peers had little incentive to take that risk again. Mao was now reported to have said, "Cadres are the decisive factor." Shanghai's new editorialists claimed, "Any viewpoint that sets revolution against production is wrong."[130] Zhang intoned, "Young people have contributed much to the Cultural Revolution, but they cannot be expected to take over at once the duties of the [leading] secretaries."[131] To reverse the withdrawal of cadres from their work, the Revolutionary Committee used policies like those the Party had employed in 1956. A few prominent old warhorses from the Municipal Party Committee, notably Wang Shaoyong and Ma Tianshui, retained very high posts (after minor self-criticisms), to show other cadres that their flag was still there.[132] The administrative personnel shortage behind the quick-fix policies that caused the Cultural Revolution, however, had not disappeared. On the contrary, the violence worsened this problem by inducing passivity among experts who had tried to be loyal. Here again, the policies of pressure had led to an unexpected reduction of their own effectiveness.

When the top Party cadre in a unit came under criticism for acting like a dictator rather than a good patron, second-in-command cadres would often take over—and might receive blessings from revolutionary committees irrespective of their origins. At high levels such as municipal bureaus, districts, and counties, many top leaders were retained after merely pro forma sessions of criticism. When local Party secretaries had made themselves unacceptable, because of resentments after they applied the old policies of pres-

---

[127] *Zhezhong zhuyizhe, zongpai zhuyizhe gailiang zhuyizhe, xiaotuanti zhuyizhe, fensan zhuyizhe, fenlie zhuyizhe; Jidian zhanbao*, February 9, 1967. At this point, the tabloid was ex-Geng but not yet pro-Zhang.

[128] *WHB*, February 21, 1967.

[129] An example is the Shanghai Aquatics Products Bureau; see *NCNA*, April 14, 1967.

[130] *WHB*, February 12, 1967.

[131] *Ziliao zhuanji*, February 10, 1968.

[132] On the rehabilitation of Wang Shaoyong and Ma Tianshui, see *Xinxing hongse* (Rising redness) (Guangzhou), February 27, 1968.

sure, other managers had to be sought for the revolutionary committees.[133] If no others who could be trusted by the new regime were available, the mantle tended to fall again on bosses whom their constituents knew well.

Local committees were sometimes announced without any leaders at all, if the new regime needed a show of influence in a place but had no personnel there whom it could trust. Such fiascoes could occur in units as big as whole districts (of which the city had only ten). For example in Xuhui District, the most cosmopolitan large residential section of Shanghai, a revolutionary committee was proclaimed on March 6, but without a clue as to who led it.[134] Some revolutionary committees were formed in new administrative areas that had not existed on maps before.[135]

By April 1967, "revolutionary leading cadres" from many areas and enterprises were brought to a large conference. They were asked, despite all the past conflict, "to recognize the importance of leaders of revolutionary mass organizations." They were flattered as "the core and mainstay of the revolutionary three-way alliance"[136]—but everyone knew the army was. Even the label "cadre" was worth less than before the chaos.

NEW ORDER WITH OLD TENSIONS
AFTER MID-1967

In one sense, the trauma of the Cultural Revolution was only beginning. The twists and turns of the movement, after mid-1967, are many and fascinating. Institutional change continued, because the revolutionary committees were obviously temporary. The suicides and killings had not ended.[137]

---

[133] The Huangpu District Revolutionary Committee was formed only three weeks after the municipal one, and *SHWB*, March 20, 1967, announced that the head of the previous district Party, Wang Zuhua, was its new chairman. Next to be established was the "preparatory committee" in Jing'an District; the new head Hu Huaqing had been deputy district head before the Cultural Revolution. See *RMRB*, April 3, 1967. Zhang Zhenyan, the new "responsible person" (*zerenzhe*) of the Chuansha County Revolutionary Committee had been deputy head there before the holocaust. Yen Hao, the responsible person of the preparatory group at the Shanghai Instruments, Meters, and Telecommunications Bureau, had been that bureau's deputy director before January. Cong Jie, chairman of the Revolutionary Committee of the Shanghai No. 1 Iron and Steel Factory, had been deputy director of that factory before. Wang Kun, new responsible person of the Shanghai Municipal Foodstuffs Corporation, had even been Party secretary in that company before. See *RMRB*, April 3, 1967.

[134] *SHWB*, March 6, 1967.

[135] As late as February 23, 1968, *RMRB* announced a revolutionary committee in Xujiang District, which was a new unit. On March 29, the same paper proclaimed the Anning Area (*diqu*) committee. These jurisdictions were temporary.

[136] *NCNA*, April 1, 1967.

[137] A sufficient source for this sad topic, referring to interviews and previous publications,

The violence had begun because short-term accomplishments of the campaign method suggested it was legitimate, because labels gave people interests in group revenge, and because patronage made individual relationships a widespread problem. Such policies continued for a decade more, but with decreasing rather than increasing results.

The army, which was China's main means of holding together by mid-1967, had never been entirely unified on these methods, even when it had followed orders loyally. And soldiers were restless in 1967, because of all the chaos they saw. Shanghai's radical *Liberation Daily* warned against

> resistance coming primarily from a handful of people who have wormed their way into the army, acting one way to people's faces and another behind their backs. . . . They even talk of revolutionary actions as "emotional," "excessive," and "straying from principles." . . . The high-level leading organs, military academies and schools, and artistic troupes of our army, where the Cultural Revolution is not unfolding, must respond to the great call of Chairman Mao and learn from the experiences of the revolutionary rebel groups in Shanghai.[138]

But for the most part, the army "supported the left" anyway, and increasingly this meant a new establishment with radical rhetoric but law-and-order aims. When rebel groups became angry at military repression, a revolutionary committee blandly advised, "If people have complaints against the army, they should send their big character posters to the PLA through representatives."[139] Soldiers' participation in the new government's work teams gave those units a credibility and prestige they could not otherwise have garnered. Many a "great alliance" in factories and offices held together mainly because of soldiers' efforts, if at all.[140] Yet the army could not monitor everything.

The building of the new order was slow, because the revolutionary committees were at least as short of usable cadres as the old Party committees had been. By July 1967, 30 percent of Shanghai's state factories still had no "alliances," even of a nominal sort, to link them with the city's Revolutionary Committee.[141] About that time, news came of military opposition to radicals in Wuhan. In August, resentment at the continuing political chaos was

---

is Anne F. Thurston's *Enemies of the People: The Ordeal of the Intellectuals in China's Great Cultural Revolution* (New York: Knopf, 1987).

[138] *JFRB*, January 14, 1967.

[139] *WHB*, February 22, 1967.

[140] For a fine summary of soldiers' roles in reunifying Zhabei District, see *RMRB*, October 16, 1967. On the work of "military representatives" in factories, see *XDRB*, March 30, 1967.

[141] *RMRB*, July 3, 1967.

especially evident in the most professional of China's armed services, the air force. Air units in nearby Wuxi covered the attack of one civilian group against another that was apparently more radical.[142] In Shanghai, the army became a vital monitor, but a reluctant campaigner.

The Shanghai suburbs and other cities on the Yangzi Delta were generally more establishmentarian than the metropolis, except for urban rusticates (mostly with bad family labels) who had been sent to those places. Suburban areas continued in 1967 to host intense army training of factory militias, on the 1964 model.[143] Especially in July and August, these militias were revived as teams for "civil offense and armed defense" (*wengong wuwei*), that is, for monitoring units the Revolutionary Committee wanted to control better. Well into 1968, these military corps organized "joint revolutionary actions on a big scale" to defend the new establishment.[144] A few PLA officers could coordinate many civilians, who enjoyed less trust from the Revolutionary Committee but could fill out such teams. This practice slightly alleviated the overall cadre shortage.

There was so much resistance to the Revolutionary Committee's revival of pre-1966 categories that in an August 3 incident, dissidents put up posters saying, "Shanghai must have a second chaos [after January], thoroughly reforming the Shanghai Revolutionary Committee."[145] On that day, according to a Red Guard paper, a propaganda team of eighty drove in three trucks to the Shanghai Diesel Oil Plant, with the intention of making the factory loyal to the Revolutionary Committee. Within an hour, all three trucks had been smashed, and the propagandists had trouble leaving the scene. About thirty were arrested by local "rascals and bullies," but there was no report that later revenge could be taken against such independence.[146]

The formation of revolutionary committees in most of Shanghai's urban districts and rural counties was delayed by the obviousness of the dissidence

---

[142] General Yu Lijin, leader of the air force, had long been stationed near Shanghai; and he allegedly condoned the use of air troops at Wuxi. But a telephone call from Yao Wenyuan is said to have prevented this intervention, just as it was about to take place (*Cankao ziliao* [Reference materials] [Guangzhou], an issue of July 1968 in *SCMP* 4222 [1968]: 1; this was a Red Guard tabloid, not the important limited-edition Party newspaper of the same name.)

[143] See *NCNA*, October 23, 1967, for information concerning the garrison's activities in early April. This article also mentions the director of a factory militia in Xuhui District who "fought his way under white terror" (i.e., Xuhui's ex-capitalist managers) until he became a member of the "revolutionary group," thereafter "slackening his self-transformation and regarding himself as a veteran rebel"—until "the masses" set him straight again. This little novel represents the Cultural Revolution in many factories.

[144] *WHB*, March 26, 1968.

[145] *1969 Zhonggong nianbao* (1969 Chinese Communist yearbook) (Taipei: Institute for the Study of Chinese Communist Problems, 1969), 4:22.

[146] *Peking Informer* (Hong Kong), 16, no. 5 (March 1, 1968): 5.

in that hot summer. Downtown Huangpu District set up its revolutionary committee as early as March 20, and central Hongkou did the same on July 1. Only two other districts (and two that both had relatively large portions of bourgeois-labeled populations, Changning on April 9 and Xuhui on November 8) set up such bodies in 1967.[147] The portion of proletarian-labeled people in the other six districts was generally higher than in these four—and even in these four places, where some members of old elite families could now achieve positions in the new order, the revolutionary committees were not stable.

Because the new regime was trying to restore order with old policies of pressure whose utility had declined, Zhang's "General Headquarters" remained severely split. It could not simultaneously co-opt leaders from labeled groups whose interests its policies still kept separate, from potential leaderships that no longer desired to be either patrons or clients, or from the previous officialdom that had experiences to show no one was safe from campaigns. These problems were especially evident in Yangpu, Putuo, and Jing'an districts. Their district offices reported "civil wars" (*neizhan*), although by October nominal alliances were functioning in a few major factories in these areas.[148] From December 3 to 5, 1967, the Municipal Revolutionary Committee called a conference of "workers' representatives and soldiers" to fight the influence of nonproletarians in Shanghai factories.[149]

Ambiguities of the new regime in Shanghai were typified by the politician Wang Hongwen (later infamous as the only worker-background member of the Gang of Four), who led proletarian meetings for a Revolutionary Committee whose most prominent other members came from families that originally had bourgeois labels. Wang planned a victory over "anarchism." He intended to lead, on behalf of the proletarian dictatorship, a campaign against workers who would not submit to the Revolutionary Committee.

---

[147] *1968 Feiqing nianbao* (1968 Chinese Communist yearbook) (Taipei: Institute for the Study of Chinese Communist Problems, 1968), p. 294. Of Shanghai's ten counties, only two established revolutionary committees in 1967: Songjiang on March 27 and Chuansha two days later. Shanghai County set up a third on February 17, 1968. These three, with Baoshan County, must have the smallest portions of agricultural population.

[148] *Dapipan tongxun* (Great criticism bulletin) (Guangzhou), October 5, 1967.

[149] *NCNA*, December 6, 1967. This conference coincided with a purge from the Municipal Revolutionary Committee of three representatives, including the head of the committee's propaganda group. The names of those removed are not identical in different sources, some of which are transcriptions from radio broadcasts. But the late-1967 purge apparently involved Political Propaganda Group chief Zhu Xiqi and his lieutenants Hu Zhihong, Li Fugen, and Min Kaosi, who were also accused of being "bad heads" (*huai toutou*) of a workers' group called Communists Facing the East (*gong xiang dong*). See *1969 Zhonggong nianbao* 3:71. But also, *Dongfang hong dianxun* (The East is red telegram) (Guangzhou), 3 (July 1968), and *Jiu yiliu tongxun* (September 16 Bulletin) (Guangzhou), August 1968.

Early in 1968, he said he had a little list of three thousand Shanghai worker "lords" who needed to be struggled against, although other "little devils" who had just been hoodwinked might safely go free.[150] These political tactics still stressed labels and campaigns, though they were now slow to bring order.

"Three-way alliances" of workers, cadres, and especially soldiers were supposed to be the pillars of new revolutionary committees in all units. The alliances where hard to stabilize, even when they could be created. Zhang mused that such organizations worked better in unimportant than in important units:

> I am thinking of this problem all the time. Why are the great alliances more difficult to achieve in Shanghai's most vital departments, especially those dealing with problems of security and secrecy [*baomi*]? There are enemies inside these, especially in state-run defense industries. . . . In units which are pools of stagnant water, appropriate struggle must be carried out against conservative power.[151]

These "old, big, difficult" units remained recalcitrant through 1968, despite the sending of worker propaganda teams to factories like the Yangshupu Power Plant, the Guanghui Electric Bulb Factory, the May 1 Electric Machines Factory, and many other firms that could not be brought to heel.[152] Even when these factories "did their [production] work well," they often opposed propaganda teams sent by the army, struggled against the Revolutionary Committee envoys, "spread rumors," and conducted work slowdowns to get attention.[153] By no means was all this resistance open; much of it used "weapons of the weak." But its effect on the resources of the Revolutionary Committee was very strong.[154]

State violence in decreasingly effective campaigns was the committee's usual response. Sometimes, as on April 27, 1968, the police held "public judgment meetings" to put dissident leaders on show trial, giving death sentences that "were carried out immediately," while the crowds shouted "Long live Chairman Mao!"[155] In June, the committee held a conference of military from air, sea, and land units at Shanghai, all swearing they would

---

[150] *Wenge tongxun* (Cultural Revolution bulletin), no. 13 (March 1968).

[151] *Yiyue fengpao* (January storm) (Guangzhou), March 24, 1968.

[152] *XDRB*, December 11, 1968. "Old, big, difficult" is *laodanan*; "worker propaganda team" is *gongren xuanchuan dui*.

[153] *JFRB*, August 25, 1968.

[154] See James C. Scott, *Weapons of the Weak: Everyday Forms of Peasant Resistance* (New Haven: Yale University Press, 1985).

[155] *WHB*, April 28, 1968.

"defend to the death" the new authorities.[156] But talking did not eliminate the problems of labeled groups and repressed individuals that had festered for years and had come out in late 1966. When the navy that same month sent a propaganda team to the strategically important Hudong Shipyard, struggle sessions for a long time thereafter remained intense.[157] The military, having to intervene in civilian politics, lost some of the acclaim it had earned from all sectors of Shanghai's society during earlier years.

Calls for "revolution" against revolutionary committees were heard in many parts of China at this time. In Shanghai, the dissidence was divided. It came from some groups whose members were largely bourgeois-labeled, and oppositely from associations of those who were labeled proletarian. The most powerful single opposition group was called the "Support Station of the United Headquarters."[158] This proletarian faction bitterly attacked Zhang in handbills, saying he "spread the doctrine of the extinction of classes" and "supported rightist elements."[159] Others attacked him, because they saw (more accurately) that he was trying to restore the 1963–65 order, albeit without much success.

For a decade and a half, the Party had relied on administrative policies that threatened too much and promised too much. For more than a year after it let these bees out of the bonnet in 1966, giving everyone rights to threaten and to promise, even police coercion could not put them back. The Revolutionary Committee's response to the situation was to use the old administrative policies. These imposed further repression on a divided Shanghai, but they could not bring order quickly.

CONTINUED PROLETARIAN LABELS AND TRADE UNIONS IN 1968

The city emerged in 1968 from its first, most violent bouts of a Cultural Revolution that lasted, at least officially, a decade. Zhang's Committee tried to reestablish hierarchy between managers and workers, as well as hierarchy between different kinds of workers. But the question of how much affirmative action proletarian families should enjoy remained unanswered.

[156] *WHB*, June 30, 1968.

[157] *NCNA*, June 25, 1968.

[158] This *Zhilian zhan* was similar to a "Communist Small Group" (*Gongchan zhuyi xiaozu*) at Beijing University, a "Polaris Study Society" (*Beidouxing xuehui*) in Hubei, the October Revolution Small Group (*Shiyue geming xiaozu*) in Shandong, and the famous Provincial Union of Proletarians (*Sheng wu lian*) in Hunan (Xi, "Zhongguo wenhua," p. 14).

[159] *XDRB*, May 20, 1968.

Ex–Scarlet Guard organizations of proletarian workers remained active in early 1968, at least as informal clubs; and they partially replaced Shanghai's trade unions, which had largely crumbled along with the Party. In many places, such as the Shanghai Rubber Molding Factory, propaganda teams arranged an agreement between opposing rebel and unionist groups, under which the leaders of both agreed to dissolve their factions. But when the work team left, the factions were still there—and simple threats of force against them were ineffective, because they were locally strong. By 1968, newspapers assured ex–Scarlet Guard leaders that rumors of their imminent arrest for maintaining informal activities were unfounded.[160] Wang Hongwen complained that too many nonproletarian people had entered factories. He said their influence was poisonous, because they inevitably brought capitalist ideas.[161] He was seeking proletarian constituents, who were none too eager to follow him and who were in any case still opposed by intractable mixed-label blocs in factories.

"Trade unions of the entire people" were disapproved by the Revolutionary Committee. This ban was chancy, however, because Mao had once said unions should include "all hired working people, including progressives, middle-roaders, and backward elements, with the exception of a tiny number of reactionaries."[162] It was feasible to quote Mao for almost any policy. Liu Shaoqi had said democratic party members could even have leadership positions in trade unions. He felt that landlords, rich peasants, counterrevolutionaries, and bad elements who remolded their thinking could join unions. With Liu's authority to discredit a policy, nothing more was needed by 1968. Therefore ex-bourgeois and contract workers were ousted from unions, so that they could not organize themselves to fight such discrimination. The Revolutionary Committee tried to restore the old union structure, with a fresh emphasis on labels, rather than create a fairer one.

A document from its allies in the Central Committee aimed at monitoring entry to urban jobs, as before 1966.

With regard to the cases of temporary workers, contract workers, rotated workers, and out-contract workers, the Center is prepared to make reforms according to different circumstances, after investigation and study. Before any new decision is taken, none of them shall be changed to the status of permanent workers. They must not form independent organiza-

---

[160] *WHB*, February 13, 1968.

[161] *NCNA*, December 6, 1967.

[162] *Gongren zaofan bao*, December 1, 1967. The article concerns the Shanghai Watch Factory.

tions. They must not exchange experiences, establish revolutionary ties with one another, or organize visits of delegations to higher levels.[163]

By the same token, any policy that increased production pressure or justified recruiting new kinds of workers was condemned. The idea that trade unions should hold competitions in production, or should work under slogans like "quotas in command," "professional skill in command," or "mechanization" were all deemed capitalist.[164] People who had good-label heritages asserted their rights to privileges even more strenuously in 1968 than before the Cultural Revolution. But after such hard use and public questioning, the labels became less legitimate.

CONTINUED FRUSTRATIONS
OF INDIVIDUAL CLIENTS IN 1968

The Revolutionary Committee in 1968 was trying as hard as it could to acquire patron-client networks. The previous year had deeply shaken many personalist mazes, because leaders fell and sets of them betrayed each other. The emergent regime met fierce resistance from lower leaders, who wanted to keep their groups intact and did not want interference from work teams of the Revolutionary Committee. As one of the official papers said, "There is still a minority of unit leaders . . . who cherish old viewpoints and are reluctant to jump out of their old circles [*lao taozi*]."[165]

High revolutionary committees had a hard time getting information from lower ones, which were more independent than the old basic Party committees had been. A newspaper warned as late as September 1968:

> Revolutionary committees of all areas, counties, bureaus, and institutions . . . and all revolutionary mass organizations must promptly report their situations to the Municipal Revolutionary Committee, seek advice from it, and notify it of things. They should make special reports on any new problems. . . . They must make separate reports on important matters. . . . If a unit under our supervision does not seek advice before doing something, or make a report afterwards, it is establishing an independent kingdom.[166]

[163] Central Committee and State Council notice in *Guangtie zongsi* (Guangzhou Railroad General Headquarters), no. 28 (February 1968).

[164] *Gongren zaofan bao*, December 1, 1967.

[165] *JFRB*, February 21, 1967.

[166] *WHB*, September 25, 1968.

The author of this admonition felt a need to specify that the content of such reports "must be true." Even in late 1968, hierarchy among the revolutionary committees was imperfect, and the committees together did not control all of Shanghai.

Management ideals of the early Cultural Revolution—reducing staff, ranks, and rules[167]—tended to militate against technical bureaucracies. Expert agencies often have weak personalist networks, because their bureaucracies can grow so large, coordinating so much, that face-to-face links between patrons and clients become infeasible. The Cultural Revolution encouraged smaller clientelist networks than had existed before. It tended to break up modern hierarchies that previously knit traditional patronage groups together. For example at the municipal level, the economic offices of the central government were "investigated" and closed during the CR by Shanghai groups. The press sometimes described these offices as spy stations, where weapons, radios, and "a good deal of contraband goods and commodities in short supply" were unearthed by Red Guard bands.[168] Large factories could forbid entrance by work teams from higher levels.[169] In the Sujiahang Vegetable Market, which contains many small booths, the Zhabei District office (which was supposed to oversee that bazaar) had lost all its authority by 1968. Its only recourse was to call policemen to arrest the "rascals and hoodlums who had infiltrated the rebel group of the market . . . the rotten eggs" and send them to jail. However, the police simply could not catch the main local leader in that market. "Secret agents tipped him off, allowing him to get away without a trace."[170] Old Shanghai was alive and well in 1968.

The Revolutionary Committee tried hard to reestablish a politics of personal loyalty and protection, but its propaganda teams were snubbed even in lower committees it helped to legitimate.[171] Many knew Party leaders in their units had taken unfair advantage of other local leaders in the past. Army-led teams might breeze in, trying to reconcile these elites. But "in a place where Party members and non-Party rebels are more or less hostile to each other in feelings, . . . an open-door campaign should be carried out."[172]

[167] *NCNA*, November 21, 1967.

[168] *Chengjian hongsi* (Urban construction red headquarters) (Guangzhou), no. 8 (January 1968), in *SCMP* 4127 (1968): 11; and *Hong dianxun* (Red telegram), no. 2 (March 1968), in *SCMP* 4143 (1968): 12–13.

[169] *JFRB*, August 1, 1968, about the Shanghai Food Machines Factory.

[170] *Caimao zhanbao* (Finance and trade war report), August 14, 1968.

[171] *XDRB*, December 23, 1968, quoting the broadcast of a *JFRB* editorial.

[172] *WHB*, October 19, 1968. This is the work method adopted by the No. 3 Workshop of Xianfeng Motor Plant in Shanghai, as well as by an air force team at the Shanghai Oil Refinery.

People in basically different patronage networks (as well as in differently labeled groups) found they were happier if they used less energy in mutual fighting.

For most of the next decade, Shanghai under the Gang of Four continued to sponsor old ideals of solidarity. The Cultural Revolution, however, strongly suggested that no such group could ultimately win. Puritans and Anglicans had also discovered something like that, by the end of the English Revolution. A loss of interest in fighting can establish guarantees for different kinds of leaders.

CONTINUED CAMPAIGNS
AND CADRE WITHDRAWAL IN 1968

The Shanghai Revolutionary Committee sponsored movements to frighten local leaders who might become its rivals, just as the previous Party committee had done for many years. But the use of campaigns to instill fear met declining returns. By 1968, constituencies were splintered. Unofficial ones had begun to use violence. The result was familiar, however, in another respect: Campaigns still made ambitious people more activist, and ordinary managers and workers more withdrawn.

Campaigns did not work at all for the CR economy, as they had (at least temporarily and in cities) for the Leap. Work discipline lapsed in 1966–68. A small fabric mill reported, "Anarchic ideas go unchecked among some employees: They come to work late and leave early, they are often absent without leave, and they defy interference by anyone."[173] At the Shanghai Rubber Factory, chess, poker, singing, dancing, and storytelling occupied a good deal of "work" time. Some employees even tore down, in secret, notices of the meetings held to study Mao's thoughts.[174]

At the Water Conservation Machine Factory, sleeping, knitting, and "basking in the sun" were added to these "anarchic" sins.[175] At the Deep Sea Fisheries Corporation, "hundreds of employees are on dry land, doing nothing all day long. . . . Trawlers are now moored in the harbor for as many as five to seven days before they go out to sea." The average catch was

---

[173] *WHB,* February 13, 1968.
[174] *WHB,* February 15, 1968.
[175] *WHB,* March 16, 1968.

reportedly one-quarter of what it could be.[176] At the Gexin Electric Motors Plant, "sick leaves" rose in 1968.[177] By that year, "many factories abolished the old practice of cadres setting the targets and workers meeting them."[178] Thus the local epidemic of loafing would violate no rules, because the rules had been repealed. Campaigns, which are by definition extraordinary means to get results, had never before become so subtle. In this form, however, they were no longer useful.

Financial institutions in 1968 were still disorganized by campaign fervor. When a revolutionary "combat group" induced a member (who was also a bank clerk) to steal some bank funds, its loyalists found plenty of political justification for this embezzlement.[179] By early 1969, the army tried to take over the many "dens of tigers" in Shanghai's finance and trade departments.[180] A basis had been laid for the realization, not to be implemented until a decade later, that campaigns have severe limits as tools for financial control.

Campaign violence also rejuvenated a tradition of school gang fights. Many young "rebels," clearly deserted by the Revolutionary Committee in 1968, lost hope for successful careers. So they formed street gangs and called themselves campaigners. One band of them looted heaters, clocks, and telephones from a chemical factory.[181] At a commune, another gang trampled fields and had a good time spoiling melons and peppers.[182] Regular workers and peasants protested against the "troublemakers," but youth gangs are not easy to repress in any society.[183] When the campaign tradition of "making revolution" was legitimate, and could be defined in almost any way, this problem was worse.

Continued campaigning in the Cultural Revolution also made cadres withdraw their energy from work. Even local Party leaders, by October 1968, often wanted to resign from the Party rather than be "rectified" in it. They "had grievances, were downcast, and did not submit themselves to rectification."[184] The propaganda teams sporadically "urged the broad masses to accept cadres. . . . They used to denounce cadres, with the result

[176] Ibid.
[177] *WHB*, October 18, 1968.
[178] *NCNA*, December 28, 1968.
[179] *WHB*, March 11, 1968.
[180] *Shanghai Radio*, January 31, 1969.
[181] *XDRB*, December 12, 1968.
[182] *WHB*, August 4, 1968.
[183] *JFRB*, August 1, 1968.
[184] *WHB*, October 19, 1968, example from the Shanghai Oil Refinery.

that the latter became very timid and did not dare to work boldly."[185] But technical managers of bourgeois backgrounds, and many Communists who could work with them, had suffered too much. By late 1967, more than two-fifths of Shanghai's department heads and bureau chiefs had yet to be "liberated."[186] Some, at that point, preferred to retire rather than resume their posts.

Restoring the authority of cadres was a major campaign goal of many work teams. But one purpose of a campaign is to mobilize support for a regime that has few cadres. This administrative policy had been carried to a point of negative returns by 1968. Cadre withdrawal was so severe that the propaganda teams were understaffed. These groups had to move around quickly from one factory to another, unable to do their jobs well anywhere. Some called for "the planned absorption of a proper number of cadres into workers' propaganda teams," but many managers did not qualify—mainly because they lacked will for the task.[187]

In the autumn of 1968 "May 7 Cadre Schools" began to absorb in rural areas large sections of the city's alternative elite—not just those who wished to serve, but also those who now demurred from doing so with any forcefulness. This send-down of former government, Party, and mass organization cadres, including many from street and residents' committees, was organized by urban districts. All cadres from a particular corporation or part of the city would go to a particular place, often a village not far from Shanghai.[188] This campaign was ostensibly designed to educate rather than stratify people. But the different periods of rustication for different cadres undermined that goal. As a 1969 article admitted, "Some people think that those who enter Party schools are superior persons, and those who enter cadre schools are inferior."[189] Shortly before the turn of the decade, some cadres were drafted for ordinary send-down to frontier areas.[190] Eventually, many Chinese leaders at all levels realized it was unwise for a poor country to throw away talented people. Campaigns were not, in the long run, an effective means to mobilize them.

[185] *WHB*, August 19, 1967.

[186] *Zhengfa hongqi* (Politics and Law Red Flag) (Guangzhou), October 17, 1967.

[187] See *SCMM*, no. 650 (March 13, 1969): 32, quoting *HQ*.

[188] *WHB*, October 9, 1968, describes the exodus of five hundred cadres from Nanshi District to Liuhe School in Chuansha County.

[189] *JFRB*, July 14, 1969.

[190] *Shanghai Radio*, September 19, 1969. For more, see Yang Jiang, *A Cadre School Life: Six Chapters*, trans. Geremie Barmé (Hong Kong: Joint Publishing Company, 1982).

CONCLUSION: ORDER RESTORED,
LEADERSHIPS EXHAUSTED

The Chinese Communist Party had been smashed in 1966–68 as an effective institution, if not as a symbol. It needed either a requiem or a repair. So in March 1968, the Shanghai Revolutionary Committee set up its "Party Small Group."[191] At lower levels, later that year, demobilized soldiers and "outstanding rebels" joined Party rectification teams in factories. These leaders were generally chosen on the basis of recommendations from visiting work teams.[192]

What was needed, at this time, were new policies that would work, rather than a resurrected institution based on old ideas whose usefulness had declined. Because no fresh vision informed the effort, the campaign to restore the Party was widely seen as humdrum. Many leaders were still considered overly "conservative." Newspapers openly complained the Cultural Revolution had had no effect. The previous "middle party" (*zhongjian pai*) and "good old men" (*lao hao ren*) were generally readmitted to the Party. They were capable, needed, and usually hurt. There was only a limited "strengthening" of the membership by further absorption of proletarians. As before, movements in the name of the workers largely benefited people who could claim to be their vanguard.[193] Labels, monitors, and campaigns were still the order of the day, but all were now passé.

A diluted version of the "blood pedigree theory" was evident in 1968 discussions of the new Party. Newspapers said it should not be just a "production party" or a "citizens' party" but should recruit "advanced elements of the proletariat."[194] Since so many kinds of people had been violent and unfair in 1967, a tabloid's editors felt it necessary to add that "bad people doing bad things must be distinguished from good people doing bad things."[195] The latter, presumably, were acceptable new Party members.

Class struggle campaigns did not end, but quotas of victims were not as stylish as before: "We must not drag out the enemy merely for the sake of satisfying the organization." "Class clearance troops" (*qingli jieji duiwu*)

---

[191] Dang xiaozu; see *Wenge fenglei* (Cultural Revolution storm) (Guangzhou), no. 3 (March 1968).

[192] *WHB*, October 16, 1968, refers to the case of the No. 1 Shanghai Tire Factory.

[193] *JFRB*, October 25, 1968.

[194] *Wenge fengyun* (Cultural Revolution winds and clouds), no. 2 (February 1968).

[195] *Gongren zaofan bao*, August 17, 1968.

were nonetheless supposed to live up to their names.[196] This mandate was difficult in Shanghai, where many talents (beginning then with Zhang Chunqiao) came from bourgeois family backgrounds. The old ideas were still touted as effective; but after the violence, they no longer served their purposes well.

Labeled groups, patronage networks, and violent campaigns persisted both as long-term sources of disorder and as short-term instruments of order. The balance between these two opposite results slowly became clearer: the policies mainly created disorder. They were all retained by the would-be-revolutionary Party for a decade after 1968, after most of Shanghai's population had tired of them.

When did the Cultural Revolution end? Many say it lasted a whole decade, 1966–76. But its mass violence was in slow decline by 1968. During April 1969, the CCP's Ninth Congress was held in Beijing and was called "the congress of victory." In that month, Hong Kong's main Communist newspaper mentioned "the completion of the Cultural Revolution." But a Chengdu journal at the same time said the congress marked "a new stage in the Cultural Revolution," not its end. A Henan source quoted Mao: "It must not be thought that peace will come after the second or even the third Cultural Revolution." A Fujian paper ambiguously hoped, "The congress will certainly lead us forward to seize all-around victory." A Shanghai newspaper only asked "whether or not the Cultural Revolution can be carried through to the end." Mao, at the congress, was guarded: "We hope that the present congress will be one of unity and of victory, and that after its conclusion still greater victories will be won throughout the country."[197]

This implied more of the same old policies, after a period of consolidation. Yet Shanghai had potential in China's economy. Labeling, patronizing, and campaigning were mostly irrelevant to the contribution this city might make to the nation's development. New policies were needed to realize this potential. When a group of technicians from another part of China in 1969 visited the Shanghai Machine Tool Factory (a bastion of the Cultural Revolution), they noted it did not have the best technologies in the world for tool making—but it had the best in China. This modernity was criticized on the grounds of overly complex technology. Using it tended to split the labor force into skilled and unskilled groups.[198] But Shanghai has to emphasize high quality, to assure markets for its products competing with those of in-

[196] Ibid.; *Caimao zhanbao*, August 14, 1968; *JFRB*, August 20, 1968.
[197] See *South China Morning Post*, April 20, 1969, p. 10.
[198] NCNA, July 21, 1969.

land factories. Even this machine tool plant, more famous for its radicalism than any other factory in the city, would not exist for long on the principles of the Cultural Revolution.

This kind of natural selection in economics, as well as workers' and managers' exhaustion with the onerous policies of pressure, now reduced the use of old administrative styles. As Wang Hongwen said at the Tenth Party Congress in August 1973, quoting Mao, "Great disorder across the land leads to great order." Wang and Mao were right, though the future order was not the kind they had in mind.[199]

[199] *The Tenth National Congress of the Communist Party of China (Documents)* (Beijing: Foreign Languages Press, 1973), p. 45.

CHAPTER 11

Conflict among Local
Symbol Makers, 1966–1968

Ample make this bed,
Make this bed with awe;
In it wait till judgement break. . . .
—EMILY DICKINSON

The Cultural Revolution seems oddly named. Culture, ideals, and enthusiasm had less to do with the event than many accounts suggest. The Cultural
Revolution nonetheless was cultural in the sense that life-styles were at
stake, and it encompassed spectacular symbols. The previous chapter gives
its history; so the main means of presentation here can shift to types of
activities. Because the CR's striking images have so deeply affected past
analyses of events then, these visions should be related to the argument
of this book. The way to accomplish that, following the method used earlier, is to study the structure of public symbols in 1966–68 and to associate
them with the people who used them, who were urban residents and intellectuals.

What is the link between such symbols and the policies of pressure that
caused the Cultural Revolution? The images of this time were regular, in
their way. They were coherent along predictable, abstract dimensions: Red
was always opposed to black; and light, to darkness. Excess and thoroughness (*chedi*) were repeatedly praised, whereas golden means or limiting criteria were always damned. Movement was good; stability was bad. The link
between the CR's symbols and the policies of pressure depends on why such
passionate colors and dichotomies were so wildly popular in 1966–68.

People chose these symbols to express the intensity of their frustration at
having been manipulated by government categories, bosses, and threats.
They were mad. Pastels would not do; so they chose red. Quiet sutras and
relaxed muscles could not let out enough of their anger, after their lives had
been exploited so egregiously for years; thus they shouted loud slogans and
clenched their fists, instead. A formal consistency of many symbols in the
Cultural Revolution is evident. This pattern came not because uniformity is
natural, or because such things are random, but because of the need for a

language to express intense motives among people who felt sharp pain at specifiable kinds of state coercion.[1]

These symbols were just options. Different, quietistic emblems have been sometimes chosen by Chinese people. Symbols do not cause events. Their selection is a thing to be explained (as the whole CR is), not an explainer. Their availability tells nothing, because their opposites were also available. But they did summarize their time, and they help us understand how the people who made the CR saw it.

The same administrative policies that caused rebellion among workers and cadres affected residents and students too. Labeling had created status groups; and in the freedom of late 1966, these groups organized in schools and neighborhoods, not just factories. Monitoring, especially by 1966, had sponsored two kinds of personalities, which may be called the dominant and subservient types. Campaign violence divided precincts and schools more severely than ever before, causing ordinary residents to choose a symbolic language in which it was easy to express hate for neighbors. This chapter deals with symbols that students and residents selected in different contexts of high and popular culture, in their preferences for jobs and housing, in decisions to travel or stay at home, and in arrangements for schooling.

INTELLECTUALS' CHOICES IN HIGH CULTURE

Intellectuals were major victims of Shanghai's Cultural Revolution, and the literature in English on 1966–68 persecution of them is extensive.[2]

---

[1] The logic attempted here relates symbols to experiences and is generally inspired by Suzanne K. Langer, *Philosophy in a New Key: A Study in the Symbolism of Reason, Rite, and Art* (New York: Penguin, 1942). Langer paid more attention to the link between experienced meaning and symbolic form than do many recent philosophical analysts, who are more eager to be praised as pure mathematicians in disguise.

[2] The most famous account has become Nien Cheng's *Life and Death in Shanghai* (London: Collins, 1986). On these problems nationally, see Anne F. Thurston, *Enemies of the People* (New York: Knopf, 1987). Two detailed accounts are Yue Daiyun, with Carolyn Wakeman, *To the Storm* (Berkeley and Los Angeles: University of California Press, 1985), and Ruth Earnshaw Lo, *In the Eye of the Typhoon* (New York: Harcourt Brace Jovanovich, 1980). Further cases are described in Vera Schwarcz, *Long Road Home* (New Haven: Yale University Press, 1984), and Merle Goldman, *China's Intellectuals: Advise and Dissent* (Cambridge: Harvard University Press, 1981). A list of repressions is in Ting Wang, *Niugui sheshen ji* (A collection of ghosts and monsters) (Hong Kong: Sanjiadian Shuwu, 1967). He Lüting was chosen as a representative here, because academics had paid more attention to writers than musicians or visual artists. Richard Kraus then sent the author part of a forthcoming work entitled *Pianos and*

Among the best-known in Shanghai was He Lüting, who headed the Music Conservatory. This composer had published "The East Is Red," a magnificent tune that became China's unofficial national anthem during the Cultural Revolution, as part of a 1957 collection of his songs. One of his later problems was an accusation of plagiarism, because he had not fully credited a North Shansi peasant who wrote the tune in 1942.[3] The words begin, "The East is red, the sun is shining / From China comes a Mao Zedong." He Lüting knew Mao at Yan'an and was professor of music at the Lu Xun Arts Academy there. The anthem for which he claimed credit is like a Chinese folk song, but also stately; and its musical quality is a clear reason for its popularity. Even after He was violently attacked, his song remained a hallmark of the Cultural Revolution.

In its field, the Shanghai Music Conservatory is equaled only by a similar academy in Beijing. Located on a large campus in an old, well-to-do area of the city, this elite institution in the mid-1960s had only six hundred students but employed a staff of three hundred.[4] He Lüting had opposed the Party's educational policies after 1963.[5] So the attack against him was led by students of the "five red kinds," apparently aided by political department cadres. From June 1966 on, he was "dragged out" in struggle meetings. In the late summer, Red Guards ransacked He's house, destroying sheet music by Western composers. They arranged several public sessions of criticism against He and forced him to put on a humiliating signboard and walk around the conservatory. This composer was, by most reports, not a retiring man; and he tried in December 1966 to discredit his attackers. They reportedly served him poisoned tea at one point, though he did not die from it. Such persecutions continued through the spring of 1968, when he said in a televised criticism against him that ten Red Guards had once ganged up to beat him.[6] Campaigns of this sort were not polite or abstract.

Musical talent was the basis He had espoused for conservatory admis-

---

Politics in China: Class, Nationalism, and the Controversy over Western Music, which will change this situation as regards musicians. There are several good books on theater. Visual critics, who are in such obvious danger of intellectual corruption because of political conservatism among people with money to buy objects and endow museums, have too often disdained analysis of PRC art. Arnold Chang, *Painting in the PRC: The Politics of Style* (Boulder, Colo.: Westview, 1980), thus enters a field with great potential.

[3] See Kraus, *Pianos and Politics*, chap. 4.

[4] Interview with a Kampuchean Overseas Chinese woman who studied at the Shanghai Music Conservatory before 1965, URI, Hong Kong. The Conservatory is on Huaihai Road, in the previous "French Concession."

[5] *GMRB*, June 9, 1966.

[6] Kraus, *Pianos and Politics*, chap. 4.

sions. This composer favored the full-time regimen of practice that is normal at conservatories throughout the world. Teacher-student relations in music are traditionally close, in any country. This propensity was strengthened by Chinese family styles and Communist policies, and He Lüting had many supporters among his conservatory's faculty and students. Before the harshest attack against him, one of his pupils obtained "an important post in the information section of the Shanghai Conservatory's Cultural Revolution Liaison Office." This disciple warned He that criticisms were being prepared. Reportedly at the urging of He's wife, his daughter became involved in "discussions of ideological problems" with this pupil and induced the latter to pass on "all the details of the secret investigations."[7]

He Lüting thus obtained photostats of the relevant documents.[8] The musician learned that Red Guards from the conservatory had gone to his native city of Shaoyang, Hunan, to gather old information against him.[9] Clandestine files, distant investigations, vying between factions, and the involvement of family members were all central features of He Lüting's case—and many others during the Cultural Revolution. These became the standard operating procedures of the time, as they had been in the Antirightist and Four Cleans eras.

He Lüting had his own network of "lackeys and reactionary relatives, who shadowed the investigators." For their part, the Red Guards found that in 1927, this composer had shown "frenzied opposition to the Hunan peasant movement. A light and cheerful tune of his, called the 'Cowherd's Flute,' had been composed and played in 1934; but by 1962, he played a sad tune, 'Night Flute in a Desolate Village.' "[10] The Red Guards were interested in aesthetics, but along a somewhat narrow set of dimensions. Young people in 1966 Shanghai had such uncertain prospects—and if they had been in bad situations before, such potentially better ones—that they thought quietude and melancholy were unbeautiful in public. Fury seemed aesthetically right to them.

Campaigning uses minimal resources to aim at quick results; thus, as a style, it conflicts with the norm of regular practice over many years that is prerequisite to good musicianship. He Lüting held that "some people stress the transformation of the thoughts of players too much and require musi-

---

[7] *WHB*, April 24, 1968.

[8] Ibid.

[9] Ibid. Shaoshan, which is Mao Zedong's birthplace in Hunan, differs from Shaoyang. He Lüting's place is a railhead and county seat in the watershed of the Zu River, far to the southwest of either Mao's old home or the provincial capital, Changsha.

[10] *WHB*, June 8, 1966.

cians to give up regular training in technique. . . . They will find it impossible not only to perform musical works, but also to know the content." His outspoken case for the need to recruit good players and give them time to practice—in a profession for which technical levels of accomplishment are easily detectable—laid him wide open to attacks. To the frustrated and the patriotic, slowness seemed a betrayal.

Campaigning also, as a concept derived from war, stresses the usefulness of destruction; but most artists, if given a choice, talk more about "creation." After leftist critic Yao Wenyuan published a 1963 article berating Debussy, He Lüting used a pseudonym to defend the French impressionist and call Yao a "bruiser, who would use a club to knock down anything."[11] This puts in formal terms a difference between the ideal styles of the Cultural Revolution and of those who disliked it. Enthusiasm for "smashing" campaigns was common among underlings who disliked their old patrons and bad-labeled people who wanted freedom, even though it competed with increasing doubts about the usefulness of so much destruction.

Members of the conservatory spoke against He, but the style of early 1966 was also to recruit critics from all walks of life. On a single day, a soldier from the local garrison, a worker from the Yangshupu Power Plant, a police clerk, a music publisher, and a suburban propaganda team member all lambasted He Lüting.[12] On another day, the struggle came from two other soldiers, a middle-school student, and staff of the cultural center in a suburban county.[13] On yet a third day, the denouncers were two more military men, a worker in an electric appliance factory, a commune representative, and musicians from the Shanghai Philharmonic and the Shanghai Choir.[14]

Suicides were reported among several Shanghai musicians in 1966. Lu

---

[11] Ibid. Yao Wenyuan, later renowned as a member of the Gang of Four, was in 1963 a Shanghai art critic, and he published this critique of Debussy under a pen name. Yao had the sharpest polemical pen in modern Chinese letters. Composer He Lüting's reference to a "club" gave Yao's identity away. A 1962 speech by writer Ba Jin at the Second Shanghai Congress of Writers and Artists had criticized Yao, while not naming him, as a man who, "holding a hoop in one hand and a club in the other, goes everywhere looking for men with mistakes." See Lynn White, "Leadership in Shanghai, 1955–69," in *Elites in the People's Republic of China*, ed. Robert A. Scalapino (Seattle: University of Washington Press, 1962). For more, see Lars Ragvald, *Yao Wenyuan as a Literary Critic and Theorist: The Emergence of Chinese Zhdanovism* (Stockholm: University of Stockholm, 1978), and Stephen O. Huff, "Literary Policy in Communist China and the Rise of Yao Wen-yuan" (Senior thesis, Department of East Asian Studies, Princeton University, 1975).

[12] *XMWB*, June 13, 1966.

[13] *XMWB*, June 22, 1966.

[14] *XMWB*, June 28, 1966.

Zuzhen, on the conservatory's faculty, took poison in November. Composer Yang Jiaren and his wife gassed themselves in their Shanghai flat, because their son had been conducting a "hate campaign" against them (partly on account of the capitalist educations they had received in the United States). Musicologist Fu Lei of the Shanghai Academy of Arts, famous for his biography of Beethoven, also committed suicide in Shanghai after his persecution by Red Guards.[15]

Many prominent Shanghai intellectuals suffered harsh campaign attacks, beginning in June 1966. There is no space to detail all their tortures here. Because Jiang Qing, Mao's wife, had long been working with the Shanghai Municipal Beijing Opera Troupe and Municipal Dancing School (the corresponding establishments in Beijing were unwilling to follow her politics or aesthetics), these institutions were busy by the spring of 1966 giving performances in many cities.[16] Radicals also used Shanghai's Shaoxing Opera Troupe for revolutionized productions.[17]

Prominent professors were almost all labeled "capitalist" and, often worse, "intellectual." So they were less fortunate. Li Pingxin of the East China Normal University History Department was accused of having advocated "counterrevolutionary theories" in 1957, of having called the Great Leap policy "a slave system," and of having advocated a need for "honest officials" in 1965.[18] Any cultural leader with doubts about the Antirightist Campaign, the Great Leap, or the Four Cleans was an obvious candidate for grief in the spring of 1966. The Cultural Revolution, before August, looked like yet another case of the Party rounding up the usual suspects. The 1957

---

[15] *Star* (Hong Kong), October 22, November 24, 1966. Fu Lei was the father of Fu Cong (Fou Ts'ong), who won an important piano prize in Warsaw in 1955, married Yehudi Menuhin's daughter Zamira in 1960, defected from China, and had sometimes strained relations with Fu Lei.

[16] *GMRB*, June 17, 1966, indicates that the Shanghai Dancing School put on thirty-three performances of Jiang's revolutionized version of the ballet *The White Haired Girl* (*Baimao nü*) in Beijing during late April and early June. The revolutionized ballet *The Red Detachment of Women* (*Hongse niangzi jun*) accounted for most of their other performances. Shanghai's Beijing Opera Troupe played *The Red Lantern* (*Hong deng ji*) and later the more distinctively Shanghainese *On the Docks* (*Haigang*). Recordings of the first, third, and fourth of these items were available from the Zhongguo Changpian She (China Recording Society), issues M-817, BM-6169, and M-839, respectively.

[17] *XMWB*, August 6, 1966, notes that the city's Shaoxing troupe was still "in discussion," trying "to be art workers with abilities in culture and labor, guided by Chairman Mao."

[18] *WHB*, June 20, 1966. "Honest officials" refers to brave bureaucrats who criticize emperors. Further reports of struggles against Li Pingxin are available in *XMWB*, June 21, 24, 1966. The list of his attackers is as varied as in the case of He Lüting, except that the June 20 *WHB* concentrates on critics within the university itself, from the departments of history, politics, biology, education, and even the university farm.

precedent was obvious, except that the scope of personal violence against intellectuals in this new campaign was already greater.

Attacks on a Fudan University historian, Zhou Yutong, received national publicity because he supported the study of historic "honest officials" who had censored the bad policies of past emperors.[19] Playwrights, moviemakers, and all other kinds of intellectuals were subject to similar accusations, supported by flimsy evidence that often extended back for decades.[20] The articles reporting struggle meetings were more notable for the variety of people who had untoward things to say about intellectuals than for details on their crimes. Often the main problem lay in intellectuals' views that their professional fields gave them rights to advisory roles in politics. Newspaper readers in 1966 were clearly supposed to be impressed by the isolation of intellectuals from other kinds of citizens. Once they (and their families) were labeled and set off from "the people," social ostracism and physical attack followed. People with intellectual labels often led the fray, lest they be thought unprogressive.

INTELLECTUALS' SUICIDES: ANOMIE BY POLICY

Suicide was the only means by which some victims of struggle could express themselves.[21] Statistics are not available, but confirmation that the suicide rate was high in the spring and summer of 1966 comes from a wide variety of sources. Zhou Enlai, berating a group of Shanghai Red Guards for violating the home of Mme. Sun Yat-sen, said they should not attack people solely on the basis of class origins: "Some youngsters have acted like hooligans."[22]

Reports from foreign residents in China during 1966 stressed their concern about common information on suicides and killings. Soviets, for example, dwelt on this topic even more than on other aspects of the Cultural

---

[19] Zhou's main analogy was to Peng Dehuai, who censored Mao's Great Leap Forward. His faults, as described by investigators who opposed him, began in a period when he allegedly "sided with Wang Jingwei," China's chief collaborator with Japan during the war. A national article is in *GMRB*, July 13, 1966; a local one is in *XMWB*, July 5, 1966.

[20] Against Wei Xinfang, who wrote the play *Hai Rui's Memorial to the Emperor* in 1959, see *NCNA*, June 14, 1966, and *XMWB*, July 11, 1966. Against Qu Baiyin and his film *Creative Monologue* (*Chuangxin dubai*), see *XMWB*, June 17, 19, 1966, and July 8, 1966. Against the film *A Thousand Miles of Adverse Wind* (*Nifeng qianli*), see *XMWB*, June 17, July 7, 1966.

[21] The prime account is Thurston's *Enemies of the People*.

[22] Stanley Karnow, *Mao and China: From Revolution to Revolution* (New York: Viking, 1969), p. 210.

Revolution that they criticized. *Pravda* spoke with some authority when it called the Cultural Revolution a "pogrom."[23] Even a young British teacher sympathetic to the ideals of the Cultural Revolution deplored the "rough handling" of victims at criticism meetings, and reported the common knowledge that Shanghai was then suffering an epidemic of suicides.[24]

A Western journalist, collating numerous reports, believed the suicide rate among ex-bourgeois "during the initial eruption of the Cultural Revolution was extremely high." Many comments from the time tell as much about the mentalities of the commentators as about the subject of their report. Lin Biao said, "Many people have committed suicide or been killed." As Public Security Minister Xie Fuzhi explained, many killed themselves "out of fear of punishment for their crimes."[25]

When Zhang Chunqiao received a report from East China Normal University on the suicides of ten people there within a short period, he considered this "a grave situation." Even the secretary of the university's Party committee had jumped from a building. Zhang nonetheless took a hard line:

> Despite the fact that most of those who died were not good people, there is still need for work to be carried out better among those who must be toppled. . . . If a few people are wronged in cleaning out the class ranks of educational workers, the problem will not be too serious. But it would be very serious if we let real enemies get away.[26]

Information about deaths among intellectuals spread through unofficial billboards. "A poster would appear announcing that someone had refused to be reformed and decided to remain an enemy permanently. We knew then that the person had allegedly killed himself, but we never knew if the death was self-inflicted or whether such a person had in fact been killed or forced to commit suicide by the Red Guards."[27] Others heard about suicides through their families.[28] Channels of communication for such news were mainly unofficial, including many new tabloids that various conflicting revolutionary groups published. A new system of media replaced the Party

---

[23] *Pravda*, January 15, 1967; cf. A. Zhelokhovtsev, *The Cultural Revolution: A Close-up Eyewitness Account* (Moscow: Progress Publishers, 1975), pp. 137ff., 200–2.

[24] Sophia Knight, *Window on Shanghai* (London: Deutsch, 1967), p. 226.

[25] Ibid., pp. 215, 300, 431. For scattered further reports of suicides, see also pp. 187, 212, 215, 266, 301, 344.

[26] *Hongsi tongxun*, no. 4/5 (July 12, 1968). See also *XDRB*, September 28, 1968.

[27] Yue and Wakeman, *To the Storm*, p. 184.

[28] Liang Heng and Judith Shapiro, *Son of the Revolution* (New York: Random House, 1983), pp. 248–49.

press, whose potency declined along with that of many other pre-1966 policies.

The classic analysis of suicide is by Émile Durkheim, who catalogs three types of causes: "Altruistic" suicide is a duty, when an individual is part of a society that requires this act in specific circumstances, as codes of honor in war have often done.[29] "Egoistic" suicide, on the contrary, is caused by an individual's detachment from social norms; it arises basically from personal reasons rather than social pressure. "Anomic" suicide expresses anger and frustration because of unfulfilled hopes; it occurs not because of too much or too little social integration of the individual, but because the social norms the person wants to follow disallow the attainment of personal goals.[30]

Although no sociological category will bring back the dead, suicide in the Cultural Revolution was mainly anomic. Durkheim associated this type with temporary states of social deregulation (such as occurred in China during 1966). He thought that modern markets might cause suicidal anxiety by holding out unwinnable prizes: "The state of crisis and anomie is constant and, so to speak, normal. From the top to the bottom of the ladder, greed is aroused without knowing where to find an ultimate foothold. Nothing can calm it, since its goal is far beyond all it can attain."[31] Apparently Durkheim did not imagine that a political system, as much as an economic system, could burden individuals with such impossible demands on a constant basis. It could also raise hopes without raising the chances of their fulfillment.

Altruistic or egoistic suicides come from a society's tendency to bond its members either too much or too little. But it would be hard to make a strong case for codes like the "samurai ethic" or the "Protestant ethic" in contemporary China. China's Cultural Revolution norms never approved suicide, which did not result from "altruism." Neither did these suicides derive just from individuals' "egoism," because social pressures are clearly needed to explain the 1966–67 epidemic. Instead, they were "anomic," in Durkheim's terms. They resulted not from deep links between individuals and society, but from temporary social policies that shattered individuals' hopes of attaining goals. These suicides as described by Durkheim's theory echo the

[29] Chinese examples of this form are less well known than Japanese ones, but they are stressed in Étienne Balazs's *Chinese Civilization and Bureaucracy* (New Haven: Yale University Press, 1964), p. 6.

[30] Émile Durkheim, *Suicide: A Study in Sociology*, trans. J. Spaulding and G. Simpson (New York: Free Press of Glencoe, 1951).

[31] Translated from Durkheim's *Suicide* in Robert A. Jones, *Émile Durkheim* (Beverly Hills, Calif.: Sage, 1986), p. 100.

argument of this book because they suggest not a value consensus or individual deviances, but specific frustrations.

The policies that led to this result could have been chosen otherwise. The means of administration that created the Cultural Revolution were not inexorable patterns of political culture that will haunt China forever. As labels, patronage, and campaigns have gone somewhat out of style, suicides in China have declined, too.

STUDENTS' RAMPAGES: PRECEDENTS, INCENTIVES, AND EFFECTS

Proletarian youths knew, by the early summer of 1966, the educational benefits that post-1963 educational policies had brought them in middle schools and universities. They formed groups to ransack the houses of the Cultural Revolution's victims, who at first were mostly intellectuals from capitalist or landlord backgrounds. Good-label youths could more easily rise to leadership posts, even in gangs composed mostly of repenting-label activists. But some prominent Red Guard leaders, both in Shanghai and nationally, came from bad-label backgrounds.[32]

Red Guards raided offices and homes to "check up" (*waidiao*) on persons who offended them for any reason.[33] They inventoried materials in shops and plants, and they used "big character posters" (*dazibao*) to detail the wrongdoings of campaign targets. These unfortunates acquired entirely new bad labels—often animalistic, such as "monsters and freaks"—that their persecutors added to any old bad labels found in their records.

None of these activities was trailblazing. Investigations by youth activists dated back to "tiger hunting" in the 1952 Five Anti Campaign against businessmen. Big character posters were prominent in both the Hundred Flowers and Antirightist campaigns of 1957. Mobilizing masses had long been the

---

[32] On the national scene, interviewees report that Nie Yuanzi (probably the most prominent single Red Guard leader, a young woman philosophy instructor at Beijing University who led the radical group that attacked the university president and so won public favor with Mao Zedong) was from a landlord family. Hu Shoujun, leader of a prominent rebel group at Fudan University in Shanghai by August 1966, was reportedly from a family of petty bourgeois. Many nonstudent leaders who were often radical, notably Zhang Chunqiao and Yao Wenyuan in Shanghai, also had capitalist and intellectual family origins.

[33] "House searches" (*chao jia*) were old means of harassing the families of discredited officials in China. The use of "big character posters" also relates to old Chinese traditions of public petitioning. Nothing in this book should be read to claim that particular means and language of action in the CR are unlinked to Chinese traditions—only that the basic motives and extent of violence then cannot be explained by traditions.

Party's standard operating procedure, especially since the 1958 Leap. Inquisitions on past misdeeds and categorizations of the guilty by labels were also old habits, though the Four Cleans Campaign and Socialist Education Movement set particularly high standards of thoroughness in labeling during 1964. All the main campaigns of earlier PRC eras contributed to the start of the Cultural Revolution. By August 1966, the Politburo's resolution assured that the struggle would be chaotic, because it allowed non-Party people to participate (as they had in the Hundred Flowers). The levels of local violence were unprecedented, in schools and even residential neighborhoods, because past policies of control had angered so many.

Weather was a factor too, as in many Chinese affairs. The summer of 1966 in Shanghai was especially hot.[34] Although the first stages of the CR were largely indoors, especially in schools, struggle meetings soon tended to spill outside, as local Party committees authorized marches with drums and gongs. Red Guards on hot days easily entered dwellings through open doors and windows. In late August, as their numbers multiplied and their types diversified, some searched houses practically at random.[35]

The August decision increased the diversity of family backgrounds among Red Guards, and it also increased the range of their ages. Students from universities and middle schools, who had conducted earlier searches, were generally less violent than Young Pioneer groups. Mayor Cao had to leave a meeting in September, when young Red Guards started shouting, "Beat him! Beat him!" They might have overwhelmed him, except for bodyguards. They did beat Deputy Mayor Song Jiwen. The city's leaders would probably have reacted more strongly to such attacks, if violence had not been in the air for many years.

During a raid on a residence, a group of young Red Guards found only a caretaker; so they "destroyed everything and went away." As an interviewee said,

> In Shanghai, the Red Guards from secondary schools or universities are more reasonable. But those from the Pioneers are very wild. . . . In a struggle meeting, if the people in charge can't control them, they will beat the person being criticized. Authorities who stop them are accused of being counterrevolutionaries. This is a major reason why different groups of Red Guards fight.[36]

---

[34] *Far Eastern Economic Review*, September 8, 1966.

[35] Hans Granqvist, *The Red Guard* (New York: Praeger, 1967), pp. 117–19, based on reports of a non-Soviet Russian who was a long-term resident of Shanghai.

[36] Interview with a Zhejiang man, URI, Hong Kong, based also on discussions with his sister and nephew in Shanghai at that time.

Young Red Guards, ranging in age from eight to fifteen, formed especially puritan and intemperate groups. When they found a shop that would not comply with the new standards they wished to enforce, they would paste critical posters over its walls, often sealing the door of an especially objectionable firm with a portrait of Chairman Mao (which could not be torn to gain entrance).[37] Even into the next year, Shanghai primary school students were accused of damaging property, fighting among themselves, cursing their rivals, and ignoring teachers and elders who attempted to discipline them. Many learned to fear retaliation from them.[38]

STUDENTS' CHOICES IN POPULAR CULTURE

The Red Guards were careless about old intellectuals, but they were passionately concerned about anything new. This pattern was evident also in the English and French revolutions. There, as in China, purely symbolic changes (often changes of names) were thought to have power for human betterment. Labels became more diverse than ever.

Youths in Shanghai by 1966 found many titles in need of progress. Red Guards suggested that the Yong'an (Eternal Peace) Department Store, long the city's largest, should be renamed Yongdou (Eternal Struggle), Yonghong (Eternal Red), or even Hongwei (Red Guard).[39] Inscriptions in foreign languages, carved in stone on the facades of many buildings during the 1920s and 1930s, were chiseled off; and the bronze lions in front of an ex-British bank were put into storage. Because Shanghai had grown most quickly under foreign sponsorship, some Red Guards even proposed that the name of the city be changed to "Fandi" (Anti-Imperialism), that the Huangpu River leading to its port be renamed the "Anti-Imperialist River," and that the main shopping street, Nanjing Road, become "Anti-Imperialist Road."[40] Any Chinese wearing "Hong Kong clothes," meaning Western attire, could be stopped on the street for criticism. If Red Guards spotted tapering trousers, pointed shoes, elastic laces, jeans, or white collars, they would give lectures on fashion to the wearers. Long-haired people were escorted to barber shops for involuntary clippings. There was a short-hair campaign.

Red Guards closed parks that courting couples used. When they needed space for "liaison stations," to arrange accommodation for visiting Red

---

[37] *Far Eastern Economic Review*, September 8, 1966.
[38] *RMRB*, July 10, 1967.
[39] *NCNA*, August 24, 1966.
[40] Granqvist, *Red Guard*, pp. 114–16. See also *Far Eastern Economic Review*, September 8, 1966.

Guards from other cities, they pestered the occupants into leaving.[41] The bells of the Shanghai Customs House tower, which once chimed the carillon of Big Ben at Westminster, were reprogrammed in 1966 to ring "The East Is Red."

Not all such changes were permanent; but new signs, posters, and pictures of Chairman Mao appeared on all available street-level wall space. "The stores on Nanjing Road are not just service units; they are also propaganda units."[42] All of them removed "strange" goods such as Western-style clothing from public sight. One attired its clerks in sandwich boards, sporting quotations from the Chairman. Another put portraits of Mao in display cases.

Red Guards entered trams and trains without paying fares—except spiritual fares, "reading the sayings of Chairman Mao loudly."[43] After August, people from any class background could form "propaganda teams" to travel around the country. An organization called the "Shanghai People's Criticism and Accusation Group," for example, put on free skits.[44] Members of such groups felt themselves entitled to raise criticisms in work units where they performed. At the West City Second Junior Middle School, "small generals" formed a propaganda team of thirty members, which helped to patrol its part of town against "bourgeois" deviations. Youths at the Shanghai Internal Rivers Navigation Office formed a team to "wander" on Suzhou Creek in small steamboats, "publicizing the thought of Chairman Mao" to residents in boats along that waterway. Formal rules prescribed that Red Guards, entering houses for inspection, should belong to the same work unit as the household head,[45] but these strictures were widely honored in the breach. Campaigning was out of control.

Symbols of cheer and color, at this time, blended with those of trauma. For many—especially ex-bourgeois youths whom the previous system had treated badly, but whose own families seemed safe—August was a real liberation. The city's Shanghainese Language Drama Troupe divided into propaganda groups and gave frequent skits. The teams of two middle schools "grouped together to publicize the thought of Chairman Mao to passengers"—not because they had been organized to do so together, but because

[41] SHNL, March 30, 1967.

[42] *SHWB*, September 30, 1966.

[43] Ibid. See also Gordon A. Bennett and Ronald N. Montaperto, *Red Guard: The Political Biography of Dai Hsiao-ai* (Garden City, N.Y.: Doubleday, 1971), chap. 4.

[44] *Shanghai renmin pingtan tuan*; *SHWB*, September 16, 1966.

[45] Knight, *Window on Shanghai*, p. 222.

they met by chance on a tram.[46] "Small arts teams" (*wenyi xiao fendui*) were widespread. When a woman was overheard, on trolley route no. 25, singing a foreign lullaby called "Darling" to her baby, the "passengers joined in criticism. . . . One passenger tried to defend the woman, but even the conductor endorsed the comrades' opinion."[47] If the rations of independence and privacy were to be skimpy, at least they would be equal.

RESIDENTS' RELIGIOUS CHOICES IN THE CULTURAL REVOLUTION

All foreign things, especially foreign religions, came under severe attack. Churches, active or inactive, were "stripped of crosses, statues, icons, decorations, and all church paraphenalia" about August 24, 1966.[48] Although one Roman Catholic church, with broken windows and no cross, continued services into March 1967 for nearly one hundred longtime parishioners, the priest became an employee of the "Anti-Religious Combat Office." He could not hear confessions. After each once-a-week mass, he read a new benediction, from the *Quotations of Chairman Mao*.[49]

Muslims in Shanghai protected themselves from these onslaughts more successfully than others, and the reason is clear. Unlike Christians or Buddhists, they are recognized as a national minority; and in Shanghai, they had a Muslim Middle School (*Huimin Zhongxue*). This academy formed its own Red Guard groups. One of the factions, called the *Baozi hao*, was strong enough to assure respect for Muslim rights. It eventually settled down to studying the "three great disciplines and eight points to attend to," under army representatives who also helped keep order.[50]

[46] *SHWB*, September 15, 1966.

[47] *WHB*, May 4, 1968.

[48] SHNL, August 30, 1966. The elderly Russian correspondent who wrote the SHNL piece toured Shanghai on August 24 and saw Red Guards at work on St. Ignatius Cathedral in Xuhui, the Church of the Sacred Heart in Hongkou, St. Joseph's in Sichuan Road, St. Peter's at the former Aurora University, and churches in Dongjiadu, Qiaojou Road, and Datong Road, in addition to the Anglican cathedral on Jiangxi Road, the International Church (formerly American Community Church) on Hengshan Road, and even a school in a former church building on Tibet Road. Books and religious tracts fueled bonfires in front of churches on that day, and also in front of ex-missionary buildings on Yuanmingyuan Road.

[49] Report of Louis Barcata, *China News* (Hong Kong), March 1967. A more doubtful or unique report in *Tiantian ribao* (Hong Kong), September 28, 1967, said that earlier in the month Red Guards found a man with a crucifix, tied him to a cross, erected this in a school playground, and harassed him until his cries brought soldiers who rescued him.

[50] *WHB*, March 3, 1967.

Buddhism and Taoism in the late 1960s still claimed allegiance from a much larger portion of Shanghai's citizens than any of the more recently imported religions, but they suffered Red Guard attacks also. Many Buddhist and Taoist temples suspended services for the duration. Their monks and priests fended as they could. A popular resurgence of Buddhism and Taoism in recent years, however, makes clear that private piety on a widespread basis did not end. Most Red Guards, still very much in Chinese families, knew what their parents honored. Belief comes in many degrees.[51]

A seventy-six-year-old woman was made a model in Luwan District because she ceased to praise Buddha. Before the Cultural Revolution, she had fasted and repeated the holy name of that ancient teacher regularly, to pay homage. But after two years of Cultural Revolution, she "changed her faith." She knew only fifty Chinese characters well, but she was able to decipher Mao's "Three Constantly Read Articles" with the help of her granddaughter. She studied them one sentence at a time, trying to memorize them for recitation, and she had dreams about them. This method did not work, however, because the sentences were too long. So her son taught her to divide each sentence into parts, and she would study this way all day, while waiting in lines at shops, reciting the disconnected phrases aloud. Reportedly, people thought she had gone crazy; but in the end, she could recite all three articles.[52] With the new sutra, as with the old, understanding often took second place to piety. Not everyone in Shanghai during the Cultural Revolution was frenzied, because the old cultural options were a breakwater for some against the campaign wave.

Traditional family religion, too, was compatible with certain aspects of the Cultural Revolution, especially for people whose lineages were proletarian. "Blood doctrine" remained strong among worker-label students throughout these years, despite halfhearted official denunciations of belief in the inheritability of class virtue by blood.[53] Well into 1968, in a part of Luwan District where 90 percent of the residents were proletarians, the local neighborhood committee organized a village-like ritual: every night, a walker rang a curfew bell, and each family paid a few minutes' respect to

[51] Clifford Geertz discusses the greater "force" of Islam in Morocco and a greater "scope" for it among social contexts in Indonesia. He quotes Frank O'Connor: "No Irishman is really interesting until he has begun to lose his faith" (*Islam Observed: Religious Development in Morocco and Indonesia* [Chicago: University of Chicago Press, 1968], p. 117).

[52] Example adapted from Bruce MacFarlane, "Notes from Wuliqiao Rd., Luwan District," April 20, 1968, in Universities Service Center Library, Hong Kong.

[53] *RMRB*, April 26, 1967, documents this for the Shanghai No. 6 Girls' Middle School, where the factions seem to have been based almost exclusively on family labels.

the picture of Chairman Mao in each kitchen, where the shelf of ancestral totems had once been, singing "The East Is Red" and reading from the *Quotations of Chairman Mao* before going to bed.[54] If everyone, of any family background, could be labeled loyal, then all questions about solidarity could be answered positively.

STUDENTS' PREFERENCES IN PROMOTIONS

Families naturally react to changes in the ability of members to obtain good educations or salaries, and the Cultural Revolution sharply affected these opportunities. On June 3, 1966, a national decision decreed that entrance exams for universities would not be held that spring. The enrollment of the fall 1966 class was to be postponed for six months.[55] This was to be a temporary campaign, though youths who wanted more schooling could not know, then, that the country's education system was about to close for years.

Shanghai secondary school graduates now had nothing to do but make Cultural Revolution. Local papers reported that street cadres from rich residential areas "sent letters to support the decision on admission exams."[56] Considering what these bureaucrats for rustication had to lose by keeping youths who disliked them unoccupied, the street cadres' enthusiasm for the lapse in promotions seems forced. Clearly protesting too much, graduating seniors, even from prestigious high schools, also praised this decision.[57] They owed at least some credit to their own chances of winning even better labels in the future.

Before August, all such expressions were determined by the agencies for socialist education. Approved "proletarian" and "cadre" groups were at first the ones able to have their opinions published. They had no great liking for the admission exams, and they could expect benefits for loyalty in a turbulent time. They were in more secure positions than bad-label youths. Above all, they could express themselves plainly, in "blood doctrine" terms:

---

[54] *WHB*, June 7, 1968.

[55] Peter Cheng, *A Chronology of the People's Republic of China* (Totowa, N.J.: Littlefield Adams, 1972), p. 223.

[56] *XMWB*, June 19, 1966, published letters from a street in Hongkou District, which a map shows in a central location near the confluence of Suzhou Creek and the Huangpu River.

[57] Support for the admissions postponement came from the best schools in Shanghai: Tongji, Bile, Jinling, Hongqi, Shidong, Shinan, Gezhi, Huimin, Mingde, Kongjiang (in a workers' housing project financed by large state corporations), and Jiaotong University Affiliated Middle School (which is a magnet school for science) (*XMWB*, June 19, 20, 1966).

All revolutionary teachers and students unanimously think the former admissions exam system was not good socialism. To carry out this system, the anti-Party class line kept a great number of excellent workers, poor and lower peasants, revolutionary cadres, soldiers, and sons and daughters of martyrs from being admitted to universities. This only fostered successors from the bourgeois class. Students are grateful for the reform of the system. They take Chairman Mao's writing as their supreme instruction, and this course in class education as the first important political lesson.[58]

Final exams were canceled in the spring of 1966 at secondary and primary levels. All students due for promotion were passed to the next grade wholesale, without tests or scores, and their transfer to the next level of schooling in 1967 was also promised to be automatic.[59] What happened to these students' actual careers is a later story.

RESIDENTS' PREFERENCES
IN PLACES TO LIVE

Residential rustication was always an option for ex-students with nothing else to do. Young members of families already under attack in 1966 had seriously to consider going to live in villages. A Shanghai deputy mayor (soon to be criticized) indicated as early as April that the Municipal Committee was planning a 1966 send-down of "unemployed youths" to Xinjiang on much larger scale than usual.

Most youths have inherited the spirit of endurance and revolution from the People's Liberation Army. They are equally successful in severe cold and very hot weather. Formerly, some young girls dreaded the hot sun, wind, and rain. But now they are quite indifferent. They consider it a great honor to have brown, sunburned skins.[60]

This call of the wild, with patriotic ideals and Party organization behind it, was enough to inspire some Shanghai youths to move elsewhere. Going to Xinjiang was depicted as a glorious and fun campaign, as well as a way to get a better label than any ordinary family could provide.

[58] *XMWB*, June 19, 1966.
[59] SHNL, July 23, 1966.
[60] Deputy Mayor Song Richang is quoted in *XDRB*, April 20, 1966. Xinjiang may be recognized by some readers only under its old romanization, Sinkiang.

Oral guarantees were given to others, though not published in newspapers, to offer further encouragement: The normal term of service in Xinjiang was to be three years. Some youths were told they could travel back to Shanghai for visits to their families during that time.[61] Residence committees sometimes even offered "household guarantee certificates" (*hukou bao-zheng shu*) to assure rusticates of their legal ability to regain registrations in Shanghai later.[62] Many youths were then uncertain whether they could happily live for long periods in rural places. They were attracted, however, by the future options that household guarantee certificates suggested. If they left the city, and the Cultural Revolution became more severe, they might benefit from rustication. Some interviewees report figuring that if the campaign moderated after mid-1966, they would be able to return to Shanghai anyway.

There were three stages in the send-down process. First, a youth would sign up (*bao ming*) for rustication. Later, after an administrative process, the legal household registration would be moved (*qian hukou*), so that the person's rations and rights to jobs and education in Shanghai would end. Lastly, a youth might actually go to the assigned rural place. But it was easier for local monitors to reach their quotas for the early, merely promissory stages of this process than to persuade youths finally to depart.[63]

An intense campaign for volunteering, that is, for going through at least the first of the three stages, took place in June 1966. Street committee cadres pledged in big character posters to go to Xinjiang themselves, or to send their children.[64] Rural counties, which had charge of many "worker and peasant" contract laborers (who wanted regular jobs in Shanghai), were increasingly asked to send these discontents far away to Xinjiang. On June 23, local newspapers reported that large groups of youths would leave on trains

---

[61] SHNL, June 12, 1965.

[62] Interview with an ex–Red Guard who had done rustication labor and said he knew definitely that "organs of the Shanghai People's Committee" had issued household guarantee certificates. Written confirmation of such documents has not been found, but several interviewees report them.

[63] In 1976, the author photographed a bulletin board at a silk factory in Wuxi showing the names of employees, their "intellectual-youth" offspring, the children's years of graduation, and whether each of the targeted youths had passed through these three processes. Although a majority had volunteered in principle, only a minority had left for rural areas. The photo of this board has been published in the best book concerning the send-down: Thomas P. Bernstein, *Up to the Mountains and Down to the Villages: The Transfer of Youth from Urban to Rural China* (New Haven: Yale University Press, 1977).

[64] XMWB, June 22, 1966, quotes "street blackboard newspapers" that name nine street committee members who "guarantee to hand their children over to the Party" and three who "say they will go themselves."

every three days. The first batch of 950 departed that very day, under military escort, to go work on the Xinjiang army-run farms.[65]

Resistance to this campaign started even before the bitter, unofficial countercampaign of rural violence against residential cadres, which began in August. During July, official sources had admitted that many youths were reluctant to leave their homes and "break their family shackles."[66] Local newspapers printed stories about families in which parents and children "struggled" to overcome this reluctance. For example, a girl postponed her departure for a time because she caught tuberculosis. Then she stayed for a further time because she got a job in a radio shop, and still further (after volunteering in principle to live in Xinjiang) when the Party sent her to a school for a one-month preparation course. Her father wrote letters to "the department concerned" to stop her going, but the girl finally left for Shihezi Farm in the wild west.[67]

How many Shanghainese volunteered to leave their city in the summer of 1966, how many registrations were transferred on paper only, and how many actually moved out are difficult data to obtain. This intense campaign among Shanghai youth was an immediate, precipitating cause of the Cultural Revolution's violence. The pressures organized for rustication by long-cumulating policies, but then increased in mid-1966, may have been almost as important for the onset of chaos as the August directive restraining police.

This does not mean the rustication campaign brought big results under the conditions of chaos in 1966. Send-down was then much less effective than it became later. Boarding trains for Xinjiang led smoothly to boarding trains for "exchanging revolutionary experiences" in other Chinese cities. One campaign led to others, for very different goals, when purposes were decentralized in practice after August.

Attacks on lane cadres and local education bureaucrats intensified steadily through the autumn and into January. "Talk and practice" sessions (*jiangyong hui*), held for street committee members and people's policemen to teach rustication propaganda techniques, provided ready lists of bureaucrats for Red Guard struggle sessions.[68] Because rustication was widely unpopular, and because it was widely perceived as indistinguishable from the post-1963 admissions bias against bourgeois-background students, Shanghai's residential officials came under early attack.

[65] *XMWB*, June 23, 1966.

[66] *ZGQNB*, July 29, 1966.

[67] *XMWB*, June 3, 1966. Shihezi Farm, like many other locations in Xinjiang, is populated mainly by Shanghai people.

[68] *XMWB*, August 17, 1966.

At Fudan University, which is the equal of any in China, major conflict developed in September and October over the disposition of "black materials" in students' files. These could be used to determine rustication or job assignments. Now that "rebels" could organize against the allocation system—and had obvious incentives to do so—they staged a hunger strike. They surrounded the Youth League Committee at Fudan and held a sit-down siege of that office for four days and nights. Finally, they attacked the files and "seized black material by force."[69]

Most bureaucrats inside schools and large offices were still protected by their buildings, but residence and lane committee cadres were more vulnerable. A low-level functionary in Hongkou District complained that, in December, the ex-rusticates attacked Party cadres in lanes, not higher bureaucrats who were responsible for the rustication policies. He had personally suffered at four accusation meetings, but "I really never expected that I should be called a counterrevolutionary."[70]

Anti-rustication ideas appealed more widely to different kinds of Shanghai youths than any other platform, and Red Guards not wanting to become farmers tended to spread the Cultural Revolution quickly. Elite youths, who could aspire to good careers, started the most severe conflicts of the movement, but the bitterness of ordinary, nonelite rusticates against cadres also brought violence to many local lanes.[71] Shanghai's returned youths generally refused to leave the city in the autumn of 1966, and they demanded urban jobs.[72]

Union worker organizations, such as Geng Jinzhang's, therefore had a conflict of interest with returned nonunion rusticates who wanted city jobs. But the members of unions were also angry that lane cadres had to fill quotas of send-downs—even from areas where proletarians lived. In the Wangjia Wharf area of Nanshi District (as true-red a workers' precinct as any in

---

[69] Based on an interview of January 27, 1967, at Fudan University by Australian students J. Perlez and J. Tennant, in mimeographed notes, pp. 39–40, at Universities Service Centre, Hong Kong.

[70] Quoted from *WHB* in *CNA*, April 7, 1967.

[71] Stanley Rosen, *Red Guard Factionalism*, has shown that students at Guangzhou's elite schools participated in the Cultural Revolution far more than students at other schools. Susan Shirk, *Competitive Comrades: Career Incentives and Student Strategies in China* (Berkeley and Los Angeles: University of California Press, 1982), has shown that students at full-time urban high schools even after 1963 had to hedge their bets about the final value of either political or academic criteria used to judge them, but those at "people-run" (*minban*) schools did not, because they had no real hope of good jobs. This uncertainty at some elite schools led to nervousness and conflict in the Cultural Revolution there.

[72] Evelyn Anderson, "Shanghai: The Masses Unleashed," *Problems of Communism* 27, no. 1 (1968): 17–18.

Shanghai), the lane cadres who had sent workers' children out of the city found themselves in very deep trouble by January. "Class revenge" (*jieji baofu*) was the war cry of a local tabloid there called *Haibao*. According to a rival Rebel newspaper that supported the Revolutionary Committee (and thus opposed both the old Party cadres and the Scarlet Guard–like organizations in Nanshi), this local proletarian tabloid

> told the masses who had been struggled [*sic*] by the street Party committees and police posts to submit relevant material for reopening their cases [that is, to reestablish household registrations in Shanghai]. Their struggle against the lane cadres took the form of force, and they created a reign of white terror in that area. . . . They ignored the First Circular Order of the Shanghai Municipal Revolutionary Committee. When this notice asked people to stop struggling lane cadres, they incited the masses to attack our [pro-rustication] press.[73]

In another lane, proletarian cadres who were caught by returned rusticates had to bow their heads and kneel for several hours, "to pay back the blood debt" (*taohuan xuezhai*).[74] The label system had not, originally, been designed for use against bureaucrats.

Scarlet Guards were the most powerful civilian organizations in Shanghai by January. Zhang Chunqiao needed all the help he could get against them— and he accepted it even from returned rusticates. His papers nonetheless still published lyrical descriptions of how gloriously the Cultural Revolution was faring in Xinjiang, and how much the rusticates would miss until they went back there. As his *Wenhui bao* sometimes admitted, "The handful of persons in power at the Shanghai Municipal Committee and the Xinjiang Production and Construction Corps received, corrupted, and trampled on the youths supporting construction." So this newspaper urged more people to "rise in rebellion for the purpose of getting more Shanghai youths to respond, of their own accord, to the great call for building and defending the border regions."[75] The paper also denounced "parents who were allowed to send petitions that once children had fulfilled their terms, they should be demobilized for return to Shanghai."[76] It had to concede, " 'Returning to Shanghai to rebel' appears superficially to refer to rebellion against mistakes in

[73] *WHB*, March 1, 1967. This issue names four leaders of these worker organizations who were arrested.
[74] *CNA*, April 7, 1967.
[75] *WHB*, January 25, 1967.
[76] *WHB*, January 18, 1967.

work of moving people to the interior, [but] those who return to Shanghai are deceived because of selfish and impure ideas in their minds."[77]

Criticism campaigns could not be faulted abstractly, though. This same newspaper lamely suggested, a few days later, "If these revolutionary workers have any complaints against the power holders in their original [Shanghai] areas or units, they can expose and criticize these by writing letters and big character posters [in Xinjiang]. Or if necessary, they may send a few representatives back to take part in the movement."[78] Mainly, though, the youths were urged to "fight their way back home to Xinjiang."[79] Few followed the advice.[80] When five did so, in mid-February, newspapers headlined that they were "sent off to Xinjiang by an enthusiastic and happy crowd" that obviously outnumbered them.[81]

Lest ideals fail to inspire returns to the country, the Revolutionary Committee tried to introduce penalties for staying in Shanghai. When factory wages had been paid to returnees, the payroll clerks "should be required to recall the payments; this may be by installments."[82] Rations, as well as money, were supposed to be kept from returnees. "The fixed standard of grain consumption for people must not be raised at will. . . . Temporary residents must take care of their own meals. . . . Those who have come to exchange revolutionary experience, if they have received extra grain allowances, should return the loans. . . ."[83]

Food and housing supplies could not meet the needs of returned rusticates, the regular population, and outside Red Guards. The February 1967 meat shortage in Shanghai occurred partly because peasants were concerned by reports of Leap-like urban radicalism and had therefore sold their hogs prematurely.[84] Housing was also a problem for returnees who could not stay with their families. The influx of Red Guards from other cities and the long-standing low rents and lack of upkeep by the Shanghai Real Estate Management Bureau created something like true communism for low-quality, crowded residential space in Shanghai. A free-supply system prevailed all but formally in housing. Many people squatted after August 1966. The head of an eight-person Shanghai household was asked by his neighbors, "Why

[77] *WHB*, February 12, 1967.
[78] *WHB*, February 19, 1967.
[79] *WHB*, February 11, 1967.
[80] Good statistics are unavailable, but this conclusion is based on statements from several interviewees whom other evidence has not been found to contradict.
[81] *WHB*, February 16, 1967.
[82] *NCNA*, January 30, 1967.
[83] *WHB*, February 20, 1967.
[84] *JFRB*, February 17, 1967.

don't you go out and 'occupy' some house space right away?" When he did not, he was publicized in a national Party journal as an exemplar of virtue.[85]

Few ex-rusticates went back to the boondocks. Remaining in Shanghai, ex-rural youths continued in 1967 and 1968 to attack authorities of both the old and new regimes. Parents of returned Xinjiang youths descended on lane cadres, demanding approval of household registrations in the metropolis. Some used violence, if these living licenses were refused. The new regime's press could only grieve:

> The struggle against lane cadres, to get back one's children who are frontier youths, is extremely wrong. Selfish "rebellion" is very shameful. Recently, another batch of Xinjiang youths have returned to Shanghai. They should immediately fight their way back home. . . . Parents of youths supporting Xinjiang should urge them to go back. . . . They are actually harming them, though they say they "love" them.[86]

The repetition of such editorials, from late 1966 to mid-1968, suggests that government resources to enforce this policy had declined during the Cultural Revolution.

Neighborhood cadres were caught in the middle. The official press insisted they were "not power holders, therefore struggle must not be waged against them. . . . A neighborhood committee is a mass organization of inhabitants for self-rule." Residents did not believe this, however, of the neighborhood cadres they attacked. The press admitted that "mistakes cannot be avoided" and that errors had been made. But it pleaded that most of the neighborhood cadres were "activists working on a non-paid basis."[87] Physical attacks against them dampened their enthusiasm for this volunteer work.

Factories had priority over street offices, in the revolutionary committees' efforts to establish police controls. By the end of 1967, a "people's war of encirclement and oppression of hoodlums and delinquents" was nonetheless waged by officials in Shanghai neighborhoods.[88] Struggles spread so that "whole streets have become kilometers-long galleries of big character post-

---

[85] *HQ*, no. 2 (January 16, 1967), in *SCMM*, no. 563 (1967): 11. For more on house squatting in Shanghai, whose normalcy the Cultural Revolution furthered but previous policies started, see "My Neighborhood: City Life and the Residents' Committee," in B. Michael Frolic, *Mao's People: Sixteen Portraits of Life in Revolutionary China* (Cambridge: Harvard University Press, 1980), pp. 224–41.

[86] *WHB*, February 11, 1967.

[87] *WHB*, February 10, 1967.

[88] *JFRB*, December 27, 1967.

ers."[89] But there was also an increase of ritual rebellion, directed against distant figures like Liu Shaoqi, now irrelevant to lives in Shanghai. Real politics still simmered, under all the attempts to guide participation. As Zhang Chunqiao admitted in March 1968, "Several hundred thousand middle school graduates have still not been handled well. . . . Enemies will take a chance to provoke them."[90] In the same month, his newspapers still derided "excuses" for not going back to Xinjiang. Some youths were said to claim they were staying to learn Shanghai's advanced experiences in revolution, "so that we can fight better when we return to Xinjiang." But the paper pointed out that they had "studied for more than a year in Shanghai" already. Some youths (with proletarian labels) complained, "You have no class affection for me, if you urge me to go back to Xinjiang."[91]

By the spring of 1968, the residents' committees were still not staffed with sufficient loyalists to run a large-scale rustication smoothly. New lane committee members were understandably wary of taking the path that led their predecessors into trouble. "They cherished 'fear.' "[92] They were afraid of "saying the wrong things," when talking to youths.[93] But the new regime's response to the cadre shortage, when it decided it could give rustication priority by launching a crash campaign, turned out to be entirely old: It began a coercive effort to achieve short-term benefits, regardless of long-term costs.

The largest effort at rustication in Shanghai's history occurred during the middle of 1968. A total of 450,000 secondary school leavers (from the 1967 and 1968 "graduating" classes together) were promised "employment without choice in factories or communes."[94] These half million people were scheduled to go in large groups to Jiangxi, Heilongjiang, and the Shanghai suburbs. About 100,000 people were earmarked for each of these areas (Xinjiang was not mentioned), and Shanghai was to provide jobs for only 150,000. By 1968, when local monitors could act less like patrons, they found it harder to protect particular clients, because all school graduates were now supposed to go.

These "graduates" of the Cultural Revolution did not react passively to compulsory assignment. Confucius, Lenin, the Party, and the Municipal Revolutionary Committee had all led them to understand that organization

---

[89] *NCNA*, December 14, 1967.
[90] *Wenge tongxun*, March 1968, p. 13.
[91] *WHB*, March 2, 1968.
[92] *WHB*, June 17, 1968.
[93] *WHB*, April 23, 1968.
[94] *South China Morning Post*, September 3, 1968.

could mean power. Zhang's police in 1968, though much stronger than before, still had insufficient resources to do the job alone. So the government established "teams to supervise the allocation of graduates," which tried in practice to make sure that only members of opposing, rival Red Guard cliques were actually sent out of Shanghai. As the regime's press reported with consternation, "This led to a renewal of factional fights in schools."[95]

Low-level residential revolutionary committees were finally created on the basis of "three in one combinations," involving old street committee cadres, residents, and police—often overseen by some soldiers, for good measure. Model committees were praised for organizing propaganda classes, fostering red successors, and mobilizing people against "the enemy."[96] But none of these councils was cited for prowess in successfully rusticating youths. Police officers, instead, sent ex-students out of town, when the latter could be found and induced or compelled to go. Urban registrations were in no case supposed to be given to rusticates who returned.[97] Sometimes membership in the prestigious army was granted to persons who would go in military units to the country's frontiers.[98]

Beginning at this time, Shanghai exported a higher portion of its youths to rural areas than ever before, or its cadres achieved higher rates of double counting, or both.[99] Shanghai also reported sending out a greater portion of its youth than any other city. The three factors contributing most to these achievements were the use after 1968 of more soldiers and police, the high number of Shanghai schools accepting students from outside the city, and the geographic distance back to the city from frontier areas.[100]

Only coercion could have fended off the violent resistance among residents to government policies for mass send-down in 1968. At a Wusong District school in August 1968, armed "hooligans . . . set up kangaroo courts, kidnapped and tortured students, teachers, and school employees, as well as children of poor and lower middle peasants and dependents of rev-

---

[95] *WHB*, April 20, 1968.

[96] *WHB*, May 4, 1968.

[97] *WHB*, February 25, 1968.

[98] *WHB*, September 11, 1968, describes the experience of a recent graduate named Wu Songnian, who came "from prosperous Shanghai" to a distant mountain area as a member of the PLA.

[99] The best evidence is in Bernstein's *Up to the Mountains*, p. 30, which shows that Shanghai had sent out 1,000,000 youths by mid-1974. This would be 18 percent of the urban population (or 9 percent of the whole municipality, including suburbs). Among cities, the next highest portion (for Wuhan) was only two-thirds as much of the core urban population.

[100] See also Lynn White, "The Road to Urumchi," *China Quarterly* 79 (September 1979): 481–510.

olutionary soldiers." At another, they "broke almost all the window panes and wrecked a large amount of equipment."[101] Vandalism by school gangs is common in many countries, but its sharp rise in Shanghai during 1968 suggests that the usefulness of political propaganda and campaigns to guide these youths had been exhausted.

The new regime had no new residential policies. It only started a larger, fresh campaign to send out youths, especially members of families with bad labels. In ex-capitalist Xuhui District in 1968, a "bad element" distributed leaflets claiming that lane cadres received eight hundred to a thousand yuan in cash for each youth they sent to the frontier. He told the parents of one volunteer, in this ex-Catholic area, that their son had been nailed to death on a wooden plank in Xinjiang. He persuaded other families to telegraph their children there, asking them to return to Shanghai—and many did so.[102] Everything this "bad element" said may have been untrue, but the official press confirms that he was believed by the Xuhui people with whom he spoke. By 1969, the regime's newspapers called for "more worker-propagandists" in street committees.[103] Such policies, though they were continued until 1978, had reached limits of effectiveness by the late 1960s.

STUDENTS' CHOICES IN REVOLUTIONARY TOURISM AND EDUCATION

Beijing radicals, especially Mao, inspired traveling bands of students. These people made the Cultural Revolution a national event. But the students also took trips for their own reasons, which were not all political. Their movement was based on common symbols, as much as on common substantive policies. They were engaged in one campaign with a single name, "Cultural Revolution," and that was now enough to justify it. Since groups and individuals "revolted" for different reasons against different targets, their frequent conflicts with each other are not surprising.

Members of the Shanghai Municipal Committee, at least through the end of August 1966, received travelers from the capital with public hospitality.[104] On August 30, for example, Mayor Cao and most of his fellow Municipal Committee secretaries held a meeting on Culture Square for three thousand revolutionary students from Beijing—even though this group

---

101 *WHB*, August 4, 1968.
102 *WHB*, May 26, 1968, in *SCMP* 4207 (1968): 16.
103 *WHB*, October 5, 1969.
104 One of many examples is reported in *SHWB*, August 27, 1966.

openly proposed to overthrow Cao's committee. The mayor also invited an even larger number of Shanghai students from cadre backgrounds. This rally was guarded by students of a "Red for Generations" (*daidai hong*) organization from Jiaotong University. They failed, however, to keep out other students from Fudan and Tongji Universities, "some of whom were not invited," and many of whom were disenchanted by Cao and his cadres.

This meeting was by all accounts a disorderly one. At the end of it, one of Cao's Red Guards announced "decisions" that reflected an emphasis on localism, labels, and the desires of youths to travel:[105]

To order the sons and brothers of the non-five-red types [*fei hongwulei*] from Beijing to get out

To order that the Shanghai Municipal Committee allow students from Shanghai's five-red types to go to other places and exchange experiences [*chuanlian*]

To set up a Shanghai Liaison Headquarters for the Beijing Red Guards

Soon Beijing establishmentarians began sending Red Guards to Shanghai too. One of these groups linked up with "more than two hundred children of high-ranking cadres in Shanghai" and set up a Red Guard group of their own. The members wore armbands that displayed the bureaucratic grades of their parents.[106] Labeling was alive and well, but groups in opposition to each other no longer accepted the same sets of labels as important.

Ex-students, by the fall of 1966, had a great deal of free time on their hands. Their classes could not meet, because "four million copies of textbooks in Chinese language, history, philosophy, economics, pedagogy, political education, and foreign languages were . . . now branded as big poisonous weeds."[107] The teachers no longer could use any approved curricula in these subjects. Students at boarding institutions had been told to continue living in their dorms over the summer for the first time in 1966; and they studied Mao's thought in that hot season. But by cool October, they wanted a change of pace, as did the large numbers of youths from many class backgrounds who left Shanghai. By then, they were ready for a vacation.

For student travelers, October and November were less chaotic than the summer or winter. In this pleasant autumn time (always best for trips in

---

[105] Mimeographed announcement of the Sixth Brigade of the Jiaotong University branch of the "Red for Generations" Red Guards of Jiaotong University, August 31, 1966.

[106] *Hongwei zhanbao* (Red Guard war report) (Shanghai), February 16, 1967.

[107] *JFRB*, August 11, 1966.

China), Shanghai organizations created practical facilities for revolutionary tourism. A lane committee in Sichuan South Road established a voluntary "sewing and mending station." Young Pioneers of the Railway Bureau's No. 1 Primary School staffed ten information desks at the North Railway Terminal. A minor office of Huangpu District at the center of town set up a "Red Guard haircut station," convenient for Red Guards and a credible threat to others.[108] An air force unit in the suburbs established a reception office to welcome youths "exchanging experiences on foot."[109] Over six hundred ex-students came to this office in about eighty touring teams, each of which thus averaged only seven or eight members. These bands had political aims, but they were also circles of friends traveling in a campaign that became a national lark.

No authority could effectively use class labels to check the family purity of participants at any large rally, especially in a distant city. Individual students who remained in Shanghai and wanted to make academic progress found their careers blocked; so they tended to gather together with their school chums, even when their interest in politics was not overwhelming. As few as 15 percent from some of the less prestigious schools actively took part in Red Guard organizations.[110] At other schools, especially those whose students expected elite careers, participation was much higher. Future monitors thought they knew who they were going to be, and they were as ill-served by the CR campaign as future technocrats who could get no education.

The Cultural Revolution was also a time of trial for school administrators. This had not much later effect on staffing, however, because most such cadres (Party secretaries and academics alike) were restored to their posts by the Municipal Revolutionary Committee during the 1967 efforts to reestablish schools with any personnel whatever, so as to induce youths to get off the streets. Since intellectuals and academic pursuits had so often been declared illegitimate, however, unofficial norms among youths even after the autumn and winter of 1966 favored "stopping lessons and making revolution" (*tingke naogeming*). The most interesting activities of students were not in schools, and travel was foremost among them.

By February 15, 1967, the new regime's main newspaper entitled an editorial "Resume Classes and Make Revolution" (*fuke naogeming*). But few

---

[108] *SHWB*, November 22, 1966. The sewing station was a *yiwu fengbu zhan*; the Pioneers's railway desk was a *Honglingjin tielu wenxun tai*; and for haircuts, the Red Guards provided a *Hongweibing lifa zhan*.

[109] *Buxing chuanlian*; *SHWB*, November 30, 1966.

[110] Estimate from the Shanghai No. 6 Girls' Middle School, *CNA*, no. 660, p. 7.

followed this advice. As an ex-Communist interviewee put it, "That movement never took hold. It was still, by 1969, in a dormant state. Classes were simply not renewed at full speed."[111] A teacher at the East China Normal University said his students came to campus only occasionally, just to read what was posted on the walls.[112] Crash campaigning was a vogue that could not easily be turned off like a faucet. Education is hard work for long-term goals, not a crash campaign. The CR made those goals probably unattainable and the work illegitimate. Students learned that lesson and therefore skipped school.

The press in mid-March 1967 tried to convince parents that they should send their offspring back to the academies. A father of three sons shot back a letter saying that the classes of only two sons had by then been resumed, in each case just two days a week for two hours. The rest of the time, "they have nothing to do." The school of the third son had not yet reinstated its lessons at all.[113] By mid-July, Fudan University and the East China Normal University were still just "partially" offering classes.[114] By October 1967, the city's Party organ declared that even middle-school teachers who had returned to classes were "rather timid in performing their work."[115] In November, *Wenhui bao* assured its readers that "the broad masses . . . have been fully mobilized to resume classes."[116] But this now required a campaign, another effort with an ambitious aim that might well not be attained, many months after it was first ordered to be done.

The Municipal Revolutionary Committee's supply of loyal, competent staff to control Shanghai's schools and factories was as limited as the previous Party committee's had been. In this pinch, high leaders cared more about factories than about schools. Coercion, not just persuasion, proved necessary to amalgamate groups that were divided by several years' emphasis on proletarian backgrounds for admissions. The Revolutionary Committee avoided putting resources into this project for a long time, because it lacked staff to do both that job and more urgent tasks in the economy.

Labeling among students also slowed the restoration of schools. As early as mid-February, 1967, *Wenhui bao* decried "enemies who divide students into 'five-red types' or 'black types.' Some students are so poisoned by this

---

[111] Interview, Hong Kong, with a cadre whose main experience had been in economic work.
[112] Interview, Hong Kong, with an ex–faculty member from East China Normal University.
[113] *WHB*, March 17, 1967.
[114] *NCNA*, July 11, 1967.
[115] *JFRB*, October 30, 1967.
[116] *WHB*, November 11, 1967.

theory that they deny the need to remold themselves and deny others the ability to remold themselves."[117] By April, in a girls' school,

> evil people . . . persuaded students with poor or proletarian family backgrounds that they were the only true revolutionaries and encouraged them to exclude those whose parents were members of the former exploiting classes. . . . The pupils were divided into two camps. Each would occupy its half of the classroom and refuse to speak to those from the other side.[118]

By May 1967, at middle schools in worker areas to which the Revolutionary Committee bothered to send a pacification team, cadre- and worker-origin students who had enjoyed educational benefits during previous years again donned old armbands from Red Guard groups that the Municipal Party Committee had formed before its demise. This "greatly angered" the Revolutionary Committee's work team members, but they were far outnumbered by the students and could do little to repress these proletarians' continuing faith in "blood doctrine."[119] As late as October 1967, only the most senior grades at these schools had achieved "great alliances."[120] With rare frankness, an official paper admitted,

> There are many factions and organizations among students. Unity is impossible. . . . Relations between teachers and students are still abnormal, and these groups are far apart in their feelings. . . . Students spend their time organizing "command headquarters" outside schools, or they organize underground factories, or they idle away time at home. They do not attend the revolutions made in their schools.[121]

Even at Fudan University, the seat of the most radical Red Guard groups during the January Revolution and a supplier of many cadres for "worker" propaganda teams in later months, no "great alliance" could be formed until October 1967.[122] By August 1968, Fudan's continuing disunity was evident in the need for a written "agreement" among various student factions to be

---

[117] *WHB*, February 17, 1967.

[118] *NCNA* (Beijing), April 13, 1967, concerning the Shanghai No. 6 Girls' School.

[119] *Hongse zaofanzhe* (Red rebel) (Shanghai), May 13, 1967.

[120] *NCNA*, October 29, 1967.

[121] *WHB*, March 12, 1967.

[122] *Hongse zaofanzhe tongxun* (Red rebel bulletin) (Shanghai), December 4, 1967. This tabloid contains a fascinating note on a telegram from Yao Wenyuan to students in Shanghai who were doing research to "struggle" early Communist Party leader Li Dazhao. Yao said, "We should struggle the living." But he could never miss the opportunity for a barb: "If we struggle the dead, Qu Qiubai should have been struggled long ago."

led by a propaganda team that had not even arrived on campus yet.[123] There and at other universities, Red Guards and teachers signed "letters of determination" and "letters of guarantee" to welcome propaganda teams from the city government.[124] Finally the propaganda teams were to "stay permanently in the schools . . . and they will always lead the schools."[125] The campaign method had reached the limits of its usefulness in this call for permanent bureaucracy; but finding staff for such institutions throughout the city would have been a big task.

The secondary schools were so numerous that the regime's only hope of overseeing them, even by late 1968, was to turn the task of discipline in particular schools over to nearby factories (when, indeed, control had been reestablished there). When a small molding factory was put in charge of a school, for example, it had to "encircle and suppress anarchism."[126] Not until late 1968 did the Revolutionary Committee announce a plan to send such teams from neighboring plants into all of Shanghai's secondary schools.[127]

Worker and soldier involvement in restoring order rebuilt the local power of constituencies for affirmative action that had prevailed before mid-1966. In education as in other fields, Zhang's regime ended with positions practically identical to those of the government it had overthrown—but now with less legitimacy for them, because of intervening violence, uncertainty, and free discussion. Zhang himself was clear about this: "In Shanghai, it is workers who have the greatest right to speak. Students cannot dictate."[128] His *Wenhui bao* averred in mid-1968, "The majority of the students, especially university students, have their world outlook confined to the sphere of the bourgeoisie."[129] One of his work teams proclaimed, "Bourgeois elements and small proprietors may not join rebel groups' backbone elements."[130]

The old labels were restored for nonproletarians, and a forceful anticrime campaign in mid-1968 also suggested that coercion might be used again on

---

[123] *Hongwei zhanbao*, August 15, 1958.

[124] *Juexin shu, baozheng shu; Gongren zaofan bao* (Worker rebel report), August 25, 1968.

[125] *WHB*, August 31, 1968. See also *WHB*, August 27, 1968.

[126] *Gongren zaofan bao*, August 17, 1968.

[127] *WHB*, September 3, 1968.

[128] *China News Summary*, no. 202 (January 4, 1968): 5.

[129] *WHB*, August 29, 1968.

[130] *Dongfanghong dianxun* (The East is red telegram) (Guangzhou), 2 (July 1968), article about Shanghai.

the holders of bad political labels who were not yet in jail.[131] One survey suggests that three-quarters of Chinese urban neighborhoods by the 1970s had at least one resident who was still under political supervision, at least formally; and at least 10 percent of all urban families were directly affected.[132]

But proletarian cadres were not happy either, after two years of challenge to their legitimacy and rule. Now the gloss was off the pride that workers had celebrated in the mid-1960s. They may have suspected their leaders had dealt unjustly with fellow citizens. A Shanghai worker implied this lack of self-respect and lack of respect from others, which turned out to be the main, sad upshot of earlier efforts for worker pride: "Many of the sons and brothers of workers and peasants who raised their opinions in schools were expelled without reason. Some were expelled because the result of their study was poor. The party in power said we were society's garbage."[133] Then he added with revealing pathos, "We go to the [half-time] industrial schools, because no one wants us."

In official terms, this worker's label became as good under the Revolutionary Committee as it had been before the Cultural Revolution. But in social terms, everyone now knew Shanghai's structure was more complex than any mere victory in the state structure could sustain, for a would-be elite without the size and expertise to make the city run. A visiting reporter wrote in late 1968, "In China, Shanghai is something special. There is almost a 'bourgeois' air of budding prosperity. The crowds stroll aimlessly, and there is a constant click of cameras."[134] A 1969 "Purification of Class Ranks" effort to stress old labels met strong resistance in all ten districts of Shanghai.[135] Leaderships in some local groups apparently began to think they might gain more by trying to get along with each other than by using tags and offices and violence to compete in ways that ignored their diverse talents.

---

[131] On April 27, 1968, ten thousand people attended a rally in Culture Square, Shanghai, where death sentences were passed on several "counterrevolutionary culprits" and "carried out immediately" (*WHB*, April 28, 1968).

[132] Martin King Whyte and William L. Parish, *Urban Life in Contemporary China* (Chicago: University of Chicago Press, 1984), p. 281.

[133] "Letter to Chairman Mao," by a student at the Industrial Middle School of the Shanghai Municipal Committee, *Kangda zhanbao* (Resistance university war report) (Beijing), April 1, 1967.

[134] Edouard Dillon for Agence France Presse, in *South China Morning Post*, November 24, 1968.

[135] Shanghai Radio, January 3, 1969.

CONCLUSION: FAILED SYMBOLS
AND NEW BELIEFS

As Michael Walzer has written,

> At a certain point in the transition from one to another form of traditional
> society (feudal, hierarchical, patriarchal, corporate) to one or another
> form of modern society, there appears a band of "strangers" who view
> themselves as chosen men, saints. . . . The band of the chosen confronts
> the existing world as if in war. Its members interpret the strains and ten-
> sions of social change in terms of conflict and contention. The saints sense
> enmity all about them. . . . One day, however, security becomes a habit,
> and zeal is no longer a worldly necessity.[136]

China's norm-makers during the Cultural Revolution—both intellectuals in
its great tradition and informal social leaders in low-level social groups—
were at a stage similar to that of the "saints" in England's Puritan Commonwealth, which Walzer describes. For these Chinese saints too, the worldly
and transcendental spheres were temporarily joined. Mao badges for a while
became currency, used by Red Guards in lieu of money. Then a deflation
came.

When heaven and earth were seen to be so close, everything was mean-
ingful. Tongji University students during the Cultural Revolution built a
huge statue of Chairman Mao at the front of their campus. It was 10.1 meters high from the base to the top, in honor of the PRC's founding day of
October 1. It was 7.1 meters from foot to head, in memory of the CCP's
founding (in 1921) on July 1.[137] An urge to make the cosmos uniform and
right was clearly symbolized by such efforts. It may have been a natural
reaction against the differentiation that affects any modernizing society.
However that may be, the earlier policies of categorizing, monitoring, and
threatening people had used administrative coercion that bred an intensity
of purpose in people who received or were denied modern benefits. They all
wanted to prove their total loyalty to a state that had gained so much power
over them. Because so many were in conflict with others over those benefits,
however, the result was symbolic unity and actual chaos.

Understanding the world's whole meaning, how all its virtue holds
together and is different from its evil, may be finally impossible for anyone.

---

[136] Michael Walzer, *The Revolution of the Saints: A Study in the Origins of Radical Politics*
(Cambridge: Harvard University Press, 1965), pp. 317–19.

[137] MacFarlane interviews (see note 52, above), April 19, 1966.

The Cultural Revolution nonetheless fostered rituals of piety, to put people in tune with the general good. Some rites were collective. A platoon of the Shanghai Garrison put together a short liturgy of songs to the words of Chairman Mao, to be sung at all "five-before" (*wu qian*) times: before lessons, meals, roll calls, drills, and assemblies.[138] Further prayer was individual. At 5:30 A.M. on a 1968 spring morning, a Shanghai hotel porter was unaware of being observed as he approached the Maoist "shrine" in his unit. He bowed and read some of the *Quotations* quietly for fifteen minutes, thinking he was alone.[139]

The religion of the Cultural Revolution may be described formally.[140] Like most compelling beliefs, it contained tensions to allow a creative application of its precepts to real-life situations.[141] Cultural Revolution symbols were full of dichotomies, like Mazdism, which described a strict separation of light from dark, East from West, appearance from reality, purity from dirt. Imaginations were stirred then by the metaphysics of splitting and rebellion. These symbols were seen as relevant at high levels of abstraction. "Dividing one into two" (*yi fen wei er*) was moral, while syntheses of ambiguous things were immoral. Vividness was good, to the point that gaudiness (as seen by Chinese in less enthusiastic times) was not gaudy. Redness or bright color, the sun or fire, and simple completeness were always approved. Blackness or whiteness, coolness, and complex discovery were seen as subterfuges for bad. All humanity was supposed to be one and uniform, and animals (especially insects, turtles, and snakes) provided evil names. Motion, travel, and parading were good, while fixity was disapproved in general. These were not several contrasts; they were closely interwoven.

They suggested an ideal personality. If these beliefs subsisted in clouds, rather than in people's heads, this would all have been irrelevant to the frustrations over policies that caused Cultural Revolution. Those anxieties were in people's heads too, and the choice of symbols helped structure the way they saw their plights as labeled people, networked clients, and campaign targets. The general type of images that appealed to them, as a framework to make sense of their lives, affected their perceptions of what had hap-

---

[138] *SHWB*, October 31, 1966.

[139] MacFarlane (note 52, above) indicates in this report that he was not seen by the man at prayer.

[140] Lowell Dittmer, "Thought Reform and the Cultural Revolution: An Analysis of the Symbolism of Chinese Polemics," *American Political Science Review* 71, no. 1 (1977): 67–85.

[141] In Chinese studies, the classic statement of the link between options and credibility—and of the end of choices as a sign of decay—is Joseph R. Levenson's *Confucian China and its Modern Fate* (Berkeley and Los Angeles: University of California Press, 1958).

pened.[142] The concrete causes and normative organizers of this experience were inseparable.[143]

As modern philosophers tell us, symbols reflect real things, even while they allow us to try out alternative reflections.[144] Even at the height of the Cultural Revolution, there were important options that people had, to help them deal with different situations. One example is the contradiction between imagining Mao or his thought as an unchanging guide for Chinese society, while also imagining China in constant change. As a Shanghai Red Guard put it in 1968, "We are all in the most agitated state of mind, and we most respectfully wish Chairman Mao a very peaceful, long, long life."[145] Contentment is not what tensions created by policies over the previous seventeen years had bequeathed, but it was a long-term personal goal of many who had suffered manipulation in that whole time.

As zeal very slowly became less necessary in China during the 1970s, norms changed. Shanghai Radio complained as early as 1968 that some Red Guards used force to demand money in exchange for their revolutionary emblems.[146] Ambition turned to cynicism, for many in the Cultural Revolution. Dynamic ex-CCP activists had to "break down and weep" when the Party in which they believed was shown to be so full of corrupt cadres.[147] "Rebels" fared no better; a group of them by 1968 said that workers' propaganda teams had come to repress the student movement, and that "the epoch of the Red Guards is over."[148]

A "new tide of thought" (*xin sichao*), among a very few Shanghai intellectuals, compared the Cultural Revolution with "a change of dynasty." These dissidents demanded popular representation and "genuine socializa-

---

[142] Anthony Wallace calls this kind of framework a "mazeway" in "Revitalization Movements," *American Anthropologist* 58 (April 1956): 264–81. Talcott Parsons, less famous for catchy phrases, calls it the "normative order" in *The Social System* (Glencoe, N.Y.: Free Press, 1951), p. 11, and in *The Structure of Social Action* (New York: Free Press, 1937), p. 91.

[143] The disjunction between symbolic analysis and systematic analysis has been exaggerated by Clifford Geertz and his opponents alike. Only an overemphasis on scientific method rather than scientific knowledge can sustain a debate in which symbols are treated as separate from functions. There has been some confusion between the point that neither symbols nor functions in a context need be entirely consistent, and the point that they are not quite the same. They can be inconsistent, and they can relate to each other. See Geertz, *The Interpretation of Cultures* (New York: Basic Books, 1973), but see also one of his system theory books, *Agricultural Involution* (Berkeley and Los Angeles: University of California Press, 1971).

[144] See Langer, *Philosophy in a New Key*.

[145] *WHB*, March 29, 1968.

[146] Shanghai Radio, February 24, 1968, said Mao badges were on the "black market" (though maybe black was turning gray).

[147] *Far Eastern Economic Review*, June 1, 1967, p. 491.

[148] *WHB*, September 5, 1968, quotes and criticizes this notion.

tion" (*zhenzheng gongyou*). They said wealth should be distributed more fairly. This movement denounced "power holders and people who ignore the masses."[149]

The official press called this "ultrademocracy."[150] For most of the next decade, the old organizational policies were restored. But by the late 1970s, interests and groups in China had changed. Ideas from the Cultural Revolution did not effectively guide China's development after that, and their simplicity was a framework that China's newly complex elite came to reject. This rejection deeply shaped local leaders' ideas during the era that followed, in the 1980s.

[149] *WHB*, June 4, 1967.
[150] Ibid.

CHAPTER 12

Conclusion: Causes and Lessons of the Tragedy

Many people are aware that we in China have gone through a ten-year holocaust. . . . We have a right as well as a responsibility to write down what happened to us. Such a record is not merely for our own sake, but for the benefit of others as well as future generations.
—BA JIN

For each participant, the Cultural Revolution meant something different. For many, it was an attempt to realize political ideals: socialism, equality, a responsive modern state, or rule by the people. For Party leaders, it was largely a struggle for personal power. For most youths, it was a period of traveling and politicking. Many managed to sit on the sidelines, taking cover until the storm cleared. The perceived meaning of this event could change at different times like a kaleidoscope, even for a single person.[1] Yet an overarching significance of the Cultural Revolution for most people, no matter what else it meant, lay in seemingly arbitrary violence. Many Chinese now feel that such destructive chaos should never be allowed to occur again.

The policies that led to social danger in this movement can be specified, no matter what broad cultural or instinctual traits they may have channeled. Once these kinds of policies are clear, then social science can turn to something more practical—good advocacy—because better policies can be contrived to reduce the likelihood of such dangers, both in the future and in any place. There are at least partial similarities between events like the Cultural Revolution, the Holocaust, and recent mass bigotries in countries as different as Uganda, Cambodia, and Iran. None of these disasters arose instantly. To the partial extent they can be compared, we might look for common patterns in their causes in order to identify warning signs, and try to act against them wherever they may appear. The only obvious alternative is to treat them as inevitable.

That large project obviously goes beyond the scope of the present book,

---

[1] This paragraph derives from a conversation with Mr. Feng Shengping, who suffered during the Cultural Revolution. For this source and many discussions with Mr. Li Cheng, it is hard to know where to put the footnotes.

but China in the late 1960s suffices as a place to begin the search. The chapters above have emphasized three policies as main causes of the Cultural Revolution: measures for labeling people, putting people under monitors, and increasing compliance in fearsome campaigns. Political constituencies by the mid-1960s were created officially, by status labels. The mass extent of conflict among such groups was exacerbated by official sponsorship of family-like dependence under patrons. Campaigns gave legitimacy to violence.[2] What unifies labels, monitors, and campaigns is that they are all implementing means of administration.

The Cultural Revolution was thus a policy mistake. Such an understanding does not trivialize the tragedy but, on the contrary, provides a way to draw better policies from this painful experience.[3] The Cultural Revolution

---

[2] Nothing here should be interpreted as a claim that the factors cited in this book have been completely neglected by earlier studies. The present effort relies on previous works, comparing Shanghai data with some of their points under the rubric of social reactions to administrative techniques. On the importance of labeled groups, for example, the best detailed study of conflict in a local Chinese organization at this time is Marc J. Blecher and Gordon White's *Micropolitics in Contemporary China: A Technical Unit during and after the Cultural Revolution* (White Plains, N.Y.: Sharpe, 1979). A larger unit, albeit rural, is the object of another study that also provides evidence for this view: Anita Chan, Richard Madsen, and Jonathan Unger's *Chen Village: The Recent History of a Peasant Community in Mao's China* (Berkeley and Los Angeles: University of California Press, 1984). The same village is also the scene of an analysis that cleverly combines culturalist and "rational-actor" methods (by using symbols that represent leadership styles among which peasants chose) in Richard Madsen, *Morality and Power in a Chinese Village* (Berkeley and Los Angeles: University of California Press, 1984). Two other books that provide data emphasizing labeled groups are Hong Yung Lee's *The Politics of the Chinese Cultural Revolution: A Case Study* [in Kwangtung] (Berkeley and Los Angeles: University of California Press, 1978), and Stanley Rosen's *Red Guard Factionalism and the Cultural Revolution in Guangzhou (Canton)* (Boulder, Colo.: Westview, 1982). None of these emphasizes the patronage factor, however, as much as a book by Andrew G. Walder, *Communist Neo-Traditionalism: Work and Authority in Chinese Industry* (Berkeley and Los Angeles: University of California Press, 1986), which does not, however, assign importance to the group factor, and which may be followed by a new volume by Walder about the Cultural Revolution. These studies look beyond Beijing to explain events. The present book is partly designed to put their discussions of groups' and individuals' motives in the perspective of more usual researches emphasizing top politics and campaigns. This book pays more attention to pre-1966 history, and it tries to combine the different emphases of other studies into a more unified approach based on the sometimes understated importance, in all of them, of policy.

[3] It could be argued that alternative approaches trivialize the tragedy more than this policy approach does. For example, too much emphasis on Mao randomizes the causes of the CR, because one or a few crazy leaders might appear in any society anytime. An overweening emphasis on cultural factors, which similarly seem endemic and unavoidable by definition, would also randomize the event by putting its causes beyond control. Assuming they are not so, the policy approach offers criteria for judging other and future dangers (e.g., the current danger for labeled Chinese in Indonesia, a case mentioned later in this chapter). "Policy mistakes" do not imply a total lack of consciousness about the faults of the chosen course among those who select it. In fact, they are most interesting when contrary advice is heard and rejected, as histo-

in its main meaning (its widespread violence) and as a particular historical event (rather than an outcome of any inflexible Chinese culture or Communist ideology) was mainly an unintended consequence of policies for labels, monitors, and campaigns. Most Chinese habits of discourse about politics, like most Western ones, treat major political events in terms of the intentions and ideologies of high leaders.

Mass protest movements such as the CR, however, are acts of collective defiance. The groups that engage in them are "crowds," whose formation is often a matter of historical circumstance, not a result of anybody's conscious plans.[4] Unarticulated goals, expressed through unorganized and conflicting groups, are often as important in such movements as are conscious intentions.[5] These protests are not just deviance from authority; they are expressions of different authorities.

The Cultural Revolution was aimed at political adversaries that included parts of the state apparatus—and called for support from other state agencies. Its politics were conflicts whose results depended largely on the "scope" and resources of the local actors involved.[6] The state was not unified. Both state and society were, in the end, deeply affected by the diverse wills of local actors. This generalized protest became a means by which China's society and state were both reproduced for the future. One purpose of the present book is to suggest that we need a new kind of political science—one that takes seriously not just reactions to state coercion by "weak" leaders in many small collectivites, but also their own sovereign initiatives—to explain major political events.[7]

---

ries like that of Pan Hannian suggest above in chapter 2. Such mistakes imply a numbness that may be self-induced, beneficial to immediate ambitions, blinkered, semiconscious, complex, usually more stupid than malicious. See Barbara Tuchman's *The March of Folly* (New York: Ballantine, 1984), which discusses the policies of Troy on the horse, of King Rehoboam on dishonoring the Israelite chiefs, of Renaissance popes on the proto-Protestants, of Montezuma on letting Cortés's militia into his palace, of Charles XII and Napoleon on invading Russia, of George III on America, of the United States on Vietnam, and other rich examples of governments taking people unseriously. Policy is a more important category, as compared with power or culture, than many scholars admit.

[4] See George Rudé, *The Crowd in History* (New York: Wiley, 1964).

[5] See Frances Fox Piven and Richard A. Cloward, *Poor People's Movements* (New York: Vintage Books, 1979).

[6] E. E. Schattschneider, *The Semi-Sovereign People* (Hinsdale, Ill.: Dryden Press, 1960), shows the importance of "scope" in determining outcomes. For a refined view that makes clear why the state (even if unified) cannot always control the scope of conflict, see Alain Touraine, *The Voice and the Eye* (Cambridge: Cambridge University Press, 1981). A student at Princeton, Julie Faber, brought these points to the author's attention.

[7] The job is furthered in James C. Scott, *Weapons of the Weak: Everyday Forms of Peasant Resistance* (New Haven: Yale University Press, 1985). For an old definition of "influence" that

HOW MUCH WAS MAO TO BLAME?

High politics played some role, though. The narrative above has implied a fourth factor, beyond the three that affected many work units and millions of individuals. One man *can* influence the course of history—if larger factors are in place—even though Thomas Carlyle said so. This fourth, more immediate, instigator of the CR is also a kind of policy, and it is epitomized best by Mao's August 1966 constraints on the police system. Public security forces might, in their normal fashion, have prevented political expression by frustrated groups and individuals at that time. They might have kept political violence focused on its usual pre-1966 targets. Because of Mao's role in the bureaucracy, especially in August 1966, the state temporarily restrained its usual police repression. And popular organizations sprang up immediately to vent grievances that the three policies of pressure had spawned for many years.

This top-leadership factor, necessary but insufficient as a cause of the whole event, had a big precipitating role in its timing.[8] Mao's instructions for a "Cultural Revolution" are sometimes adduced as enough to motivate the chaos. This is true only if the movement is seen mainly as a power struggle among small groups in Beijing. Even then, Mao's intentions were often as flexible or unclear as his resources. A writer such as Stuart Schram, who knows best the difficulties of reading Mao's mind, can still say of the Cultural Revolution that "Mao's central and crucial role in bringing it about is not subject to discussion, but there were those who argued that he was merely the instrument, or the catalyst, of objective forces rooted in Chinese history, and/or in the logic of a western-inspired revolutionary process."[9] Part of the job of this book, which aims to complement previously published ideas about the Chairman's importance by citing broader origins for the Cultural Revolution, is to show more precisely the role that Mao did play.

---

avoids the word "power" but shows it to be the creation of effects that would otherwise not occur, such as local leaders often bring, see Robert A. Dahl, *Modern Political Analysis* (Englewood Cliffs, N.J.: Prentice-Hall, 1963). Just as real sovereignty or independence exists in non-"sovereign" sizes of collectivity smaller than the nation-state, so also it exists in larger collectivities. This is one of the emphases in the work of Richard A. Falk, for example in *Legal Order in a Violent World* (Princeton: Princeton University Press, 1968).

[8] This link justifies the best book on the high politics of this movement, Roderick Mac-Farquhar's *The Origins of the Cultural Revolution*, 2 vols. (New York: Columbia University Press, 1972, 1983); the third volume covering the 1960s is forthcoming. Volume 1, page 3, says plainly that Mao "made" the Cultural Revolution. But see note 10 below.

[9] Stuart R. Schram, "The Limits of Cataclysmic Change: Reflections on the Place of the 'Great Proletarian Cultural Revolution' in the Political Development of the People's Republic of China," *China Quarterly* 108 (December 1986): 613.

He was crucial as a spark in August 1966, and he was one of thousands of Party leaders (including his rivals, who often excelled him in this) who advocated policies for labeling, monitoring, and campaigning from the start of the PRC.

Official status groups, tight patronage, and policies of fear were the main causes of the Cultural Revolution as trauma. What Beijing politics added was an occasion for social forces to organize. Mao's restrictions on police of August 8, 1966, affected politics even months after they were reversed. But that does not mean Mao's initiatives, or even the collective actions of all the top leaders over any short period, are enough to explain all of the sequel.

Differences between top leaders in Beijing do not constantly sway the whole country. Even the agreements between them can prove ineffective in the short term or countereffective to their own plans over long times. Their policies since 1949 created an accumulation of dynamite whose explosion they could not fully control. Mao's role was to pull the pin on a grenade that he did not make alone, and whose effects no one could surely predict. Liu Shaoqi and Mao Zedong *together* supported most of the means, most of the time, which brought this Cultural Revolution.[10] Similar administrative habits had helped the whole Party win the Civil War. They underlay many victories in domestic politics thereafter. Long-term pressure, exerted by such policies on millions of local leaders, was more important for the Cultural Revolution's violence than were the immediate effects of particular small movements or the personal ambitions of national leaders.

Mao was, of course, important as a vague symbol of the need for unity. As Karl Marx wrote, describing Louis Bonaparte's dictatorship over France's largest class (the peasants) in 1852, "Their representative must at the same time appear as their master, as an authority over them, as an unlimited governmental power that protects them against the other classes and sends them the rain and the sunshine from above."[11] This was an appearance, not a full reality. It is important in explaining only part of what happened.

No kind of cause is more basic or less so, but different causes relate to different parts of the effect. To explain mass violence, we have to get beyond Mao, power struggle among a few men, egalitarian ideals, and any constant Chinese or Communist political culture. Over a long time, national leaders

---

[10] MacFarquhar in *Origins* is definitely not among the many authors who imply that Mao and Liu were in fairly constant disagreement. His work shows great care and voracious research on politics at the top in China.

[11] Karl Marx, "The Eighteenth Brumaire of Louis Bonaparte," in *The Marx-Engels Reader*, ed. Robert C. Tucker, 2d ed. (New York: Norton, 1978), p. 608.

did make policy, and thus helped to make the effects of policies on individuals. But that does not mean they understood what they were doing, or that no power was exercised on them from "below." The "important people" were not the only important people, in the making of this event.

HOW MUCH WAS SOCIALISM TO BLAME?

This book places guilt for the CR on three ancillary, implementing policies of China's Communists after 1949. These measures were used because they reduced the Party's need for manpower to achieve quick results toward socialist goals. The Party's dogmas, however, did not absolutely disallow a more gentle recruitment of talent from larger groups in society. CCP leaders together chose to interpret their ideology otherwise. Peculiarly impatient administrative policies are to blame for the CR, but this does not prohibit Communists like Deng Xiaoping from changing their minds now about China's policies—while remaining Communists. Their ideology did not preclude such a choice then; and now, Chinese public revulsion at past excesses militates for it. Memories of CR injustice have helped China's Communists to reinterpret their ideas, to advocate a broadening reform of local leaderships, and generally to reject the policies of pressure they used before. Socialism has been too malleable to blame for the Cultural Revolution.

The three implementing policies to which the CCP became addicted after 1949 could be (and have been) also followed by non-Communists in other countries. Such habits might be called "Leninist"; but some forms of socialism reject them, and non-Marxist leaders have sometimes adopted them. Communist ideals concern liberation and freedom, not the kind of oppression that labels, bosses, and campaigns bring. Marx did, to be sure, join many other nineteenth-century philosophers in the romantic hope that political will and social violence would have good ends. His class analysis seems to suggest labeling, in particular; but he was an analyst, not the leader of a coercive state that could have used these categories far more lightly and pragmatically (and in China, is now doing so). Marx's writings underestimate the extent of regress, by his own standards, that precedes the progress he thought inevitable.[12] But at least conscious progressives could be free, not bound by their class cultures or intimidated by violence. Lenin, not Marx,

---

[12] A striking example is Marx's optimistic assessment of the long-term effects of the proto-fascist Louis Bonaparte, who was seen as perfecting an executive power that the proletariat could later overthrow ("The Eighteenth Brumaire," pp. 594–617).

was the main Communist organizer of ideas about the use of force.[13] Yet even Lenin's notions were inconsistent enough to have real practicality in Russia; his "ism" can be accused of begetting the policies of pressure only on the understanding that it was not perfectly coherent.

Recent Chinese reformers within the CCP have blamed Lenin by name. As Liao Gailong of the Party Secretariat's Policy Research Office said in 1980, "Lenin's political theory neglected the democratic aspect of proletarian dictatorship but attached too much importance to the aspect of violent suppression."[14] In *What Is to Be Done?* (1902), Lenin called for a "small, compact core of the most reliable, experienced, and hardened workers, with responsible representatives in the principal districts, and connected by all the rules of strict secrecy with the organization of revolutionaries."[15] Lenin's most distinctive contributions to socialism emphasized mere tactics: how to use the "organizational weapon" of the Party to bring Communism more quickly than history would do, if left alone. Labels, monitors, and temporary campaigns grew out of this interest, but Lenin's own later experiences gave him opposite concerns too.

This is most obvious in Lenin by the 1920s, just before his death. When he became aghast at Stalin and the effects of Russian administrative habits, he urged as an afterthought to revolution

> that learning shall really become part of our very being. . . . "Measure your cloth seven times before you cut." . . . Better fewer, but better. . . . Better get good human material in two or even three years than work in haste [*sic*] without hope of getting any at all. . . . there are such heaps of old lumber. . . . we have bureaucrats in our Party offices as well as in our Soviet offices.[16]

He stormed that "one has to swear at Russians twenty times and check up on them thirty times in order to get the simplest thing done in the right way. . . . bureaucratism cannot be 'sent packing' from a peasant country, cannot be 'swept from the face of the earth.' One can only reduce it by slow, stubborn effort." But it was a tad late to think of all that.

Soviet factory and trade union practices, imported to China especially in the First Five-Year Plan after 1952, set up allocative systems cementing ties

---

[13] See A. J. Polan, *Lenin and the End of Politics* (Berkeley and Los Angeles: University of California Press, 1984), and Sheldon S. Wolin, *Politics and Vision* (Boston: Little, Brown, 1960), esp. chap. 10.

[14] Liao Gailong, quoted in *Issues and Studies* 17, no. 11 (1981): 73.

[15] Robert C. Tucker, ed., *The Lenin Anthology* (New York: Norton, 1975), p. 72.

[16] Ibid., pp. 715–16, 736, 740.

within work units.[17] Bureaucratic benefit and pay systems were also taken largely from Soviet models, and sometimes mechanically from Soviet institutions. The state sponsored clientelism as legitimate. Its policies did not just call forth old bossism, but added to it and exacerbated it in new ways.

This does not mean socialism of any kind could explain the Cultural Revolution. Leninism, even in a narrow sense that neglects some patient phases of Lenin's actual history, is just one possible set of Communist policies. There are other sets too, and they could easily underlie less categorizing, less monitoring, and more quietude. It is doubtful that "Communist culture" can be said to exist (in the same sense that "Chinese culture" exists, for example). Socialist interests arise among people, usually in middle classes, who have other options too. Communism has never supplied so total a range of choices for individuals identifying with it as Chineseness has.[18] Communism is an ideology, coexisting for its believers with alternatives, not a complete environment or culture.

Socialism might best be defined by the history in which it arose—as a product of the development of efficient markets that called for regulation. When human time, wealth, and environs become market commodities, people feel threatened and want government regulation.[19] Not all labor services are legitimately on the market, in any country. Efficient resource markets may threaten the environment in which people have to live, even though its cleanliness is difficult to price. Financial markets may threaten the wealth people thought they had rightly earned. Protection and markets are both state projects, in Polanyi's analysis. "Socialism" in this sense may just be one side of the modern coin of progressing efficiency. (The other side is called "capitalism," except in Deng's China or Gorbachev's Russia. But most now agree that the whole coin, with both sides, is most important.) Such a definition of socialism certainly need not include policies of organization for labels, patrons, and campaigns.

---

[17] The most important work in this area is Walder's *Communist Neo-Traditionalism*.

[18] This relies on Geertz's notion of "culture" as an inconsistent, not systematic, array. The present book, all about a problem of causation, does not contravene that anthropologist's bias against talking about causes, because it explicitly discusses them in terms of policies that are much less general than all of culture.

[19] Karl Polanyi uses anthropological and historical data to show that commoditization of land, labor, and money was not natural—and needed to be restrained by government controls of the market, so that efficiency could be maximized with full accounting of its costs. His analysis of British economic history suggests that, in many countries, periods of quick market growth have alternated with periods for protecting people against some effects of such growth (as the enclosures led to more commoditization, the Speedhamland Laws led to less, and the Corn Laws meant more again; or in the United States, the 1865–1929 period was followed by the FDR era; or in China, Mao's time was succeeded by Deng's). See Polanyi, *The Great Transformation: The Social and Economic Origins of Our Time* (New York: Rinehart, 1944).

Socialism in this sense also need not be joined to a theory of history that claims to be a science. Deterministic notions of the future may be more responsible for holocausts than are markets or socialism. Fixed ideas about what moves history can give leaders a cocksureness, an arrogance toward groups and mores their science proves moribund. These can encourage careless use of administrative techniques such as official tags, forced dependence, or violence. Many authors have suggested a link between historical determinism and overweening government.[20] Ideologies that predict history tend to legitimate "organizational weapons" rather than functional systems.[21]

The main findings here berate the organizational measures that some Communists—and Nazis, and others—have used to press their wills on large populations. Tags, imposed dependence, and organized threats have been frequent administrative techniques in many countries. Nonsocialists use them, and Communism does not require them. In China, such organizational tricks have been mainly used by revolutionary leftists (rather than by visionaries on the right); but that may be coincidental. Although Marxists often adopt quick-fix administrative policies with hidden costs, there is nothing inherent in generic socialism to make them do this. Only when politicians of any bent think they know what the future holds—and decide to speed it by using specifiable policies—are tragedies like the Cultural Revolution likely to arise.

Such rule, severe as it is within its scope, has eventual limits. Totalitarianism describes a situation in which "all social ties have been entirely replaced by State-imposed organizations."[22] This can pertain only partly in any country—especially a large one. The state in China has often aimed at the totalitarian form.[23] But it has often fallen short of it, largely because the regime lacked sufficient loyal staff or other resources to use in attracting support. When the political costs of the effort exceed the political benefits,

[20] For example, see Karl R. Popper, *The Open Society and Its Enemies* (Princeton: Princeton University Press, 1950).

[21] Franz Schurmann, citing Philip Selznick and basing his ideas on Karl Mannheim, distinguishes "pure ideology" (Mannheim's "ideology") that stabilizes an organization from "practical ideology" ("utopia") that encourages a unit to expand beyond its system boundaries (Schurmann, *Ideology and Organization in Communist China* [Berkeley and Los Angeles: University of California Press, 1966]).

[22] Leszek Kolakowski, a Platonist philosopher, writes on "Marxist Roots of Stalinism" in *Stalinism*, ed. Robert C. Tucker (New York: Norton, 1977), p. 285. This is quoted in the clearest essay by Pierre Ryckmans [Simon Leys], "Human Rights in China," *Quadrant*, November 1978, pp. 70–76.

[23] The classic studies are Étienne Balazs, *Chinese Civilization and Bureaucracy*, ed. A. F. Wright, trans. H. M. Wright (New Haven: Yale University Press, 1964), and Karl A. Wittfogel, *Oriental Despotism* (New Haven: Yale University Press, 1957)—both suggestive, learned, but not much help on what can be done.

policy changes.[24] A good example has occurred since 1978; label classifications, designations of monitor-satraps, and campaigning have all been reduced.

Much writing about China overstates the effectiveness of control, however, because PRC newspaper articles suggest as much and academics need footnotes. By the same token, many descriptions underemphasize the social responses, ecological constraints, and administrative aspects to policy. This criticism of the scholarly literature is even more applicable today than in Mao's time, for which many data show the crucial importance of control institutions to the daily lives of millions. Once the legitimacy of organized intervention in day-to-day civil life became entirely normal, by August 1966, then labels, forced clientelism, and campaign violence could be used by anybody. The bee was out of the bonnet. Fear among some people, in the hope of historical progress for many, was a tactic that in the long run did not work.

Mao and his high rivals were less effective as long-term egalitarian socialists than as short-term political strategists. These leaders were all passionately fascinated with techniques to inspire unified action in their big country, so long divided, and they found some applicable policies. This book is about the three most important, which all involve distinguishing "the enemy and ourselves." Seeing conspiracy, having an enemy, defining the clean people and the unsalvageably dirty ones, "dividing one into two," all became state policy. But that affected people not because it was psychology or ideology, but because it was policy. It meant labeling people with good and bad names, monitoring them so that the good ones might be nurtured and the bad restricted, and running campaigns to inspire some and scare others. The top PRC leaders (irrespective of their rivalries) were more political technicians than social philosophers. They had ideals, but their main problem was implementation.

HOW MUCH WAS TRADITION TO BLAME?

To what extent did Chinese culture contribute to the Cultural Revolution? The 1981 Party *Resolution* on CCP history largely explained this event on the basis of "feudal remnants" in Chinese authority relations. Analyses like those by Wang Xizhe or the Party *Resolution* have obvious merits; but their limits also need to be specified, now, in light of the evidence from

---

[24] This generalizes the main logic used in a more specific sphere by Merle Goldman, *Literary Dissent in Communist China* (Cambridge: Harvard University Press, 1967).

Shanghai presented above.[25] Even if Chinese tradition deserves some blame for the Cultural Revolution, its role is hard to assess. Some particular traditions are easy to suspect. If labels damaged people (and they did), Confucian philosophers were ardently interested in specifying moral "names" for everything. If China's traditionally strong families and lineages have fostered patron-client relations (and they have), "feudalism" contributed to the disaster, as the *Resolution* says. If norms of organizational loyalty were at fault (and arguably they were), the Confucian temple was a model of loyal organization; the living sons sat before ancestral tablets, also arranged by generation, as if a cult of loyalty alone could lead to strength. Or if Confucianism seemed too quietistic to justify campaigns, especially of youths against elders, then there was always the Legalist tradition to cite.

The part of "tradition" in causing the CR is still hard to specify for two reasons: First, how could Chinese culture as a whole have brought about this specific episode, as distinct from other, different, Chinese events before and after it? "Tradition" refers to a cluster of things that by definition change very slowly. If the Cultural Revolution were crucially a result of Chinese habits, then China would have cultural revolutions all the time. Yet this does not occur. A tradition-based explanation of the event does not explain why the mid-1960s were unique.

Second, is Chinese culture consistent, so that deductions can be made from it? It is rich, diverse, comprised of flexible elements. It is not unified or monotone. Labeling, for example, has hoary roots in China. Confucius was very concerned with "names" of categories of people, but he did not succeed in structuring all relations between Chinese—even if he tried to do so. Confucianism specifically concerns links between people who have family ties (as fathers and sons, elder brothers and younger brothers, or husbands and wives), relations among people who are friends, and the need for a subject to be loyal to his civil ruler. If China is a "heap of sand," as Sun Yat-sen said, this should help structure it. But most of the modern patron-client links do *not* fall into kin categories that Confucianists see as natural. Loyalty-oath societies in imperial and republican China were also not of this type, even if they often called on analogues to it. Chinese norms are flexible and useful enough to offer different options. Taoism emphasized the naturalness of individuals, rather than the extension of families by ethical education. Legalism emphasized the need for force in social solidarity. All of these traditions were available parts of Chinese political culture—despite their historical opposition.

---

[25] On Wang Xizhe and the *Resolution on CPC History (1949–81)*, see the first chapter of this book.

Monitoring, similarly, is no new Chinese topic. A master (*shifu*) might replace a natural father to lead a millenarian sect, for example; but other traditions also give respect to natural parents. The individual has been heard of, in China. Many Chinese mores are collectivist, but others are nearly liberal.[26] It is difficult to draw sure deductions from so rich a premise as Chinese culture.

The traditional bases for campaigning are the opposite of those for labeling and monitoring—which may, when enforced zealously, reduce rather than increase fears of disorder (*luan*). The campaigns may well draw on traditional Chinese conceptions of evil as free-floating and exorcisable. But this habit seems to conflict with other mores about the naturalness of good, as well as with old ideas about fate being separate from human intentions. An analyst may readily pick a tradition, any tradition. General Chinese penchants for careful labeling, group networks, or timely moralizing may be old habits; but they do not preclude their alternatives. If "tradition" caused the cr, then which of China's many conflicting traditions caused it? Why did the people who made the movement not choose the others instead?

The kind of bossism that is blamed in this book, as one of the chief causes of the Cultural Revolution, builds on various Chinese traditions, especially extended family-Confucian and Legalist ones. But its more specific origins can be found in the Party's shortage of monitors. Patronage has both new and old aspects in China. Parallel things could be said about labels and campaigns.[27] Specific policies, which were rather immediate in their causes and results after 1949, institutionalized some of the many options that Chinese culture makes available.

THE INTERACTION OF LABELS, MONITORS, AND CAMPAIGNS

The Cultural Revolution arose not just because labeled groups were consciously frustrated or advantaged by 1966, or just because individuals were dependent or powerful in patron-client networks, or just because campaigns

[26] Vitaly A. Rubin, *Individual and State in Ancient China: Essays on Four Chinese Philosophers* [Confucius, Mo Zi, Shang Yang, and Zhuang Zi], trans. Steven I. Levine (New York: Columbia University Press, 1976). See also, W. Theodore de Bary, *The Liberal Tradition in China* (New York: Columbia University Press, 1983).

[27] The present author has argued elsewhere that campaigns are understandable, at least to peasants, in terms of the quick communitarian work that the crop cycles for rice and wheat require, to maintain food supplies for so large a population. See White, "Agricultural and Industrial Values in China," in *Value Change in Chinese Society*, ed. Richard Wilson, Sidney Greenblatt, and Amy Wilson (New York: Praeger, 1979), pp. 141–54.

legitimated violence. These three factors interacted to produce the melee. Political labeling made status groups clear; dependence made underlings follow or attack their unit bosses, often on the basis of label categories; and campaigns made such action seem ineffective unless violent. The synergy of these policies is as important as their separate effects.

A group-interest approach, based on labels, does not fully explain why the "rebel" groups should have become so conscious and active, as soon as they were allowed to organize in August 1966. A rational-actor approach, based here on the individual interests of clients and monitors, cannot fully explain why people coalesced as they did, to oppose enemies as a mass. An approach that emphasizes only the propriety campaigns gave to violence cannot explain how such coercion was directed, or who suffered from it. These separate analyses imply basically different logics of action, which could be given names like collective, rational, or habitual (if such abstractions help). More important, they all refer to types of administrative policy.

Methodological differences between these approaches are worth describing, if only for the purpose of showing how analytic diversions can hide concrete synergies. Labels create politically different groups; clientelism creates politically linked ones. Authors who emphasize labels tend to think about specific, varied group interests.[28] Those who stress patronage think about the networks that serve personal interests of supply and protection. But these approaches are not mutually exclusive. They show most when used together, because both individual and collective interests are relevant to politics. Interest approaches and clientelist approaches are complementary and reinforcing, because they explain different things. They can ascribe nonexclusive predicates to the same subject.

They both depict patterns of individual action, but the labeled-group approach does so on the basis of collective understandings that unify people. The patron-client approach does so on the basis of personal relations, especially between leaders and followers.[29] Whether a local leader "rebelled," or

---

[28] But see Rosen, *Red Guard Factionalism*, which is superior to any other book in this field for its attention to the links between group formation *timing* and group interests.

[29] This distinction is not quite the same as Durkheim's between social integration based on functional similarities between people ("mechanical solidarity," to use his term) or on functional differences ("organic solidarity"). Durkheim tried to derive kinds of behavior from types of social bonds. He points to the importance of analyzing results in terms of personal similarities or dissimilarities; but this can be done without his emphasis on solidarity, which is an "intervening variable" between collections of individuals and behavior. The first focus here is directly on patterns of action. To see an inconsistency in talking about labels and patronage at the same time is to take solidarity as a concrete rather than an analytic category. Actually, it is just a notion. See Émile Durkheim, *The Division of Labor in Society* (New York: Macmillan,

instead defended the status quo, depended on personal background, on clientelist relations with other local actors, and on roles in the revolutionary political structure—not necessarily just one of these.[30]

The problem with individual-action models alone is like that with group-consciousness models alone. In reducing explanations of behavior to the personal or the collective level only, they both ignore institutional habits that can join them. Rational-action models, by stressing the motives of individuals over groups and the externality of facts to values, do not explain organizations forming decisive policies based in ideologies; they tend to treat ironic results of such decisions only as residuals, not as data deserving real explanation. Group-consciousness theories, on the other hand, often neglect individual motives that can stymie public intentions; these ironies are seen as ephemeral snags to group will, rather than serious problems in the decision process. Both these approaches are useful—if they are taken together, and if the blindness in each is remedied by attention to the other and to policies.

The third kind of policy emphasized in this book is campaigning, and it differs from monitoring and labeling just as the sociologist Max Weber's concept of "charisma" differs respectively from "tradition" and "legal rationality." These three types exhaust the kinds of authority that leaders use (or conversely, the kinds of motives that induce people to follow). In addition to "campaigns," "monitors," and "labels," it is easy to think of fourth words that suggest policies used in pre-1966 China; for instance, "slogans" or "propaganda" were evident. But their substantive content (which may differ from one example to another) is included in labeling, monitoring, and campaigning. Slogans, for instance, may label people, may encourage them to obey their bosses, or may be designed to scare them. Fourth or fifth types of policy can be conflated into the main three.

Other studies of the PRC have often discussed the campaign method, because it is the hallmark of totalitarianism. Andrew Walder, who has pioneered research on "neo-traditionalist" patronage in industrial China, has downplayed the need to consider either "group" or "totalitarian" bases of action there.[31] He chides the totalitarian model, epitomized by campaigns, for failing to show positive incentives to compliance and for suggesting that a system can run on negative incentives alone. But if the main aspect of to-

1933). For another critique of Durkheim, along these lines but excessive because it rejects the use of integration even as a merely analytic tool, see Charles Tilly, *Big Structures, Large Processes, Huge Comparisons* (New York: Russell Sage Foundation, 1985).

[30] From an interview with a PRC "reformer," in Princeton.

[31] See Walder, *Communist Neo-Traditionalism*, 5–7.

talitarianism is specified in terms of its most typical administrative instrument—that is, campaigns—then its positive incentives to ambitious activists are evident. Also, totalitarianism is always imperfect.[32] The main way to talk about it is to cite policies that increase or decrease it. In operational terms, it is like other policies, including neo-traditionalist ones; but it complements these, describing sanctions, impersonal rather than family-like ties, and the modern atomization that coexisted with China's new patronage networks.

Walder similarly criticizes the "group/pluralist" model, saying collectives are less regularly articulated than face-to-face networks. Actually, though, group labeling affected the opportunities of millions of people on a daily basis, just as the patronage system did. Political articulation was bottled up, because of government measures to repress it. When it came, the result was a Cultural Revolution.[33] The problem with excluding totalitarian and group models, while considering only clientelist ones, is that all three operated concurrently as state policies. Their analytic logics differ as types of explanation, but that does not prevent them from coexisting as traits of the same set of actions.

TIME: ADMINISTRATIVE RESOURCES
PACE THE REVOLUTION

Much of the PRC's history can be conceived as a flow of events pushed by two conflicting factors: the Party's organizational need for loyalists, and its need for experts (often ex-bourgeois) to help modernization. The CCP's shortage of personnel was not absolute but was relative to ambitious goals. In that broad sense, the will to revolution was partially responsible for policies of "blind advance"[34] that used labels, monitors, and violence as administrative tools. Yet the ideology for quick change often arose in revolutionaries' minds through a logic of inversion—a vision of what China was not,

[32] See the Platonist cited in note 22, above.

[33] Probably because of afterthoughts about evidence on groups in works by Rosen, Lee, and others, Walder, *Communist Neo-Traditionalism*, adds a sensitive and revealing footnote on page 7: "An adequate political sociology of communist states, and of their distinctive variety of 'pluralism,' would require an elaboration of the central tension between group politics and vertical loyalties, and it would involve a conceptual reordering that recognizes the distinction between the identity and interest of social aggregates and how political activity is organized and the actors defined." Such a project is declared "beyond the scope of this book," but proposing it so honestly has got to affect interpretation of the main idea there.

[34] This phrase (*mao jin*) is used by some interviewees.

but should be.[35] The shortage of "red experts" was soluble, with enough time. The whole CCP leadership was insufficiently patient, in view of its limited means.

Revolution has never been sudden, and the Party's resources after 1949 grew slowly. Hopes and editorials have long obscured how gradual and incomplete the business of a revolution always is. CCP leaders who emphasized the consolidation of resources, before advances, contributed to the cumulative process as much as the leaders like Mao who were more famous for reckless phases. Advances and retreats were two sides of the same building process. The attacks of 1966 took place only after a climate of campaigns put these actions within common bounds set by the CCP leadership as a whole. The Party's various factions had long used tactics of political surprise. Labor and materials were under ever-more-centralized control; so organizations were better able to support obedience to bosses. Quick critique, combining police coercion and mass struggle, had by the mid-1960s become standard operating procedure. Most countries have not seen this slow cumulation of the campaign-and-consolidation habit that preceded the 1966 purges at many levels, but such moves were ordinary in China by then.

Once violent ostracism was established as normal politics by 1967, many other factors turned the political kaleidoscope. Red Guard factions split or formed alliances on many grounds. Among the most important were political labels.[36] The local sequences in which these groups were formed, and the timing of such events in relation to Beijing leaders' directives, often affected their political positions. The personalities of local leaders were also important. This book does not attempt to provide an explanation of all these events, only of the violence, especially at its beginning. Impatience with the slowness of social change, and thus policies of pressure to speed it before the Party had a personnel infrastructure strong enough to support them well, brought social reactions that explain the strength of the Cultural Revolution tide—and many of its eddies too. The leadership style of the whole CCP during its first quarter century in state power often seems clever, happy, forceful, attractive—and it did serve the people in some ways. But it miscalculated, also. It discounted too sharply the future costs of policies that manipulated people, and it overvalued the immediate benefits of coercion. This was not clever, even though Mao Zedong put a cheerful face on it.

[35] See Sheldon Wolin's *Politics and Vision* (Boston: Little, Brown, 1960) for more about seeing traits not present.
[36] See material here as well as in Blecher and White, *Micropolitics of a Technical Unit*, and Lee, *Politics of the Chinese Cultural Revolution*, cited in note 2 above.

SPACE: LOW POWER
CONFOUNDS HIGH RULE

For many analysts, "[t]he origins of the Cultural Revolution, both political and ideological, should be traced back to the fall of Peng Dehuai, the
Great Leap Forward, and the extremism within the Central Committee during that period."[37] Yet the Cultural Revolution was not just a sequel to the
Great Leap Forward.[38] Insofar as the CR was a mobilization of participants
based on unspecific follow-the-leader propaganda, there may be some value
in pointing to similarities between these two huge movements. But these parallels do not explain why CR groups were first urban rather than rural, and
why they were based mostly on political labels. In order to account for the
CR as a mass movement, not just a top-to-bottom effort, we must look at the
interests and motives of local city folk who made it.

"Weapons of the weak" have best been studied by James Scott in a village
of a fairly small country, and mostly for their effects on matters like grain
thefts, slanders, arsons, feigned compliances, and machine smashings under
cover of darkness.[39] Such contexts are myriad, often endemic, in poor
places.[40] They show the wide scope over which power is actually spread;
and the number of people involved makes these "weapons" important, even
when used by uncoordinated and separate actors. A message of this book is
that they can explain very large political results, not just small ones. Pat-
terned social reactions to elite policies can shape crucible events in gigantic
countries, as well as subterfuges in villages.[41]

Such reactions may be "unintended" from a government's viewpoint, but

[37] Qi Xin, " 'Leftism' and the Cultural Revolution," in Qi Xin et al., *China's New Democracy* (Hong Kong: Cosmos Books, 1979), p. 127.

[38] MacFarquhar, *The Origins*, has also shown many dissimilarities between the Leap and
the CR, while still emphasizing the importance of their sequence. This book follows him but
deemphasizes the sequence, because the Leap and the CR were different (even opposite) outside
Beijing.

[39] See Scott, *Weapons of the Weak*, which is an empirical and theoretical look at this in
Malaya.

[40] See also Eric J. Hobsbawm, *Primitive Rebels* (Manchester: University of Manchester
Press, 1959); and contrast Carlo Levi, *Christ Stopped at Eboli* (New York: Farrar, Straus, 1947)
with Edward Banfield, *The Moral Basis of a Backward Society* (New York: Free Press, 1958).

[41] Besides the Cultural Revolution, another huge national change that can best be explained
by the action of "weapons of the weak," forged in long years of oppression by high elites, is the
overthrow of Russian czarism. Peasant anarchists did this. Lenin was an urban organizer and
coup maker; but rural antiorganizers made the basic change. A recent set of essays that show
how policies in Mao's time strengthened the compartmentalized "honeycomb" of rural Chinese
communities is Vivienne Shue's *The Reach of the State: Sketches of the Chinese Body Politic*
(Stanford, Calif.: Stanford University Press, 1988).

they are intended by the people who make them. Political scientists who view power narrowly, thinking it most naturally resides at the top of a system, may have difficulty seeing the occasions when governments are weak because their resources become constrained and people want to be left alone. When "the weak" then bring about effects that otherwise would not occur,[42] together they are not weak at all, but strong.

Policies come from leaders, but at many levels. Implementing them, to affect millions, requires more than one leader and more than one size of collectivity. Mao alone did not make the policies for labels, bosses, and campaigns; these measures came from all the top leaders, over a long period of time. Their power over behavior that otherwise would have been different was deeply conditioned by the unarticulated policies of the heads of small groups.

Local people in the Cultural Revolution seldom formed self-conscious lobbies. Their power, though "low" in political level, was great in amount. As Arthur Bentley wrote,

> We cannot possibly advance to an understanding of [the despotic ruler] except in terms of the group activities of his society, which are most directly represented through him. . . . [There are] no slaves, not the most abused of all, but help to form the government. They are an interest group within it.[43]

Mao may have used members of discontented groups cynically, for purposes of his power struggle against Liu. But they used him, too, as a symbol of legitimacy against the local bosses who had oppressed them. Distant Mao was at least as handy for them, as their tumult was for Mao's own agenda. Their adulation of the godlike Chairman created a context in which they could lay claim to new rights.

Hannah Arendt has described a "temporary alliance between the mob and the elite" in totalist regimes.[44] Her work, like most scholarship about totalitarianism, has depended mainly on data from Europe. The Chinese case can show how important local leaders within "the mob" become, when totalist policies rule a country presenting the central leader with gigantic

---

[42] See Dahl, *Modern Political Analysis*, p. 40.

[43] Arthur F. Bentley, *The Governmental Process* (1907; Cambridge: Harvard University Press, 1967), p. 270, quoted in Michael Waller, "Communist Politics and the Group Process: Some Comparative Conclusions," in David S. G. Goodman, *Groups and Politics in the People's Republic of China* (Armonk, N.Y.: Sharpe, 1984), p. 200.

[44] Hannah Arendt, *The Origins of Totalitarianism* (New York: Meridian, 1951), pp. 326ff.

span-of-control problems and inheriting traditions of strong authority in lin-eages. Ideologically too, European totalisms were designed to organize a German, Italian, or Russian-Soviet "people" (a *Volksgemeinschaft*), and to make that whole community loyal to the state. But Mao's ideology some-what varied this model, because it divided such large groups of urban people against each other and legitimated so much opposition to the system.[45] Be-cause labels, patrons, and campaigns in China were imposed on people in a way they could not effectively resist, these policies specify in operational terms—not just ideological ones—the ways "masses" are atomized and dis-ordered.[46] That result is not an event of natural history; it is the consequence of specifiable kinds of state action.

The power of labels to make bourgeois people radical, for example, stems largely from these people's lack of standing to resist such categories. Any denial of the system's legitimacy, from them, seems self-serving. As a Chinese liberal has written, "Communism like Christianity contains some mechanism against which objection is powerless. . . . An explanation of all opposition."[47] Just as a Christian fundamentalist may claim that faithless-ness is the work of the devil, a Communist can attribute to family back-ground any bourgeois objections. So "capitalists" in the PRC had incentives to become super-conforming radicals.

State policies to control behavior can be effective, if they create new local resources that attract people to do what the government wants. But such efforts may backfire when they impose punishments that local people dislike and can evade, or when they promote solidarities that people support in public but subvert in private. They can also prove ineffective and ironic, when their categories or procedures inadvertently create resources that or-dinary people use against the regime.[48] Kenneth Jowitt has written about a

---

[45] This is partly from Maura Wong, Princeton, '88.

[46] Quick social change—urbanization, democratization, and industrialization—is often blamed for the atomized and incoherent societies that support dictators. See, for example, the classic by William Kornhauser, *The Politics of Mass Society* (Glencoe, N.Y.: Free Press, 1959), esp. pp. 173–74, 223. But an aim of the present book is to suggest that good industrial, democratic, and urban policies could be concurrent with good implementing policies (for flex-ible labeling, choice of monitors, and no terror), in a try for both modernity and justice. Even if the correlations that many books on totalitarianism show are accurate, they are insufficient for telling governments—and citizens—what to do and what to avoid.

[47] Mu Fu-sheng, *The Wilting of the Hundred Flowers* (New York: Praeger, 1962), p. 137.

[48] See also Susan Shirk, *Competitive Comrades* (Berkeley and Los Angeles: University of California Press, 1982). Shirk's book is sensitive to ironic results of policy in mid-1960s China. Some authors see the rational-actor logic that explains such patterns as incompatible with the group-consciousness logic that can treat other patterns in the CR. Different analytic types may often be used together.

frequent gap between public compliance with Party rule and private avoidance of it.[49] The labeling process that created important groups in the Cultural Revolution was a top-down policy process, not an upwelling from social bases—even though these formations arose inadvertently, as an unintended consequence of Party rule. Social reaction to monitoring, likewise, was neither pure compliance to Leninist rules nor complete avoidance of them; instead, it was an irony that mixed them: People actively used for their own benefit things the state had created for itself.

The label system motivated people to think about groups in avaricious ways. Labeling encouraged them to acquire the best names they could, and to fight for their social legitimacy in those terms. The patronage system made each person more "other-directed," more solicitous of designated leaders' wishes—which were usually collectivist, because the monitors were subject to higher authorities too. But it inspired personal enmities as often as personal loyalties. Campaigns taught people to be more wary of their larger social environments, even though public campaigns also advanced private vendettas. A common trait of these policies was that when they became administrative habits, they threatened individuals. Another common trait was that they encouraged a mixing of individual and collective values; so people talked about that difference but increasingly acted for themselves.

The full tale of groups in Shanghai's Cultural Revolution will require more research, which is likely to find overlaps between official and unofficial labels. Quasi-ethnic communities, for example those distinguishing North and South Jiangsu people (the "Subei" and "Jiangnan" groups), probably affected some actions in the CR, but scant data are yet available on this subject.[50] Subei people comprised much of Shanghai's contract proletariat. Jiangnan workers and cadres, at least before 1949, considered the northerners uncouth because of their dialect, bright clothing, fondness for garlic, and willingness to take jobs in transport, night-soil hauling, and other menial work. Subei labor had concentrated in certain factories before Liberation, especially foreign-managed ones where administrators were less condescending than Jiangnan managers. This rift became practically a taboo topic

[49] Kenneth Jowitt, "An Organizational Approach to the Study of Political Culture in Marxist-Leninist Systems," *American Political Science Review* 68, no. 1 (1974): 171–91. One of the arguments here is that "culture" offers a more total, flexible array of options than Marxism-Leninism (which grows as one option in a larger cultural context) can possibly provide. Communism is an ideology, not a culture.

[50] Emily Honig is currently studying it. There is more evidence from pre-1949 years; cf. her *Sisters and Strangers* (Stanford, Calif.: Stanford University Press, 1986), which unlike her current research concerns mainly the pre-1949 period.

in public discourse during later years. Further research could well show it to remain important as a division at least within Shanghai's proletariat. Party policies of patronage and labeling did not create this split, but they may have exacerbated it.

Ethnic groups were otherwise unimportant for Shanghai's Cultural Revolution, if only because practically all the people are Han Chinese. Campaigns for pride in the proletarian "family" after 1963 nonetheless created something like racial prejudice, which clearly contributed to the violence after 1966 as several chapters above show. Unionized workers crucially aided the Party in its pressures against capitalists during the early 1950s, its recovery after the Hundred Flowers, and its need to maintain order in the post-Leap depression. Favored union workers were politically central to the urban Party, in crisis after crisis. The official sponsorship of the proletariat as the salt of the earth led to rationalized injustice for others. Although ethnic conflict was hardly germane in a city over 99 percent Han, the movements for proletarian familism created something like a moral equivalent of tribal divisions.

China's holocaust raised—and still raises—basic questions of identity for its participants. For individuals and families, this movement concerned what kind of person to be, how to name oneself, how to fit into a community. If the Cultural Revolution deserves its title, though, the main meanings are ironic. In the long run, the violence confused identities and cultures far more than it clarified them.

NORMAL POLICIES
AND ABNORMAL EXCESSES

Labels may be necessities for any government. There would be no way to concoct rules without them.[51] Pasting adjectives on groups is an unavoidable part of many administrative processes. Especially when a government's staff is short-handed, a continuous reviewing of these tags would be prohibitively expensive. But fixed labels bear no clear relation to current and potential behavior. Such categories can give the people they treat an interest in seizing benefits or avoiding sanctions implied by the policies using them—without any reference to the reasons for which the categories first arose. Labels that

[51] Geof Wood, ed., *Labeling in Development Policy: Essays in Honor of Bernard Schaffer* (The Hague: Institute of Social Studies, 1985), uses the late Dr. Schaffer's ideas on the "culture of poverty" to criticize policies in Ireland, Colombia, Cyprus, Fiji, Bangladesh, and India.

are unresponsive to present or coming behavior, especially names based on ethnicity, religion, or family background, lead to expectations and frustrations that divide people. Leaders of one such interest can organize their constituents to get the better of others. Labeling that seems an administrative necessity can be put to uses that create long-term problems.

Bossism, similarly, saves short-run costs. If an organization has big plans but few loyal or active personnel, it must spread its resources thinly over the population it is trying to influence. "Line authority" increases, even at low administrative levels, and loyalist local monitors get freedom to do their work.[52] Such cadres' hands are strengthened, if subordinates cannot normally expect to change to another patron. Also, an organization with scarce staff is reluctant to retire these local leaders; so work units remain stable over many years. The short-term administrative benefits of such a system can hide long-term costs, which arise because dependence hinders flows of accurate information and fosters lethargy among members who do not get along with their superiors. Bossism is traditional in China, not just in theory, and it may be difficult to modernize systems based on patronage.

Campaign violence has been seen as a potential servant of order by thinkers ranging from Li Si to Machiavelli.[53] For example, Georges Sorel advocated violence in a "general strike" by which workers would purge society's faults.[54] Lenin and Hitler both endorsed violence by parties whose members were committed to suspend their individual wills for the sake of a central discipline. This was supposed to rejuvenate society. The social psychologist Erich Fromm, studying such phenomena in the early 1940s, related it to individuals' fears of displacement by modern industry. He thought people might seek to restore old community relations in a modern society by joining centralized movements that forcibly put down local rivals.[55]

The habit of campaigns, however, is also largely understandable on rational grounds, from the viewpoints of both low and high officials. This habit became a policy (not just in China, but also earlier in Germany and Russia). Campaigns require activists, and activists are potential leaders. They are usually younger than the people whose ways they are mandated to

[52] Many theorists of administration contrast regular "line" and specialist "staff" personnel. Relevant articles are collected in Amitai Etzioni, *A Sociological Reader on Complex Organizations*, 2d ed. (New York: Holt, Rinehart, 1969), e.g., pp. 266–91.

[53] Li Si was prime minister under the First Emperor of Chin (famous for burning books, killing scholars, and "building" the Great Wall) in the late third century B.C. His writings may be sampled in Wm. Theodore de Bary, ed., *Sources of Chinese Tradition* (New York: Columbia University Press, 1960), 1: 136–44.

[54] Georges Sorel, *Reflections on Violence* (New York: Macmillan, 1961).

[55] Erich Fromm, *Escape from Freedom* (New York: Avon Books, 1965).

change. They expect career advancement from their contributions. For top leaders, the value of these fearful exercises is that they reduce resistance to directives. If violence in campaigns, for example in China before the mid-1960s, seems irrational for individual and group logics of ends and means, that is because it had more consequences than its perpetrators intended and because they were careless of others. What was irrational (and worse) is that the activists knew they were dealing harshly with people, and some of them suspected they did not know fully what they were doing. But they did it anyway.[56]

The effectiveness of campaigns springs not just from force, but from individuals' uncertainty about whether it will be applied. Campaigns have a general form: They build in waves of alternating threats and relaxations.[57] Legitimate violence is still normal in all large communities, for example against murderers or war enemies. There is nothing especially communistic about this habit, and there is nothing exclusively Chinese in it. But the effect of unpredictable, random applications of violence is to increase compliance with authority among those who feel they may be threatened. Violence has this effect, at least, until its victims realize together that the weapon threatening them will lose the capacity to elicit compliance if they organize against it. That realization is what happened in the Cultural Revolution, and it has been institutionalized broadly in Chinese urban society during the past decade. Experience in violence is the normal basis of nonviolence and tolerance.

The policy means emphasized in this book may seem linked to ideal types of authority such as Weber proposed, but they came out of the heads of the politicians who tried them and the citizens who reacted to them. Their main link is to understandings of authority and compliance options among the Chinese actors then, not just to scientific premises that allow formal tests by others now. Policies are intentions; they are not just analyses. The Cultural Revolution resulted from an elite's interest in identifying rivals, monitoring order, and gaining mass compliance. Such interests are usual, but they result in tumult when policies for them are carried much further than usual and are coupled with state coercion. The kinds of policies that boded tragedy were measures that gave people tags unconnected with their present behavior, measures that set them under satraps, and measures using random force

[56] Examples of evidence for second thoughts are included in earlier chapters' references to politicians like Pan Hannian and Chen Yi.

[57] The best treatment is still Ezra Vogel's description of the land reform in Guangdong, in *Canton under Communism* (Cambridge: Harvard University Press, 1969), pp. 91–124.

to make them docile. The tragedy may well be blamed on a climate of anxiety in Chinese cities by 1966—as in Massachusetts Bay in the 1690s or Germany in the 1930s or Kampuchea in the 1970s. But observing a climate of anxiety does not tell much, unless we can determine what created it. An answer seems to lie in resource-constrained and coercive policies that bred fear among people over a number of years.

THE ETHICAL NEED FOR RESEARCH ABOUT CAUSES

It is slightly old-hat, in discussing revolutions, to talk about their causes. The best literature on any revolution, the French, has practically abandoned the narrative of history to concentrate on broad forces and symbols.[58] Interpreting texts is now more à la mode than seeking causes. This current approach is as useful as any other analysis of consciousness; but comparison is not among its aims, and the beauties of the textual approach need not obscure an equal need to find why things happened.

"Cause" is a big word. There is much danger of hubris in using it, because of difficulties in knowing links between historical factors. But to give warnings when policies are harmful, people need to discover what brings effects. Clear definitions, along with attempts to distinguish necessary, sufficient, and auxiliary causes, should allow some progress without making too many claims. Readers will finally judge the credibility of asserted links on the basis of their own experiences.

Systematic explanation may often be a less vivid means to organize understanding about a situation than is a narrative of the options people have, when facing it. But such a tale can be combined with "hypothetical analysis" that seeks causes.[59] People are usually less interested in consistency than results. They do not just adhere to a particular psychology, "deep structure," or unified culture; they also think of alternatives. The nub of the task here is not to show all options that the Chinese people had, as they began the violence of the CR. Nor is it only to show a few of the factors (for example, in Beijing politics) that led to the result. Instead, it is to show a sufficient set of

[58] See Robert Darnton, "Revolution sans Revolutionaries," *New York Review*, January 31, 1985, pp. 21–23, which reviews Lynn Hunt's *Politics, Culture, and Class in the French Revolution* (Berkeley and Los Angeles: University of California Press, 1984).

[59] On Weber's "hypothetical analysis," see H. Stuart Hughes, *Consciousness and Society* (New York: Vintage Books, 1961), chap. 8. More is in Reinhard Bendix, *Max Weber: An Intellectual Portrait* (Garden City, N.Y.: Doubleday, 1960). See above, chapter 1, note 106, on related ideas by Richard Madsen.

factors that would have precluded the violence of what followed, if they had been absent. These precipitating, intermediate vectors are less diverse than "culture" but more comprehensive than the motives of a few top leaders. They show clearly in the policies for labels, monitors, and campaigns, which are all means of administrative implementation. The thesis is that if these policies had been less salient before 1966, the extensive violence of the Cultural Revolution would not have occurred.

To become overinterested in the difficulties of explaining causation would probably be to evade the task of attempting to show what the experience of the Cultural Revolution means for the future, and for other countries. An aim of research on a tragedy of this size should naturally be to go beyond interpretations and take lessons. For example, can the kind of analysis in this book tell anything about the disaster that befell Jews under Hitler? No writing can bring back the dead. Academic treatments are not likely to comprehend all aspects of catastrophes. Many will object to comparing the Holocaust with anything else, even the Cultural Revolution or the Kampuchean killing after 1976 (the most recent instance of such an offense against millions).[60] Formal comparison of such events is not the sole valid reaction to them, but several recent phenomena bear at least some resemblance to this type.[61] It would also serve no clear purpose to speculate which of these calamities was worst. They were not the same. More people died in the Holocaust than in the Cultural Revolution, because of Hitler's bureaucracy for running murder camps.[62] More people suffered in the Cultural Revolution,

---

[60] The Kampuchean killing has received too little scholarly attention, but a major recent book is David A. Ablin and Marlowe Hood, eds., *The Cambodian Agony* (Armonk, N.Y.: Sharpe, 1987); both editors have been students of the present author, and they organized a conference at Princeton to discuss the draft chapters of their book. See also Ben Kiernan and Chanthou Boua, eds., *Peasants and Politics in Kampuchea, 1942–1981* (Armonk, N.Y.: Sharpe, 1982), and William Shawcross, *The Quality of Mercy: Cambodia, Holocaust, and Modern Conscience* (New York: Simon and Schuster, 1984).

[61] The persecution in Iran of Ba'hais and the persecution of East Indians in Uganda are cases in point. The lower number of victims in those instances made the result no better for them. No catalog will be attempted, here, of all such tragedies. They do, however, form a phenomenon that deserves more extensive comparative study for the purpose of preventing future examples—even if each affected group feels an understandable claim to unique attention after such an experience.

[62] See Gerald Fleming's *Hitler and the Final Solution* (Berkeley and Los Angeles: University of California Press, 1982), which proves Hitler's detailed personal involvement in ordering the Holocaust. This contrasts with Mao's more indirect involvement in the less-organized murders and suicides of the Cultural Revolution. The recent Kampuchean case is closer to Germany's; the recent Ugandan and Iranian cases are apparently closer to China's. (A greater portion of the targeted group dies if the state bureaucracy assumes a more direct role; but the suffering among many is severe in any case. The larger number of survivors in the less-organized cases

if only because of China's gigantic urban population. Statistics tend to trivialize thinking about such problems, but the tragedy common to all these events is their main feature.

To the extent they are comparable, it is useful to look for causes, so as to identify, predict, and resist them. But there are moral problems in not analyzing causes, too. "Never again" means nothing, with respect to the Cultural Revolution or the Holocaust, until we know the traits of what must never again happen, how its parts link into a system. This book cannot dwell on the German, Iranian, Kampuchean, or other semi-analogues to the Cultural Revolution. But labeled groups, new officials, and violent campaigns are identifiable in all of them, even though the directness of the state's involvement in each of them varies greatly.

The trauma of 1933–45 in Europe was based on German government policies that gave people inflexible labels (such as Jew, Gypsy, or Slav), put them under official overseers, and threatened them with increasing violence in waves of campaigns. Resentment of clientelist relations was apparently less important in Germany than in China. The levels of modern development of these two countries were different when the two tragedies occurred, even though impatience for modernization undoubtedly gave rise to some forces behind the disasters in each. The ruling party's shortage of loyal professionals was somewhat parallel. As Hitler once said, "When I look at the intellectual classes here in Germany, . . . we need them. Otherwise, I don't know, we could wipe them out or something. But unfortunately we need them."[63] The use of state coercion on behalf of local bosses identified with the ruling party—and against other local people who could have done their jobs—seems to be closely parallel in these two cases.

An obvious dissimilarity lies in the extent to which Hitler's government directly organized killings. The anarchy of the Cultural Revolution was encouraged, but not tightly coordinated, by Mao's regime. Social ideals did not motivate the movement that led to the Holocaust; and this exploration of the Cultural Revolution suggests immediate ideological goals also did not determine what happened in 1966–68 as crucially as many publications have implied. Careerism and frustrations raised by long-term official attempts to implement ideals from 1949 to 1965 were more important to the event than has generally been recognized. To the extent ideals caused the

---

may affect later political development, though more research would be needed to show this.) Nor do such differences gainsay the general importance of group categories, local bosses, and preceding violent campaigns in all these disasters.

[63] David Schoenbaum, *Hitler's Social Revolution: Class and Status in Nazi Germany, 1933–39* (New York: Norton, 1980), p. 276; see also the comment about Himmler, p. 279.

violence and did not merely rationalize it, they did so in a heavily institutionalized, unimmediate form. Whether they should be called "ideals" in that form is moot. If so, this question becomes less relevant as a point of comparison with the German and other cases.

Cultural factors, long thought to be crucial in the German event, seem to deserve less attention in light of the fact that broadly similar rampages have befallen cultures as different as those in Germany, China, Kampuchea, Iran, and Uganda. It is unclear, at least, what kind of culture might preclude such a tragedy. Specific policies may explain more about the beginnings of social violence (if not all its later results) than culture, ideology, symbols, or maybe even the leader's psychology. If so, analogues to the three policies of pressure outlined here for China's case might be worth researching more thoroughly, to assess their importance in other countries' disasters.

It is possible that such violence will again haunt Chinese people, but on an unexpected, international scene. Chinese in Southeast Asia may well include the world's largest groups now at high risk of major pogroms. In a country like Indonesia, local leaders might benefit from violent campaigns against Chinese residents they envy. These might be justified in the name of Islam, or socialism, or nationalism, or an ideological combination; that would make no difference to any victims. Patriotic revolutions in such countries could easily develop—and the one that has done so, in Vietnam, soon became anti-shopkeeper (which, throughout Southeast Asia, unfailingly also means anti-Chinese). The portion of "Hoa" among boat people from Vietnam was far greater than the percentage of Chinese in Vietnam's population. In other countries of Southeast Asia, this pattern of upheaval against the most wealthy and cosmopolitan ethnic group—which is easy for majorities to label and resent—could turn up again. In Indonesia, where the Chinese minority is economically crucial, not thoroughly assimilated, different in religion, involved in some corruption, and numerically too small to defend itself, there is potential for a movement of this kind. When such a danger is evident but not activated, we might look for ways to prevent it.

The framework of this book suggests warning signals before such disasters. If governments move toward more official group classification schemes, toward mandating more structured dependence in politics, or toward more unpredictable use of violence, then the onset of disaster should be resisted. The outside world should use whatever leverage it has to promote equal protection norms, interest-based (rather than network-based) politics, and steady, noncampaign development in such countries. Foreign influence may often be trivial in these situations, however, especially in big countries if the danger develops over any length of time. Better consciousness of these situations may still offer some hope of heading off tragedy or reducing its effects. Then at least some people may sense their peril and avoid it—by emigration, if need be. More comparative research is needed on the general conditions of such risks; but official labels, monitors, and campaigns are clear signs for alarm.

COMPARISONS AS A BASIS FOR PREDICTIONS ABOUT CHINA

China has usually been compared with Russia for the purpose of answering almost any modern question, not just about tragedies like the Cultural Revolution. On the other hand, China and Russia also differ in structural respects. The USSR and PRC states share Leninist traditions, and these societies' two revolutions also have some similarities. But their political experiences are in many ways disparate. China's communications network in 1949 was even slower than that connecting the most important parts of Russia in 1917, and China's per-capita income was lower at the time of its revolution. China's Party has strained even more obviously against its limited resources than has the CPSU in Russia, at least since Stalin's time. China's revolution was less thorough in social terms than Russia's (even though Soviet scholars of China say so!).[64] The surviving prestige of non-Communist informal elites in China after Mao contrasts with the end of most non-Party elites in Russia after Stalin.

That Soviet dictator actually killed many of his country's non-Communist local leaders, as well as leaders within the CPSU who would not follow his policies. He created Soviet groups of professionals in all fields, from the military to the arts. Mao may have wished to do the same, but he succeeded in this effort far less completely. Stalin's official critics, notably Khrushchev, all came out of a Stalinist system in which they had not personally suffered (and some paroled from the gulag became dissidents against the post-Stalin Soviet regimes). Most of Mao's post-1976 official critics, on the other hand, personally suffered for at least part of the time he ruled.

The corps of professionals, which the Chinese government needed for modernization, has grown from both pre- and post-1949 elites, despite all

---

[64] Gilbert Rozman, *A Mirror for Socialism: Soviet Criticisms of China* (Princeton: Princeton University Press, 1985), e.g., p. 143, shows that some Soviet academics, especially in the Institute of the Far East, rue the continuing social prestige of the old intelligentsia and related capitalists. The impact of Chinese non-Communist elites has become even more evident since the period Rozman's pioneering book reports.

the political turmoils in the first quarter-century of CCP rule. The relative uniformity of urban elites' backgrounds in the USSR contrasts with the relative variation of these in China. This dissimilarity in the structure of informal elites distinguishes the two socialist powers from each other, and it must be considered alongside their obvious similarity: they both still have disciplined ruling parties. Many writings refer only to the similarity and ignore the difference.

The disparity comes from the two countries' recent political experiences, especially the uniqueness of China's Cultural Revolution. The CCP's shortage of professionals caused pre-1966 Chinese administrators to rely on labels, patrons, and campaigns. These policies allowed them to make progress in their tasks of social change. But the resulting Cultural Revolution created such havoc that, in its aftermath, the legitimacy of diverseness in China's elite is now confirmed, despite Leninist norms against pluralism.

Comparisons with other great revolutions, such as the French and especially the English, deserve more study than they have received. The English parallels are especially intriguing. In Britain, as in China, a period of group classification, personal distrust, and iconoclastic violence was followed by a widespread and surprisingly sudden reconciliation between two very large local elites (Anglo-Catholic and Puritan). Only eleven years after chopping off a king's head, Britons restored his son to the throne. Although the English Republic was far from liberal in its Commonwealth and Protectorate stages (which have many similarities to the Cultural Revolution), the long-term reaction to this experience loosened British society. There is evidence that China may be under some roughly similar forces—though many other differences between these countries surely affect their histories also.

In France, after mass revolutionary turmoil, the purge of alternative local elites was incomplete. Even the guillotines were less thoroughgoing than, for example, was that most perfectionist revolutionary, Stalin. In any comparison of China with France, there are again of course huge differences. The rest of the world does not hope now for a Chinese Napoleon. But French families that produced local leaders before 1789 were able, under Napoleon and later, to continue their participation in politics alongside members of families that rose during the revolution. This fairness toward talent, no matter whence it comes, is a usual pattern toward the ends of revolutions—and that tolerance is a natural reaction to unfairness at the height of social violence. Because China's previous elites have not completely lost out at the local level, the winding down of China's revolution could prove quicker and less subject to control by a unified party than the same process has been in Russia.

NEARING THE END OF CHINA'S REVOLUTION

Will another Cultural Revolution occur in China? This book suggests not. Extensive mass violence is now unlikely, because CR experiences have disinclined Chinese local leaders, especially in cities, to permit very forceful use of policies that categorize people, control people, and scare people. The Maoist policies did not ultimately work, as many local leaders now sense. Because the decision makers have that experience, such policies are even less likely to work now.[65] Low-level elites, some of which encouraged intergroup conflict during the 1960s, have now become tired of fighting each other. "Never again" is their motto, too. The Puritans and Royalists became satiated in England during the 1650s. Even French factions did, in the 1790s. A similar thing has now happened in China.

Divisions of the top leadership, as severe as that between Mao Zedong and Liu Shaoqi, could easily arise again. Without as much mass frustration in cities, however, the results would be entirely different. Chinese local leaders' retrospective reactions against pressures that led to the CR will continue to affect politics in that country, even though no one can be sure how these memories will mesh with other reasons for future change there.

OPTIMISM FOR THE FUTURE

In China, the end of the Cultural Revolution meant rehabilitation—not just for the victims of that movement, but for the targets of all earlier campaigns too. An important casualty, of course, was public enthusiasm about how much political will and leadership could achieve for China.[66] The CR bred cynicism on that point; it dashed the hopes of some who hoped a lot. It was a sharp public lesson in the fact that policies can have unintended consequences.

Dry and realistic optimism, not just alienated cynicism, can nonetheless come out of this. The best proof that the violence of the late 1960s affects China's present and future lies in the extent to which it has already affected thinking about the past. A single example may suffice: Pan Hannian, the

---

[65] See also Merle Goldman, "Wenhua da geming de fei xiaoji yingxiang" (The non-adverse influences of the great Cultural Revolution), *Zhishi fenzi* (The Chinese intellectual), 2, no. 3 (1986): 47–49.

[66] Regret at this loss of enthusiasm is also reflected in some hopeful Western writings, for example, Edoarda Masi's *China Winter: Workers, Mandarins, and the Purge of the Gang of Four*, trans. Adrienne Foulke (New York: Dutton, 1982).

Shanghai Party's early liaison with capitalists, was purged in 1955 for his close links to non-Communists.[67] He was posthumously restored to honor in 1983, explicitly for "his ability to unite with other comrades and non-Party personnel, to work in full cooperation with them."[68] China's CCP elite made the policies that created a climate for Cultural Revolution, even though most of these leaders did not intend, predict, or control such widespread violence. That elite may reform itself, and since 1978 it seems to be doing so.

Political conflict in China has changed since the Cultural Revolution. The resources of political actors, as well as the issues dividing them, were largely reshuffled by the chaos of that experience. A decrease of labeling and less state sponsorship for bossism has somewhat reduced the importance of political status groups. Nascent "interest groups" based in cultural or economic constituencies have become more important, even though both Chinese and Westerners (for different reasons) have great disinclination to talk about them. Recent policies of decentralization in the economy, if they become thorough, may make assets available to a wider variety of political actors. If recurring tensions between "reform" and "conservative" factions in Beijing continue to be resolved in favor of the new technocrats, political arenas might also become less bifurcated than in the past, and political representatives of geographic or functional units might not so regularly find themselves in set clusters of tactical alliances.[69] If ever there were a country large enough to "expand the sphere," as Madison put it, China could do that.

This does not mean that the CCP is about to close up shop. This Communist Party is in a position to evolve independently of any other, and its relation with broader forces in Chinese society will affect such changes. Since that society will soon include Hong Kong, and already includes great diversity at the local level in other Chinese cities, the Party itself has already begun to show more variation, at least in terms of functional specialties. Does a one-party system inevitably generate problems of the sort China's local elites faced after 1949? It may tend to correlate with them, but the CCP has implemented the three policies of chaos much less in the past decade than before. Even some policies for Party discipline, mandating bosses for

[67] See the paragraph about Pan toward the end of chapter 2, above.

[68] *NCNA* (Beijing), February 28, 1983. See also chapter 2, above. Pan died in 1977 as a disgraced man. Yang Fan, also exonerated in 1983, was still alive to speak at Pan's rehabilitation meeting (*NCNA*, issue above).

[69] See Li Cheng and Lynn White, "The Thirteenth Central Committee of the Chinese Communist Party: From Mobilizers of Managers," *Asian Survey* 28, no. 4 (1988).

each section, can bring higher costs now. A loosely organized one-party system could omit such policies. China's leaders will be responsible for their own decisions in this matter, as they have been in the past.

CAREFUL POLICY AS THE
IRREPLACEABLE CONCLUSION

The roots of Cultural Revolution reached to low-level units in Shanghai, but policy causes (not less specific social causes) were crucial. Government measures created new status groups, personal networks, and a climate of violence before 1966. The social conditions that gave rise to the Cultural Revolution did not come from thin air, and probably not from long-lost cultural or psychological links that are too complex to trace well. Instead, they came from specific, identifiable state policies. Better planning could have obviated these and could have prevented the massive political explosion of 1966.

It is possible to ask whether revolutionary social violence should be generally planned against, but one need not be conservative to see that a lack of planning has in some cases brought grief for too many, too randomly. The issue is human, not just political. The main aim of this book is to help policy makers realize that administrative measures using inflexible labels, fixed patronage, and fearsome movements create long-term costs, even if they seem to save short-term costs. The insight that the CCP leaders mostly missed, from 1949 to 1966, is that policies should be designed for eventual benefit, not just immediate convenience. Implementing means should, if possible, avoid categorization of people, manipulation of people, and campaigns to unnerve people. Of course, this is a moral matter. Because it is commonly seen as such, it becomes by the same token also a matter of administrative efficiency. The former is more important. But the two are not separate.

No vision of historical "convergence" among societies is necessary to underlie this concept. The reason why China's government in Deng's time has reversed the unfair policies that caused violence after 1966 almost surely lies in a sense, not just among the new leaders but also among the broad elites on which they depend, that the earlier policies of pressure did not work. That political consensus now, rather than any inevitable convergence, is the basis of this change and the reason it is likely to continue. The Cultural Revolution of the past is the best insurance against a Cultural Revolution of the future.

There seem to be two different types of political participation and leadership. One of these ignores the levels of human community. It fixes people in categories, forces them to depend on officials, and uses haphazard fears to reduce short-term administrative costs. Another, better, kind of leadership acknowledges the quantum of sovereignty in small groups, not just large ones.

The findings here throw no cold water on hopes for political reform—or revolution, when problems call for so much change. Political tactics that aim at good results will always be necessary. Such tactics can avoid hasty labels, monitors, and campaigns. Better policies will make for better results. This is not a matter of any particular culture, or of inchoate human aggressiveness, or of universal history. It is a matter of the need to care about people and to figure the effects of causes.

Bibliography

Most books cited in the footnotes are on the list below, but the most useful sources for this research were articles in the Chinese newspapers and journals listed in the roster of abbreviations. These PRC sources are in most cases less thoroughly edited than Chinese books, and thus are often more informative about politics. Other essential bases of this study were interviews in Princeton and elsewhere, especially at Universities Service Centre, Hong Kong.

Ablin, David A., and Marlowe Hood, eds. *The Cambodian Agony*. Armonk, N.Y.: Sharpe, 1987.

Ahn Byung-joon. *Chinese Politics and the Cultural Revolution: The Dynamics of Policy Processes*. Seattle: University of Washington Press, 1966.

Anderson, Evelyn. "Shanghai: The Masses Unleashed." *Problems of Communism* 27, no. 1 (1968): 12–21.

Arendt, Hannah. *The Origins of Totalitarianism*. New York: Meridian, 1951.

Azrael, Jeremy. *Managerial Power and Soviet Politics*. Cambridge: Harvard University Press, 1966.

Ba Jin. *Random Thoughts*. Translated by Geremie Barmé. Hong Kong: Joint Publishing Co., 1984.

Bachman, David M. *Chen Yun and the Chinese Political System*. Berkeley: University of California Center for Chinese Studies, 1985.

Balazs, Étienne. *Chinese Civilization and Bureaucracy*. Edited by A. F. Wright and translated by H. M. Wright. New Haven: Yale University Press, 1964.

Banfield, Edward. *The Moral Basis of a Backward Society*. New York: Free Press, 1958.

Barmé, Geremie, and John Minford, eds. *Seeds of Fire: Chinese Voices of Conscience*. Hong Kong: Far Eastern Economic Review, 1986.

Barnett, Doak A. *China after Mao*. Princeton: Princeton University Press, 1967.

Baum, Richard D., and Frederick C. Teiwes. *Ssu-Ch'ing: The Socialist Education Movement of 1962–1966*. Berkeley: University of California Center for Chinese Studies, 1968.

Baum, Richard D. "Ideology Redivivus." *Problems of Communism* 16, no. 3 (1967): 1–11.

––––––. *Prelude to Revolution: Mao, the Party, and the Peasant Question, 1962–66*. New York: Columbia University Press, 1975.

––––––. " 'Red and Expert': The Politico-Ideological Foundations of China's Great Leap Forward." *Asian Survey* 4, no. 9 (September 1964): 148–57.

Bendix, Reinhard. *Max Weber: An Intellectual Portrait*. Garden City, N.Y.: Doubleday, 1960.

Bennett, Gordon A., and Ronald N. Montaperto. *Red Guard: The Political Biography of Dai Hsiao-ai*. Garden City, N.Y.: Doubleday, 1972.

Bentley, Arthur F. *The Governmental Process*. 1907. Cambridge: Harvard University Press, 1967.

Bergère, Marie-Claire. " 'The Other China': Shanghai from 1919 to 1949." In *Shanghai: Revolution and Development in an Asian Metropolis*, edited by Christopher Howe, pp. 1–34. Cambridge: Cambridge University Press, 1981.

Bernstein, Thomas P. "Cadre and Peasant Behavior under Conditions of Insecurity and Deprivation: The Grain Supply Crisis of the Spring of 1955." In *Chinese Communist Politics in Action*, edited by A. Doak Barnett, pp. 365–99. Seattle: University of Washington Press, 1969.

——. *Up to the Mountains and Down to the Villages: The Transfer of Youth from Urban to Rural China*. New Haven: Yale University Press, 1977.

Bianco, Lucian. *The Origins of the Chinese Revolution, 1915–1949*. Stanford, Calif.: Stanford University Press, 1971.

Carnoy, Martin. *The State and Political Theory*. Princeton: Princeton University Press, 1984.

Ch'en Nai-ruenn, ed. *Chinese Economic Statistics: A Handbook for Mainland China*. Chicago: Aldine, 1967.

Chan, Anita. *Childen of Mao: Personality Development and Political Activism in the Red Guard Generation*. Seattle: University of Washington Press, 1985.

Chan, Anita, Richard Madsen, and Jonathan Unger. *Chen Village: The Recent History of a Peasant Community in Mao's China*. Berkeley and Los Angeles: University of California Press, 1984.

Chan, Anita, Stanley Rosen, and Jonathan Unger. "Students and Class Warfare: The Social Roots of the Red Guard Conflict in Guangzhou (Canton)." *China Quarterly* 83 (September 1980): 397–446.

——, eds. *On Socialist Democracy and the Chinese Legal System*. Armonk, N.Y.: Sharpe, 1985.

Chang, Arnold. *Painting in the PRC: The Politics of Style*. Boulder, Colo.: Westview, 1980.

Chang, Parris H. *Power and Policy in China*. Enlarged ed. University Park: Pennsylvania State University Press, 1978.

Chen Gang [pseud.]. *Shanghai gang matou de bianqian* (Change on the Shanghai docks). Shanghai: Shanghai Renmin Chuban She, 1966.

Chen Yuan-tsung. *The Dragon's Village*. New York: Pantheon, 1980.

Cheng Chu-yuan. "The Power Struggle in Red China." *Asian Survey* 6, no. 9 (1966): 469–83.

Cheng, Nien. *Life and Death in Shanghai*. London: Collins, 1986.

Cheng, Peter. *A Chronology of the People's Republic of China*. Totowa, N.J.: Littlefield Adams, 1972.

Chesneaux, Jean. *The Chinese Labor Movement, 1919–1927*. Translated by Hope M. Wright. Stanford, Calif.: Stanford University Press, 1968.

Chi Wang. *Mainland China Organizations of Higher Learning in Science and Technology and their Publications.* Washington, D.C.: Library of Congress, 1961.

Chinese Communist Party, Central Committee. *Resolution on CCP History (1949–81).* Beijing: Foreign Languages Press, 1981.

Cobban, Alfred. *The Social Interpretation of the French Revolution.* Cambridge: Cambridge University Press, 1964.

Coble, Parks M., Jr. *The Shanghai Capitalists and the Nationalist Government, 1927–1937.* Cambridge: Harvard University Press, 1980.

Cohen, Arthur A. *The Communism of Mao Tse-tung.* Chicago: University of Chicago Press, 1964.

Committee of Concerned Asian Scholars. *China! Inside the People's Republic.* New York: Bantam Books, 1972.

Cornelius, Wayne. "Urbanization and Political Demand-Making." *American Political Science Review* 68 (September 1974): 1125–46.

Coser, Lewis. *The Functions of Social Conflict.* Glencoe, N.Y.: Free Press, 1956.

Crozier, Michael. *The Bureaucratic Phenomenon.* Chicago: University of Chicago Press, 1964.

Dahl, Robert A. *Modern Political Analysis.* Englewood Cliffs, N.J.: Prentice-Hall, 1963.

Dahrendorf, Ralf. "Out of Utopia: Toward a Reorientation of Sociological Analysis." *American Journal of Sociology* 64 (September 1958): 115–27.

Dai Houying. *Stones of the Wall.* New York: St. Martin's Press, 1985.

Daubier, Jean. *A History of the Chinese Cultural Revolution.* Translated by Richard Seaver. New York: Random House, 1974.

de Bary, Wm. Theodore. *The Liberal Tradition in China.* New York: Columbia University Press, 1983.

————, ed. *Sources of Chinese Tradition.* Vol. 1. New York: Columbia University Press, 1960.

Deutsch, Karl. *The Nerves of Government: Models of Political Communication and Control.* Glencoe, N.Y.: Free Press, 1963.

Ding Wang. *Niugui sheshen ji* (Collection of ghosts and monsters). Hong Kong: Sanjia Dian Shuwu, 1967.

Dittmer, Lowell. "The Cultural Revolution and the Fall of Liu Shao-ch'i." *Current Scene* 11, no. 1 (1973): 1–13.

————. *Liu Shao-ch'i and the Chinese Cultural Revolution: The Politics of Mass Criticism.* Berkeley and Los Angeles: University of California Press, 1974.

————. "Thought Reform and Cultural Revolution: An Analysis of the Symbolism of Chinese Polemics." *American Political Science Review* 71, no. 1 (1977): 67–85.

Donnithorne, Audrey. *China's Economic System.* New York: Praeger, 1967.

Durkheim, Émile. *The Division of Labor in Society.* Translated by George Simpson. New York: Macmillan, 1933.

_____. *Suicide: A Study in Sociology*. Translated by J. Spaulding and G. Simpson. New York: Free Press of Glencoe, 1951.

Eberhard, Wolfram. *Guilt and Sin in Traditional China*. Berkeley and Los Angeles: University of California Press, 1967.

Eckstein, Alexander, Walter Galenson, and Ta-chung Liu, eds. *Economic Trends in Communist China*. Chicago: Aldine, 1968.

Eckstein, Harry. "The Idea of Political Development: From Dignity to Efficiency." *World Politics* 34, no. 4 (1982): 451–86.

Elkins, David, and Richard Simeon. "A Cause in Search of Its Effect, or What Does Political Culture Explain?" *Comparative Politics* 11 (January 1979): 127–46.

Erikson, Erik H. *Childhood and Society*. 2d ed. New York: Norton, 1963.

_____. *Young Man Luther*. New York: Norton, 1958.

Erikson, Kai T. *Wayward Puritans: A Study in the Sociology of Deviance*. New York: Wiley, 1966.

Falkenheim, Victor C., ed. *Citizens and Groups in the Policy Process of the People's Republic of China*. Ann Arbor: University of Michigan Press, 1987.

Fleming, Gerald. *Hitler and the Final Solution*. Berkeley and Los Angeles: University of California Press, 1982.

Friedman, Edward. "After Mao: Maoism and Post-Mao China." *Telos* 65 (Fall 1985): 23–46.

_____. "Cultural Limits of the Cultural Revolution." *Asian Survey* 9, no. 3 (1969): 188–201.

Frolic, B. Michael. *Mao's People: Sixteen Portraits of Life in Revolutionary China*. Cambridge: Harvard University Press, 1980.

Fung, Ka-iu. "The Spatial Development of Shanghai." In *Shanghai: Revolution and Development in an Asian Metropolis*, edited by Christopher Howe, pp. 269–99. Cambridge: Cambridge University Press, 1981.

Gao Yuan. *Born Red*. Stanford, Calif.: Stanford University Press, 1987.

Gardner, John. "The Wu-fan Campaign in Shanghai: A Study in the Consolidation of Urban Control." In *Chinese Communist Politics in Action*, edited by A. Doak Barnett, pp. 447–76. Seattle: University of Washington Press, 1969.

Gaulton, Richard. "Political Mobilization in Shanghai, 1949–51." In *Shanghai: Revolution and Development in an Asian Metropolis*, edited by Christopher Howe, pp. 35–65. Cambridge: Cambridge University Press, 1981.

Geddes, W. R. *Peasant Life in Communist China*. Ithaca: Cornell Society for Applied Anthropology, 1963.

Geertz, Clifford. *The Interpretation of Cultures*. New York: Basic Books, 1973.

_____. *Islam Observed: Religious Development in Morocco and Indonesia*. Chicago: University of Chicago Press, 1968.

_____. *Local Knowledge*. New York: Basic Books, 1983.

_____. *Negara: The Theatre State in Nineteenth-Century Bali*. Princeton: Princeton University Press, 1980.

_____. *The Social History of an Indonesian Town*. Cambridge: Harvard University Press, 1965.

Goldman, Merle. *China's Intellectuals: Advise and Dissent*. Cambridge: Harvard University Press, 1981.

_____. *Literary Dissent in Communist China*. Cambridge: Harvard University Press, 1967.

Goodman, David S. G., ed. *Groups and Politics in the People's Republic of China*. Armonk, N.Y.: Sharpe, 1985.

Granqvist, Hans. *The Red Guard*. New York: Praeger, 1967.

Griffin, Patricia E. *The Chinese Communist Treatment of Counter-Revolutionaries, 1924–1949*. Princeton: Princeton University Press, 1976.

Harding, Harry, Jr. "China: Toward Revolutionary Pragmatism." *Asian Survey* 11, no. 1 (1971): 51–67.

_____. *Organizing China: The Problem of Bureaucracy, 1949–76*. Stanford, Calif.: Stanford University Press, 1981.

Henderson, Gail E., and Myron Cohen. *The Chinese Hospital: A Socialist Work Unit*. New Haven: Yale University Press, 1984.

Henze, Jürgen. "Higher Education: The Tension between Quality and Equality." In *Contemporary Chinese Education*, edited by Ruth Hayhoe, pp. 93–153. Armonk, N.Y.: Sharpe, 1984.

Hinton, Harold C. *An Introduction to Chinese Politics*. New York: Praeger, 1973.

Hinton, William. *Hundred Day War: The Cultural Revolution at Tsinghua University*. New York: Monthly Review Press, 1972.

_____. *Turning Point in China: An Essay on the Cultural Revolution*. New York: Monthly Review Press, 1972.

Hobsbawm, Eric J. *Primitive Rebels*. Manchester: University of Manchester Press, 1959.

Hoffman, Charles. *Work Incentive Practices and Policies in the People's Republic of China, 1953–1965*. Albany: State University of New York Press, 1967.

Honig, Emily. *Sisters and Strangers: Women in the Cotton Mills of Shanghai, 1919–1949*. Stanford, Calif.: Stanford University Press, 1986.

Hook, Brian. "China's Cultural Revolution: The Preconditions in Historical Perspective." *World Today* 23, no. 11 (1967): 454–64.

_____. "The Post-Plenum Development of China's Proletarian Cultural Revolution." *World Today* 22, no. 11 (1966): 467–75.

Howe, Christopher. "Industrialization under Conditions of Long-Term Population Stability: Shanghai's Achievement and Prospects." In *Shanghai: Revolution and Development in an Asian Metropolis*, edited by Christopher Howe, pp. 153–87. Cambridge: Cambridge University Press, 1981.

_____. *Urban Employment and Economic Growth in Communist China, 1949–1957*. Cambridge: Cambridge University Press, 1971.

Hsiao, Gene T. "The Background and Development of 'The Proletarian Cultural Revolution.'" *Asian Survey* 7, no. 6 (1967): 389–404.

Hsü, Kai-yu. *Chou En-lai: China's Grey Eminence*. Garden City, N.Y.: Doubleday, 1968.

Huang Yifeng and Zhou Shangwen. *Shanghai gongren sanci wuzhuang qiyi* (Three armed uprisings of the Shanghai workers). Shanghai: Renmin chuban she, 1979.

Huberman, Leo, and Paul Sweezy. "The Cultural Revolution in China." *Monthly Review* 18, no. 8 (1967): 1–17.

Huff, Stephen O. "Literary Policy in Communist China and the Rise of Yao Wen-yuan." Senior thesis, Department of East Asian Studies, Princeton University, 1975.

Hughes, H. Stuart. *Consciousness and Society*. New York: Vintage Books, 1961.

Hunter, Neale. *Shanghai Journal: An Eyewitness Account of the Cultural Revolution*. New York: Praeger, 1969.

Johnson, Chalmers A. "China: The Cultural Revolution in Structural Perspective." *Asian Survey* 8, no. 1 (1968): 1–15.

––––––. *Peasant Nationalism and Communist Power: The Emergence of Revolutionary China, 1937–1945*. Stanford, Calif.: Stanford University Press, 1962.

Joseph, William, Christine Wong, and David Zweig, eds. *New Perspectives on the Cultural Revolution*. Cambridge: Harvard University Press, 1988.

Jowitt, Kenneth. "An Organizational Approach to the Study of Political Culture in Marxist-Leninist Systems." *American Political Science Review* 68, no. 1 (1974): 171–91.

Kallgren, Joyce K. "Public Policy and Life in China." In *The People's Republic of China after Thirty Years: An Overview*, edited by Joyce K. Kallgren, pp. 95–122. Berkeley: University of California Center for Chinese Studies, 1979.

––––––. "Social Welfare and China's Industrial Workers." In *Chinese Communist Politics in Action*, edited by Doak Barnett, pp. 540–75. Seattle: University of Washington Press, 1969.

Karnow, Stanley. *Mao and China: From Revolution to Revolution*. New York: Viking, 1972.

Karol, K. S. *The Second Chinese Revolution*. Translated by M. Jones. New York: Hill and Wang, 1974.

Kau Ying-mao. "Governmental Bureaucracy and Cadres in Urban China under Communist Rule, 1949–1965." Ph.D. diss., Department of Political Science Cornell University, 1968.

––––––. *The People's Liberation Army and China's Nation-Building*. White Plains, N.Y.: International Arts and Sciences Press, 1973.

Kiernan, Ben, and Chanthou Boua, eds. *Peasants and Politics in Kampuchea, 1942–1981*. Armonk, N.Y.: Sharpe, 1982.

Kirby, E. Stuart. "The Framework of the Crisis in Communist China." *Current Scene* 6, no. 2 (1968): 1–10.

Klein, Donald W. "A Question of Leadership: Problems of Mobility Control and Policy-making in China." *Current Scene* 5, no. 7 (1967): 1–8.

Klein, Donald W. and Anne B. Clark. *Biographic Dictionary of Chinese Communism*. Cambridge: Harvard University Press, 1971.

Kleinman, Arthur. *Social Origins of Stress and Disease: Depression, Neurasthenia, and Pain in Modern China*. New Haven: Yale University Press, 1985.

Knight, Nick. "The Marxism of Mao Zedong: Empiricism and Discourse in the Field of Mao Studies." *Australian Journal of Chinese Affairs* 16 (July 1986): 18–19.

Knight, Sophia. *Window on Shanghai: Letters from China, 1965–67*. London: Deutsch, 1967.

Kornhauser, William. *The Politics of Mass Society*. Glencoe, N.Y.: Free Press, 1959.

Kraus, Richard Curt. *Class Conflict in Chinese Socialism*. New York: Columbia University Press, 1981.

_____. *Pianos and Politics in China: Class, Nationalism, and the Controversy over Western Music* (forthcoming).

Kuo Tai-chün and Ramon H. Myers. *Understanding Communist China: Communist China Studies in the United States and the Republic of China, 1949–1978*. Stanford, Calif.: Hoover Institution Press, 1986.

Kwok, Reginald Yin Wang. "Trends of Urban Planning and Development in China." In *Urban Development in Modern China*, edited by Laurence J. C. Ma and Edward W. Hanten, pp. 147–93. Boulder, Colo.: Westview, 1981.

Langer, Suzanne K. *Philosophy in a New Key: A Study in the Symbolism of Reason, Rite, and Art*. New York: Penguin, 1942.

Lardy, Nicholas R. *Economic Growth and Distribution in China*. Cambridge: Cambridge University Press, 1978.

Lee, Hong Yung. *The Politics of the Chinese Cultural Revolution: A Case Study*. Berkeley and Los Angeles: University of California Press, 1978.

Levi, Carlo. *Christ Stopped at Eboli*. New York: Farrar, Straus, 1947.

Lewis, John Wilson. "Commerce, Education, and Political Development in Tangshan, 1956–69." In *The City in Communist China*, ed. J. W. Lewis. Stanford: Stanford University Press, 1971.

_____. *Political Networks and the Chinese Policy Process*. Stanford, Calif.: Northeast Asia-United States Forum, 1986.

Li Cheng and Lynn White. "The Thirteenth Central Committee of the Chinese Communist Party: From Mobilizers of Managers." *Asian Survey* 28, no. 4 (1988): 371–99.

Liang Heng and Judith Shapiro. *Son of the Revolution*. New York: Random House, 1983.

Lieberthal, Jane Lindsay. "From Cooperative to Commune: An Analysis of Rural Administrative Policy in China, 1955–58." M.A. thesis, Department of Political Science, Columbia University, ca. 1971.

Lieberthal, Kenneth G. *Revolution and Tradition in Tientsin, 1949–1952*. Stanford, Calif.: Stanford University Press, 1980.

Lifton, Robert J. *Revolutionary Immortality: Mao Tse-tung and the Cultural Revolution*. New York: Vintage Books, 1968.

Ling, Ken. *The Revenge of Heaven: Journal of a Young Chinese.* New York: Putnam, 1972.

Link, Perry, ed. *Stubborn Weeds: Popular and Controversial Chinese Literature after the Cultural Revolution.* Bloomington: Indiana University Press, 1983.

Liu Binyan. *People or Monsters? And Other Stories and Reportage from China after Mao.* Edited by Perry Link. Bloomington: Indiana University Press, 1983.

Liu, Alan P. L. *How China is Ruled.* Englewood Cliffs, N.J.: Prentice-Hall, 1986.

Loh, Robert, as told to Humphrey Evans. *Escape from Red China.* New York: Coward-McCann, 1962.

Lu Ken. "Hu Yaobang fangwen ji" (Interview with Hu Yaobang). *Baixing Monthly* (Hong Kong), December 1985.

Lu Xinhua et al., *The Wounded: New Stories of the Cultural Revolution.* Translated by Geremie Barmé and Bennet Lee. Hong Kong: Joint Publishing Co., 1979.

Luard, D.E.T. "The Urban Communes." *China Quarterly* 3 (July–September 1960): 76–86.

Lyons, Thomas. *Economic Integration and Planning in Maoist China.* New York: Columbia University Press, 1987.

MacFarquhar, Roderick. *The Origins of the Cultural Revolution.* Vol. 1, *Contradictions among the People, 1956–1957*; Vol. 2, *The Great Leap Forward, 1958–1960.* New York: Columbia University Press, 1974, 1983.

MacInnis, Donald. *Religious Policy and Practice in Communist China.* New York: Macmillan, 1972.

Mackerras, Colin, and Neale Hunter. *China Observed: 1964–1967.* London: Pall Mall, 1968.

Madsen, Richard. *Morality and Power in a Chinese Village.* Berkeley and Los Angeles: University of California Press, 1984.

Malraux, André. *Man's Fate (La condition humaine).* Translated by Haakon Chevalier. New York: Random House, 1934.

Mannheim, Karl. *Ideology and Utopia: An Introduction to the Sociology of Knowledge.* London: Routledge, 1936.

Mao Tun. *Midnight.* Beijing: Foreign Languages Press, 1957.

Masi, Edoarda. *China Winter: Workers, Mandarins, and the Purge of the Gang of Four.* Translated by Adrienne Foulke. New York: Dutton, 1982.

Mehnert, Klaus. *Peking and the New Left: At Home and Abroad.* Berkeley: University of California Center for Chinese Studies, 1969.

Michael, Franz. "The Struggle for Power." *Problems of Communism* 16, no. 3 (1967): 12–21.

Montaperto, Ronald N. "From Revolutionary Successors to Revolutionaries." In *Elites in the People's Republic of China*, edited by Robert A. Scalapino, pp. 592–93. Seattle: University of Washington Press, 1972.

Mu Fu-sheng. *The Wilting of the Hundred Flowers.* New York: Praeger, 1962.

Munro, Donald J. "Egalitarian Ideal and Educational Fact in Communist China." In

China: The Management of a Revolutionary Society, edited by John Lindbeck, pp. 256–303. Seattle: University of Washington Press, 1971.

_____. "Man, State, and School." In *China's Developmental Experience*, edited by Michel Oksenberg. New York: Praeger, 1973.

Murphey, Rhoads. *Shanghai: Key to Modern China*. Cambridge: Harvard University Press, 1953.

Myers, James T. "The Fall of Chairman Mao." *Current Scene* 6, no. 10 (1968): 1–18.

Nathan, Andrew J. *Chinese Democracy*. New York: Knopf, 1985.

Nee, Victor. *The Cultural Revolution at Peking University*. New York: Monthly Review Press, 1969.

Nivison, David. "The Criteria of Excellence." In *The Chinese Civil Service: Career Open to Talent?*, edited by Johanna M. Menzel, pp. 92–106. Boston: Heath, 1963.

Nossal, Frederick. *Dateline—Peking*. London: Macdonald, 1962.

Oi, Jean C. "Communism and Clientelism: Rural Politics in China." *World Politics* 37, no. 2 (1985): 238–66.

Oksenberg, Michel. "China: Forcing the Revolution to a New Stage." *Asian Survey* 7, no. 1 (1967): 1–15.

_____. "Chinese Policy Process and the Public Health Issue: An Arena Approach." *Comparative Studies of Communism* (April 1974): 375–412.

_____. "Occupational Groups in Chinese Society and the Cultural Revolution." In *The Cultural Revolution: 1967 in Review*, edited by Chang Chun-shu, James Crump, and Rhodes Murphey, pp. 1–44. Ann Arbor: University of Michigan Center for Chinese Studies, 1968.

Orleans, Leo. *Every Fifth Child: The Population of China*. Stanford, Calif.: Stanford University Press, 1972.

Pan Ling. *In Search of Old Shanghai*. Hong Kong: Joint Publishing Co., 1982.

_____. *Old Shanghai: Gangsters in Paradise*. Hong Kong: Heinemann, 1984.

Parish, William L. "The View from the Factory." In *The China Difference*, edited by Ross Terrill, pp. 185–98. New York: Harper and Row, 1972.

Parsons, Talcott. *The Social System*. Glencoe, N.Y.: Free Press, 1951.

_____. *The Structure of Social Action*. New York: McGraw-Hill, 1937.

Pepper, Stephen. *World Hypotheses: A Study in Evidence*. Berkeley and Los Angeles: University of California Press, 1970.

Pepper, Suzanne. *Civil War in China: The Political Struggle, 1945–1949*. Berkeley and Los Angeles: University of California Press, 1978.

Pfeffer, Richard. "The Pursuit of Purity: Mao's Cultural Revolution." *Problems of Communism* 18, no. 6 (1969): 12–25.

Polan, A. J. *Lenin and the End of Politics*. Berkeley and Los Angeles: University of California Press, 1984.

Polanyi, Karl. *The Great Transformation: The Social and Economic Origins of Our Time*. New York: Rinehart, 1944.

Popper, Karl R. *The Open Society and Its Enemies.* 2 vols. Princeton: Princeton University Press, 1950.

Possony, Stephan T. "The Chinese Communist Cauldron." *Orbis* 13, no. 3 (1969): 783–821.

Pye, Lucian W. *China: An Introduction.* 3d ed. Boston: Little, Brown, 1984.

———. "Reassessing the Cultural Revolution." *China Quarterly* 108 (December 1986): 597–612.

———. *The Spirit of Chinese Politics: A Psychocultural Study of the Authority Crisis in Political Development.* Cambridge: MIT Press, 1968.

Qi Xin et al. *China's New Democracy.* Hong Kong: Cosmos Books, 1979.

Raddock, David M. *Political Behavior in Adolescents in China: The Cultural Revolution in Kwangchow.* Tucson: University of Arizona Press, 1977.

Ragvald, Lars. *Yao Wenyuan as a Literary Critic and Theorist: The Emergence of Chinese Zhdanovism.* Stockholm: University of Stockholm, 1978.

Rice, Edward E. *Mao's Way.* Berkeley and Los Angeles: University of California Press, 1972.

Richman, Barry. *Industrial Society in Communist China.* New York: Random House, 1969.

Rosen, Stanley. *Red Guard Factionalism and the Cultural Revolution in Guangzhou (Canton).* Boulder, Colo.: Westview, 1982.

Rosenberg, William G. *Bolshevik Visions: The First Phase of the Cultural Revolution in Soviet Russia.* Ann Arbor, Mich.: Ardis, 1984.

Rozman, Gilbert. *A Mirror for Socialism: Soviet Criticisms of China.* Princeton: Princeton University Press, 1985.

Rubin, Vitaly A. *Individual and State in Ancient China: Essays on Four Chinese Philosophers.* Translated by Steven I. Levine. New York: Columbia University Press, 1976.

Ryckmans, Pierre [Simon Leys]. "Human Rights in China." *Quadrant,* November 1978, pp. 70–76.

Schoenbaum, David. *Hitler's Social Revolution: Class and Status in Nazi Germany, 1933–39.* New York: Norton, 1980.

Schram, Stuart R. "The Limits of Cataclysmic Change: Reflections on the Place of the 'Great Proletarian Cultural Revolution' in the Political Development of the People's Republic of China." *China Quarterly* 108 (December 1986): 613–24.

———, ed. *Chairman Mao Talks to the People.* New York: Pantheon, 1974.

Schurmann, Franz. *Ideology and Organization in Communist China.* Berkeley and Los Angeles: University of California Press, 1966.

Schwarcz, Vera. *Long Road Home.* New Haven: Yale University Press, 1984.

Scott, James C. *Weapons of the Weak: Everyday Forms of Peasant Resistance.* New Haven: Yale University Press, 1985.

Selden, Mark. *The Yenan Way in Revolutionary China.* Cambridge: Harvard University Press, 1971.

Selznick, Philip. *The Organizational Weapon: A Study of Bolshevik Strategy and Tactics*. New York: McGraw-Hill, 1952.

Shalom, Stephen Rosskamm. *Deaths in China Due to Communism: Propaganda versus Reality*. Tempe: Center for Asian Studies, Arizona State University, 1984.

Shanghai shehui kexue yuan, jingji yanjiu suo, Chengshih jingji zu (Shanghai Academy of Social Sciences, Economic Research Institute, Urban Economy Group). *Shanghai penghu qu de bianqian* (The transformation of Shanghai's shack districts). Shanghai: Renmin chuban she, 1965.

Shanghai zonggonghui caimao chu (Shanghai General Federation of Trade Unions, Finance Division). *Gonghui caimao gongzuo* (Union finance work). Shanghai: Laodong chuban she, 1951.

Shanghai zonggonghui diaocha yanjiu shi (Shanghai General Labor Federation, Investigation and Research Office). *Gonghui qinggong gongzuo* (Youth work in the unions). Shanghai: Laodong chuban she, 1951.

Shanghai zonggonghui wenjiao bu (Shanghai General Federation of Labor, Culture and Education Department). *Quanguo gonghui gongzuo huiyi teji* (Speeches from the National Union Work Conference). Shanghai: Laodong chuban she, 1950.

Shanghai zonggonghui wenjiao bu (Shanghai General Federation of Trade Unions, Culture and Education Department. *Gongchang zhong de xuanquan gudong gongzuo: gonghui gongzuo cankao ziliao* (Propaganda and education work in factories: Reference documents for union work). Shanghai: Laodong chuban she, 1950.

Shawcross, William. *The Quality of Mercy: Cambodia, Holocaust, and Modern Conscience*. New York: Simon and Schuster, 1984.

Sherrard, Michael. *A Lexical Survey of the Shanghai Dialect*. Tokyo: Institute of Asian and African Languages and Cultures, 1982.

Shirk, Susan L. *Competitive Comrades: Career Incentives and Student Strategies in China*. Berkeley and Los Angeles: University of California Press, 1981.

Shue, Vivienne. *Peasant China in Transition: The Dynamics of Development toward Socialism, 1949–1956*. Berkeley and Los Angeles: University of California Press, 1980.

———. *The Reach of the State: Sketches of the Chinese Body Politic*. Stanford, Calif.: Stanford University Press, 1988.

Sima Lu. *Douzheng shiba nian* (Eighteen years of struggle). Hong Kong: Zilian chuban she, 1967.

Simon, Herbert A. *Models of Man: Social and Rational*. New York: Wiley, 1957.

Skinner, G. William. "Marketing and Social Structure in Rural China." *Journal of Asian Studies* 24, nos. 1–3 (1964–65).

Snow, Edgar. *The Other Side of the River: Red China Today*. New York: Random House, 1961.

Solinger, Dorothy J. *Chinese Business under Socialism*. Berkeley and Los Angeles: University of California Press, 1984.

Solomon, Richard H., in collaboration with Talbott Huey. *A Revolution Is Not a*

Dinner Party: A Feast of Images of the Maoist Transformation of China. Garden City, N.Y.: Doubleday, 1975.

Solomon, Richard H. *Mao's Revolution and the Chinese Political Culture.* Berkeley and Los Angeles: University of California Press, 1971.

Stanford University China Project. *East China.* Subcontractor's Monograph *HRAF-29*, Stanford 3. New Haven: Human Relations Area Files, 1956.

Stone, Lawrence. *The Causes of the English Revolution, 1529–1642.* New York: Harper and Row, 1972.

Storry, Richard. *A History of Modern Japan.* Harmondsworth, Eng.: Penguin, 1960.

Sun Longji. *Zhongguo wenhua de "shenceng jiegou" (The "deep structure" of Chinese culture).* Hong Kong: Jixian she, 1983.

Tai Sung An. *Mao Tsetung's Cultural Revolution.* Indianapolis, Ind.: Bobbs-Merrill, 1972.

Tannebaum, Gerald. "The 1967 Shanghai January Revolution Recounted." *Eastern Horizon* 7, no. 3 (1968): 7–25.

Taylor, Robert. *China's Intellectual Dilemma: Politics and University Enrolment, 1949–1978.* Vancouver: University of British Columbia Press, 1981.

Terrill, Ross. *Mao: A Biography.* New York: Harper and Row, 1980.

Thurston, Anne F. *Enemies of the People: The Ordeal of the Intellectuals in China's Great Cultural Revolution.* New York: Knopf, 1987.

———. "Victims of China's Cultural Revolution: The Invisible Wounds." Parts 1, 2. *Pacific Affairs* 57, no. 4, 58, no. 1 (1984–85, 1985): 599–620, 5–27.

Tilly, Charles. *Big Structures, Large Processes, Huge Comparisons.* New York: Russell Sage Foundation, 1985.

Townsend, James R. *Political Participation in Communist China.* Berkeley and Los Angeles: University of California Press, 1967.

———. *The Revolutionization of Chinese Youth: A Study of Chung-kuo Ch'ing-nien.* Berkeley: University of California Center for Chinese Studies, 1967.

Tuchman, Barbara. *The March of Folly.* New York: Ballantine, 1984.

Tucker, Robert C. "Does Big Brother Really Exist?" *Wilson Quarterly* 8, no. 1 (1984): 106–17.

———, ed. *Stalinism.* New York: Norton, 1977.

Vogel, Ezra F. *Canton under Communism: Programs and Politics in a Provincial Capital, 1949–1968.* Cambridge: Harvard University Press, 1969.

Wakeman, Frederic, Jr. *Strangers at the Gate: Social Disorder in South China, 1839–1861.* Berkeley and Los Angeles: University of California Press, 1966.

Walder, Andrew G. *Chang Ch'un-ch'iao and Shanghai's January Revolution.* Ann Arbor: Center for Chinese Studies at the University of Michigan, 1978.

———. *Communist Neo-Traditionalism: Work and Authority in Chinese Industry.* Berkeley and Los Angeles: University of California Press, 1986.

Wallace, Anthony. "Revitalization Movements." *American Anthropologist* 58 (April 1956): 264–81.

Walter, Carl E. "Party-State Relations in the People's Republic of China: The Role of the People's Bank and the Local Party in Economic Development." Ph.D. diss., Department of Political Science, Stanford University, 1981.

Walzer, Michael. *The Revolution of the Saints: A Study in the Origins of Radical Politics*. Cambridge: Harvard University Press, 1965.

Wang, James C. F. *The Cultural Revolution in China: An Annotated Bibliography*. New York: Garland, 1976.

Weber, Max. *From Max Weber*. Edited by H. H. Gerth and C. Wright Mills. New York: Oxford University Press, 1958.

Wedeman, Andrew Hall. *The East Wind Subsides: Chinese Foreign Policy and the Origins of the Cultural Revolution*. Washington, D.C.: Washington Institute Press, 1987.

White, Gordon. *The Politics of Class and Class Origin: The Case of the Cultural Revolution*. Canberra: Australian National University Contemporary China Centre, 1976.

White, Lynn T., III. "Agricultural and Industrial Values in China." In *Value Change in Chinese Society* edited by Richard Wilson, Sidney Greenblatt, and Amy Wilson. New York: Praeger, 1979.

_____. "Bourgeois Radicalism in the 'New Class' of Shanghai." In *Class and Social Stratification in Post-Revolution China*, edited by James L. Watson, pp. 142–74. Cambridge: Cambridge University Press, 1984.

_____. *Careers in Shanghai: The Social Guidance of Individual Energies in a Developing Chinese City*. Berkeley and Los Angeles: University of California Press, 1978.

_____. "Changing Concepts of Corruption in Communist China." In *Changes and Continuities in Chinese Communism: The Economy, Society, and Technology*, edited by Yu-ming Shaw. Boulder, Colo.: Westview, 1988.

_____. "Deviance, Modernization, Rations, and Household Registration in Chinese Cities." In *Deviance and Social Control in Chinese Society*, edited by R.W. Wilson, S. Greenblatt, and A. Wilson, pp. 151–72. New York: Praeger, 1977.

_____. "Leadership in Shanghai, 1955–69." In *Elites in the People's Republic of China*, edited by Robert A. Scalapino, pp. 302–77. Seattle: University of Washington Press, 1972.

_____. "The Liberation Army and the Chinese People." *Armed Forces and Society* 1, no. 3 (1975): 364–83.

_____. "Low Power: Small Enterprises in Shanghai." *China Quarterly* 73 (March 1978): 45–76.

_____. "Non-Governmentalism in the Historical Development of Modern Shanghai." In *Urban Development in Modern China*, edited by Laurence J. C. Ma and Edward W. Hanten, pp. 19–57. Boulder, Colo.: Westview, 1981.

_____. "The Road to Urumchi: Approved Institutions in Search of Attainable Goals during Pre-1968 Rustication." *China Quarterly* 79 (October 1979): 481–510.

_____. "Shanghai-Suburb Relations, 1949–1966." In *Shanghai: Revolution and*

Development in an Asian Metropolis, edited by Christopher Howe, pp. 241–68. Cambridge: Cambridge University Press, 1981.

_____. "Shanghai's Polity in Cultural Revolution." In *The City in Communist China*, edited by John W. Lewis, pp. 325–70. Stanford, Calif.: Stanford University Press, 1971.

_____. "Workers' Politics in Shanghai." *Journal of Asian Studies* 26, no. 1 (1976): 99–116.

Whyte, Martin King, and William L. Parish. *Urban Life in Contemporary China*. Chicago: University of Chicago Press, 1984.

Wickeri, Philip. "Seeking the Common Ground." Ph.D. Diss., Princeton Theological Seminary, 1984.

Wittfogel, Karl A. *Oriental Despotism*. New Haven: Yale University Press, 1957.

Wolin, Sheldon S. *Politics and Vision*. Boston: Little, Brown, 1960.

Wood, Geof, ed. *Labeling in Development Policy: Essays in Honor of Bernard Schaffer*. The Hague: Institute of Social Studies, 1985.

Wylie, Raymond F. *The Emergence of Maoism: Mao Tse-tung, Ch'en Po-ta, and the Search for Chinese Theory, 1935–1945*. Stanford, Calif.: Stanford University Press, 1980.

_____. "Shanghai Dockers in the Cultural Revolution." In *Shanghai: Revolution and Development in an Asian Metropolis*, edited by Christopher Howe, pp. 91–124. Cambridge: Cambridge University Press, 1981.

Yan Jiaqi and Gao Gao. *Zhongguo "wenge" shinian shi* (A history of the decade of China's "Cultural Revolution"). Hong Kong: Dagongbao Press, 1986.

Yang Jiang. *A Cadre School Life: Six Chapters*. Translated by Geremie Barmé. Hong Kong: Joint Publishing Co., 1982.

Yang Xiaokai [Xi Guang]. "Zhungguo wenhua tageming de shehuizhuyi zhidu de tu po" (The Cultural Revolution's disruption of the socialist system). *Zhishi fenzi* (The Chinese intellectual), no. 7 (Spring 1986): 13–15.

Yue Daiyun, with Carolyn Wakeman. *To the Storm: The Odyssey of a Revolutionary Chinese Woman*. Berkeley and Los Angeles: University of California Press, 1985.

Zhelokhovtsev, A. *The Cultural Revolution: A Close-up Eyewitness Account*. Moscow: Progress Publishers, 1975.

Zhu Yuanzheng. *Zhonggong caiqing zhengce xin dongxiang* (New trends in Chinese Communist fiscal and economic policies). Hong Kong: Ziyou chuban she, 1953.

Index

Index